Few are as well qualified to write about Kipling in India as **Charles Allen**, best known for such chronicles of British India as *Plain Tales from the Raj*, *The Buddha and the Sahibs* and *Soldier Sahibs*. Born in India in the twilight years of the British Raj, Allen experienced an early childhood very similar to that enjoyed by Kipling several generations earlier. Subsequently he has lived and travelled in virtually every corner of the Indian sub-continent.

Praise for *Kipling Sahib*

'A delightful evocation of late 19th century India and an acute study of Kipling's genius; utterly absorbing'
Allan Massie, Books of the Year, *Spectator*

'*Kipling Sahib* is the best book on its subject, and on British India, for years'
Sunday Herald

'[Kipling was] a writer of genius whose development and work Allen describes with sympathy and penetration . . . A fascinating book, one of the best on Kipling I have read . . . Anyone who has ever fallen under Kipling's spell will delight in this book. It extends our knowledge, and depends our understanding, of the greatest English writer of his generation'
Daily Telegraph

'This compelling portrait of Kipling . . . provides a vibrant picture. Charles Allen's book, which plumbs the depth of Kipling's Indian inspiration, should help to restore him to his rightful place in the literary pantheon'
Literary Review

'This stimulating biography of Kipling's early life, before the arrant imperialism took hold, gives us the feel of a fascinating, awkward and ugly young man who was half a satirist of the hidebound Raj and half an oriental mystic'
Oldie

'Allen has done his subject proud with a biography of great sensitivity, insight and rare charm'
Mail on Sunday

KIPLING SAHIB

*India and the Making of
Rudyard Kipling*

Charles Allen

ABACUS

First published in Great Britain in 2007 by Little, Brown
This paperback edition published in 2008 by Abacus

Maps drawn by John Gilkes

A CIP catalogue record for this book
is available from the British Library.

ISBN 978-0-349-11685-3

Typeset in Bembo by M Rules
Printed and bound in Great Britain by
Clays Ltd, St Ives plc

Papers used by Abacus are natural, renewable and recyclable
products made from wood grown in sustainable forests and certified
in accordance with the rules of the Forest Stewardship Council.

Mixed Sources
Product group from well-managed
forests and other controlled sources
www.fsc.org Cert no. SGS-COC-004081
© 1996 Forest Stewardship Council
FSC

Abacus
An imprint of
Little, Brown Book Group
100 Victoria Embankment
London EC4Y 0DY

An Hachette Livre UK Company
www.hachettelivre.co.uk

www.littlebrown.co.uk

To my children

'O beloved kids'

Contents

Preface: Blowing the Family Trumpet

Immodest as it sounds, I was born to write this book. My most formative years were spent in an India not so far removed from Rudyard Kipling's as the place and time might suggest – Assam and Bihar in the 1940s. The *Just So Stories* and *The Jungle Book* were real to me to a degree denied most children: I suffered malaria, dhobi itch and snakes in the bathroom; I rode elephants, played on tiger skins, was spoiled rotten by servants unstinting in their affection, watched my father dispense justice on the verandah, was lulled to sleep under mosquito nets by my ayah to the creak and swish of the punkah and the howling of jackals. Like the boy Ruddy, I became an orphan of the Raj, cast out of Paradise at an early age and seemingly abandoned by my parents in an alien land among unknown people, although in my case they were my paternal grandparents, who themselves had been born in India and had gone through the same cycle – as, indeed, had my parents.

At my grandparents' home in East Sussex I grew up surrounded by Kiplingiana. Hanging among the watercolours of Simla and the Himalayan foothills in the dining room were two of ten plaster plaques made by John Lockwood Kipling for his son to illustrate the first edition of *Kim*. One I remember was of the Pathan horse-trader Mahbub Ali who befriends the boy Kim and initiates him into the 'Great Game'; the other of the old Sikh soldier identified as 'the Ressaldar'. Just outside the dining room stood a garishly painted chest bearing an inscription which declared it to be the property of J. L. Kipling, made for him by his students at the Mayo School of Art and Industry in Lahore. In my grandfather's library an entire shelf was packed with Kipling first editions, many carrying inscriptions on the title page with the author's name crossed out in black ink and signed with the initials 'R. K.' – among them a nondescript tome with dull olive-green covers which I'm told is one of half a dozen surviving copies of the first edition of *Plain Tales from the Hills*.

As I grew older I became more aware of the Kipling connection. Two of the oil paintings in my grandfather's house were of his father, always spoken of as 'Sir George'. One was painted in 1851 before his departure for India and showed a dandified twenty-one-year-old at a game of cricket; the other, painted half a century later, was of the same man, returned, now a stern, white-whiskered patriarch. The illegitimate son of an Islington solicitor, George Allen had been packed off to India to seek his fortune, which he achieved twice over, initially as a newspaper magnate and then as an industrialist. In the former capacity he gave journalistic employment first of all to John Lockwood Kipling as a special correspondent of the *Pioneer* in Bombay and subsequently to his sixteen-year-old son as an assistant editor of the *Civil and Military Gazette* in Lahore.

The fortune made by Sir George in India was subsequently lost in India by his youngest son, my grandfather and namesake Charles Allen. 'C. T.', as he was always called, was born of Sir George's second wife, Maud, the daughter of an Indian Civil Service judge and of a very different social class from that of his first wife, a sixteen-year-old seamstress whom George Allen had met on Delhi Ridge in 1857, when both were in fear for their lives. I remember C. T.'s irritation when Charles Carrington's *Rudyard Kipling: His Life and Work* was first published in 1955. Carrington's was the first proper biography of Kipling, but in my grandfather's view he had been hoodwinked by the playwright Sir Terence Rattigan, who had exaggerated the role played by his barrister grandfather, William Rattigan. Subsequent biographers followed suit, with the result that George Allen was all but written out of the Kipling story. Andrew Lycett's masterly and monumental life, *Rudyard Kipling*, published in 1999, restored the balance, placing Allen as

primus inter pares in a triumvirate made up of himself, William
Rattigan and the Simla banker James Walker, joint owners of the
Pioneer and the *Civil and Military Gazette*.

The George Allen that Rudyard Kipling knew was a somewhat Olympian figure, presiding over an extensive business
empire of which his newspaper interests formed only a part, a
man with strong political views, used to getting his way and prepared to spend large sums of money to buy the best, whether it
was influence, news or journalists. Rudyard Kipling once
described Allen as a 'full mouthed man', which suggests that he
spoke his mind. And although he wrote of loving him and of
being willing to do anything for him, yet he lived in awe of him
and never felt at ease with him. James Walker, by contrast, was
kind-hearted and approachable, as was Mrs Walker, who made
something of a pet of the adolescent Kipling whenever he stayed
with them in Simla. At that time James Walker was very much the
burra sahib in Simla and only slightly less influential than the
Viceroy and the Commander-in-Chief, just as George Allen was
the *burra sahib* of Allahabad, the plains city where Rudyard
Kipling was based for the last sixteen months of his six and a half
years as a working journalist in India.

My grandfather claimed to have played with Rudyard Kipling in
Simla in 1884 when he was five and the latter eighteen. But in
truth, his contacts with his father's famous protégé were few. Their
last communication took place in 1936, a matter of months before
Kipling's death, when C. T. appealed to him for financial help to
keep his old newspaper, the *Civil and Military Gazette*, going. Three
months later Kipling was dead and the *CMG* passed into the hands
of a group of *talukdars* in Lucknow who ran it into bankruptcy.

After my grandfather's death in 1958 the Brighton dealers
descended, and much of the family's Kipling material was dispersed. In the process, some vandal worked his way through the
Kipling first editions with a razor blade, slicing out the
autographed title pages, which rendered them all but valueless.
Most of George Allen's papers had already been lost, either in a

shipwreck in 1887 or in the London Blitz, so that from that point on the Kipling connection was effectively severed.

Then fate intervened. In 1974 the distinguished radio producer Michael Mason asked me to work for him on a new oral-history project for BBC Radio 4. *Plain Tales from the Raj* was eventually broadcast in eleven episodes, and it made an enormous impact. The book that followed was briefly a best-seller and gave me a start as an oral historian. The magic that illuminated the radio series was Mason's alone, my role being limited to that of researcher and field-interviewer. But in the process of gathering material I travelled the length and breadth of England listening to elderly men and women who had spent most of their working lives in British India. None had known Rudyard Kipling personally, but in many instances their parents had belonged to the generation of sahibs and memsahibs whose lives Kipling had chronicled in his short stories and satirised in his verses. Indeed, some considered Kipling a cad: a vulgar, socially inferior interloper who had abused the Anglo-Indian community's hospitality by writing about the seamier side of the British Raj (the term 'Anglo-Indian' being used by them to describe the British in India, as it is throughout this book). One of my interviewees even assured me that the reason why Kipling could write so well about the borderline between the British and the Indians was because he was 'eight annas to the rupee' – a derogatory term for a person of mixed British and Indian ancestry ('Eurasians' as they were called then; confusingly, 'Anglo-Indians' as they are now). Despite these lingering prejudices the spirit of Kipling invested the radio series, and the knowledge I gained at the feet of Mason and our 'survivors' gave me a new and more sympathetic understanding of the British in India. So began a process of learning about India, past and present, that continues to this day.

In 1987 I was lucky enough to be given my head in assembling an anthology of the best of Kipling's Indian stories. While researching and writing the accompanying text to *Kipling's Kingdom* I made two important discoveries: first, that a large corpus of Kipling's early writing remained unread and awaiting rediscovery, and, secondly, that he wrote as much about Indian India as British India. The notion of writing a biography of Kipling in India and India in Kipling entered my head, and it has taken the best part of two decades to bring that idea to fruition; that I have finally done so is thanks in large part to the encouragement initially of Tim Whiting at Little, Brown, subsequently of his successor Steve Guise.

During my research a great many authorities on Kipling and his India have given me invaluable assistance, directly and indirectly. Among them two stand head and shoulders above the rest: first, the eminent Professor of English at Pomona College, Claremont, California, Thomas Pinney, who has devoted much of his professional life to tracking down and setting in context the letters of Rudyard Kipling; secondly, Andrew Lycett, author of the definitive biography of Rudyard Kipling, referred to above. Scores of biographies, critical studies and literary deconstructions, ancient and modern, have been consulted, and among these I must highlight four as being particularly valuable in cutting paths through the jungle – or the *rukh*, to use Kipling's preferred word: Charles Carrington's pioneering model of how to assemble a 'life and work' (with Lord Birkenhead's suppressed earlier biography *Rudyard Kipling*, finally published in 1978, serving as a model of how not to go about it); Louis Cornell's all too slim *Kipling in India*, published in 1966, which first demonstrated the diversity of Kipling's early writing and first set it in context; Andrew Rutherford's scholarly *Early Verse by Rudyard Kipling 1879–1889*, published in 1986, which showed that in addition to the collected verse, ballads and poems and the supposedly definitive editions authorised by Kipling in his later years, there was a mass of 'Unpublished, Uncollected and Rarely Collected Poems' from Kipling's Indian years; and, lastly, Judith Flanders's delightful book about the four Macdonald sisters and their families, *A Circle of Sisters*, published in 2001, which set Rudyard Kipling's parents Alice Macdonald and John Lockwood Kipling in their social and artistic contexts.

However, all these biographers would be quick to acknowledge the invaluable assistance to their researches provided by that extraordinary band of devotees who make up the backbone of the Kipling Society, and who since 1927 have worked collectively to publish each quarter, in the pages of the *Kipling Journal*, the latest research into the life and work of Rudyard Kipling. Each generation of members has provided its leading lights: enthusiastic collectors, dogged compilers, learned scholars and meticulous editors united in their devotion to 'R. K.'. McMunn, Martindale and Harbord are just three of the many names that come up time and again as one thumbs through past copies of the *Kipling Journal*, runs one's hand along the shelves of the Kipling Society Library at the City University or scrolls through the *New Readers' Guide* on the Society's scrupulously maintained website: www.kipling.org.uk. However, the present generation of movers and shakers within the Kipling Society merits equal gratitude from those of us who make use of their industry freely given. My thanks, in particular, to (in strictly alphabetical order): Roger Ayers, Sir John Chapple, Sir George Engle, Norman Entract, Emanul Karim, Jane and Sharad Keskar, Lisa Lewis, John McGivering, David Page, John Radcliffe, John Sherwood, John Slater, Mike Smith, John Walker, George Webb and Alasdair Wilson – and my apologies to anyone inadvertently left out.

Two years after the death in 1976 of Kipling's last surviving child, Mrs Elsie Bambridge, the papers accumulated by her were passed by the National Trust to the University of Sussex, where they were first collated and catalogued by John Burt. Every Kipling scholar knows what riches are there to be pored over in the Library's Special Collections and what unstinting help is given by its staff, including Karen Watson, Simon Homes and Adam Harwood, under the direction of Fiona Courage, Special Collections Manager. My thanks to them and to the Director and staff at the absurdly renamed Asia, Pacific and Africa Collection (the India Office Library, as was) at the British Library, and the Senior Librarian and staff at the City University (where the Kipling

Society's Library and Archive is housed). My thanks to the National Trust for permission to quote from and use illustrations from material in its ownership, and to the following institutions for permissions to quote from Kipling letters in their collections: the US Library of Congress, Princeton University, Dalhousie University, the Houghton Collection at Harvard University, the Ray Collection at the Morgan Library, the Huntingdon Library, and the Berg Collection at the New York Public Library.

A great many kind persons assisted me with my researches either directly or indirectly as I followed the Kipling trail on a number of journeys through India and Pakistan. My particular thanks to: F. S. Aijazuddin of Lahore, whose scholarly recovery of his city's past proved invaluable to me; William Dalrymple in Delhi; Professor Srivastava and members of the Department of English at the University of Allahabad; Ram Advani of Advani Books, Lahore; the Indian Army officers and wives who since the 1970s have taken the lead in restoring and maintaining the Gaiety Theatre in Simla as members of the Simla Amateur Dramatic Club (Colonel Ranbir Singh being the Hon. Secretary at the time of my most recent visit); in Bombay, Farooq Issa, and, most especially, my former collaborator and fellow writer Sharada Dwivedi, who dug out of Government of Maharashtra archives a wealth of new information about the Kiplings' early days in that fair city; in the United States, Ron Rosner and Omar Khan, author of *From Kashmir to Kabul*; and closer to home, Lindy, Marchioness of Dufferin and Ava, and Lola Armstrong, Curator of the Dufferin and Ava Archive at Clandeboye, for access to the Dufferin Collection, Sue Farrington and Merilyn Hywel-Jones for their help with maps of old Lahore and Simla, Helen MacDonald for her kindness in lending me a photograph of Trix Kipling, and Lorna Lee, author of *Trix: Kipling's Forgotten Sister*, for her guidance. A special thanks also to the Society of Authors for the writing award which gave me a vital breathing space at an early stage of this project, and, closer to home, Vivien Green, staunchest of agents; Liz Robinson, sternest of defenders of literary standards; Charlotte Purton for providing an editorial long-stop; indexer Patricia Hymans; map artist John Gilkes and Linda Silverman and Iain Hunt, tip of the iceberg of the Little, Brown editorial team, whose combined efforts invariably go unnoticed except when things go wrong. Lastly my loving thanks to my first reader, Liz Allen, best friend, life partner and mother of our children.

Since Carrington, scores of Kipling biographies and critical studies have been written, most recently David Gilmour's *The Long Recessional: The Imperial Life of Rudyard Kipling* (2002), which focused on Kipling as the embodiment of the spirit of the British Empire. So what more is there to say about the man that should be said?

My own view is that one area of his life demands closer scrutiny: the five years of his Bombay childhood, and the six and a half years of his apprenticeship as a journalist in Upper India which Kipling termed his 'seven years hard'. Even the magnificently comprehensive Andrew Lycett could not afford to devote more than five chapters out of twenty to these twelve crucial Indian years. India was where Rudyard Kipling was happiest, where he learned his craft, where he rediscovered himself through his writing and came of age as a writer. India made him, charged his imagination, and after he left India in March 1889 at the age of twenty-three he was most completely himself as an artist when reinhabiting the two Indian worlds he had left behind. He lived thereafter on borrowed time, a state of higher creativity he was unable to maintain once he had exhausted his Indian memories with the writing of his masterwork *Kim*. For this man who was never emotionally robust, now locked in an increasingly bleak marriage, the death of his beloved eldest daughter Josephine in 1899 accelerated his withdrawal from human intimacy. He became thereafter increasingly, obsessively private, much preferring in his writing to deal with the workings of machinery rather than with human feelings, his undoubted genius sparking only fitfully but sustained by his mastery of his craft.

I am very conscious of what the novelist Martin Amis has called the 'biographical fallacy' – the misapprehension that an author's creation either as a character or as the narrator of a story is a reflection of himself or herself. However, all writers draw from their own experience to a greater or lesser degree, even if they afterwards reshape that experience within their own imagination. With Kipling it is a case of the greater degree. He himself was happy to admit that he had 'a cold-blooded trick of turning most things and experiences into print'[1] and it would be no exaggeration to describe him as one of the great magpies of English literature – although the mynah bird would be a more appropriate comparison, since he was as much a mimic as a borrower.

Exploring and illuminating the sources of Kipling's literary output and the degree to which he placed himself within his writing is central to our understanding of the man and his work. For example, returning from Simla to Allahabad in late July 1888 at the height of the Rains, Kipling found the River Gugger in flood and had to kick his heels until the waters had abated. He passed the time talking to the crossing-keeper who lived in a shack beside the ford. Kipling the journalist turned the experience into a complaint about the wretched state of the Umballa–Kalka road, published in the *Pioneer* a few days later on 28 July. A bridge had stood at the crossing point but had been washed away in a flood many years previously, and part of his complaint was that it was high time a new bridge was raised. Kipling the writer then developed the same experience into a short story, 'In Flood-Time', which he placed in the *Week's News* on 11 August. The form he used was one which he had made his own: a dramatic monologue from the crossing-keeper as he makes his guest comfortable, set within a framework provided by the listening journalist-sahib, the tale gaining verisimilitude by appearing to be jotted down word for word exactly as recounted.

The old man has a story to tell from his youth, which turns out to be a reworking of the classical tale of Hero and Leander. In this Indian version Leander is the Muslim crossing-keeper and his

Hero a Hindu widow whom he visits illicitly at night by swimming across the river. Desperate to see her one night, he sets out when the river is in full spate and discovers too late that he has been caught up in 'the Great Flood about which men talk still' which has brought down the local bridge. But unlike Leander, the crossing-keeper does not drown. Instead, the author adds his own 'Kiplingesque' touch, for as the crossing-keeper is about to be swallowed up by the waters his fingers grasp the knotted hair of his rival in love: 'He had been dead full two days, for he rode high, wallowing, and was an aid to me. I laughed then, knowing for a surety that I should yet see Her and take no harm; and I twisted my fingers in the hair of the man, for I was far spent, and together we went down the stream – he the dead and I the living.' Ever the recycler, Kipling hangs on to his crossing-keeper and serves him up again as Gobind, the one-eyed story-teller who provides the Preface to *Life's Handicap*. Some years on, the Great Flood reappears as a wrathful manifestation of Mother Ganges in 'The Bridge-Builders' – that compelling parable of the old, Gods-fearing Asia pitted against the modern, practical West.

Unlike his friends Sir Arthur Conan Doyle and Sir Rider Haggard, Kipling was incapable of compartmentalising his life and his work. Taking this as my cue, I have resisted the temptation to deal with him in segments. Everything is set down here in strict chronological order. The disadvantage of this method is that it becomes a juggling act; the huge advantage, that it gives a truer picture of how it came about that the myopic, clumsy school runt 'Gigger' was transformed within the space of six and a half years into 'Ruddy', the literary prodigy; of how the same Ruddy then became within a second span of six and a half years England's best-beloved man of letters; and of how Ruddy lost and found and lost again his Daemon and became Kipling, spokesman of Empire, all but done for at thirty-five. To emphasise the difference between these two Kiplings I refer to the younger man as 'Ruddy', while the man he became at thirty-five is always 'Kipling'.

I make no apologies for quoting directly from original sources more liberally than is usual in a biography. Perhaps this comes from having learned my trade as an oral historian, but it seems only proper that the words of a biographer's subject should always take precedence over his own, particularly in dealing with a man whose entire adult life was built around what he wrote. Young Ruddy stands alongside Byron as one of the great letter-writers of the nineteenth century, besides being far more versatile in his literary output, and my aim has been to let this writing speak for itself as far as possible.

Finally, I have included Anglo-Indian argot wherever appropriate. A number of Anglo-Indian words, such as the Station, the Club, the Rains, the Hills, the Hot Weather, the Cold Weather, Society, Home, Civilians, Natives and Season (as in Simla Season), had their own local meaning, and were always spoken as if written with a capital letter, although not always set down that way. To avoid confusion I have followed suit. A glossary is attached.

Charles Allen,
Spring 2007,
Somerset

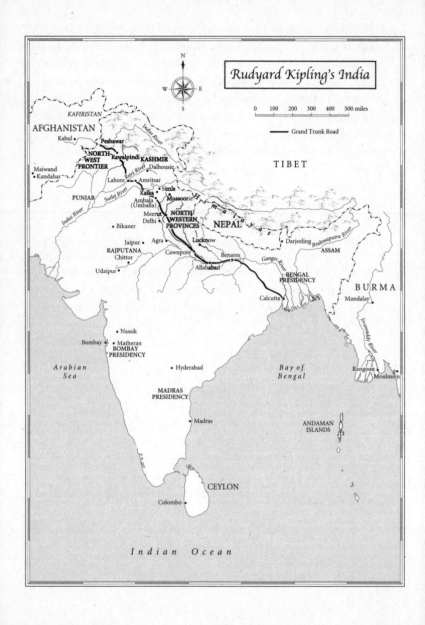

Rudyard Kipling's India

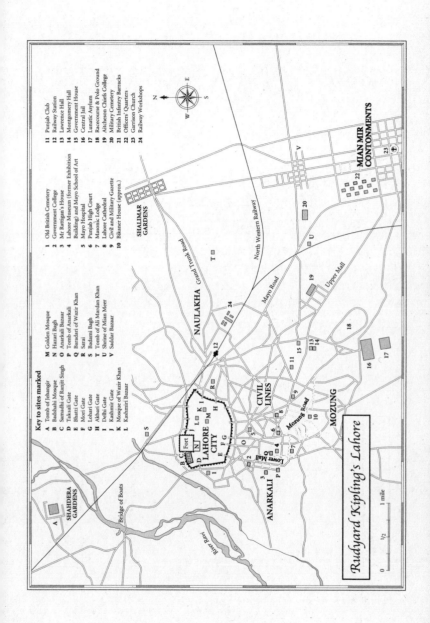

Key to sites marked

A Tomb of Jehangir
B Badshahi Mosque
C Samadhi of Ranjit Singh
D Taksali Gate
E Mori Gate
F Bhatti Gate
G Lohari Gate
H Akbari Gate
I Delhi Gate
K Mosque of Wazir Khan
L Kashmiri Bazaar

M Golden Mosque
N Hazari Bagh
O Anarkali Bazaar
P Tomb of Anarkali
Q Baradari of Wazir Khan
R Sarai
S Badami Bagh
T Tomb of Ali Mardan Khan
U Shrine of Mian Meer
V Saddar Bazaar

1   Old British Cemetery
2   Government College
4   Mr Rattigan's House
4   Lahore Museum (former Exhibition Building, and Mayo School of Art
5   Mayo Hospital
6   Punjab High Court
7   Masonic Lodge
8   Lahore Cathedral
9   Civil and Military Gazette
10 Bikaner House (approx.)

11 Punjab Club
12 Railway Station
13 Lawrence Hall
14 Montgomery Hall
15 Government House
16 Central Jail
17 Lunatic Asylum
18 Racecourse & Polo Ground
19 Aitcheson Chiefs College
20 Military Cemetery
21 British Infantry Barracks
22 Officers' Quarters
23 Garrison Church
24 Railway Workshops

Rudyard Kipling's Lahore

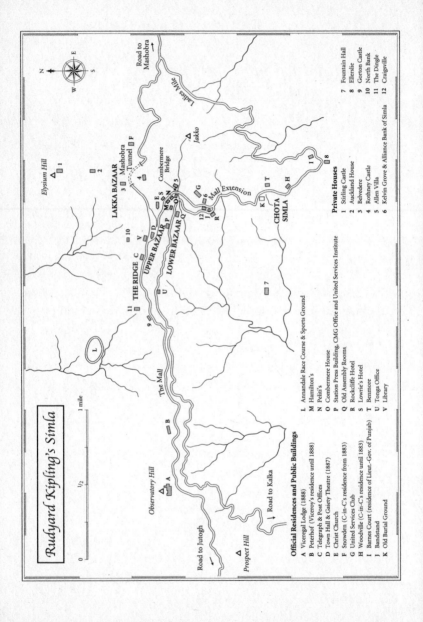

Rudyard Kipling's Simla

Official Residences and Public Buildings

A Viceregal Lodge (1888)
B Peterhof (Viceroy's residence until 1888)
C Telegraph & Post Offices
D Town Hall & Gaiety Theatre (1887)
E Christ Church
F Snowden (C-in-C's residence from 1883)
G United Services Club
H Woodville (C-in-C's residence until 1883)
I Barnes Court (residence of Lieut.-Gov. of Punjab)
J Bandstand
K Old Burial Ground

L Annandale Race Course & Sports Ground
M Hamilton's
N Peliti's
O Combermere House
P Station Press Building, CMG Office and United Services Institute
Q Old Assembly Rooms
R Rockcliffe Hotel
S Lowrie's Hotel
T Benmore
U Tonga Office
V Library

Private Houses

1 Stirling Castle
2 Auckland House
3 Belvedere
4 Rothney Castle
5 Allen Villa
6 Kelvin Grove & Alliance Bank of Simla

7 Fountain Hall
8 Ellerslie
9 Gorton Castle
10 North Bank
11 The Dingle
12 Craigville

Introduction: 'Seek not to question'

And for the little, little span
  The dead are borne in mind,
      Seek not to question other than
  The books I leave behind.

Rudyard Kipling, 'The Appeal', set down at the end
of his final revision of his collected poetry, published
posthumously as the *Sussex Edition*, 1937–9

It is hard to grasp the extent to which Rudyard Kipling dominated the popular imagination of the English-speaking world just over a century ago. It can best be judged by reading what his literary contemporaries thought of him. 'I'm getting just a wee bit tired of Mr Kipling,' declared the humorist Jerome K. Jerome in the *Sun* on 7 May 1900:

He appears to have dominated the universe to the exclusion of all other beliefs. Kipling day by day has grown into a sort of nightmare. 'Kipling and the Queen', 'Kipling and the German Emperor', 'Kipling and Tommy Atkins', 'Kipling in the Hospital', 'Kipling in the train that's going to the Hospital', 'Kipling before he got into the train that went to the Hospital', 'Kipling on the Boers', 'Kipling on People who dare to express an Opinion on the Boers', etc.

A more thoughtful account of the phenomenon was given by the socialist writer H. G. Wells, as set down in his novel *The New Machiavelli*. 'It is a little difficult now to get back to the feelings of that period,' Wells has the novel's hero explain:

The prevailing force of my undergraduate days was not Socialism but Kiplingism ... Never was a man so violently exalted and then, himself assisting, so relentlessly called down. But in the middle nineties this spectacled and moustached little figure with ... its wild shouts of boyish enthusiasm for effective force, its lyric delight in the sounds and colours, in the very odours of empire ... became almost a national symbol. He got hold of us wonderfully, he filled us with tinkling and haunting quotations ... he coloured the very idiom of our conversation ... He helped to broaden my geographical sense immensely, and he provided phrases for just that desire for discipline and devotion and organised effort the Socialism of our times failed to express.

Throughout the 1890s the editors of middlebrow monthly journals in Britain and America such as *Macmillan's Magazine*, *Lippincott's Monthly Magazine*, *McClure's Magazine*, *Century Magazine*, *Ladies Home Journal* and *St Nicholas Magazine for Children* had competed to publish the latest story from Kipling's pen. His finest work of fiction, *Kim*, first appeared in serialised form in *McClure's Magazine*, beginning at Christmas 1900. Having begun his writing career as a journalist, he continued to use the popular press as his preferred first outlet. In September 1895 Kipling offered *The Times* some verses in support of the Royal Navy, and such was the popular response that its editor was happy to publish thereafter whatever Kipling sent him. In the following year, after much badgering for something to mark the Queen's Jubilee, Kipling wrote the five stanzas that came to be known as 'The Recessional'. From that time onwards the other national dailies joined *The Times* and the monthlies in the queue, happy to clear a space for whatever Mr Kipling had to offer.

An outpouring of trenchant polemical verses followed, each of which hit the public nerve square on, whether it was a call for America to join Britain as the world's lawgiver in 'The White Man's Burden' or a reminder of the nation's duty to look after its soldiery – 'The Absent-Minded Beggar' raising the then enormous sum of a quarter of a million pounds for the *Daily Mail*'s Absent-Minded Beggar Fund. In 1897 Kipling was formally enrolled as a member of the British Establishment when he was elected to the Athenaeum Club, its youngest member at thirty-one. Although he declined the Poet Laureateship and a knighthood, everyone knew that Kipling spoke for England and was Laureate of Empire in all but name.

In February 1899 disaster struck the Kiplings in New York, and the English-speaking world held its collective breath. First their beloved eldest daughter, six-year-old Josephine, died of whooping-cough, then the writer himself developed pneumonia in both lungs. Over ten days of crisis in early March, with Kipling unconscious or in delirium, the newspapers carried daily bulletins charting his progress. Crowds gathered outside his hotel, to stand in silence or kneel in prayer. His illness coincided with that of Pope Leo XIII, so that the news-stands carried the joint banner 'KIPLING and POPE'. 'Two nations have watched, by proxy, beside the sick-bed of the man that has so endeared himself to all Anglo-Saxon hearts,' wrote a contemporary. 'Knowledge of his fight with Death is the property of the public. He does not belong to himself, as do you and I; he is part of the Country . . . It is indisputable that, had Rudyard Kipling died, the hearts of millions of men would have ached with an agony of loss . . . There are thousands that *do* write; there are dozens that *can* write; but there is only one Rudyard Kipling.'[1] *The Times* devoted a leader to him, crediting Kipling with having enabled the West to understand the East as never before, and declaring him 'a patriot poet' who had 'sung the pride of Empire' while also preaching its obligations. The *Morning Post* paid its own tribute by printing, centre-page across three columns, a facsimile of the manuscript of Kipling's 'The English Flag'.[2]

Never had a writer been accorded such public affection, and when his recovery was known to be certain, telegrams and messages of goodwill poured in from every corner of the globe, their senders ranging from world leaders such as Theodore Roosevelt, Kaiser Wilhelm and Lord Curzon to the Sergeants' Mess of the Suffolk Regiment and the Soldiers' Institute at Allahabad. Nevertheless, with the death of his eldest and 'best-beloved' the blinds were lowered on the outside world. 'Much of the beloved Cousin Ruddy of our childhood died with Josephine,' wrote his niece Angela Thirkell, 'and I feel I have never seen him as a real person since that year.'[3]

Soon afterwards Kipling became the first celebrity to acquire a stalker. When he sailed to South Africa to winter there with his family in December 1901, he was tracked by a lunatic armed with a revolver who gained entry to the house in Cape Town lent Kipling by his admirer Cecil Rhodes. Only by administering copious draughts of whisky to the would-be assassin did Britain's most famous writer avert an untimely death at the age of thirty-five.[4]

Had Rudyard Kipling died in December 1901 in South Africa, instead of living on for another thirty-five years, our image of him would have been very different. This book is an account of that first half of his life: from his birth in Bombay on the evening of 30 December 1865 to the completion in 1900 of *Kim*, his greatest work and his last word on India. By the time *Kim* appeared in book form in October 1901 Kipling's extraordinary powers of imagination were already on the wane. The craftsmanship stayed with him for the rest of his life, particularly in his verse, but the spark of genius that gave his writing its sharp, dangerous crackle was almost gone, along with the desire to jolt that had made the best of his early work so electrifying to his Victorian readership.

More importantly, the seams he had mined so thoroughly for the best of his writing were all but exhausted. Long before his death in January 1936 Kipling's reputation was in eclipse. To liberals and literary figures alike he had become a hate-figure, in George Orwell's ugly phrasing, the 'morally insensitive . . . aesthetically disgusting . . . gutter patriot', the very embodiment of Little England jingoism. When his ashes were immured in

Westminster Abbey's Poets' Corner not a single important literary figure troubled to attend. He might almost have been, in the words of the title of his own flawed early novel, *The Light that Failed*.

And yet today the name of Rudyard Kipling is stuck as firmly in the public mind as that of any of the literary greats of his age, from Tennyson and Hardy at one end of the time frame to T. S. Eliot and D. H. Lawrence at the other, even if part of that familiarity comes second-hand from the Disneyfication of *The Jungle Book* and the dozens of turns of phrase or memorable lines that are now part of everyday speech: 'East is East and West is West', 'Good hunting', ''satiable curtiosity', 'The White Man's burden', 'Steady the Buffs', 'He travels the fastest who travels alone', 'As immutable as the hills', 'The most ancient profession in the world', 'The female of the species is deadlier than the male', 'The Colonel's Lady and Judy O'Grady are sisters under their skins', 'A woman is only a woman, but a good cigar is a smoke', 'You're a better man than I am, Gunga Din', 'Words are the most powerful drug used by mankind', 'A soldier known only to God', 'Lest we forget' and, above all, the opening lines of what is consistently voted Britain's most popular poem: 'If you can keep your head when all about you / Are losing theirs and blaming it on you.'

The last of the half-dozen generations reared on the *Just So Stories*, *The Jungle Book*, *Puck of Pook's Hill*, *Kim* and the collections of short stories that appeared under such titles as *Land and Sea Tales for Scouts and Guides* are now either dead or fast entering their dotage – the present writer among them. Yet, from the steady stream of biographies, critical studies, Kipling anthologies and reprints that continue to be published, it is clear that both the man and his work continue to command an audience.

What made Kipling so hugely popular in the 1890s was his seemingly unerring instinct for saying, not exactly what the public wanted to hear but what most needed to be said, and for saying it directly and in a way that was instantly quotable, if not singable. Among his contemporaries he was the most accessible of writers in what he wrote but, equally, the most private in his personal life, demanding to be judged by his writing alone. 'When I have any-thing to say, I write it down and sell it. My brains are my own,' he once declared to an American newspaper reporter. When he first became a public figure in 1891 he reacted to any perceived breach of his privacy with a hostility that bordered on paranoia, and that distrust grew more pointed with each passing year. The thought of his life and the lives of those closest to him coming under the scrutiny of biographers filled him with horror. In 1934 he was vis-ited at Bateman's, his home in East Sussex, by his old friend and publisher Frank Doubleday, who found him shovelling piles of his papers on to an open fire. When asked why, he declared that no one was going to make a monkey out of him after his death.

This was only the culmination of a process of covering his tracks which had begun in the 1890s when his old school friends and a fellow journalist from his India days started writing about him. In 1896 his one-time editor from Lahore, Kay Robinson, had writ-ten with his grudging approval a series of articles about their early days together in India. But then, when Kipling suffered his double pneumonia in February–March 1899 and seemed at death's door, Robinson wrote a follow-up, quoting extensively from an early letter in which Kipling had spoken frankly about his future hopes as a writer. Once recovered, Kipling made it plain that he regarded Robinson's behaviour as a breach of trust, paid him £50 for the return of his letter and never spoke to his old friend again. At much the same time he wrote to his old chum George Beresford ('M'Turk' in the *Stalky* stories), who had been writing articles about the background to the *Stalky* tales, imploring him to aban-don a projected autobiographical account of his schooldays with Kipling: 'If you love me don't publish them.'

Rudyard's sister Trix was the next to be approached, being warned by letter to be careful what she said about him: 'When they sound you out about my views, you must not repeat any of the things I told you.' According to Trix, 'Ruddy passed through a phase of almost morbid desire to throw veils over his perfectly respectable past. It used to sadden our parents a little – for after all he was not a bastard brought up in a gutter. I think it was the result of living in America and being badgered by the journalists.'[5] Whatever the cause, the urge to seek and destroy continued, and in the years that followed Kipling made strenuous efforts to recover his early letters and manuscripts and to warn off anyone who wanted to write about him. In this he was greatly assisted by his wife Carrie, staunchest of proctors.

In May 1910 the death occurred of 'Uncle Crom' Price, who had been the boy Ruddy's mentor and *in loco parentis* at United Services College in Devon. Six months later his mother, Alice, died, swiftly followed by the complete mental collapse of his sister Trix and then, two months later, the death of his beloved father, John Lockwood Kipling. Mother, father and only sister had made up three of the four corners of what the Kiplings had always called the 'Family Square', and the combination of tragedies had an effect scarcely less devastating than the loss of little Josephine a decade earlier. Rudyard Kipling tore up his parents' wills, broke off all communications with his mother's surviving sisters, and with the help of his wife Carrie set about burning his parents' papers over a three-day period – including all his letters to them and theirs to him.

Of the thousands of letters that passed between Ruddy and his parents, just two survive: one from father to son and one from son to father. 'If Rud had been a criminal,' wrote Trix of her brother's behaviour, 'he could not have been fonder of destroying any family papers that came his way.' But it was not just the immediate family papers that were destroyed. After the earlier death of his uncle Ned Burne-Jones in 1898 Rudyard had taken the opportunity to destroy the considerable correspondence between the two of them – and, while he was about it, most of his letters to the beloved aunt, Georgie Burne-Jones (née Macdonald), who had nurtured him at her London home every Christmas during his darkest years.

The setting up of a Kipling Society was vigorously opposed by

Kipling for many years but in 1927 it was formed with the active support of his oldest friend, Lionel 'Stalky' Dunsterville, causing its subject to complain bitterly: 'As to your damn Society, how would you like to be turned into an anatomical specimen, before you were dead, and shown up on a table once a quarter? . . . Seriously, old man, when a man has given all that he has to give to the public in his work, he is the keener to keep to himself the little (and it is very little) that remains.'[6] In 1931 Kipling's niece Angela Thirkell published *Three Houses*, reminiscences of her childhood days at the Burne-Jones's family house at Rottingdean, East Sussex. She was the daughter of Margaret, youngest of the Burne-Jones cousins, and Ruddy's confidante as the 'Wop of Albion'. In Kipling's eyes it was yet another betrayal and another breach of his privacy.

Eventually Rudyard Kipling felt he had no option but to write about himself, which he did in the last months of his life in a disingenuous autobiography entitled *Something of Myself*, which might more accurately have been called *As Little About Myself As I Can Get Away With*. It said a lot about the craft of writing but gave away almost nothing about his private life beyond what was already known or touched on in his fiction. The manuscript was unfinished when Rudyard Kipling died on 18 January 1936. Carrie Kipling read it and declared that as it stood it was 'too offensive' for publication and would require the editing out of 'anything that people can ride off and dispute about'. After extensive cutting and rewriting, first by Carrie and then by Kipling's close friend H. A. Gwynne working to her instructions, a version was published in February 1937.

Although Carrie donated a number of her late husband's manuscripts to various libraries, these gifts were bound in some cases by stipulations that made it virtually impossible for scholars to publish any studies based on them; the manuscript of *Kim*, donated to the British Library, was a notorious case in point. Carrie also felt duty bound to continue the incineration of letters initiated by her husband, buying up his correspondence wherever and whenever the opportunity arose and setting matches to it. She also burned at least one notebook containing unpublished work and, according to their surviving daughter Elsie, also destroyed 'a large canvas-covered case labelled "Notions". . . containing unfinished stories and poems, notes and ideas, collected through the years'.[7] Carrie's last act of faith to her husband was to order in her will that the diaries which she had kept throughout their married life should be destroyed.

By these concerted means a mass of Kipling material was lost to literature, most significantly Ruddy's letters written between the ages of fifteen and thirty-five to those closest to him. From this period only one cache survived the flames: a bundle of letters mostly written between the ages of twenty-one and twenty-three to Mrs Edmonia Hill, the most doted-on of several older married women to whom the young writer poured out his soul, and the most influential. When Edmonia Hill fell on hard times in her old age she put the letters on the open market and they were bought by an American collector. Carrie Kipling got to hear of it, bought the letters back and destroyed them – unaware that copies had been made.

When Carrie Kipling died in 1937 the Kipling legacy passed to Mrs Elsie Bambridge. Fortunately for literature Elsie did not inherit her parents' literary pyromania. Indeed, she went to some trouble to preserve and collate her father's papers, tracking down the copies of her father's letters to Edmonia Hill and adding other Kipling material to her collection. When in 1940 Trix learned that Elsie had located one of her father's early notebooks, she wrote to congratulate her and to express delight at its survival: 'How wonderful to see that black MS book again! I think Mother gave it to him when she went back to India in 1881 – he had it at U. S. Col [United Services College]. And it was known and loved by me when I was 13 or 14. I'm so glad it escaped the frenzy of burning any letters and papers connected with his youth (and mine too, alas) which possessed him directly after Mother's death.'[8] Sadly, Mrs Bambridge felt obliged to carry out her mother's wishes by destroying the forty-five volumes of her diaries – although not before she had allowed Charles Carrington to read them through and make notes.

As her father's executor Elsie Bambridge was determined to preserve his good name, and in authorising a biography she demanded of its author, Lord Birkenhead, such stringent conditions that it should have come as no surprise to him when she rejected his first draft and paid him off. When the 'suppressed' Birkenhead biography was finally published in 1978 it contained no great revelations, but did show that Mrs Bambridge had been correct in believing that it did no justice to her father. Fortunately, after Birkenhead she turned to the historian Charles Carrington, who, despite the many obstacles, produced a biography that was a milestone of objective truth-gathering. When Elsie Bambridge died in 1976 what remained of the Kipling papers went to the National Trust – and thence to the University of Sussex.

In the event, the purges and the bonfires were not enough. So prolific was 'Gigadibs the literary man' that enough survives in the way of manuscripts, lesser works published and long forgotten and, above all, letters and scraps of letters to allow the biographer to put solid flesh on bone – and more than enough to show that the Ruddy who grew prematurely into adulthood in the 1880s and achieved enormous fame in the 1890s was a far more complex, troubled and troubling individual than the man he presented himself to be in *Something of Myself*. However Kipling may have wished to be remembered, this is Ruddy humanised: his complications are the man; they are, to a great extent, what make him a writer of genius.

I

'Mother of cities'

BOMBAY AND A BEGINNING, 1865–7

> Mother of cities to me
>   For I was born at her gate,
> Between the palms and the sea
>   Where the world-end steamers wait.
>
> Rudyard Kipling, 'To the City of Bombay',
> *The Song of the Cities*, 1894

The 'world-end steamers' that carried generations of Anglo-Indians between Britain and India are long gone, but shipping still crowds the roads in Bombay Harbour, and passengers still disembark at the quay known as the Apollo Bunder, even if most of them are day-trippers returning from Elephanta Island. But apart from the Bunder little remains of the Bombay seafront as it was when its most famous British son was born. To find the Bombay of Rudyard Kipling you must strike inland to the open space in front of the Maharashtra State Police Headquarters, formerly the Royal Alfred Sailors' Home. Six broad avenues converge here, requiring the traffic to circle a modest fountain erected in the year of Kipling's birth, 1865. Given the stranglehold now exerted by Maharashtran political lobbies on the city, it is probably just as well that so few people know that the fountain celebrates General Arthur Wellesley's victories over the Marathas.

Walk on past the Indo-Saracenic domes of what was the Prince of Wales Museum and is now the Chhatrapati Shivaji Maharaj

Vastu Sangrahalaya, in honour of the Maratha warlord Shivaji. The museum was built after the city's craze for Gothic and Romanesque Transitional had begun to subside, but on the opposite side of the road the arcades of Elphinstone College and the David Sassoon Mechanics' Institute and Library give the first hint of architectural excesses to come. The avenue widens at a section known today as the *Kala Ghoda*, the Black Horse, after an equestrian statue of another Prince of Wales that stood here before relegation to the Byculla Zoological Gardens, Bombay's graveyard of the British Raj.

Push on through the traffic along Mahatma Gandhi Road and follow the curve of the ghostly ramparts of Bombay Fort. Time was when no building was allowed within a thousand yards of the Fort's walls, in order to provide a clear field of fire, so that this was all open land and coconut palms, a grassy crescent known to Bombay's British residents as the Esplanade and to everyone else as the *maidan*. Most of the buildings here date from the building spree that followed the levelling of the ramparts in the early 1860s.[1]

Now we are getting closer to Kipling country, but first another intersection, laid over the foundations of Bombay Fort's Church Gate, and another fountain: the city's much-loved Flora Fountain, which only the politicians call Hutatma Chowk. Who remembers today that it was paid for by public subscription to honour the departing Governor, Sir Bartle Frere, the man who more than any other individual created modern Bombay? But press on. From Flora Fountain continue to trace the curve of the old ramparts to the point where Bazaar Gate stood – and where suddenly and dramatically the Victoria Terminus explodes into view in all its High Gothic extravagance. What else could it be called today except the Chhatrapati Shivaji Terminus, even if some stubborn citizens insist on sticking to 'VT'?

But ignore VT and ignore, if you must, on the other side of the street, F. W. Stevens' other architectural glory: the Bombay Municipality Building with its absurdly elongated central dome. Carry on up what was formerly Esplanade Road, past the Times of India Building on the left, and past the Anjuman-i-Islam Muslim School next to it – which might not be so easy if it's break time and the children are out. Once safely past, cast your eyes over the generous acreage of land to your left, with its abundance of mature trees and shrubs: banyan, mango, jacaranda, bougain-villaea, frangipani and palms of every order. Young men and women throng the paths that criss-cross the site, mostly in jeans but a number wearing brightly coloured saris or *salwar-kameez*, with shawls over the shoulders. A notice at the entrance identi-fies them as students of the Sir Jamsetji Jijibhoy School of Applied Art.

Enter the grounds. Best to make an appointment, but no one will really mind if you do not. Set well back from the traffic you will find an oasis hidden among the trees, where the loudest sounds are of mynahs, parakeets, crows and fruit-bats, and at its heart, in what is still 'a garden full of sunshine and birds',[2] a two-storey bungalow with a tiled roof, upstairs verandah and faded, green-painted gables. In the back porch is a head cast in bronze which bears a startling resemblance to Mahatma Gandhi. A plaque on the wall declares this to be the birthplace of Rudyard Kipling – which, strictly speaking, it is not.

Neither the bungalow with the faded green gables nor any of the present buildings in the grounds of the Sir Jamsetji Jijibhoy School of Art had been built when the Kiplings first arrived in Bombay. The city then stood poised on the cusp. An island of plans, marked-out plots, new-laid avenues and railway lines – and new acres fast being reclaimed from the sea. A city of dreams and great expectations.

In the early hours of 11 May 1865 the P&O mail steamer *Rangoon* was piloted through the crowded shipping lanes to anchor some distance off the stone pier of the Apollo Bunder. Later that morn-ing relays of *gallibats* and *dhangis* – already corrupted by British mariners into 'jolly-boats' and 'dinghies' – ferried the passengers and their baggage ashore, among them a European couple both of that indeterminate age when youth shades into maturity. A shrewd observer might have hazarded a number of guesses: that they were newcomers to India, not particularly well off, quite possibly newly-wed. A prematurely greying beard combined with a bald pate made the man appear the older by some years, but in reality both he and his wife had been born in the same year, 1837, and it was she who was the older by three months – a seniority she afterwards concealed to the extent of requiring her husband to add an extra year to his age.

Of the two, it was the woman who would have made an immediate impression, even though we may picture her sporting a 'desert hat of the foulest appearance' that was part of the tropical trousseau selected before they had set sail from Southampton a month earlier. According to the youngest of her four sisters, she was of 'pale complexion, dark brown hair and grey eyes with black lashes, and delicately pencilled eyebrows. In those eyes lay the chief fascination of her face, so expressive were they that they seemed to deepen or pale in colour according to passing emotion.' No less striking, but tactfully overlooked, was the firm mouth and set jaw that marked Alice as the most determined of the five Macdonald sisters.

As well as being the eldest and tallest, Alice was held to be the most 'Irish' in temperament: 'She had the ready wit and power of repartee, the sentiment, and I may say the unexpectedness which one associates with that race. It was impossible to predict how she would act at any given point. There was a certain fascination in this, and fascinating she certainly was. Needless to say she had many admirers, and it must be confessed was a flirt.'[3] Alice's younger brother took the same view, believing his sister to possess 'the nimblest mind' he had ever known, together with 'the kind of vision that is afforded by flashes of lightning. She saw things in a moment and did not so much reason as pounce on her conclusions ... Her power of speech was unsurpassed – her chief difficulty being that she found language a slow-moving medium of expression that failed to keep up with her thought.' But Alice's wit was also sharp-edged – 'a weapon of whose keenness of point there could be no doubt, and foolish or mischievous people were made to feel it'.[4] This 'sprightly, if occasionally caustic, wit' made her very good company – 'except, perhaps, to those who had cause to fear the lash of her epigrams'.[5] Perhaps not surprisingly, Alice's favourite character in fiction was Thackeray's mercurial, ambitious Becky Sharp.

At first sight her companion did not impress, standing no more than five foot three inches in his boots; one contemporary in India described him as 'a little man with a big head, and eyes for everything'.[6] But John Lockwood Kipling was someone who improved enormously on acquaintance. His new brother-in-law had very soon warmed to 'his gentleness of spirit, his unselfish affection and general lovableness', and had been equally impressed by his mental powers: 'His power of acquiring and retaining knowledge was extraordinary. His curiosity, in the nobler sense of the term, was alive and active in almost every field of knowledge. All things interested him . . . He was widely read, and what he read he remembered and had at his disposal.'[7] These characteristics were to stand John Lockwood Kipling in good stead in India, where he would become known as a gentle, easy-going, even-tempered man with an encyclopaedic knowledge. 'One of the sweetest characters I have ever known' was how one of his friends was later to sum him up,[8] while one of his son's fellow journalists would remember him as 'a rare, genial soul, with happy artistic instincts . . . and a generous, cynical sense of humour'.[9]

Alice Macdonald and John Lockwood Kipling had met two years earlier at a picnic beside a small reservoir named Lake Rudyard, outside Burslem in the Staffordshire Potteries; he of solid Yorkshire stock, she part Scot and part Welsh – 'all Celt and three parts fire', as her son later put it.[10] He was the eldest of six children, she the eldest of five daughters in a family of seven children. A common nonconformist background, with two generations of Methodist ministers or lay-preachers in both families, had given them very similar upbringings of austere gentility, where reading, self-improvement and fireside entertainment were the order of the day. Both had experienced a 'highly developed family life' which had encouraged them to think well of themselves – perhaps too much so. In the opinion of Alice's younger brother Fred, it had led his sisters to think 'more highly of their common gifts and qualities than is altogether good for them, and to undervalue other qualities'.[11] In Alice Macdonald and John Lockwood their close family circles had also developed a common love of music and literature, a shared dislike of chapel cant and a cheerful cynicism. In Alice's case, it had also led to an abiding fascination with table-rapping, spiritualism and the occult.

With her agile mind, Alice was yet clumsy on her feet; the very opposite, in fact, of John Lockwood Kipling, who was nimble on the dance floor but had a mind that 'moved more slowly, and was patient and meditative'. 'The result', according to Fred Macdonald, 'was a kinship of thought and feeling that soon ripened into something more.'[12] It was John Lockwood Kipling who provided the solid foundation upon which their marriage was built. Although he was as keen on poetry and literature as Alice, his creativity found its best expression in drawing and modelling. In the summer of 1851, when John Lockwood was fourteen, he had visited London on a Cook's Excursion to see the Great Exhibition and was so inspired that he had decided there and then to make a career as a modeller in pottery. He left school and through a friend of his father's was taken on by a local firm in Burslem, while at the same time going to evening classes at Stoke School of Art.

A seven-year apprenticeship turned John Lockwood into a thoroughly capable draughtsman and modeller in clay. The Stoke School of Art became linked to the South Kensington Museum when it opened in 1857, which led to John spending two years in London as a junior assistant to the sculptor J. Birnie Philip as he worked on the frieze on the podium of the Albert Memorial and other designs. The South Kensington Museum then became the headquarters of the School of Ornamental Art (later the Royal

College of Art), set up to establish a national standard and curriculum for art teaching based on solid craftsmanship and classical draughtsmanship. After developing the skills in modelling and carving bas-reliefs which became his speciality, John worked as an assistant in the Department of Science and Art, where he further refined his techniques as a modeller in terracotta.

During this same period Alice Macdonald's social horizons widened dramatically when she and her sisters were introduced by their eldest brother, Harry, to his school friends at the King Edward VI Grammar School in Birmingham, among them a close-knit group of aspiring artists and writers which included William Fulford, Cormell Price and Edward 'Ned' Jones. When Harry moved on to Oxford his circle of friends widened to include William Morris and other followers of the Pre-Raphaelite movement inspired by Ruskin. Their father's move to a new parish in London continued the Macdonald sisters' emancipation, bringing the two eldest, Alice and Georgie, into contact with an ever-widening coterie of young painters and poets based in Bloomsbury and Red Lion Square. Fired by a shared passion for all things 'holy and beautiful and true',[13] these termed themselves the 'The Brotherhood' and besides Ned Jones – now calling himself Burne-Jones – they included Dante Gabriel Rossetti, Ford Madox Brown, Edward Poynter and, from time to time, their chief mentor, John Ruskin.

Hard on the heels of Alice and Georgie, and no less eager, came their younger sisters, Agnes and Louie, all four becoming committed Brotherhood groupies. Alice was quick to fall in and out of love. She was twice engaged to the writer William Fulford and once to the Irish poet William Allingham, prompting Edith to declare that she 'never seemed to go on a visit without becoming engaged to some wild cad of the desert'.[14] Georgie was more committed, going one step further than her elder sister by marrying Ned Burne-Jones in 1860 and setting an example that Agnes subsequently followed by marrying Edward Poynter. Alice, however, chose to go her own way – until the increasing ill-health of their father, now based in Wolverhampton, obliged her to abandon London and return to her parents' side.

Earlier that year John Lockwood Kipling's ambitions had also suffered a setback with the sudden death of his father. He too was forced to leave London and go home, to support his mother and four unmarried sisters by working for his former employers in Burslem as a modeller and designer in their pottery. So it came about that Alice Macdonald and John Lockwood Kipling first set eyes on each other just when both had seen their hopes dimmed. In April 1863 Alice went to visit her brother Fred in Burslem, where the latter had recently begun his first ministry after deciding to follow in his father's and grandfather's footsteps. Soon after her arrival she and Fred joined a picnic party beside the reservoir of Lake Rudyard organised by John Lockwood Kipling's employer. According to John Lockwood, he looked across the spread and saw 'a beauteous creature, pensively eating salad'.[15] The catalyst that drew them together is said to have been an emaciated grey horse standing in a nearby field: John murmured an apposite line from Browning's *Childe Harold* which Alice continued. By midsummer they were engaged. Alice's only regret, as later given to an old friend, was that 'I ought to have met John earlier.'[16]

Their future happiness now lay in John securing a post with long-term prospects that would remove them from the provincial confines of Yorkshire and the Potteries and ideally provide Alice with the company of kindred spirits such as those she had known in London. By the end of June 1863 John was back in West Kensington assisting the architectural decorator Godfrey Sykes with the modelling of the terracottas at the Museum.[17] A frieze of unglazed hard-baked red clay set high on the wall in the courtyard of what is today the Victoria and Albert Museum shows the twenty-seven-year-old John Lockwood Kipling among the designers and craftsmen who had worked on the architectural decorations of the South Kensington Museum: an unmistakable stocky figure with full beard and deep-sunk eyes.

John continued to work intermittently at the Museum until

December 1864. On the third day of that month the Honourable Claude Erskine, a senior judge of the Bombay High Court with a long-standing interest in public education in Bombay and then on leave in England, wrote to the Chief Secretary to the Government of Bombay to say he had found just the man to fill the second of three new posts at the Sir Jamsetjee Jeejeebhoy School of Art and Industry: 'As Architectural Sculptor, we have been fortunate in securing the services of Mr J. Lockwood Kipling . . . For the last four years he has been in the service of the Department of Science and Art at South Kensington, and most of the modelling for the Terra Cotta decorations of the Museum there have been executed by him . . . He appears to be specially qualified for the duties now allotted to him.'[18] Besides setting out the future course of John Lockwood Kipling's career, this letter also gave notice of its subject's decision to abandon 'John' in favour of his more formal second given name, derived from his mother's maiden name. At their marriage, in Kensington on 18 March 1865, his wife followed suit in her own fashion, signing herself 'Alice Macdonald Kipling'.

It is hard to understand why any young couple without local connections would have wanted to exile themselves in India at this time. British India in the mid-1860s was a far cry from the land of the nabob and the pagoda tree of earlier years. Barely seven years had elapsed since the hideous eruption of violence known as the Sepoy or Indian Mutiny, when British men, women and children in scores of isolated communities scattered across the northern and central Indian plains had been put to the *tulwar* and bayonet. In the words of the Mutiny's first historian, the British had experienced 'the degradation of fearing those we had taught to fear us'.[19]

The degradation had been followed by bloody retribution, with the avenging armies of the British often failing to make any distinction between rebels and innocent bystanders. The result was a legacy of bitter distrust and a drawing apart of the two races that was to last for decades. As one of the most widely read Anglo-Indian writers of the time put it, 'a terrible abyss has opened between the rulers and the ruled; and every huckster, every pettifogger who wears a hat and breeches, looks down upon the noblest of the natives'.[20] But it was not only hucksters and pettifoggers who held such prejudices. Writing to a friend at this time, Bombay's former Governor, Sir Bartle Frere, bewailed the fact that attitudes had changed for the worse. 'You have no idea how much India has altered. The sympathy which Englishmen felt for the natives has changed to a general feeling of repugnance.'[21]

Before 1857 the British in India had habitually referred to themselves as 'Indians' and to Indians as 'Natives', a word employed without negative connotations. After 1857 it became 'Anglo-Indians' and – among a sizeable segment of the British population – 'Niggers'. Two of the most popular writers of the period were Captain George Atkinson, whose *'Curry and Rice' on Forty Plates: or The Ingredients of Social Life at 'Our Station' in India* was to be found on the bookshelves of every well-established Anglo-Indian household, and Major Walter Yeldham, whose first volume of collected verse, *Lays of Ind*, was published in 1871 under the pen-name of 'Aliph Cheem'. Both use the N-word casually and unashamedly. Indeed, one of 'Aliph Cheem's' lays is entitled 'Those Niggers' and tells of Colonel Thunder's distrust of every category of Indian. It begins:

> Old Colonel Thunder used to say,
>   And fetch his bearer's head a whack,
> That if they'd let him have his way,
>   He'd murder every mortal black.

And ends:

> In fact, throughout our whole dominion,
>   No honest nigger could be got,
> And never would, in his opinion,
>   Until we'd polished off the lot.

After an initial outpouring of memorials and personal reminiscences the Mutiny of '57 became a taboo subject among Anglo-Indians, something not to be spoken about but always there at the back of one's mind, along with the unspoken fear that what had happened once could happen again, and that Indians were to be neither trusted nor respected. These were attitudes that the Kiplings soon came to share.

Whatever doubts the young couple may have had were evidently outweighed by the prospect of financial independence. To a penurious couple whose fathers had never earned more than £160 in a year, the terms of the Article of Agreement that Lockwood Kipling signed on 14 January 1865 with Judge Erskine must have seemed generous: an appointment for three years on a fixed salary of four hundred rupees per mensem, amounting to just over £400 per annum, together with free accommodation, sea passages paid and a further £200 for kitting-out. On the face of it, this would allow Lockwood to remit a small sum home every month and, with careful housekeeping, put something aside for the future.

But what he may not have grasped, for neither his nor Alice's families had links with India, was that he would be working for the Government of Bombay's Department of Public Instruction in the lower of two tiers of government service. The upper level was made up of Civilians, members of the Indian Civil Service who formed the 'first firing line' of British India's civil and political administration, enjoying enhanced status, generous salaries, the prospect of promotion to the highest ranks of government and early retirement on a fat pension. There was a huge distinction, as much in status as in terms and conditions, between the members of this 'covenanted' service, and other government employees. A further distinction was that many of the latter were employed by provincial rather than central government services, and the terms they offered were limited and without enhanced salaries or pensions.

The young man who came out to India to escape British class

barriers found himself trapped in a caste system as inflexible as that followed by the Hindus. 'You must be "in the service" – that is either a Military man or a Civilian – to be thought anything of,' noted a young British memsahib in a letter to a friend written at this period. 'If you are an outsider, a railway engineer, or an Indigo Planter or anything else, you are supposed to be not a gentleman, and society makes a dead set against you and excludes you.'[22] However witty and amusing his wife might be, a junior officer in Bombay's Department of Public Instruction was ranked very low in the published Order of Precedence, which laid down the exact standing and salary of every grade in every department of government service.

It may be that a twinge of desperation had entered the young couple's minds, as they approached their twenty-eighth birthdays without that financial security deemed a prerequisite for marriage in middle-class society. Or perhaps it was quite simply that Bombay, for all its unknowns and uncertainties, represented a huge gamble. After all, a quite extraordinary metamorphosis was under way there, attracting worldwide attention and drawing adventurers from every corner of the globe. Bombay in the spring of 1865 was widely recognised as a boom town, a trading port which played by its own rules, a beacon of opportunity whereby an independent-minded young couple – British or Indian – might make their own way free of many of the constraints that held them back in their own country.

Nor would Lockwood and Alice be entirely without friends, for the last of the three teaching posts was filled by one of Lockwood's fellow artists from the South Kensington Museum, a Welshman named John Griffiths, of the same age as Lockwood Kipling and also an expert in terracotta sculpture, although hired for his drawing and painting skills. Together with an art-metalworker named Higgins, these two were being hired to introduce 'South Kensington principles' to India, with the goal of establishing a centre of artistic excellence in Bombay that would bring about a revival of India's traditional arts and crafts skills, considered by

Erskine and other like-minded officials to be in serious decline as a result of an excess of mass-produced imported goods from Europe. Here was a worthy purpose that must have appealed to the evangelical in Lockwood Kipling's nature. His desire to get young Indian craftsmen and artisans to abandon their slapdash Indian ways and learn to draw, hew, chisel, mould and paint things the way it ought to be done was to become an abiding obsession that stayed with him throughout his years in India.

Bombay had always been a place of escape and opportunity. Unlike the two other Indian Presidency capitals, Calcutta and Madras, it was an island city, blessed with the finest natural harbour on India's western seaboard but handicapped by poor communications with the mainland. Its nucleus was Mumbai, the largest of seven islets formerly separated from both the mainland and each other by tidal flats and mangrove swamps but now linked by causeways and bold reclamation schemes into one island some eight miles long and three miles wide, popularly likened to a right hand 'laid palm upwards, with the fingers stretching southwards into the sea and the thumb representing Malabar Hill, with Back Bay between the thumb and forefinger'.[23]

The Portuguese had been the first to recognise Mumbai's strategic value, establishing a toehold on its southern tip in the form of a fort that commanded the great harbour and renaming it Bom Bahia, the 'good bay'. Bombay had then fallen into the lap of King Charles the Second as part of his marriage dowry from the sister of the king of Portugal, and he had passed it on to the East India Company for an annual rent of £10. Initially it had proved a disastrous investment, the belligerent Marathas of the Deccan frustrating all attempts by 'John Company' to penetrate the Indian interior while at the same time the island's malarious swamps and foul waters killed off its servants as fast as they could be replaced. However, these setbacks helped to turn Bombay into the most cosmopolitan city in Asia – by forcing its governors to offer inducements to settlers from the mainland, including the right of traders to 'deal freely and without restraint with whoever they think proper'.[24]

Indian merchants found in Bombay a freedom from caste and race prohibitions unthinkable on the mainland, resulting in a mixing of communities that led Lockwood Kipling in later years to describe the city as 'a very unIndian, cockney sort of place'.[25] Combined with an unusual willingness in the authorities to allow Indians to play a part in the running of the municipality, this liberal spirit fostered a sense of common identity and civic pride which stood the city in good stead in the maelstrom of 1857 – although the docility of its citizens may have owed something to the activities of Bombay's Commissioner of Police, Charles Forjett. Born and bred in India, Forjett was by his own account 'a master of guise [*sic*]' who would mingle with alleged conspirators and encourage them to speak against the Government, before throwing off his disguise and arresting them the moment they did so. His actions spread such terror in the bazaars that no one dared say a seditious word, whether in public or private. Several decades later the Forjett legend became part of the composite of Indian police officers, dead and living, which went to make 'Strickland' in Rudyard Kipling's *Kim* and in half a dozen of his short stories.

The first to take advantage of the city's relaxed trading rules were the Parsis, a minority community initially based up the coast in Gujarat. A family of shipwrights, the Wadias, began turning out Bombay-built fighting ships of Malabar teak for the Royal Navy that were easier to handle than British-made men-of-war, lasted twice as long and were cheaper to produce. When Parliament ended the East India Company's trading monopoly in 1813 the Parsis were ideally placed to compete on equal terms for the hugely profitable China trade, and among them was Rustomjee Jamsetjee Battliwallah, who had migrated to Bombay as a sixteen-year-old orphan to join his uncle in the Native Quarter within the walls of Bombay Fort. Like many Parsis, Jamsetjee initially took a hybrid surname based on his occupation, which in his uncle's case and at first in his own was selling empty bottles, only reverting to traditional Parsi custom and adding his father's name of Jeejeebhoy after he had made his fortune. Within a decade Jamsetjee Jeejeebhoy had become a rupee multimillionaire, having cornered India's entire export trade to China, much of it in the form of opium.

In this same period the long struggle between the Marathas and the East India Company for possession of the Indian interior ended with a series of military victories for the latter, swiftly followed by the building of a highway over the hitherto impenetrable Western Ghat mountain range and a causeway linking the island to the mainland. Bombay at last had unimpeded access to India's hinterland, and within a decade the city's population had doubled to over half a million. The long-established and the better-off remained crammed together within the protective walls of Bombay Fort, while the newer economic migrants settled in an ever-expanding township known first as Black Town, then as Dungaree,[26] and finally as the Native Town, separated from the Fort by the *cordon sanitaire* of the Esplanade.

The China trade provided the backbone to Bombay's economy until the Opium War of 1840. A slump followed, greatly exacerbated by the collapse of the city's other mainstay, the export of calico and fine cotton muslin piece-goods manufactured on the spinning wheel and hand loom. These *swadeshi* goods now faced punishing import duties in Britain while at the same time machine-made cotton goods from Lancashire were allowed to flood the Indian market almost free of dues. Even so, immigrants continued to swell Bombay's population, putting the city's infrastructure under increasing strain. 'All round the Island of Bombay was one foul cesspool,' wrote the city's first historian, 'sewers discharging on the sands, rocks only used for the purposes of nature. To ride home to Malabar Hill along the sands of Back Bay was to encounter sights and odours too horrible to describe . . . To travel by rail from Boree Bunder to Byculla, or to go to Mody Bay, was to see in the foreshore the latrine of the whole population of the Native Town.'[27]

What reversed Bombay's decline was the American Civil War. Deprived of the American South's raw cotton by the North's blockade of its ports, the Lancashire mills turned to the cotton fields of Western India. The result was a cotton boom that expanded into a wider commercial boom, greatly helped by the completion of the Great Indian Peninsula Railway's line over the Bhor Ghat and the opening of the Bombay Baroda and Central India Railway – allowing cotton to be carried direct from the cotton fields up-country to Bombay's Cotton Green and thence by sea to the outside world. Bombay's own cotton mills began to flourish, and in four years the cotton trade brought in £80 million sterling to the city. The opium trade also revived, exports to China rising to an average of 37,000 chests per year and adding further to the fortunes of the merchants involved – predominantly Indian rather than British.

Economic migrants flocked to the island by land and sea, eager for a slice of the city's good fortune, trebling the population within less than a decade to more than 800,000. Such was the pressure on housing that by 1864 two-storey Native dwellings were occupied by an average of six families, or sixty-one persons.[28] For much of the year the greater part of Bombay's citizenry slept on rooftops or on the streets, the better-off on *charpoys* or bedsteads, the rest on the ground, but all wrapped head to foot in white sheets to keep off mosquitoes, so that at night much of the city resembled a morgue.

Presiding over this massive accumulation of both wealth and numbers as Governor of Bombay was the far-sighted Sir Henry Bartle Frere, ambitious to turn the island into the first city of Asia. In a remarkable gesture of confidence, Frere ordered the ramparts and ditches of the Fort to be levelled. The new land was then sold by auction and the money put towards the construction of a number of grandiose public buildings worthy of Bombay's new position as the 'Manchester of the East'. They were to be designed by the best English architects according to the latest style and laid out in extended line to look out across the sweep of Back Bay, like a chain of Gothic cathedrals. A modern business district was also planned, with broad avenues that broke up the Esplanade into four greens, to be serviced by two new railway termini that would allow the BB&CI and the GIP railways to deliver passengers and goods almost to the water's edge – where new docks would be built on reclaimed land.

With a little arm-twisting from Frere, the city's leading financiers and industrialists now embarked on a quite extraordinary round of public benefaction. Wealthy traders like Premchand Roychand ('the uncrowned king of Bombay'), Sir Cowasji Jehangir Readymoney ('the Peabody of the East'), Sir David Sassoon (a Sephardi Jew from Baghdad with a classic rags-to-riches story) and Sir Jamsetjee Jeejeebhoy vied with one another to fund new bridges, embankments and water tanks, and to set up and endow public institutions. Roychand paid for the construction of Bombay University's library and attached bell-tower, Jehangir set up forty drinking fountains at various points in the city, Sassoon funded schools and hospitals and Jeejeebhoy established – among much else – a School of Art and Industry that came to be known, for simplicity's sake, as the 'Sir J. J. School of Art'.

Hitherto the scarcity of land had limited the city's growth, but now the combination of excess wealth and a determined municipal government eager to support private ventures led to the setting up of scores of wildly ambitious schemes – which very quickly degenerated into a mania for speculation. James Maclean, owner and editor of the English-language *Bombay Gazette*, was one of many citizens caught up in the events that followed. 'The value of land had been trebled and quadrupled,' he later wrote. 'The population was every day increasing in numbers, and, as the available space within the island was very small, every additional foot tacked on seemed likely to be worth its weight in gold.'[29]

By the start of 1864, the year before the Kiplings' arrival in Bombay, every company in the city, as well as any individual who could rub a few silver rupees together, was deeply involved, investing in such ventures as the huge Back Bay Reclamation Scheme, set up to extend the city's western seafront deeper into the great curve of sea and sand that was one of the island's most attractive features. At first speculation was confined to ventures in cotton and land but, as the profits grew and the options diminished, all sorts of ingenious financial associations were formed, with investors clamouring to buy shares. 'The passion for speculation', wrote Maclean, 'is a contagious disease, and spreads like wildfire as soon as a few brilliant examples are on record to show with what ease fortunes may be won.' The prospect of 600 per cent returns 'sent the city quite mad . . . The Government of Bombay, not thinking what fortunes it wrecked and what lives it made miserable, and only eager to get money for the prosecution of its own public works, added fuel to the fire by inciting projections of new schemes.'

Many Britons in India found this state of affairs in Bombay extremely unsettling, not least because of the growing wealth of the Parsi community. 'Government is being jostled out of Bombay,' declared the editor of the country's newest English-language daily, the *Pioneer* of Allahabad:

> The Parsees, by their enormous profits, are making everyone discontented with Government pay, some men have degraded themselves by taking bribes in the shape of shares – others more honourable are leaving Government service to make their fortunes in commerce. Parsees splash the mud up against you as you walk; Parsees puff their smoke into your wife's face as they pass; purse-proud Parsees are admitted into English society, and delight to think that the wealth which introduced them there is the only test of power . . . If they would only keep themselves aloof from us in their social relations, as other Natives do, these annoyances would be less intimately felt.[30]

On 9 April 1865, the day before the Kiplings set sail for India, a 'horrid telegraph' announcing the surrender of General Lee's army at Appomattox brought Bombay's share-buying mania to an abrupt halt. Even before the news of the final surrender of the Confederate Army had reached Bombay the price of cotton had halved. By the time the Kiplings set foot on the Apollo Bunder three weeks later Bombay's stock market was in free fall. As Maclean saw it, 'When the crash came there was nothing but paper to meet it, and the whole elaborate edifice of speculation toppled down like a house of cards . . . Men who had been trading or speculating beyond their means found themselves unable to meet their engagement; a leading firm of Parsee merchants set the example of failing for three millions; and a panic ensued which baffles descriptions.' A brief rally towards the end of 1865 was followed by a second collapse and 'the panic at Bombay set in with renewed intensity'. By the end of 1866 virtually every bank and land company in the city had failed, leading to the collapse of scores of leading firms and leaving many individuals bankrupt. Yet the boom-funded investment that had gone into land reclamation and building over the previous five years had given the city a modern infrastructure that was of enormous advantage in years to come. As Maclean was afterwards to remind his readers, 'the splendour of the public buildings and useful and benevolent institutions of new Bombay is due to the munificence of the speculators of 1864–5'.

This was the extraordinary scene that met the Kiplings on arrival: an island in the throes of transformation, the walls of a score of public buildings half-built on every side, along with new avenues and railway lines, and acres of land freshly reclaimed or in the process of rising from the sea – while at the same time the community teetered on the brink of ruin: prices rocketing as inflation took hold, affordable housing impossible to come by, thousands thrown out of work and many households facing destitution. The crisis was encapsulated in verses that went the rounds at this time, part of which went:

> Three *Wallahs* [persons] came sailing out to the East,
> Out to the East as far as Bombay.

> Each thought to go home with a fortune at least,
>> And live like a swell meanwhile on his pay.
> But *Wallahs* must work, and *Wallahs* must swear:
>> For there's nothing to earn, and things are so dear
> That Sir Bartle Frere is starving.[31]

One of the casualties of the 1865 crash was the building programme for the School of Arts. For the purpose a generous parcel of land had been made over to Sir Jamsetjee Jeejeebhoy at the eastern end of the Esplanade beside the Mody Bay reclamations, where a hundred acres of the foreshore was in the process of being filled with earth and rubble for the foundations of the GIP Railway's Victoria Terminus. Plans for a magnificent school of art modelled on South Kensington were being drawn up but in the meantime what were known as *pendals* – described in official reports as 'a set of sheds' – would have to serve as accommodation for staff and students, and even these were going to take some weeks to put up. So, instead of moving into the roomy bungalow they had expected to occupy, the Kiplings spent their first months in India housed like refugees, joining a crowd of Europeans encamped on the Esplanade in what one observer described as 'wigwams',[32] most probably canvas tents strengthened with walls of bamboo and cane. To make matters worse, their luggage, sent out on the longer sea route via the Cape, failed to arrive, forcing Lockwood Kipling to spend his first week's wages on a dinner service and other household necessities.

Lockwood was later to call Bombay 'a blazing beauty of a place' and 'the finest city in the world so far as beauty is concerned',[33] but their first months must have been trying in the extreme. Alice Kipling was six weeks pregnant when she arrived and within days was enduring her first Indian Hot Weather – made only a little easier by the sea breezes that blew across Back Bay. Shortly before the start of the Rains in July the teaching staff and students of the Sir J. J. School of Art moved into their sheds in the School's new grounds beside Esplanade Road, an area afterwards remembered as 'thick with tropical palms and flowering trees . . . converted in May and June by the Gold Mohur into a flamboyant jungle'[34] but which Alice Kipling viewed at the time as an unhealthy swamp. When it rained the *pendals* were scarcely fit to live in, their mud floors 'saturated with wet',[35] yet the Kiplings had no option but to make the best of it. 'It's no use grumbling,' declared Alice in a letter to a Bombay friend, 'I daresay the new building will begin when we are all killed by living in the old cheap [?].'[36] Once the Rains began in earnest their conditions grew even more intolerable. 'No one,' wrote Lockwood, 'pretends to hide the fact that he is the moistest and most miserable of mortals.'[37] As for Alice, after finding toadstools growing in her bonnet and cockroaches nesting in her newest hat, she was moved to set her feelings down in verse:

> Dull in the morning, duller still at noon,
>   Dullest of all as dreary night draws round,
>   I go from mildewed couch to mouldy bed
>   And in the morning shall not feel surprise
> If from the reeking pillow, neath my head,
>   I find a crop of mushrooms when I rise.[38]

In the only complete letter to survive from their early years in India, addressed to his sister-in-law Edith Macdonald and dated 12 December 1866, Lockwood Kipling described the site of their home in some detail: 'We have as you know open sea on one side of the narrow neck of land on which we live and the ship-crowded harbour on the other – neither side further than from your house to the Market Place.'[39] And here Rudyard Kipling was born: 'between the palms and the sea',[40] as he later put it, but not in the building that today sports the plaque and bust. When asked in 1930 by the then head of the Sir J. J. School of Art if the present bungalow was the house in which he had been born, Kipling replied that the original building had stood 'on a slightly different spot some yards away'.[41] He was unwilling to add more, probably because he had no wish to draw attention to his father's lowly status at that time or to the humble conditions in which they had lived. In his unfinished autobiography, written in his seventieth year, Rudyard Kipling chose to describe his father as 'Superintendent' of the Sir J. J. School of Art and a 'Terry Sahib' as his assistant. In reality it was the other way round: Wilkins Terry, a draughtsman and wood-engraver by trade, was the School's Superintendent and Lockwood Kipling one of his three British members of staff.

Expected on Christmas Day 1865, the boy was finally delivered two hours short of midnight on 30 December – after five days of painful labour which were said to have been brought to an end by the household servants' sacrifice of a goat at one of the many shrines to the Hindu deity Shiva at the nearby temple complex of Bhuleshwar. A notice was duly placed in the *Times of India*: 'Kipling, December 30th, 1865 at Bombay, Mrs J. Lockwood Kipling, of a son.'

The boy was named Joseph, because it was the tradition in his father's family to call the eldest sons John and Joseph by turns, and Rudyard, at the insistence of one of his mother's sisters, after the reservoir where his parents had met. Rudyard very quickly became 'Ruddy' to his parents and remained so for the rest of their lives. On 22 January 1866 the boy was christened in St Thomas's Cathedral, the oldest Protestant church in Bombay and at that time the shabbiest, having been caught up in the great crash at the start of a rebuilding programme that was to take another forty years to complete. A smudgy photograph was sent home to Alice's parents showing the baby cradled in the arms of an Indian *ayah* or lady's maid, apparently causing his uncle Fred Macdonald to exclaim in dismay, 'Dear me, how dark Alice has become!'[42] From her garments and appearance this first ayah was a Madrassi, considered by many Anglo-Indian parents to make the most reliable nurses because they were said to be less indulgent. It is most likely that she also served as a *dhai* or wet nurse.

When it came to child-rearing British women in India were rarely able to draw upon the motherly advice their sisters back in England took for granted. They had little option but to follow

Anglo-Indian convention, which dictated that even nursing mothers should concentrate on their own adult preoccupations and leave it to the servants to keep their offspring fed, washed, dressed and entertained for the greater part of their waking hours. In the 1860s this often meant employing Native *dhais* to suckle European babies, as it was thought that the milk of a healthy Indian woman was superior to that of a white woman unadapted to the Indian climate and would give the baby a better chance of surviving India's many diseases.

According to Bombay's most eminent physician, Dr William Moore, author of *Health in the Tropics; or Sanitary Art as Applied to Europeans in India* and *A Manual of Family Medicine and Hygiene for*

Mother and child, J. L. Kipling (National Trust)

India, such a wet–nurse should be between twenty and thirty years of age, of temperate habits and 'not addicted to over-eating or to drink, or to smoking opium or Indian hemp'. The *dhai* was to be carefully examined before selection to ensure that she was free from piles, an enlarged spleen or skin disease. If she was found to suffer from a sore throat she was to be rejected, on the grounds that she was probably venereal. The condition of her own child had also to be examined 'and the mother of a weak, puny, badly nourished infant should be rejected; especially if there are any sores about the buttocks, privates, or corners of the mouth, which are also probably venereal'.

Whether or not the infant Ruddy benefited from such a wet-nurse, the adult Rudyard Kipling certainly looked upon them with approval. In the last of his several 'Strickland' short stories the headstrong child 'Adam' is suckled by the wife of one of his father's policemen, one of whom comments: 'Those who drink our blood become our own blood.'[43] Paradoxically, it was the fear of being tainted by Indian blood that eventually led increased numbers of Anglo-Indian parents in the post-Mutiny years to abandon the habit. The Civilian Alfred Lyall, widely regarded as British India's finest poet before Rudyard Kipling's appearance on the scene, had a son born a year after Ruddy and wrote to tell his sister that he and his wife had dispensed with the services of a local wet-nurse: 'We are determined to eschew black foster mothers, and our triumph over other households who maintain negresses is great and deserved.'[44]

In a sentence taken from a letter now lost Alice Kipling provides the briefest of glimpses of Ruddy the babe in arms: 'He notices everything he sees, and when he is not sitting up in his ayah's arms he turns round to follow things with his eyes most comically.'[45] From the solitary surviving letter spoken of earlier we have his father's portrait of Ruddy the eleven-month-old toddler:

Ruddy is a great lark but he won't be a baby much longer; he gets into imminent peril with chairs and things daily. It's the quaintest thing in life to see him eating his supper, intently watched by the three dogs to which he administers occasional blundering blows with a little whip & much shouting. His best playfellow is one 'Chang' a small Chinese pup . . . He is a beautiful tawny colour with a black nose and tongue. His hair is exactly like a thick & fine sable muff, and Ruddy buries his fat fists in it and pulls him up by the tail as a handle . . . We want to have baby photographed with him but woe's me the baby won't be long a baby & Chang will change into a big dog before we know where we are.[46]

The infant grew into a plump, bumptious child: a 'sturdy little boy', according to the sister who joined him when he was two and a half years old, 'with long straight fair hair – yes, flaxen hair – eyes like dark violets and a particularly beautiful mouth. He was thoroughly happy and genial – indeed rather too noisy and spoilt. Mother used to say that, like Kim, he was "little friend of all the world" and that's what the Indian servants in Bombay called him.'[47] This icon of the young Ruddy as 'little friend of all the world' is perfectly preserved in a story related by Alice Kipling to her son's first biographer, of the four-year-old walking hand in hand with a Maratha *ryot* or peasant cultivator over a ploughed field and calling back to his parents in the vernacular, 'Goodbye, this is my brother.'[48]

2

'Youth in the eye of the sun'

Bombay and expulsion from Eden, 1867–71

The wayside magic, the threshold spells,
   Shall soon undo what the North has done –
Because of the sights and the sounds and the smells
   That ran with our youth in the eye of the sun.

Rudyard Kipling, 'Song of the Wise Children', 1899

Rudyard Kipling came to look back on his Bombay childhood as a time of untrammelled happiness. In his unfinished autobiography he sets down his earliest recollection – 'of daybreak, light and colour and golden and purple fruits at the level of my shoulder. This would be the memory of early morning walks to the Bombay fruit market.' From the ever-widening neck of land upon which the Sir J. J. School of Art stood the Kiplings had easy access not only to the bazaars of the Native Town at the end of Esplanade Road but also to the palm-fringed sands of Back Bay. 'Our evening walks,' he wrote, 'were by the sea in the shadow of palm groves . . . When the wind blew the great nuts would tumble and we fled.' And with every sunset came the sudden nightfall of the tropics: 'I have always felt the menacing darkness of tropical eventides, as I have loved the voices of night-winds through palm or banana leaves and the song of the tree frogs.'[1]

The garden within the School's compound where Ruddy and the sister who followed him played was afterwards remembered by

Oxen drawing water, possibly Bombay, J. L. Kipling (National Trust)

both children as a lush Eden before the Fall, with flowers 'taller than chimneys' and a well 'where the green parrots lived, and where the white bullocks were always going blindfold round and round drawing up water in red waterpots to keep the roses alive, and the little grey striped squirrels nearly tame enough to eat biscuits out of his hand, used to play about in them.'[2] Along with cool interiors and harsh sunlight, this sense of closeness to the natural world stayed with Ruddy all his life, returning vividly to mind when he visited South Africa for the first time in 1899:

We shall go back by the boltless doors,
　To the life unaltered our childhood knew –
To the naked feet on the cool, dark floors,
　And the high-ceilinged rooms that the Trade blows
　　through:

To the trumpet-flowers and the moon beyond,
  And the tree-toads' chorus drowning all –
And the lisp of the split banana-frond
  That talked us to sleep when we were small.[3]

Of Lockwood Kipling's early years as a teacher of architectural sculpture and modelling little is known other than that he reported conscientiously on the progress of his students and was able to add to his earnings by giving private tuition. Among these students was a young Parsi named Pestonjee Bomanjee who subsequently became a respected artist in his own right and a teacher at the School. In old age Bomanjee recalled the infant Ruddy 'as a tiny fellow playing in the school compound'.[4] On one occasion, as the students waited in their classroom for their teacher to arrive, the boy was 'surprised by his father within the forbidden precincts of the Modelling Class where he was relieving the tedium of things by throwing pellets of clay at the students. He was firmly expelled from the temple of art, which he had thus profaned, by his scandalised parent.'[5]

Pestonjee Bomanjee had a high regard for his teacher but, initially at least, the feelings were not reciprocated. Lockwood Kipling's long years of apprenticeship in Burslem and South Kensington had given him views on art and craftsmanship which his students seemed incapable of accepting. 'A Hindoo makes a shot at the right thing & he hits or misses by chances so that no one thing is quite right,' he grumbled in an early letter home. This applied as much to craftsmanship outside the confines of the School as inside:

No masonry is square, no railings are straight, no roads are level, no dishes taste quite like what they should but a strange and curious imperfection & falling short attends everything. So that one lives as in a dream where things are just coming about but never _quite_ happen. I don't suppose if I were to talk for a week I could make you quite realise how far the brains of the native

take him and where the inevitable clog of his indolence &
that'll-do-ishness stop him short. But it is very odd & strange.[6]

The goal of reviving local tradition based on Native Indian
forms remained at the heart of the School's teaching, but combined
with a very British emphasis on precision and conformity to rules.
It was always intended that the skills learned at the Sir J. J. School
of Art should have practical applications, and the decoration of the
city's new public buildings was an obvious outlet. The first to benefit was Bombay's new covered market, built almost across the road
from the School and named Crawford Market after the municipal
commissioner, Arthur Crawford. The two magnificent semicircu-
lar marble bas-reliefs that adorn its façade are generally ascribed to
Lockwood Kipling, although probably designed by an architect
named Emerson. However, the carving of these reliefs was executed by Lockwood's students under his supervision, and the
market's decorated fountain was very much Lockwood's own creation. Sadly, its exotic birds and beasts have in recent times been
painted over and all but buried under posters and advertisements.

Under his guidance Lockwood's students subsequently worked
on the sculptural details for a number of public buildings, including the Victoria Terminus, the Royal Alfred Sailors' Home and
Bombay University.[7] The first Superintendent of Crawford Market
was a Mr Bennet, who often dined with the Kiplings in their bungalow, and a possibly apocryphal story originating from him tells
how the infant Ruddy would listen in keenly while his elders
talked, 'and how the boy would eagerly interrupt a discussion, a
reflective frown on his face, with an "I don't agree with that" or
"I don't think so", although such precocity regularly ensured for
him a rebuke from his elders!'[8] If true, this vignette suggests not
only precocity but also a distinct lack of parental discipline – as,
indeed, does the earlier story of Ruddy throwing clay at his father's
students.

The Kiplings soon discovered that, even in Bombay, Anglo-
Indian social life followed a monotonous cycle characterised by

convention and snobbery. However, one of its saving graces was hospitality. When a newcomer arrived at what outside the three Presidency cities of Bombay, Calcutta and Madras was called a Station, he would announce his arrival by leaving calling cards, beginning with the most important personages and working down through the lists as laid out in publications such as *Thacker's Directory*. He would then be invited to dine, and if his manners and background – and those of his wife, if he was married – met with approval, word would spread and more dinner invitations would follow. In Lockwood Kipling's single early letter of December 1866 he refers to one such welcoming dinner, hosted by a clergyman, where they met Lady Frere, the wife of the Governor, as well as other 'swells'. After dinner Alice Kipling had sung like a bird 'in the choruses and in the duets' and had greatly enjoyed herself.[9] At that stage the effervescent personality which was to charm Viceroys and Commanders-in-Chief had evidently failed to impress, but the combination of wit and sagacity which characterised the Kiplings as a couple was bound to make its mark and it was only a matter of time before they were welcomed by those who saw themselves as Bombay Society.

One well-connected member of this society who went out of his way to befriend the Kiplings was Henry Rivett-Carnac, whose grandfather and uncle had been governors of Bombay and whose cousin was the current Lieutenant-Governor of the Central Provinces. His memoirs reveal that Sir Bartle Frere took a close personal interest in the progress of the Sir J. J. School of Art and that it was as the Governor's aide that he came to know the Kiplings: 'During my frequent visits to them in Bombay, I often spent a morning with the Professors in the wigwams in which they lived and carried on work before the school was built.' The Kiplings struck him as an unusually good-humoured couple but what singled them out was that they 'took a very intelligent interest in everything connected with the people and the country, and . . . were better informed on all matters Indian – religions, customs, and peculiarities – than many officials who had been long in the country.'[10] Rivett-Carnac was a man of influence, and in a land where contacts counted for a great deal his patronage was to prove invaluable to the Kiplings.

In October 1867 Alice discovered that she was pregnant again. Unwilling to face the prospect of another painful delivery in difficult conditions, she went Home in February 1868 with her two-year-old boy, leaving her husband to complete the third year of his contract alone. Of that return journey, by way of the 'overland route' across the isthmus of Suez before the Canal opened in 1869, Ruddy retained a memory of 'an immense semi-circle blocking all vision': the paddle wheel of the SS *Ripon*, which took them on the first leg of their journey. By one account he was the worst-behaved of the several small children on board – a foretaste of what was in store for his mother's family in England.

Of his first eight months in England the adult Rudyard Kipling had very little to say beyond recalling a 'dark land and a darker room full of cold, in one wall of which a white woman made naked fire, and I cried aloud with dread, for I had never before seen a grate'.[11] That Kipling should have had only grim memories of this time is hardly surprising, for his mother parked him with her mother and her unmarried sister Edith at her parents' new home in the village of Bewdley, outside Kidderminster, while she went off to spend the remainder of her confinement at The Grange, the splendid mansion in Fulham in which Georgina and Ned Burne-Jones had settled with their two small children – Philip, then aged seven, and Margaret, who was five months younger than Ruddy. The Grange had just been magnificently decorated throughout by the company that William Morris had recently set up with his friends, and Alice arrived in time to join the housewarming. However, all was not well between the Burne-Joneses, and the birth of Alice's daughter on 11 June coincided with her sister Georgie's discovery of a letter revealing her husband to be besotted with a flame-haired model.[12]

Nor was Ruddy having an easy time of it. Even though his

Aunt Edith took him into her bed the boy remained thoroughly unsettled, demanding constant attention during the day and kicking her all through the night 'when he was not demanding drinks of water'. Perhaps he had good cause, having been first uprooted from his home and his beloved ayah and then abandoned by his mother among strangers in a cold, bleak land where his boisterous behaviour was checked at every turn. Nor could he have understood that his maternal grandfather was close to death and required the constant nursing of his wife and daughter. To spare the old man Rudyard was taken out of the house as often as possible, and on these enforced walks he would march down the main street of Bewdley shouting, 'Ruddy is coming! Ruddy is coming!' – and on one occasion, when his feathers had been particularly ruffled, 'An angry Ruddy is coming!'

Another of Ruddy's maternal aunts, Louisa, also lived in the village, having married Alfred Baldwin, the son of a wealthy ironmaster of the locality. The only person the two-year-old was able to get along with was the Baldwins' coachman, Reuben, whom he liked to follow as he went about his work. When at last Alice Kipling reappeared in July nursing a month-old and extremely large baby daughter, Ruddy took this blow calmly. He is said to have watched silently as the adults made a great fuss over his new sister and then, after hearing her compared to a Rubens painting, concurred in a newly acquired Worcestershire brogue, 'Ah, 'ur be very like Reuben.'[13]

Christened Alice Macdonald, the new baby had not had an easy birth, having suffered a broken arm and a black eye during her delivery and then been left for dead on a rug on the floor until her Aunt Georgie had begged the doctor to revive her with some vigorous slapping. Never then or at any time afterwards did her elder brother show the slightest sign of jealousy or sibling rivalry. On the contrary: Ruddy took his little sister to his heart and set himself up as her most devoted protector – a position he maintained in adulthood throughout her unhappy marriage and the mental breakdowns that followed.

From Bewdley Alice Kipling moved with her two small children to her mother-in-law's house in Skipton, Yorkshire. After a two-month visit they then returned to her parents for a further month before departing once more for India. Their final departure from Bewdley brought sighs of relief from both the Macdonald and Baldwin households: 'Alice and her children left us, for London, between 9 and 10, in the forenoon,' reads an entry in Mrs Macdonald's diary. 'Ruddy, after being sweet and pleasant for a little while, screamed horribly just before leaving, which had the effect of drying our tears. I cannot think how his poor mother will bear the voyage to Bombay with an infant and that self-willed rebel. I hope his father will train him better.'[14] Rudyard's aunt, Louisa Baldwin, took the same view. 'Dear old Alice left us on Monday,' she wrote in a letter to another member of the family. 'Sorry as we were to lose her personally, her children turned the house into such a bear-garden, and Ruddy's screaming tempers made Papa so ill we were thankful to see them on their way. The wretched disturbances one ill ordered child can make is a lesson for all time to me.'[15] Frederick Macdonald wrote to his brother Harry in America that the boy bullied his mother and was 'a power and a problem with strange gifts of upsetting any household'.[16] Even Ruddy's godmother and favourite aunt, Edith Macdonald, believed the boy's tantrums 'hastened and embittered' her father's end, which came just eleven days after Alice and her children had gone from Bewdley.

Alice Kipling left England all too aware of her mother's and siblings' ill opinions of her 'self-willed' son. Either out of pride or from deference to their feelings, she made sure that she never again put herself or her family in a position of such dependence, with serious consequences for her offspring.

Before the end of the year the new baby was presented to her father in Bombay, and here for the first time the four of them made up the 'Family Square' that became such an important feature at a later stage of their lives. However, baby Alice was no placid second child. She drove her mother to distraction with crying fits which only Ruddy and the ayah between them seemed able to soothe, and it was on this account that she acquired her nickname: her father thought her a 'tricksy baby'. Although as shy as her brother was outgoing, Trix(ie) was equally precocious, with a sharp mind and a quite remarkable memory. Before she was two she was showing 'a talent for apposite quotation'[17] and was able to read long before her brother. Ruddy, by contrast, 'only learned to read with the greatest difficulty', which Trix ascribed to his being too clever. 'I remember a thing he said to me quite seriously,' she afterwards wrote of his reading difficulties. 'I was probably crowing over him and he said, "No, Trix, you're too little, you see; you haven't brains enough to understand the hard things about reading. I want to know <u>why</u> "t" with "hat" after it should spell "that".'[18]

Among the qualities which Trix claimed to have inherited from her mother was second sight. 'Remember,' she wrote many years later in a letter to the *Kipling Journal*, 'my mother was the eldest of seven sisters, and a Macdonald of Skye, so her eldest daughter had a right to "the sight".' This psychic gift was apparently something that disturbed Alice Kipling greatly, but left her daughter untroubled: 'She was afraid of it. I have always found it helpful.'[19] Whatever gloss Trix may have put on it, her acute sensitivity made her a vulnerable and fearful child.

When Rudyard returned to Bombay at the age of two years and eleven months he found the beloved ayah who had nursed him as a babe in arms gone, replaced by a *budlee*, or temporary, ayah until a permanent nurse could be found. This Hindu woman, named Radha, enjoyed frightening the two children with a stuffed leopard's head mounted on the nursery wall, scaring Trixie so horribly that on one occasion Ruddy intervened and bit the *budlee* ayah. In his autobiography Rudyard assures the reader that his Hindu bearer Meeta saved him from 'night terrors or dread of the dark' by explaining that the leopard was there only to guard over him while he slept. But all the evidence points to this being wishful thinking, for he never lost his fear of the dark, and even as an adult hated being alone at night.

Fortunately for the children, the Hindu *budlee* ayah gave way to a Roman Catholic of Goan origins[20] who became the dominant figure in both their lives for as long as they remained in Bombay. Indeed, the happiness that attended their childhood in India owed far more to the companionship of their household servants than to their parents or the company of other children. It is no coincidence that in every written recollection of their first years in India, and in the fiction that drew on their Bombay childhood, both brother and sister place Ayah and Meeta centre stage, while their parents hover in the background. Indian servants were generally known by their trades rather than by their names, and although Kipling describes Meeta as a bearer, his name identifies him as a sweeper of the lowest Hindu caste. Bearers acted as valets or personal servants and were most often Muslims, so either the Kiplings were defying local conventions or, more likely, had been forced to cut their cloth according to their purse.

It was Ayah whom Rudyard remembered praying at roadside crosses, while Meeta went one stage further by taking him into Hindu temples 'where, being below the age of caste, I held his hand and looked at the dimly-seen, friendly Gods'.[21] The Bhuleshwar and Mumbadevi temples in the bazaar were both within easy perambulating distance of Crawford Market. The original shrine of the goddess Mumbai from which Mumbai Island took its name had been demolished in the mid-eighteenth century when the eastern perimeter of the Fort was enlarged. Its replacement became a focal point for Marathi-speakers and lower-caste Hindus, who would break coconuts before the shrine. The Mumbadevi temple is also unusual in containing a large number of images of the elephant-headed Ganesh and other popular Hindu folk deities: the 'dimly-seen, friendly Gods' of Ruddy's early acquaintance.

In the company of the household servants Ruddy and Trix mingled with a very different India from that of their parents, speaking not only the lingua franca known as Urdu, but also snatches of other tongues and dialects. 'In the afternoon heats,' wrote Rudyard Kipling in his autobiography, 'before we took our sleep, she [Ayah] or Meeta would tell us stories and Indian nursery songs all unforgotten, and we were sent into the dining-room after we had been dressed, with the cautions "Speak English now to Papa and Mamma." So one spoke "English" haltingly translated out of the vernacular idiom that one thought and dreamed in.'[22] Learning to move effortlessly from one language to another and one culture to another enabled Ruddy to become the child of many parts portrayed in half a dozen of his Indian stories, where he appears sometimes as 'Punch' and at other times as 'Tods', the six-year-old son of a Simla grass widow. In 'Tods' Amendment', set in Simla, the little boy is 'beyond his *ayah*'s control altogether' and 'the idol of some eighty *jhampanis* [rickshaw-pullers], and half as many *saises* [grooms]. He saluted them as "O Brother". It never entered his head that any living being could disobey his orders . . . The working of that household turned on Tods, who was adored by every one from the *dhobi* [washerman] to the dog-boy.'

Tods thinks and speaks Urdu, but has also mastered 'many side-speeches like the queer *chotee-bolee* [small talk] of the women, and held grave converse with shop keepers and Hill-coolies alike. He was precocious for his age, and his mixing with natives had taught him some of the more bitter truths of life . . . He used, over his bread and milk, to deliver solemn and serious aphorisms, translated from the vernacular into the English, that made his Mamma jump and vow that Tods *must* go Home next hot weather.'[23]

Trix's accounts of their shared childhood suggest that she had the same gift for languages – in fact, could swear in the vernacular with even greater fluency than her brother – and that both enjoyed the power this gave them over their mother, who remained unaware of their words' true meaning.

It comes as no surprise to find that the heroes of *Kim* and *The Jungle Book* tales are little boys abandoned by their birth parents – and that the most caring parents in Kipling's fiction are foster parents: in *The Jungle Book* the wolves who succour baby Mowgli, supported by the bear Baloo and the panther Bagheera; in *Kim* the widowed *Sahiba* who looks after Kim when he has a breakdown. In Rudyard Kipling's slight story 'The Potted Princes', which appeared in the American monthly the *St Nicholas Magazine* in 1892 but was afterwards suppressed by him, the two children, Punch and Judy, are playing on the verandah of their Bombay home when a large pink crane in the garden clatters his bill and frightens Judy. Ayah comforts her by singing a song, but then Punch gets pricked by the spikes of an aloe hedge as he chases the crane, and he too is comforted by Ayah, who tells him a story which begins, as in all the best children's tales in India, 'Once upon a time there was a Rajah'. When the story has been told the children rush to tell their mother, who has been out for her evening constitutional in her broom-*gharry* or open carriage. But Mama fails to understand the story and becomes confused and, in attempting to explain it to her, Punch reaches out for the bottle of eau-de-cologne on her dressing table 'that he was strictly forbidden to touch' and spills its contents down the front of his shirt, upsetting Mama.

Punch and Judy reappear in Rudyard Kipling's 'Baa, Baa, Black Sheep' and in his sister's long-overlooked version of the same events, 'Through Judy's Eyes', written after her brother's death.[24] Both tell the same story: of an Anglo-Indian brother and sister from Bombay abandoned by their parents among strangers in an English boarding house. In Trix's version her alter ego Judy can recall every detail of the servants left behind in India but finds that she has scarcely any memory of her mother. In their exile it is not her parents whom she misses most of all but the servants: 'Dear ayah who was never cross; clever Meeta, our bearer, who made toys out of oranges and nuts; Dunnoo who took charge of the fat white pony which Punch <u>would</u> call Dapple Gray; and Chokra [boy], the boy who called the other servants and only grinned and didn't mind when I pelted him with bricks.'[25]

These and other stories show two small children learning to move effortlessly between two worlds: one formal and exclusive, the other informal and all-embracing and, moreover, one in which they exercised a remarkable degree of authority, despite their ages. In their Indian world, as Trix put it, she and her brother were 'king and queen in their own country – none daring to make them afraid',[26] an analogy extended by Rudyard in his short story 'His Majesty the King', which tells of his alter ego Punch growing up in India as ruler of the nursery, spoiled by the servants but always wishing that his distant parents – 'two very terrible people who had no time to waste upon His Majesty the King'[27] – would show him more affection.

One can read too much into a work of fiction, but the signalling of parental neglect by both siblings is too marked for it to have been entirely the product of Rudyard Kipling's imagination. How else can one explain why, in an era when the three Rs were part and parcel of the nursery furniture, no effort was made to teach this highly intelligent child to read and write? 'Six and a half years old and he had never been taught to read!' wrote the long-widowed Trix in a revealing letter to her cousin, the former Prime Minister Stanley Baldwin. 'I don't know what the parents were thinking of . . . but he hadn't been taught! Mother had a very strong will but there were streaks of sand in her marble.'[28]

A recurrent theme in Anglo-Indian literature of this period is the degree to which British children were left in the care of the servants – and the dangers this represented in the misshaping of their characters. 'In the reeking atmosphere of the servants' huts,' wrote the unnamed author of an article in the *Pioneer* newspaper on the European child in India, 'he soaks in Asiatic vices and meanness through every pore of his little white skin'.[29] It was accepted as inescapable fact that European children in India must first be spoiled by servants – and then sent Home to England in order to counteract this damage. In this respect Alice and Lockwood Kipling appear to have been content to follow custom. 'We are,' wrote Lockwood, 'willing slaves to our small emperors, feeling that the best we can give them is but poor compensation for the loss of their birthright of British air'.[30] Yet there is nothing from either Rudyard's or Trix's pen to suggest that their parents

The spoilt prince in his kingdom, J. L. Kipling (National Trust)

actively gave of their best – rather the contrary. 'They said in nearly every letter that they loved their little boy and girl and missed them very much,' grumbles Judy in Trix's story. 'But Punch could have learnt to read every bit as well in India, if only Mamma had taught him, and Ayah could have shown Judy how to be "a utiful [dutiful] girl", if Mamma had really wanted her to brush her own hair, or even wipe the cups after breakfast.'

At the start of 1868 Lockwood Kipling signed a new contract to continue his teaching for another three years – but on less advantageous

terms, since he was now forbidden to give private tuition. With his
salary barely covering his domestic costs Lockwood sought to supplement his income by submitting designs for building decorations
to the Public Works Department – only to find them rejected and
then copied without his approval. To make matters worse, the
dynamic Sir Bartle Frere had been succeeded as Governor of Bombay
by a British Government placeman whose prime concern was to put
the city's finances to rights and who had no intention of wasting
money on art schools. The reluctance of Government to sanction the
funds required for the new school buildings and staff quarters meant
that the Kiplings' living conditions failed to improve. Frustrated at
every turn, Lockwood began to look outside his craft for ways of
supplementing his income.

In the artistic circles in which they had moved in England both
Lockwood and Alice Kipling had found opportunities to indulge
in what a friend termed their 'thirst for scribbling',[31] mostly in the
form of verse. In Bombay both appear to have harboured hopes of
putting their scribbling to better use, perhaps in journalism, initially without success. However, in the spring of 1870 Lockwood
secured a commission from the Government of India to tour the
North-Western Provinces to make sketches of Indian craftsmen at
work. This was thanks to the good offices of the Kiplings' Civilian
friend Henry Rivett-Carnac, who had recently moved from
Bombay up to Allahabad, capital of the North-Western Provinces,
to take up the post of Commissioner for Cotton and Commerce.
His tour took Lockwood to Allahabad and to the offices of the
Pioneer, which, under the combined leadership of its founding proprietor, George Allen, and its editor, the Reverend Julian
Robinson, was fast gaining a reputation as the most influential up-
country newspaper in India. The patronage of these two men was
to be decisive in shaping the futures of both father and son.

Allen and Robinson were what were known in Anglo-Indian
parlance as 'old *koi-hais*': experienced India hands who knew the
ropes and held deeply conservative, not to say reactionary, views on
all matters pertaining to British rule in India. Allen had begun his

Indian career as the partner of a trader in pills and patent medicines, which made him a boxwallah, the derogatory term for those engaged in trade. In May 1857 he had been among the survivors who had gathered on Delhi Ridge and, although a non-combatant, had made himself useful by setting up the British camp's one and only shop, supplying at great profit to himself '"tar bund" beer, Exshaw's brandy and Harvey's sauce, and many varieties of tinned provisions, besides Holloway's pills and ointment, and such like nostrums'.[32] The family story is that he also got hold of an abandoned printing press and began to produce a daily broadsheet, after which he and his partner set up a *dak* or postal service, employing loyal Indians to run messages through rebel-held territory. Once peace had been restored Allen returned to his former business, building up a chain of up-country stores in Allahabad, Lucknow, Simla, Umballa and Lahore that sold imported goods to a largely British clientele. But the bug of journalism had bitten and in 1865 Allen co-founded from his base in Allahabad what became up-country India's first professionally produced newspaper, modelled in format, layout and type on *The Times*.

Allen's junior partner in this enterprise and the newspaper's first editor was the Reverend Julian Robinson, an independent-minded clergyman whose political views accorded with Allen's. In the pages of the *Pioneer* they gave voice to both their own prejudices and those of the majority of their readers in northern India: planters, boxwallahs, businessmen, engineers, Europeans in the provincial services and junior officers in the ranks of the Indian Army. They not only provided the Indian and European news that their readers wanted but went to great lengths to be first with it, employing the best news services available. They also introduced a higher standard of journalism, including in every issue several leaders in which they expiated at length on every conceivable topic, from Native juries and civil service leave rules to joint stock companies and European vagrancy. In one of the earliest of these editorials the *Pioneer*'s chief proprietor set out his own position on British India:

Asiatics are, and always have been, the least democratic of men;
they care nothing for self-government: they infinitely prefer
being ruled by others; they must have some to look up to as
rulers and guides. We can but partially occupy the place, separated as we are from them by race, religion and social customs,
and it is important we should recognise the fact. The great mass
of the population is now exactly what it was three hundred years
ago, neither richer nor poorer, neither wiser nor more foolish,
while their leaders, their federal lords, the magnates of the land,
would not be men if they did not cordially hate us – so completely have their importance and power been crushed down.[33]

Within a decade Allen and Robinson had established the *Pioneer*
as northern India's premier daily, with a reputation for always being
'first with the news'. By offering generous 'fees' to highly placed
officials Allen was able to give his paper a lead over its rivals by
gaining advance notice of Government moves as well as providing
the greatest insight into what Government was thinking. This made
the '*Pi*' indispensable reading among the senior ranks of the civil
services and the military. The *Pi* also reflected the literary tastes of
its owners, and once established began to include every form of
literary expression in its pages, from essays and reviews to poetry
and fiction.

The modern popular image of British India as a cultural desert
and Anglo-Indian society as unremittingly philistine owes a great
deal to that pair of misfits E. M. Forster and George Orwell and
their monocular visions of the British Raj. But it is true to say that
the British in India in the late nineteenth century were isolated
from their cultural roots. 'No situation more unfavourable to the
development of imaginative literature could be found,' wrote the
poet and Civilian Sir Alfred Lyall in one of his many essays, 'than
that of a few thousand Europeans isolated, far from home, among
millions of Asiatics entirely different from them in race, manners,
and language.'[34]

But if their numbers were small – in Kipling's day probably no more than fifty to sixty thousand in total – and their lives too unsettled for them to be able to carry much cultural baggage, many Britons came out to India well educated and determined to continue their intellectual pursuits. From the time of Warren Hastings onwards intellectual and scientific enquiry went hand in hand with literary endeavour, with outlets such as the *Calcutta Review* and a dozen or so presses such as that of the *Pioneer*. 'Considering how short a time it is since the British began to occupy the country,' wrote a reviewer in the *Pioneer* in 1882, 'and the small number of those who are here at any given time, it is truly marvellous how many thinkers and writers of the very highest class have distinguished themselves in Anglo-Indian literature.' The same reviewer goes on to suggest that instead of reading established English literature, Indian university students would do better to read the novels of Philip Meadows Taylor and other more recent Anglo-Indian novelists: 'We should like to see the names of Keene, Chesney, Cunningham, Talboys Wheeler, and Hunter; instead of Goldsmith, Thompson and Dickens.'[35] All the above-named authors were members of either the Indian Civil Service or the Indian Army and they represented only the tip of British India's literary iceberg.

No one understood better than Rudyard Kipling that he was part of a well-established literary tradition. 'There is always an undercurrent of song, bitter for the most part, running through the Indian papers,' he declared of the quantities of verse that appeared in English-language periodicals and newspapers in his own time and before:

> The bulk of it is much better than mine, being more graceful, and is done by those less than Sir Alfred Lyall – to whom I would apologise for mentioning his name in this gallery – 'Pekin', 'Latakia', 'Cigarette', 'O', 'T. W.', 'Foresight', and others . . . Sometimes a man in Bangalore would be moved to song, and a man on the Bombay side would answer him, and a man in Bengal would echo back, till at last we would all be

crowing together, like cocks before daybreak . . . The newspaper files showed that, forty years ago, the men sang of just the
same subjects as we did – of heat, loneliness, love, lack of promotion, poverty, sport, and war.[36]

What Rudyard Kipling had to say about poetry in British India
applied equally to prose writing, where the fiercely competitive
editors of the English-language papers went out of their way to
encourage Civilians and army officers to express their views in
print as anonymous special correspondents. Among their number
were the three sons of the Reverend Julian Robinson. The middle
son, Kay, born in 1855, was to play a decisive role in encouraging
and guiding the young apprentice Rudyard Kipling. However, it
was the eldest brother whose influence was first felt by the Kiplings.

Born in India in 1849, Phil Robinson was appointed Professor
of Logic at the newly established Allahabad University in the early
1880s, but was happier as a writer and naturalist. He briefly succeeded his father as editor of the *Pi* before going his own way as
a freelance journalist, making his name as an observer of animal
and human behaviour, which he chronicled in a series of books
beginning with *Nugae Indica: On Leave in my Compound*, published
by the Pioneer Press in Allahabad in 1871. Purporting to be notes
from the field book of a visiting naturalist, it is made up of a series
of sketches of Indian birds, people and scenes, each subject carefully observed and portrayed with light humour.

What became popularly known as Robinson's Indian Garden
Series – *In My Indian Garden*, *Under the Punkah*, *Chasing a Fortune*
and *Tigers at Large* – established a genre that became hugely popular in Anglo-Indian society and was widely imitated, most
successfully by a near contemporary, Edward Aitken, born and
raised in Bombay and educated at Bombay University. Under the
initials 'E. H. A.' Aitken further extended the genre, writing
columns for the *Pioneer*'s main rival in Bombay, *The Times of India*,
and publishing such widely read books as *Tribes on my Frontier*,
Behind the Bungalow and *Naturalist on the Prowl*.

Aitken and Robinson were unusual in that they were professional writers at a time when the Anglo-Indian literary scene was almost entirely made up of gentlemen riders, amateurs who wrote for mainly pleasure and as a distraction from the cares of office. In the spring of 1870 Lockwood Kipling joined the fold to become the *Pioneer's* special correspondent in Bombay.[37] His first report appeared unsigned in April and was followed at fortnightly intervals by further articles, mostly accounts of social events in European Bombay such as the Byculla Club's summer ball, the Bombay Yacht Club's regattas, the Bombay races, and concerts and musical soirées at the Grant Theatre – which Lockwood likened to 'a detestable dog-house'.

The writing was unremarkable, but leavened by Lockwood's sense of humour. In noting the absence of mosquitoes at the Byculla Ball, where they usually gathered in clouds about the bare shoulders of the ladies, he added that had he been a mosquito he would have made the most of the succulent opportunities presented. In commenting on the Bombay Philharmonic Society's musical evenings he bewailed the shortage of talent, for amateur singers in Bombay were like 'sands in the desert, ever changing . . . The doctor orders your best tenor to England on pain of his becoming a croaker if he remains; your bass mournfully leaves you to wake the echoes of a remote jungle solitude: your lovely soprano has to lead her infant chorus back to school via the P. and O.'[38] No opportunity for reporting on social scandal was missed. 'In view of the difficulty of loving one's neighbour as oneself,' Lockwood notes in November 1870, 'some of us sought to compensate by loving our neighbour's wife better than our own!' The unhappy consequence of a Mrs Lennon's conversion to Islam was gleefully reported: 'Her paramour, who is said to be a fine-looking Pathan, was yesterday sentenced to six months' imprisonment for adultery. The punishment seems heavy for the offence.'[39]

Reading through these reports today one's eye is caught by the occasional discordant remark, such as Lockwood's aversion to the constant round of exercise and sport that was such a feature of

Anglo-Indian life. Like the son who followed him, Lockwood's stature and myopic eyesight barred him from anything that required athleticism. Forced to attend the races, he reported that 'some are born horsey but few, by taking thought, achieve horsiness'; polo he thought little better than 'hockey on horseback'; and golf he dismissed as 'a puerile, purposeless and preposterous game', adding that he 'would rather drive a hearse than walk solemnly about in a red coat after a ball'.[40] Thirty years on Rudyard was to echo these same sentiments in pouring scorn on 'the flannelled fools at the wicket or the muddied oafs at the goals'.[41]

What is even more striking about these newspaper articles is the frequency with which one particular note is sounded: that of the jaundiced observer who has seen it all before. 'Things interest us here only through persons,' was how Lockwood summed up Bombay Society. 'There is little else to furnish us with the gentle mental exercises of which we are capable . . . Thus the quarrel between Robinson and Green, which rages in official foolscap; the flirtation of Mrs Brown and Mr Jones, is my opera; the careful study of ladies' bonnets and dress in church has all the interest of the Royal Academy . . . These things, and many more, are provided by a bountiful Providence for the entertainment of mankind.'[42] Five years as a badly paid teacher in Bombay's Department of Public Instruction did not make him a seasoned *koi hai* who knew all the ropes, but that was how he presented himself. It was a trick his son picked up and improved upon, sometimes to a degree that made him almost insufferable. With both men it was a case of the outsider eager to 'pass' as an insider.[43]

However benevolent Lockwood appeared to his Indian students, his political views matched those of the proprietors of the *Pioneer*. Whatever nonconformist opinions he may have held in England, in India he trod the line, accepting the shibboleths of the day, which were that socialising with Indians was undesirable, political reforms that allowed Indians a greater share of government dangerous and Indians in general untrustworthy – particularly the educated ones. One of Lockwood's first duties as the *Pi*'s Bombay correspondent was to report on a degree ceremony at Elphinstone College. Whether out of respect for his proprietors' views or because he himself thought it right to do so, he mocked the Indian graduands in their academic gowns and mortar boards, declaring his deep veneration for 'the force of character displayed in our resolute imposition of the time-honoured forms of England on our Aryan brother. I like to see familiar folk in unfamiliar guise, especially when robes of learned state cover garments of Eastern cut.'[44] Throughout his time in India Lockwood Kipling clung to the Macaulayite view that Indian philosophy, science and history was so steeped in superstition as to be valueless: 'There are many lies in history, but Hindu writers are remarkable for having deliberately and of set principle ignored all the facts of life. All is done, however, with such an air of conviction and pious purpose that we must use Dr Johnson's kindly discrimination and say they are not inexcusable, but consecrated liars.'[45]

Not all Anglo-Indians shared these views. At this same time a small but growing number of Civilians were working to reduce the racial divide, idealists like the Bombay judge William Wedderburn, who had came out to India barely three years after his elder brother, sister-in-law and niece were murdered by mutineers in 1857. Wedderburn considered himself to be a 'servant of the Indian people', so much so that he came to be regarded by his seniors as a 'one-sided fanatic'[46] and was passed over for high office before retiring to become an active supporter of the Indian National Congress in the House of Commons. But men like Wedderburn were the exceptions. Even a liberal reformer like the scholarly administrator William Hunter believed that British rule in India meant 'order in place of anarchy'.[47]

Seen in this light, Lockwood Kipling's illiberal attitudes, however reprehensible they now appear, were no more so than those of the Anglo-Indian mainstream. Like so many of his peers, he had time only for those Indians who posed no threat, exemplified by the figure of the Indian *ryot*. It is no accident that the most offensive of his newspaper articles are those that mock Anglicised

Indians, and the most sympathetic those portraying Indian farmers and artisans. The drawings Lockwood brought back from the North-West Provinces and those he did later in the Punjab are suffused with a real understanding of the harsh lot of the Indian peasantry and the artisan. During his up-country tour of 1870 he had watched a young woman herding buffalo in the rain, presenting

> the most pathetic Arcadian figure one could possibly imagine as she flounders after her wallowing buffaloes, screaming hoarsely against the wind and sweeping rain . . . Her limbs are sometimes as smooth and as round as any that Pradier carved but slime covers them and the rain chills them to an unlovely texture of goose-flesh, and she sets the muscles of her face so hard against the bitter weather that she acquires the sullen fixity of a wild animal . . . Happily, it is not given to her to know how utterly wretched she is, and what a leaky dog-hole is the damp hutch in which she sleeps; how coarse and poor her food, how grim and hard her life.[48]

The arrival of a troop ship in Bombay Harbour in February 1871 and the landing of British troops allowed Lockwood to write no less sympathetically about the lot of the British common soldier. 'The opinions of Private Jones, Corporal McSweeney, and Sergeant Maloney,' he wrote in an uncanny anticipation of his son's 'Soldiers Three',

> on novelties of scenery, manners and customs are not perhaps so fresh and suggestive as one might imagine; indeed for all they seem to see they might as well travel in close blinkers like shy horses; but the native-and-to-the-manner-born way in which all ranks and sexes take to elephants, dhoolies, camels, tattoos, bullock-gharries, and all sorts of hitherto unimagined modes of progression, is a striking instance of our powers of adaptation which superficial foreigners insist we do not possess. Private

Jones, fresh from the soul-destroying furnaces and igneous abominations of the iron-works of England, jogs along through a medieval country, arranged, if only he knew it, on principles he has never hitherto seen in operation, and smoking his pipe gazes with incurious eyes on – Arcadia!

In April 1870 Alice gave birth to the Kiplings' third child, a boy they named John, who lived only a few days. What effect this little tragedy had on the family can only be guessed at. However, when a child's dismembered hand was found by Alice in their Bombay garden her distress was enough to frighten the children. She forbade them to ask her any questions and it was left to their ayah to explain this ghoulish mystery: that the hand had been dropped by a vulture feeding on the corpses left exposed by orthodox Parsis in their Towers of Silence on nearby Malabar Hill.

A more distant brush with death that also seems to have left its mark occurred late one night when their mother returned early from a *burra khana* or grand dinner and told Ruddy, who was still awake, that 'the big Lord Sahib had been killed and there was to be no Big Dinner'. In adulthood Kipling took this event to be the assassination of the Viceroy, Lord Mayo, knifed by a convict while on a visit to the penal colony of the Andaman Islands. However, Lord Mayo's murder took place in February 1872, ten months after the two children had left India. The identity of the victim remains a mystery, since the Indian term *Lat Sahib* was applied only to the highest in the land such as Viceroys, Lieutenant-Governors and Commanders-in-Chief. The incident could well reflect the general air of insecurity among the British community in India at a time when there was much talk of Muslim conspiracies and 'Wahabee' plots against the Government. Clearly some traumatic event – perhaps his mother's distress at the loss of her third child – took place at this time shocking enough to lodge in a sensitive child's memory and to add to the night fears that remained with Ruddy into adulthood.

Perhaps it was just as well that Lockwood's appointment as the

Pioneer's Bombay correspondent came at this same time, for it marked the start of an upward turn in his fortunes. For the first time in five years the Kiplings could afford to take a holiday, and as soon as the School's summer term ended they joined the rush of Europeans and wealthy Parsis who fled the Hot Weather by taking refuge in the Hills.

The nearest thing to a hill-station that Bombay possessed was Matheran, sited high on a ridge on the first range of the Western Ghats some fifty miles due east of Bombay, and approached only with difficulty and expense. Less exclusive but far more accessible was the Hindu pilgrimage town of Nassik, situated ninety miles away on the banks of the River Godavari. Nassik was close to the Bombay, Baroda and Central India railway line linking Bombay to northern India and was served by Deolali railway station, soon to acquire notoriety on account of its transit camp and the military sanatorium established there for British soldiers deemed to be 'doolally'. The ruler of the princely state of Bhavnagar owned a comfortable bungalow directly overlooking the Godavari, to which a friend of the Kiplings employed by the maharaja had access. Here the four Kiplings spent a blissful summer holiday, marred only by both the children and their father suffering a bout of intermittent fever, treated in the formers' case by laxatives and quinine laced with honey and jam – the subject of a pen and ink sketch by Lockwood showing an extremely chubby child with jam all over his face and captioned 'Ruddy's Idea of Heaven'.

Nassik was celebrated as one of four Hindu holy sites in India where the nectar of the gods had fallen and was visited by pilgrims in their thousands, who came to bathe in the river every morning and to cremate their dead on its banks. That the boy saw a lot more than a glimpse of this Hindu India can be judged by an interjection made by little Punch as Ayah tells her tale in 'The Potted Princess': 'Like the holy men I saw at Nasik on the mountain?' he asks. 'They were all *nungapunga* [stark naked] but they showed me their little Gods, and I burned stuff that smelt in a pot before them all, and they said I was Hindu.' That Ruddy at four years and eight months had acquired a working knowledge of Maratha as well as Urdu is shown by an exchange with his mother afterwards related to Mrs Rivett-Carnac. 'Ruddy for a while coveted the possession of a donkey, but came to me the other day saying, "Never mind of that donkey. I've seen a little white horse, & the man will let you have it for four rupees."'[49]

It was here at Nassik, too, that Alice Kipling was given the abiding image of her four-year-old son clasping the hand of a local cultivator and calling back to her, 'Goodbye, this is my brother.'[50] The word used here is *bhai*, which includes members of one's own caste or local fraternity as well as one's brother. It extends into the term *bhai-bhand*, denoting a brotherhood which binds men together as in a regiment, Masonic lodge or school and demands loyalty to an almost sacred degree. It was a concept that Ruddy came to hold very dear in his early adulthood, and it is tempting to see in this bucolic vision of child and peasant hand in hand a metaphor for the urge to reach out across cultural and class divides that was to become such a striking feature of his work.

Despite recent advances in medicine and hygiene the fear of her child contracting a fatal disease such as typhoid haunted every European mother in India. Whooping cough was rarely fatal in itself, but the paroxysms of coughing it brought so debilitated small children that they became vulnerable to other maladies. So when Ruddy contracted whooping cough after their return to Bombay he was subjected to a strict regimen of hot baths, chest and back rubs with brandy and salad oil mixed in equal parts, and a nightly purgative consisting of ipecacuanha wine. The appropriate dose for a four-year-old was one and three-quarter drams in two ounces of water, which Ruddy took in his stride. An evening routine was established whereby his mother read to him as they waited for the emetic to take effect, but under strict orders to stop reading the moment he put up his hand and said, 'Now!'

Two other vignettes from this same period have also been preserved, both testifying to the precocity of brother and sister. One is of the four-year-old boy puzzling over his identity and exclaiming, 'I cannot imagine what God made me of. It cannot be dust, because there's red blood inside me!'[51] The other, also theological, comes from Henry Rivett-Carnac:

> One day Master Ruddy had left a small quantity of pudding uneaten. 'You must finish that,' said the sister, 'or God will be angry with you.' 'Boo, boo,' replied the delinquent, 'then I shall change my God' (as he might his *dhoby* or washerman). But his sister, who claimed superior technical knowledge, replied authoritatively, 'You can't change your God, it is the *Sirkar's* [Government] God.' And Rudyard, realising even at that early age, thanks to the gorgeous *chaprassie* who accompanied him on his morning walks, that he occupied a sort of official position under the Government, which carried with it certain responsibilities, surrendered.[52]

Doubts have been cast on the authenticity of this story, first because its author evidently believed Trix to be the elder of the two children and secondly because it is unlikely that the Kiplings would have employed a *chaprassie* – a uniformed Government employee whose emblem of office was a *chaprass* or brass badge worn on a red sash. But the exchange itself, recounted by the proud father to Rivett-Carnac in a letter, seems authentic enough.

At the end of the Cold Weather of 1870–1 Lockwood was offered the renewal of his contract for a further three years and the opportunity of a six-month furlough. Despite numerous appeals, the staff and students at the Sir J. J. School of Art were still living in the temporary sheds erected in the year of the Kiplings' arrival in Bombay. 'The works had been calculated to stand for three years only,' complained Mr Terry, the School's Superintendent, to the Director of Public Instruction, adding in a subsequent letter that 'Mr Kipling and myself have frequently been laid up through the unhealthiness of the rooms in which we have lived for several years . . . and the frequent rheumatic attacks I suffer from are much aggravated if not brought on by the damp atmosphere I am obliged to live in.'[53] However, no funds were forthcoming and Lockwood and Alice Kipling had now to conclude that their children's interests would be best served by removing them from India.

On 15 April 1871 the four Kiplings sailed for England by way of the newly opened Suez Canal. For the two youngest it marked the ending of their innocence and the beginning of their years in exile. Ruddy was aged five years and fifteen weeks.

3

'A double death'

SOUTHSEA AND LAHORE, 1871–7

God's mercy is upon the young,
  God's wisdom in the baby tongue
That fears not anything.

Rudyard Kipling, from the introductory verses
to 'Tods' Amendment', April 1887

The Kiplings arrived in England in late May 1871. A wet month at the seaside in Sussex was followed by a round of family visits. The last, in mid-September, was to Bewdley, where widowed Mrs Macdonald found Ruddy to be a 'dear, good child'[1] – which makes what followed all the more puzzling.

The Anglo-Indian custom was to settle one's children with a close relative before returning to India. All Alice's sisters except the unmarried Edith had produced offspring: Georgie and Ned Burne-Jones's children Philip and Margaret were now aged ten and five. Ambrose Poynter and Stanley Baldwin, born within a month of each other, were aged four. So Ruddy and Trix had four cousins with whom they might have been expected to share more than the occasional visit. They also had their maternal grandmother living at Bewdley with their Aunt Edith, and Lockwood Kipling's mother up at Skipton, both of whom offered to have the children; as did the Baldwins, if with the proviso that Ruddy be shared out between several households. But for reasons never satisfactorily explained the Kiplings chose to leave them with strangers – a married couple who had placed an advertisement in a newspaper offering to foster children whose parents were stationed in India. That Alice Kipling was the prime mover in this can be deduced from letters which show that she saw the children's education as her responsibility rather than her husband's, but Lockwood must surely have been complicit.

According to a family friend, Alice spoke of 'complications',[2] but what these were can only be guessed at. However, all her married sisters' husbands now enjoyed a degree of financial security and public recognition denied her own spouse, and some insight into their perception of Lockwood Kipling's work can be gleaned from a comment made by Agnes Poynter in a letter in which she declared herself to be 'more and more ashamed of John's mission to that country'.[3] It may be that Alice was determined not to be beholden to her family and that she still smarted from the hostility shown towards her boy two years earlier. Years afterwards Trix was to comment to her cousin Stanley Baldwin that Ruddy was 'about as spoilt as he could be when we came home in 1871',[4] and the awkwardness of dumping this undisciplined, wayward, unlettered brat on one or other of her sisters seems to have been more than Alice was prepared to bear.

On 1 October 1871, as Lockwood's six-month leave drew to a close, the Kiplings travelled to Southsea on the south coast and handed over the children to the care of the woman they were told to call 'Auntie': Mrs Sarah Holloway, who, together with her husband, an elderly naval captain, and their twelve-year-old son Harry, occupied Lorne Lodge, at 4 Campbell Road, Havelock Park, Southsea. In Ruddy's and Trixie's semi-fiction this became the 'House of Desolation' and Mrs Holloway 'Aunty Rosa'. In Kipling's autobiography she is referred to simply as 'the Woman'.

The two children – 'a sturdy little boy not quite six and a spoilt baby of three and a half'[5]– were abandoned at Lorne Lodge without any explanation beyond Ruddy's being told that he must learn to read and write so that his parents could send him letters and books. They were woken before dawn, hugged and put back to bed again, and when they next woke it was to find that their mother and father had vanished. In their bewilderment the children turned to Mrs Holloway, only to be informed that they had been left behind 'because we were so tiresome and she had us in out of pity'. Ruddy refused to accept this explanation and questioned the kinder Captain Holloway, who told him that 'Papa had left us to be taken care of because India was too hot for small people'. But even this answer failed to satisfy: 'We knew better; we had been to Nassik, the Hill Station of Bombay. So what could be the real reason? We couldn't think and it worried us terribly.'[6]

In *Something of Myself* Kipling describes Lorne Lodge as 'an establishment run with the full vigour of the Evangelical as revealed to the Woman. I had never heard of Hell, so I was introduced to it in all its terrors.' In her determination to break his will Mrs Holloway subjected the boy to beatings, solitary confinements in the cellar or the attic, threats of eternal damnation and constant vilification that continued throughout the six and a half years he spent under her roof.

In his later years Kipling rarely let the mask slip, but at the age of twenty-three he sat down and in rage and anguish wrote the most directly autobiographical of his short stories, 'Baa, Baa, Black Sheep' – the tale of little Punch and his even littler sister Judy who are abandoned by their parents to the ministrations of Aunty Rosa at the House of Desolation. In it he came as close as he ever would to expressing his real feelings about the hurt done to him as a child. At the end of the story Punch tries to reassure his sister: 'We are just as much Mother's as if she had never gone.' To which the writer of the tale responds: 'Not altogether, O Punch, for when young lips have drunk deep of the waters of Hate, Suspicion and Despair, all the Love in the world will not wholly take away that knowledge.'

Several biographers[7] have accused Kipling of indulging in dramatic licence in writing of the House of Desolation, but his best defence comes from his sister. A few months after his death in

January 1936 she typed out her own no less harrowing account of their Southsea years in 'Through Judy's Eyes', a companion-piece to Rudyard's 'Baa, Baa, Black Sheep'. A decade later she returned to the subject in a scripted BBC radio broadcast talk entitled 'My Brother Rudyard Kipling'.[8] She also discussed it with his first biographer, Lord Birkenhead, informing him that she and her brother had never spoken of their time at Lorne Lodge because 'it hurt too much'.

Because she became something of a pet to Mrs Holloway, Trix suffered less. But in 'Through Judy's Eyes' she describes her terror when Aunty Rosa first tried to discipline her by making her stand on the high table at which the two children did their lessons. Judy finds this a terrifying ordeal: 'She was afraid of falling over the edge, and being dashed to pieces on the red and blue carpet; which used to sink further and further away while she grew colder and colder, and a funny noise, like a boiling kettle, only louder, sang in her ears. She wasn't allowed to hold on to Punch's long hair, though he offered it to her as a lifeline, or even his sleeve.' That fear, suggests Trix, will remain with Judy for ever: 'She might forget grey striped squirrels, or kind brown faces in Bombay, but anything that hurt or frightened her could not be forgotten. She was not a brooding or vindictive child, but pain and terror, especially terror, seemed to dig a groove in her brain, and she could no more efface it than she could turn her blue eyes brown.'

Outside their fiction, neither brother nor sister ever admitted to having suffered any lasting psychological damage. In Trix's case, Lorne Lodge turned an already highly strung child into a desperately insecure one. Ruddy was of made of sterner stuff and was that bit older, yet the experience undoubtedly brutalised him. Trix always clung to the illusion that the House of Desolation did her brother no lasting harm: 'My brother should have grown up morbid, misanthropic, narrow-minded, self-centred, shunning the world and bearing all men a burning grudge. Whereas, of course, he grew up just the opposite.'[9] But what Trix could not see, others did, for both as a child and as an adult Rudyard Kipling displayed traits that match precisely Trix's list of the characteristics her brother did not possess. The future Greek scholar Gilbert Murray, an exact contemporary, met Ruddy briefly in London when they were both about ten years old and retained a memory of a boy who was 'extraordinarily clever and exciting though there was something in him that repelled me'.[10] He was particularly shocked by Ruddy throwing stones at a cat. Other commentators and biographers have made much of Kipling's appetite for revenge and the unpleasant note of sadism that crops up in so many of his stories.

Of the two children, it was Trix who came closest to admitting that the real harm done to them lay not so much in Mrs Holloway's cruelty as in their parents' betrayal:

> The real tragedy . . . sprang from our inability to understand why our parents had deserted us. We had had no preparation or explanation; it was like a double death, or rather like an avalanche that had swept away everything happy and familiar . . . We felt we had been deserted 'almost as much as on a doorstep' . . . They had gone back to our own lovely home, and had not taken us with them. There was no getting out of that, as we often said.[11]

None of the Kipling and Macdonald relatives seem to have had any inkling of the ill-treatment suffered by the Kipling children. Eleven months after their arrival at Lorne Lodge their Macdonald grandmother and two of their aunts spent a fortnight at Southsea and noticed nothing untoward, Mrs Macdonald even observing in her diary that the two children were 'well and happy', seemingly 'attached to Mrs H.' – and 'much improved in manners'.[12] But as Kipling explains in his autobiography, 'Badly-treated children have a clear notion of what they are likely to get if they betray the secrets of the prison-house before they are clear of it.' His sister offered a similar explanation, with a different simile. 'She did not know,' she wrote of her grandmother, 'that well-trained animals watch their tamer's eye, and the familiar danger signals of "Aunty's" rising temper had set us both fawning upon her.'[13] The two children had learned to dissemble all too well.

In her determination to reform the two children Mrs Holloway tried turning one against the other, which had the effect of making them intensely protective towards each other. As Trix put it in 'Through Judy's Eyes', 'Punch had always been Judy's oracle, as well as her angel, so she did not love him less, only distrusted Aunty more.' Where Mrs Holloway did succeed, however, was in her efforts to teach the children to read and write. According to Trix:

> Aunty Rosa thought it would be more convenient if we both learned to read at the same time. She instructed us together, the only difference being that our punishments were different. Rudyard, being six years old, and a man, was rapped over his knuckles with a ruler, whereas I, being a lady, was only made to stand alone on the table . . . Perhaps, however, this punishment sharpened my wits, because it is my boast that I learnt to read with fair fluency some weeks before he did.[14]

Why Ruddy should have experienced such difficulty with his reading is hard to understand, but in his discovery lay his salvation. 'I was made to read without explanation,' Kipling writes in *Something of Myself*, 'under the usual fear of punishment. And on a day that I remember it came to me that "reading" was not "the Cat sat on the Mat", but a means to everything that would make me happy.' Once the breakthrough had been made the boy read voraciously and at every opportunity, and when punished by being forbidden to read, 'read by stealth and the more earnest'. Like Dickens's David Copperfield, for whom books provided his 'only' and 'constant comfort', Ruddy found solace in his reading – along with the satisfaction and sense of power that came from outwitting his tormentor. And here, at least, their parents were able to show they cared by sending books and magazines that both children pored over until they knew entire stories by heart. One of

Ruddy's favourites was an illustrated *Robinson Crusoe*, which he would take down to the basement of Lorne Lodge and use as a catalyst for his imagination: 'My apparatus was a coconut shell on a red cord, a tin trunk, and a piece of packing-case which kept off any other world. Thus fenced about, everything inside the fence was real . . . The magic, you see, lies in the ring or fence that you take refuge in.'

An even more valuable refuge was Ruddy's annual visit to the Burne-Joneses for the Christmas holidays, beginning in December 1873 and continuing every Christmas thereafter – a refuge unaccountably denied his sister: 'For a month each year I possessed a paradise which I verily believe saved me . . . At "the Grange" I had love and affection as much as the greediest, and I was not very greedy, could desire.' Here Ruddy enjoyed the company of his two elder cousins and the 'incessant come and go of young people and grown-ups all willing to play with us'. Best of all, Ruddy gained a surrogate mother in the 'beloved Aunt': Georgie Burne-Jones. Ned Burne-Jones's ever-widening circle of artistic and literary friends meant little to an eight-year-old, but with each succeeding year this month-long immersion in a house filled with laughter, music, wit, intelligent conversation and bright colours became increasingly important: a vital transfusion of life as it could be lived that gave the boy hope and the knowledge that he was still loved.

From the recollections of one of the many children born to Alice Kipling's brother Fred, it is clear that Ruddy stayed from time to time with other members of the Macdonald family – and that, for all Aunty Rosa's efforts, he remained as troublesome as ever:

> With insatiable curiosity and exhaustless enterprise, he often led the rest of us into trouble. But we in the nursery found him a delightful playfellow and storyteller, always full of enthusiasm and new ideas. I remember an occasion when he had his ears boxed by a railway porter for impudence, and he returned to our house swelling with rage and mortification. He stormed up and down the house, telling us all about it, then pulled himself

together and returned to Addison Road Station to repeat the offence.[15]

But the annual respite offered by The Grange was not enough. In Ruddy's tenth year he became increasingly and unaccountably clumsy. In 'Baa, Baa, Black Sheep' he describes his alter ego Punch, now transformed into 'Black Sheep' by his irredeemable wickedness, 'spilling everything he touched, upsetting glasses as he put his hand out, and bumping his head against doors that were manifestly shut. There was a grey haze upon all his world, and it narrowed month by month, until at last it left Black Sheep almost alone with the flapping curtains that were so like ghosts, and the nameless terrors of broad daylight that were only coats on pegs.' Ruddy's fear of this enclosing darkness grew all the more as it became increasingly hard for him to read his school books, when 'even the pages of the open-print story-books danced and were dim'. His school work suffered, leading to further confrontations with Aunty which came to a head on a Monday morning dated by Trix to March 1877, but which must have been some four or five months earlier.

Trix had been forbidden to see or speak to her brother over the preceding weekend, but on the Monday morning she was ordered to practise the piano in the front room with the curtains drawn. Disobeying orders, she peeped through the curtains and saw Ruddy walking to school 'like an old man', with a cardboard placard on the back of his jacket proclaiming him a 'LIAR' in capital letters. It has been suggested that this episode was borrowed by Kipling from *David Copperfield*, in which case Trix also entered into the deception, even to the extent of adding the detail that she ran down the street after her brother, unpicked the placard with a knife and danced on it in a rage. A screaming match then followed between her and the cane-wielding Mrs Holloway, which ended with the 'scarlet-faced virago' in tears. 'It was the end of my childhood,' Trix told her brother's first biographer. 'I was fighting for Ruddy as well as myself . . . He was too broken by fasting and beating to have any kick left in him.'[16]

Over Christmas 1876, as the boy turned eleven, his Aunt Georgie noticed him behaving very strangely, hitting out at trees in her garden as if someone was threatening him and running across the room to touch the walls 'to see if they were there'.[17] In *Something of Myself* Kipling admits to having had 'some sort of nervous breakdown, for I imagined I saw shadows and things that were not there, and they worried me more than the Woman'. His cousin Stanley Baldwin put it more bluntly: 'The boy was half-blind, and crazed to the point of suffering delusions.'[18] A retired medical friend of the Kiplings, who had known the child in Bombay, was sent down to Southsea to find out why he was suffering his hallucinations. Ruddy's condition was very speedily diagnosed as 'myopia of the seventh degree' and he was taken to an optician in Holborn to be fitted out with bottle-lensed spectacles and a pince-nez which cut painfully into his nose.

Thoroughly alarmed by the doctor's report, Georgie Burne-Jones wrote at once to Alice Kipling in Bombay to tell her to come home.

Alice Kipling had originally planned to return to England after not more than two years' separation from her children, but for reasons that probably have more to do with straitened circumstances than parental neglect, five and a half years passed before she saw them again.

Nevertheless, the Kiplings' exile had been made a lot easier to bear by their increasing participation in the Anglo-Indian literary scene. In 1871 a new literary magazine had appeared, *The Chameleon: An Anglo-Indian Periodical of Light Literature*, printed on the presses of the *Pioneer* in Allahabad, its founder and editor Phil Robinson styling himself 'Chameleon'. The magazine was made up of short stories, essays and verses, mostly by established Anglo-Indian poets and essayists such as Alfred Lyall and Henry Keene, but with enough contributions from hitherto unrecognised contributors to suggest that here was the makings of a new school of writing in India, one that was a little brash, poked fun at established authority and saw itself as defiantly Anglo-Indian.

The second issue of Phil Robinson's magazine, published in May 1872, included a short story by 'L. K.' and two poems by 'A. L. K.' The first was a romance inspired by Lockwood Kipling's visit to Yorkshire the year before. Recounted in the first person by a bored Civilian on Home leave, it tells how on the train to Scarborough he encounters a pretty young lady, whom he afterwards observes emerging from a bathing machine on the seashore. He contrives to meet her and falls in love: 'I was very far gone in what a brutal world calls spoons.' The story ends happily with the narrator's return to India with his new bride, who turns out to be the sister of his best friend. It is a tale that never quite lives up to the expectations raised by its opening aphorism, a literary trick afterwards adopted with greater facility by the son of the father: 'That man is wise and happy beyond most of his fellows who knows how to get through a long holiday without discontent.'

Alice Kipling's two contributions as 'A. L. K.' were no better, the first a poem entitled 'To Her Children at Home' which tells of 'a little girl, / Mother's bonny baby' and 'a little boy, / Mother's darling treasure'. Both 'are gone, / Leaving Mother lonely, / With the laugh, and shout, and fun, / Now remembered only'. The last verse says it all:

> Little girl and little boy,
>   Mother loves you dearly,
> It would fill her heart with joy
>   Just to see you merely.
> Far away, night and day,
>   Sadly does she miss you,
> And would give, I believe,
>   All the world to kiss you.

Today these lines read like something from a greetings card, but they would have struck a chord with *The Chameleon*'s female readers, and since Alice was never one to hide her own or her children's talents under bushels we can assume that a copy of

'To Her Children At Home' was posted to Southsea and there gave Ruddy and Trix some comfort.

The second published poem, 'A Bargain', was much more in keeping with Alice Kipling's reputation for wit and flirtatiousness. A pair of lovers plight their troth, but as they flirt the woman asks her lover if he can kiss her with lips as pure as her own, or have those lips previously made a vow 'that's broken now'? It ends:

> 'But can you give me love for love
>   And faith for faith?' said she.
> 'And is your truth like mine in sooth
>   That you should plight with me?'

Later issues of *The Chameleon* contained a more ambitious work of fiction from Lockwood Kipling entitled 'Inezilla: A Romance in Two Parts'. Set partly in the Mediterranean and partly in India, it confirms that whatever other artistic gifts he possessed, writing fiction was not among them. Intriguingly, in the same issue which carried the first part of 'Inezilla' was an essay entitled 'Concerning young men and their manners by a Lady' that was full of sharp words about the pressures a married woman in India was forced to endure. The pseudonymous 'Florence' accuses Englishmen in India of forcing married women to receive their attentions 'for politeness sake', resulting in 'those incessant flirtations which are so rife in Anglo-Indian society'. Surrounded on all sides by 'danglers' – unmarried young men thirsting for love – a married lady had 'the alternative of receiving the attentions of one or two men who make it their business to pay them to her, or of receiving none at all'. 'Florence' sounds very like 'the wittiest woman in India' of fifteen years later.

The Kiplings' initials are not found again among the latter surviving issues of *The Chameleon*. Many contributors identified themselves by initials or pen-names most of which remain unidentified, but two of their number were writers of quality whose work became a major influence though the 1870s and into the 1880s.

One was Major Walter Yeldham, writing as 'Aliph Cheem', whose verses 'Those Niggers' have already been quoted in an earlier chapter. In his *Lays of Ind* one can hear that same disconcerting change of tone which so startled readers when Rudyard Kipling's *Departmental Ditties* was first published more than a decade later, as for example in the last verse of 'Twaddle':

> You say we hold the land in trust,
>   And for a little span, sir,
> The truth is, that we'll hold it just
>   As long as ere we can, sir![19]

The other writer of consequence was 'Political Orphan', the pen-name of George Aberigh-Mackay, a member of the Education Department of the North-Western Provinces, recruited by George Allen in 1871 to be one of the *Pioneer's* special correspondents. He afterwards went on to write for the *Bombay Gazette*, in which he published the satirical essays which made him Anglo-India's leading political and social satirist, later issued in one volume as *Twenty-one Days in India: Or the Tour of Sir Ali Baba KCB*. An enthusiastic sportsman, naturalist and historian, Aberigh-Mackay was said to have only one failing as a writer: his cynicism, which he used to advantage in his portraits of Anglo-Indian 'types'. His 'grass widow' who spends her summers flirting in Simla while her husband labours on in the heat of the plains predates Rudyard Kipling's 'Mrs Hauksbee' and his other Simla *femmes fatales* by more than a decade, and is no less memorable. 'Yes, she is a source of disappointment to them,' the author declares of his grass widow and her jealous rivals:

They have watched her for three seasons going lightly and merrily through all the gaieties of Cloudland [Simla]; they have listened to the scandal of the cuckoos among the pine-trees and rhododendrons, but they have not caught her tripping . . . Her beauty has burned itself into their jealousy; her merry laughter has fanned their scorn; her bountiful presence is an affront to them, as is her ripe and lissom figure. They pronounce her morally unsound; they say her nature has a taint; they chill her popularity with silent smiles of slow disparagement. But they have no particulars.[20]

George Aberigh-Mackay was set for a distinguished literary career when in January 1881 a chill caught after a game of lawn tennis ended his life at the age of thirty-two. Had he lived on, Rudyard Kipling's impact on Anglo-Indian literature would have been far less dramatic.

No issues of *The Chameleon* survive after its sixth. It may well have folded, perhaps undermined by the success of a more down-market rival, the *Indian Charivari*, modelled on *Punch* but more down-to-earth and accurately reflecting the prejudices of its readership. A constant theme of the latter magazine's cartoons is the foolishness of Indian servants, with the verbal exchanges between them usually given in Urdu, the assumption being that its readership spoke it well enough to get the joke. Equally popular are ballads about conniving Hindu *babus* – the English-educated Indians chiefly of Bengali extraction who served as office clerks and junior functionaries in Government departments – who invariably receive their comeuppance after giving themselves too many airs. According to Harry Rivett-Carnac, Mr Terry, Lockwood Kipling's superior at the Sir J. J. School of Art, was editor of the *Indian Charivari* for a time, and he and his friends all contributed to the periodical. This would suggest that the Kiplings were involved, but since few issues survive and contributions were unsigned, it is impossible to determine if this was the case.

In March 1875 Lockwood Kipling completed his third contracted term of service at the Sir J. J. School of Art. He was thirty-seven years old, his career was stagnating and his employers had demonstrated their lack of sympathy with the school's aims by dropping 'Industry' from its title and removing the artisan element from its teaching curriculum. Again, it was Lockwood's well-connected friend Harry Rivett-Carnac who came to the rescue – by supporting his application for the post of Principal of the newly established Mayo School of Industrial Art in Lahore.

After Lord Mayo's assassination in 1872 the Government of the Punjab had decided that funds raised by public subscription to honour his memory should be used to erect two new public buildings in Lahore: a hospital and a school of art. What made the principalship of the latter particularly appealing to Lockwood Kipling was that it was combined with a second responsibility: curatorship of the Lahore Museum. He applied and secured the double post, and in April 1875 proceeded to Lahore alone, leaving Alice behind to pack up in Bombay.

The land in which Lockwood Kipling now found himself was very different from that which he had known for the last decade. The Punjab was open plains country segmented by five great rivers, its capital one over which fifty-eight kings and 173 of their satraps had ruled: a walled city whose fame in the days of the great Mughals had been acknowledged by Milton and Dryden but which had now fallen on hard times. Before the rise of the Sikh *sirdars* under Ranjit Singh, Lahore had been the home of generations of Mughal rulers and noblemen whose garden-enclosed tombs were scattered across the countryside outside the city walls. This ancient heritage was tangible to an almost intolerable degree:

> The dead at all times were around us – in the vast forgotten Muslim cemeteries round the Station, where one's horse's hoof of a morning might break through to the corpse below; skulls and bones tumbled out of our mud garden walls, and were turned up among the flowers by the Rains; and at every point were the tombs of the dead. Our chief picnic rendezvous and some of our public offices had been memorials to desired dead women, and Fort Lahore, where Runjit Singh's wives lay, was a mausoleum of ghosts.[21]

From the British perspective the Punjab constituted frontier territory, only recently won, and when Lockwood arrived in Lahore the Union flag had been flying over the rampart of Fort Lahore for barely a quarter of century. But from the moment when Governor-General Dalhousie had proclaimed British rule over the Punjab, he and his successors had set about making their mark. Lahore became the seat of a succession of Lieutenant-Governors of the Punjab Province whose names were attached to various public buildings and streets, most prominently Sir John Lawrence and his successor Sir Robert Montgomery, whose memories were preserved in the 'frigidly classical' Lawrence Hall, built as a venue for meetings and theatrical performances, and even grander Montgomery Hall, intended to provide a platform for public occasions.

Lawrence Hall (left) and Montgomery Hall (Illustrated London News)

However, the first public building to impress itself on Lockwood Kipling could only have been Lahore railway station. Completed in 1864, it had been designed both to withstand a siege and to serve as the main depot of the Punjab railway network. Behind a brick façade bristling with battlements, turrets and keeps was a complex of railway workshops and sidings extending over a hundred acres. From the railway station entrance a semicircle of roads radiated outwards like the spokes in a cartwheel, among them Railway

Road, which served as a divide between old and new Lahore. West of Railway Road rose the walls of the medieval city, within which were crammed most of Lahore's 100,000 inhabitants, and above which rose the bastions of Fort Lahore and the minarets of the city's greatest mosque, Emperor Aurangzeb's Badshahi or 'royal' mosque – said to be second in beauty only to the Taj Mahal. Access to the city was provided by twelve arched gateways, of which the first to meet Lockwood Kipling's gaze would have been the Delhi Gate, newly and clumsily restored by the British administration in 'a quasi-classical and incongruous style'. The Delhi Gate gave directly on to the enamelled façade of Wazir Khan's Masjid, Lahore's most ornate and, from the European point of view, most accessible mosque. From here the city's main thoroughfare ran on to the Moti and Kashmiri bazaars and then on again to the Kashmir Gate and the caravanserais of the Afghan horse-traders and the camel *kafilas* from the north.

Even in the Kiplings' day the city was a place to be entered with trepidation, and with lit cigarettes to mask the stench, and for as long as they remained in Lahore both father and son combined their fascination with the place with an almost obsessive interest in its drains and their dangers. Yet Lahore was a city as beautiful without as it was ugly within, inspiring the visiting Vicereine Lady Dufferin to remark that 'there is a garden five miles long surrounding the walls of the city so that whenever a Lahore cockney chooses to step out from his close dwelling and narrow street, he finds himself among plantains, and roses, and palms, and mangoes, and peepul-trees, and lovely flowering pomegranates'.[22] It was this verdant Lahore, its garden suburb lying entirely without the city walls, that the British colonised.

Like the Sikh rulers who had preceded them, the British kept clear of the city and settled initially in the tomb-strewn fields south of its walls, which came to be known as the suburb of Anarkali, after a dancing girl whose dalliance with the son of her owner, the Mughal Emperor Akbar, had caused the latter to have her killed. The son became the Emperor Jehangir and erected a fine octagonal tomb over her grave, which the Sikhs converted into a residence and the British into their first administrative head-quarters. A number of other Muslim tombs dotted about were put to similarly practical use and Anarkali very quickly became Lahore's Civil Station, the area within which the local British administration based itself. From the Bhatti Gate, on the south-west corner of the city, a road led due south to Anarkali's Tomb – a main artery which the British, in accordance with Anglo-Indian custom, named the Mall. From another of the city's southern entrances, the Lohari Gate, a second road also ran south, parallel to the Mall, and this became Court Road.

The rectangle of land between these two roads very soon became crowded with new government buildings, private residences, barracks, bazaars, and a Company *Bagh* or public garden. More space was needed and, with that confidence so characteristic of the British in India, engineers began to lay out a greatly enlarged Civil Station extending eastwards from Anarkali across the fields and tombs. Five miles away, in a marshy waste named Mian Mir after the tomb of a local Muslim saint, they plotted out a military cantonment and a raised roadway connecting it to Anarkali. This became the Upper Mall, a broad avenue planted with tamarisk shade trees, off which ran more than a dozen raised side roads, so creating a series of sunken square plots. In one of these plots, on the north side of the Upper Mall about two miles down the road from Anarkali's Tomb, stood the tomb and surrounding garden of a cousin of Emperor Akbar. This provided the nucleus for Government House, seat of the Lieutenant-Governors of the Punjab, allowing the vacated Anarkali's Tomb to be converted into Lahore's first Christian church. At this same time the first steps were initiated to preserve Lahore's heritage. The Badshahi Mosque was cleared of its Sikh occupiers and restored to its original religious function – and funds allocated for a museum.

Initially the museum's first curator had to make do with Wazir Khan's *baradari*, a handsome cuboid building with a cupola at each corner located at the south-eastern corner of the Anarkali rectangle.

Then in 1864 the Punjab Exhibition of Arts and Industry was staged in Lahore to promote the Province's arts and crafts, and a temporary structure was erected by the Public Works Department for the purpose in the gardens beside Wazir Khan's *baradari*. Once the exhibition had closed, this new building, consisting of a long, narrow hall with a series of arches on either side opening out into closed verandahs, was converted into the Punjab Museum, with the exhibits left over from the Punjab Exhibition providing the bulk of its collection. The vacated *baradari* subsequently became Lahore Public Library.

The Punjab Exhibition Building, later the Museum
(Illustrated London News)

In 1867 the museum's part-time curator, Thomas Thornton, used his authority as Secretary to the Punjab Government to issue an instruction to every official in the Punjab to send in 'any object of interest or curiosity in the way of agricultural produce, manufacture or antiquity'. As a result the museum gained a wonderfully eclectic range of exhibits, most notably an array of Graeco-Buddhist

Gandharan statues, bas-reliefs and artefacts excavated from various sites in and around Peshawar. A further addition was Lahore's famous antique cannon, known as *Zam-zamah* or the 'Hummer'. Cast in Lahore in 1762 to the orders of the Afghan invader Ahmad Shah Durrani, this awesome fourteen-foot weapon was at one time the largest artillery piece in India, and had come to be regarded as a talisman of victory. But after being damaged at the siege of Multan in 1818 it had been dragged to Lahore, to stand sentinel outside the Delhi Gate until 1870, when it was moved to a raised brick platform outside the museum – which was where Lockwood Kipling first set eyes on it. According to *Lahore as it was and is*, an early guidebook written largely by Thomas Thornton with a contributing chapter from Lockwood Kipling, the museum had by then become known to Lahore's Native inhabitants as the *Ajaib-ghar* or 'Wonder House'.[23]

Until he could find suitable accommodation to rent Lockwood took a room at the Punjab Club – not the present Punjab Gymkhana Club building with its imposing Palladian façade but its predecessor: a 'hideous barrack-like structure, with its racket court at the back', standing in its own plot of land beside the Upper Mall just west of Government House. Just across the road was the Civil Station's main recreation area, consisting of Lawrence and Montgomery Halls, Lawrence Gardens and the racecourse. From here it was a five-minute ride by pony cart to the museum – and the building immediately behind it which provided temporary accommodation for Lockwood Kipling's chief responsibility, the fledgling Mayo School of Industrial Art: a 'dilapidated building of stucco . . . painted a dull yellow . . . in a large empty compound without a tree or shrub near it'.[24]

As Rudyard Kipling was to grumble seven years later, the Punjab Club was materially no more than a place 'where bachelors, for the most part, gathered to eat meals of no merit among men whose merits they knew well', sitting down together at one table in a 'long, shabby dining-room'. Its significance lay in the fact that it was the hub around which Anglo-Indian Society in Lahore revolved, for it was an exclusive institution, open to 'none except picked men at their definite work – Civilians, Army, Education,

Canals, Forestry, Engineering, Irrigation, Railways, Doctors, and Lawyers – samples of each branch and each talking their own shop'.[25] According to the 1875 census, there were 1723 Europeans in Lahore at this time, many of them members of the railway community who lived, quite literally, on the wrong side of the tracks – in a suburb known as Naulakha beside the railway workshops. They included a large number of Eurasians of mixed race and neither they nor anyone who engaged in business or trade was eligible for the Punjab Club, so that its actual membership was less than a hundred, all white men. Had Lockwood remained a member of the provincial service, as in Bombay, it is unlikely that he would have been eligible for membership. In Lahore he was neither flesh nor fowl, since his appointment was, in the words of a friend, 'permanent but he had no official rank'.[26] But he had the support of Civilian friends and he was self-evidently a gentleman and this was enough to ensure that he was at once put up for temporary membership of the Punjab Club and subsequently voted a full member.

By the time Alice joined him in Lahore in May, Lockwood had found a bungalow to rent, although not the house that became their permanent home. The Punjab Hot Weather was now fully upon them and was like nothing the Kiplings had previously experienced. Lockwood compared it to 'a red thread' encompassing all with 'garments of fire', and ever afterwards he and other members of the family dreaded Punjab's summers. On one of the hottest nights of the year the Kiplings were invited to dine with the Deputy Commissioner of Lahore and there met an eighteen-year-old girl, Edith Plowden, who afterwards became their closest friend in India, to the extent that Alice regarded her as her 'sixth sister' and Ruddy viewed her as 'the "missing link" between Lahore and London'.

Both Miss Plowden's parents were dead and she had come out to India to live with and housekeep for her elder brother and guardian, Walter Plowden, a senior Government barrister in Lahore. Also living in Lahore at this time was a second brother, Chichele Plowden, newly enrolled in the Indian Police, and a cousin, Henry Plowden, another barrister. All were members of the closest thing that Anglo-India had to an aristocracy, based partly on class but principally on Indian service. Every Plowden in India was a descendant of Richard Plowden, who had joined the East India Company as a 'writer' or junior merchant in the 1770s and whose five sons had all become Bengal Civilians. Of their offspring five had followed their fathers as Civilians and another four had entered either the Indian Army or the Indian Police, so that by the 1870s male Plowdens were to be found comfortably placed in every Province in northern India – to say nothing of female members of the family such as Edith Plowden's aunt Katherine, whose husband Sir John Strachey was at this time Lieutenant-Governor of the North-Western Provinces.

Miss Edith Plowden was shy, prudish and insecure. Her elder brother's legal work took up most of his time and, despite her connections, she found herself friendless in Lahore – until the Kiplings took her under their wing. Fortunately for the biographer, Edith Plowden kept a number of the many letters they exchanged over the years, as well as writing an unvarnished account of their friendship which survives as an unpublished manuscript. At the dinner where they first met Edith barely noted Alice Kipling, beyond observing that she was the last to be escorted in to dinner because of her husband's lowly status and that her arms were 'bare of ornament'. But Lockwood Kipling was placed next to her and took pains to keep her amused throughout the meal. Despite his restricted stature, Edith Plowden found him 'impossible to overlook . . . with his fine head, beneficent [*sic*] expression and grey beard. I called him Socrates from his resemblance to a cast of the philosopher.' After dinner the guests moved out on to the lawn, where – since snakes liked to lie out on the warm ground after sunset – a carpet had been laid. Here Edith had her first opportunity to talk to Alice Kipling and to exchange confidences: 'No one could persuade me to enjoy a life in the Punjaub; drifting from one ugly station to another; changing communities breaking up friendships; or a broken up life in some hill station . . . Alice's cheerful philosophy rising above depressing conditions, her interest in all around her, as it seemed to me, was a rebuke to me . . . My life took a new direction that evening.'[27]

Tragedy and ill-health drew the three closer. Shortly after the dinner party the man with whom Edith Plowden's brother 'chummed' or shared house in Lahore died suddenly, leaving a widow and a small child, who had then to pack up and return to England: 'This was my first experience of the tragic partings insep-arable from Indian careers . . . The first shock was great & left me with a sense of general insecurity.' Edith took to her bed with an 'almost suicidal depression', from which she was rescued by Alice Kipling, who coaxed her into joining her on her evening drives. From then on Edith spent every Thursday evening with the Kiplings, 'John smoking and reading to us, [while] Alice & I worked embroidery from his designs with native silks – or Alice was at the piano . . . Within all was bright & artistic & bore the unmistakable stamp of that much abused word "culture".' Here she learned to share the Kiplings' enthusiasm for Robert Browning and the Pre-Raphaelites as she received a foundation course in litera-ture, art and modern ideas which frequently left her shocked, particularly when she discovered that both Alice and Lockwood Kipling had 'fallen in and out of love' before they had met and that the former owned a collection of engagement rings.

In November 1875 Lockwood began writing for the *Pioneer* as its Lahore correspondent, in his first article rejoicing at the com-mencement of the Cold Weather: 'The mornings are delightful, the evenings, chill and murky with heavy dews; the air laden with the pungent mixture of raw mist and foul-smelling smoke which every right-thinking Punjabi considers the chief delight of this splendid climate.'[28] The Prince of Wales had just embarked on a royal tour of India and as part of his duties Lockwood organised the decorations for a grand banquet and ball to be held in the Lawrence and Montgomery Halls to honour the Prince's visit to Lahore at the start of the New Year. He worked long and hard on this extra task, only to collapse on the eve of the Prince's arrival. His condition was diagnosed as typhoid and for six weeks he lay unconscious and on the brink, Alice nursing him on her own. Weeks passed before Lockwood was entirely lucid – 'I sometimes sat and talked with him but it was all fragmentary,' recorded Edith Plowden. 'This devotee of Browning and Swinburne lay reading Alice's Cookery book by the hour' – and more weeks before he was strong enough to leave the bungalow.

Lockwood's illness set its mark on both Kiplings. According to their daughter, it left him at the age of thirty-seven, 'grey and bald and prematurely old-looking'[29]; and according to Edith Plowden, Alice, too, was 'never quite the same again'.[30] When the Hot Weather came round in May there was no question of their remaining in Lahore. Before the heat had grown intolerable they left for the hill-station of Mussoorie, but hardly had they settled in before Lockwood received a summons to proceed at once to Simla to report to the office of the Viceroy.

Barely six weeks earlier a new proconsul had arrived in India whose policies were to destroy much of the good work done by his predecessors: Robert Bulwer, first Earl of Lytton, diplomat and author of a number of volumes of second-rate verse and fiction under the *nom de plume* of 'Owen Meredith'. It was said of Lord Lytton that he inherited 'insanity from one parent and limitless conceit from the other'.[31] Today he would be diagnosed as a manic depressive with wild mood swings, but at the time his behaviour was blamed on his nerves, which he calmed with heavy doses of laudanum. Lytton arrived in India 'burning with anxiety to distinguish himself in a great war'[32] but in almost every other respect he was aggressively Utilitarian. Eager to apply Disraeli's policy of non-intervention and free-market capitalism to the letter, he summarily abolished Indian import duties on British-made cotton goods, opening India to a flood of cheap Lancashire piece-goods. This might not have mattered in a strong economy, but the fact was that India's per capita income was falling dramatically as a direct consequence of a burgeoning market economy dominated by cash crops such as cotton, indigo, jute and tea grown for export. In the process it was not the peasant cultivator who benefited but the trader, so much so that British rule in India was becoming known in Native Indian circles as *Banyakiraj*, the rule of the money-lender.

Saddled with ever-mounting debts, India's rural population no longer had the means to sustain itself in hard times – and those hard times began in 1874 when India suffered the first of a series of droughts of unprecedented severity, leading to famine in Bengal and Bihar, droughts since identified as part of a worldwide weather pattern shift known today as the El Niño Southern Oscillation. In the Hot Weather of 1875 – the same summer of heatwaves the Kiplings had experienced after moving up to Lahore – the Rains failed again, resulting in the loss of the *kharif*, the autumn harvest. The authorities responded by implementing famine-relief measures: Harry Rivett-Carnac's former patron, Sir Richard Temple, was appointed famine commissioner and with the sanction of the then Viceroy, Lord Northbrook, imported rice from Burma and instituted relief measures which saved the day. But instead of being thanked, both Northbrook and Temple were castigated for profligacy by Disraeli's Home Government. Further disagreements over Disraeli's aggressive attitude towards Afghanistan and his plans to abolish Indian cotton tariffs led to Northbrook's resignation – and his replacement by the Prime Minister's fourth choice: Lord Lytton, arguably the worst Viceroy ever sent to govern India.

In the summer of 1876 the monsoon failed for a third year, leading to famine on a scale hitherto unknown in India. But when Lord Buckingham, Governor of Madras, instituted relief measures such as work camps where refugees were given food in return for their labour, he was sternly rebuked by Lytton, who ordered that no grain was to be bought by Government. So while hundreds of thousands died for lack of food in Madras and other famine-affected regions, surpluses of rice and wheat in other parts of India continued to be exported to England. In 1876 Indian wheat exports to Britain doubled, and doubled again in the following year.

To further curb the authorities in Madras Lord Lytton appointed Sir Richard Temple as special adviser to Lord Buckingham, with orders to 'tighten the reins'. Having learned his lesson in Bengal, Temple now acted with extraordinary callousness, removing half a million workers from the relief camps' rolls and reducing the rations of those who remained to the notorious 'Temple wage' of one pound of rice a day. Many thousands, if not millions, died as a consequence of these measures – for which Temple received a baronetcy and the Governorship of Bombay. Meanwhile the Great Famine rolled on. In 1877 it spread to the Deccan, Rajasthan and parts of the North-Western Provinces. Although heavy rains fell in the late summer, an unusually cold winter coupled with a cholera epidemic killed thousands worn down by hunger.

Throughout this period the *Pioneer* and other leading newspapers remained silent, persuaded by the authorities that to do otherwise would spread alarm and despondency. It was not until February 1878 that the *Statesman* newspaper in Calcutta broke ranks and published the facts. Unabashed, the Viceroy responded by setting up a Famine Commission packed with officials who shared his Malthusian view that famine was a natural phenomenon, and that attempts to mitigate its effects would only lead to over-population. The Commission duly reported that famine was indeed a natural phenomenon and had absolutely nothing to do with Government. Indeed, it praised the Government of India for the steps it had taken and recommended the establishment of a Famine Code, involving the setting up of work camps and other measures that were essentially punitive.

As a direct consequence of these and other Lyttonian policies many educated Indians who saw themselves as loyal citizens of the Crown became disillusioned with British rule and determined to work for the cause of greater Indian involvement in government. A number of British officials took the same view, among them the Civilian Allan Octavian Hume, who as Lord Lytton's Secretary of Revenue and Agriculture had become convinced that 'some definite action was called for'. Hume's plans for the imposition of an income tax to create a famine insurance fund were denounced by Lytton as penalising the 'higher income group' and were rejected in favour of indirect tax schemes which hit hardest the poorer sections of the community. Hume was demoted and resigned, and the indirect taxation he had opposed was used not for famine insurance but to create a war chest.

In the summer of 1876, however, Lord Lytton's main preoccupation was with a grand celebration which he and Disraeli had together devised: an 'Imperial Assemblage' to be held at Delhi on New Year's Day 1877, at which Queen Victoria was to be proclaimed *Kaiser-i-Hind* or Empress of India. It was to be 'gaudy enough to impress the orientals' while at the same time concealing 'the nakedness of the sword on which we really rely',[33] and one of its features was to be the presentation of armorial bearings to the maharajas, rajas and nawabs who together made up India's 'salute princes' or local rulers entitled to gun salutes of thirteen and above. It was in this connection that Lockwood Kipling had been summoned to Simla.

For some weeks the Kiplings were left kicking their heels, with no idea of why Lockwood had been sent for. In her manuscript memoir Edith Plowden hints that they came up against the wall of snobbery for which Simla was notorious. She herself had been invited to Simla by her cousin Trevor Plowden, whose family owned a fine house with a magnificent garden in Chota Simla, below Simla Bazaar. Here she went down with a second bout of fever and depression and was again rescued by the Kiplings. Walking out together one day they met a 'dreamy gentleman in a wide-brimmed soft hat walking, silent and thoughtful, accompanied by two young men respectful but alert. Something unusual about the quiet group and John's sudden silence as he removed his hat, made me ask "Who was that?" when they had passed by.' This was Lord Lytton, accompanied by his two *aides-de-camp*.

After weeks of waiting Lockwood was finally called to a meeting at the viceregal residence, Peterhof, to hear the Viceroy set out his plans for his Assemblage. Lord Lytton was in one of his better moods, and Lockwood was beguiled. 'Such a charming, gentle little Viceroy,' he wrote to Edith Plowden. 'He has a gentle lingering way of doing business – especially the double-barrelled hug.'[34] At last Lockwood learned why he had been summoned: coats of arms in the English style had been devised for each of the salute princes and it would be his task to depict these in Chinese silk embroidery on large satin banners, along with appropriate 'mottoes, titles and family mottoes in Persian characters'. Sixty-three coats of arms were required for the princes, plus another seven for the Viceroy, the Commander-in-Chief and British India's five Governors and Lieutenant-Governors – all to be delivered by Christmas.

The Kiplings left at once for Lahore, where a team of *dirzies* or tailors were hired and set to work. For the next nine weeks both Lockwood and Alice spent almost every waking hour on the project, he working up the designs and constructing the banners while she employed her skills as a needlewoman to supervise the embroidery. They and the seventy completed banners were then transported to Delhi to play their part in Lord Lytton's imperial pageant.

The site for the Assemblage had been deliberately chosen, because it was here behind Delhi Ridge that the British forces had camped in the summer of 1857 before recapturing Delhi from the rebels. It had now been transformed into one vast tented city, with the Viceroy's Camp at the centre alongside an amphitheatre with a raised dais at which the main ceremonies were to be held. As a guest of her cousin, Edith Plowden was comfortably ensconced at the camp of the Lieutenant-Governor of Bengal. The Kiplings were invited but had to make do with a modest three-roomed tent on the outer fringes.

On 30 December Ruddy celebrated his eleventh birthday in London with the Burne-Joneses, by now deeply troubled by his behaviour and 'puzzled what to do for him'.[35] On the following day in Delhi his mother watched through a curtain as Lord Lytton presented the salute princes with their banners, her husband hovering 'in the remote background producing the banners from some unseen quarter as they were wanted'. On 1 January 1877 the

Imperial Assemblage reached its climax as Queen Victoria was proclaimed Empress of India with as much pomp and display as Lord Lytton's imagination could conceive. The Kiplings' reward for their efforts was a purse of 500 rupees and a silver medal for Lockwood, which Alice considered totally inadequate. Nevertheless, they were granted an audience with the Viceroy at which Lord Lytton, ever the ladies' man, took Alice by both hands and declared her to be an angel: 'As they talked together of the Art world in London Lord Lytton learnt that Alice was the sister of Georgie Burne-Jones. "Who would have thought of meeting Mrs Burne-Jones' sister in India," said Lord Lytton. "But who would have thought of meeting Owen Meredith as Viceroy," replied Alice, who was never at a loss for a bright response.' Not altogether surprisingly, the Kiplings regarded Lord Lytton thereafter as a ruler whose 'brilliancy startled the English [community in India]', despite those who found it 'easier to criticize than to appreciate new ideas'.[36]

Friday was the day when the overseas mail came in, and one Friday shortly after the Kiplings' return to Lahore Edith Plowden went over to their bungalow as usual, so that she and Alice could open and read their letters together. 'Then the blow fell!' Edith wrote somewhat melodramatically: Georgie Burne-Jones's letter with news of Ruddy's deterioration had arrived. She reported that she had found the boy 'altered, silent, unhappy . . . One night she went upstairs to put out his light. She kissed him and said good night: he drew the bedclothes over his head and she could see he was shaking with sobs. She tried to comfort him and he appreciated it but would not say a word. She thought – had thought for some time that Alice should come home, for Rudyard was changing – more thoughtful and depressed; this break down was decisive.'[37]

Alice came to a decision within minutes: a friend was about to leave for England by P&O steamer and she would go with her.

4

'One school of many'

> One school of many, made to make
>   Men who shall hold it dearest right
> To battle for their ruler's sake,
>   And stake their being in the fight.
>
> Rudyard Kipling, 'Ave Imperatrix', March 1882

On her return to England Alice Kipling lost no time in descending on Lorne Lodge, Southsea. She found Ruddy 'shy & reserved' and Trix's affections transferred to Mrs Holloway. She spent several nights at Lorne Lodge and, according to Edith Plowden, finally broke through her son's shyness after several evenings seated at his bedside: '"Let me look at you," he said one evening & fixed his spectacled eyes steadily on her. "Your face is one grand smile," he said & put his arms round her neck & kissed her lovingly.'[1]

Alice was still unaware of the cruelty inflicted on her children by Mrs Holloway and either failed to see the warning signs or misread them. 'She told me afterwards,' wrote Rudyard in his autobiography, 'that when she first came up to my room to kiss me goodnight, I flung up my arm to guard off the cuff that I had been trained to expect.' In 'Baa, Baa, Black Sheep' Kipling's alter ego Punch does the same, but here forcing his mother to comprehend at last what she has done: "'Oh, my son – my little, little son! . . . It was my fault – *my* fault, darling – and yet how could we help it? Forgive me.'" But this was wishful thinking on the author's part, for at the time neither child gave an inkling of what they had been through. Not until Ruddy's parents read 'Baa, Baa, Black Sheep' after its publication in 1888 did they fully grasp what their children had suffered. Until that moment both children had kept their feelings entirely suppressed.

A carefree holiday on a farm in Epping Forest followed, during which the two children were given as much licence as they wished: 'I don't know how mother survived it,' wrote Trix of this time, 'we were so absolutely lawless and unchecked. Our cousin Stanley Baldwin came for a six weeks' visit and we infected him with our lawlessness too, even to donkey riding. He brought a bat and tried to teach us cricket, but we had no time for it – it entailed too much law and order.'[2] Cousin Stanley was then aged ten, his Kipling cousins eleven and eight going on nine. Desperate to make up for her absence, Alice overdid it, and went down with shingles, having to be rescued by her unmarried sister Edith. Nevertheless, the liberating effect of his mother's return helped restore Ruddy's self-confidence: 'By the end of that long holiday I understood that . . . books and pictures were among the most important affairs in the world; that I could read as much as I chose and ask the meaning of things from anyone I met. I had found out, too, that one could take pen and set down what one thought, and that nobody accused one of "showing off" by so doing.'[3]

The education Ruddy had so far received had been rudimentary. The best that the Kiplings' finances had been able to run to had been a day school in Southsea which prepared boys for entry into the Royal Navy. However, in 1874 an advertisement had appeared in the *Pioneer* which must have read like an answer to their prayers. It gave notice of the opening of a private school on the west coast of England set up by a consortium of retired Indian Army officers with the specific aim of providing an inexpensive, no-frills education for boys intending to go on to the officer-train-ing academies but unable to afford the fees of military-oriented public schools such as Wellington College. But what made United Services Proprietary College doubly attractive was that the head-master was an old family friend, Cormell Price, who had been at King Edward VI Grammar School in Birmingham with Ned Burne-Jones and Alice's brother Harry – and who may even have been among Alice's early admirers. 'Crom' as he was known to his friends, and 'Uncle Crom' as he became known to Ruddy, had been a master at Haileybury College, a school long associated with India through its original role as the East India Company's train-ing school for its administrators.

Despite this background Cormell Price was a committed rad-ical and a follower of the Pre-Raphaelite group – a most unlikely choice to be the headmaster of a public school with a strong mil-itary ethos. As one of his pupils afterwards described him, he was 'in no sense a patriotic pedagogue' but 'a keen Liberal, a truculent Gladstonian, loathing Beaconsfield [Disraeli] . . . and sniffing scornfully at his institution of the title of Empress of India. Price's attitude as headmaster was detached and philosophic, as befitted his association with the Pre-Raphaelite artists and writers in London and his friendship with Burne-Jones and Morris from his college days.'[4] Rudyard Kipling put it more succinctly: 'The Head was dif-ferent, and in our different ways we loved him.' Crom Price had an open mind and he treated each boy as an individual: 'If you went to him with any trouble you were heard out to the end, and answered without being talked at or about or around, but always *to*. So we trusted him absolutely.'[5]

Alice had been quick to write to Cormell Price to remind him of their past friendship and to enquire about the school and whether her son was eligible.[6] At the time even the modest fees demanded would have been too much for the Kiplings, but two years on their circumstances had improved considerably and in May 1877 she wrote again, giving details of Ruddy's level of education and saying that she was thinking of enrolling him as a day-boy while she herself took lodgings nearby. In the event she changed her mind and he became a boarder at the start of the spring term in January 1878.

United Services College (USC) was a 'long white barrack by the sea' made up of a row of twelve brick lodging houses on a stretch of exposed ground beside the sea at Westward Ho!, a settlement just outside the town of Bideford in north Devon. The school had opened in 1875 with some two hundred pupils on the roll, a good number of them rejects from Haileybury. In consequence there was a lot of beating and bullying of the younger boys, one of whom was ten-year-old Lionel Dunsterville, born overseas and, like so many of his fellow pupils, the son of an absent Indian Army officer. As a retired major-general he wrote that 'We were freely beaten and it did us good', yet such was his unhappiness at the time that he made repeated attempts to run away.

When Ruddy entered USC three years later as Number 264 he became an obvious target for ragging. It was not just that he was the only boy in the school to wear glasses, but they were absurdly bottle-lensed, hence his school nickname of 'Gigger', derived from giglamps. Furthermore, he was useless at games and he thought and acted differently from the other boys. As Lionel Dunsterville put it, 'With very few exceptions, of whom Kipling was one, we were all sons of officers of the Navy or Army, so we represented a more or less homogenous type, but that fact merely accentuated the individuality of those who diverged from type.'[7]

Within the first week Alice Kipling had received a cascade of tearful letters begging her to remove her son from this 'hell on earth', panicking her into writing to Cormell Price, warning him of the 'roughness of the boys' and asking him to give her son special attention: 'For old time's sake, don't laugh at me for a spoon as I write this – but the boy is different from most boys – and I can't stop worrying.' A second letter enlarged on this difference: 'The lad has a great deal that is feminine in his nature and a little sympathy – from any quarter – will reconcile him to his changed life more than anything.'[8]

Most happily for Ruddy, sympathy both from Crom Price and

a schoolmate not only reconciled him to USC but also gave him the security and encouragement he needed to flourish there. The schoolmate was Lionel Dunsterville, who took under his wing Ruddy and another new boy, George Beresford. Together the three thirteen-year-olds formed a 'triple alliance' that remained unbroken 'till we dispersed to seek our fortunes in the world', later romanticised into the schoolboy adventures of 'Stalky' (Dunsterville), 'M'Turk' (Beresford) and 'Beetle' (Kipling) in *Stalky & Co*. 'Envisage a rather podgy, easy-going, careless, soft rather than hard, laughter-loving, slightly untidy adolescent,' wrote Beresford in 1930 of his study-mate and ally, 'taking the world very easily, humming or bleating a song or tune, but with everything threaded on a literary motive or moving to the unuttered rhythm of verse. He held no convictions or decided opinions on any earthly thing, let alone patriotism or the military idea; rather he let everything come as it would so long as it afforded him raw material, or led up to his central idea of literary expression.'

Handicapped by his myopia and a degree of physical clumsiness and lack of co-ordination which today would be diagnosed as dyspaxia, Ruddy compensated by developing his own survival skills. He learned to withdraw from physical confrontation, diverting his fellow pupils with 'wonderful grotesque outline drawings of strange monsters and demons' and defusing the wrath of masters by 'removing his glasses, polishing them carefully, replacing them on his nose and gazing in placid bewilderment at the thundering tyrant, with a look which suggested, "There, there. Don't give way to your foolish tantrums."' But, above all, he found refuge in books. 'In reading,' noted Beresford, 'he was omnivorous – with his spectacles on his forehead, face to the volume, his short-sighted eyes glittering over the pages, he would hump himself to his task, and pursue his researches with an almost audible energy.' Through this dogged pursuit of the written word, much of it learned off by heart, Ruddy acquired an aura of 'complete and expert knowledge'[9] that the other boys found daunting.

It took Crom Price less than a year to recognise that nothing was to be gained by forcing this awkward boy to conform. Instead, he encouraged him to pursue what he did best, to the extent of giving him the run of his own book-lined study. 'There Beetle found a fat armchair, a silver inkstand, and unlimited pens and paper,' wrote Kipling of this remarkable gift:

> There were scores and scores of ancient dramatists; there were Hakluyt, his voyages; French translations of Muscovite authors called Pushkin and Lermontoff; little tales of a heady and bewildering nature, interspersed with unusual songs – Peacock was that writer's name; there was Borrow's *Lavengro*; an odd theme, purporting to be a translation of something called a 'Rubáiyát', which the Head said was a poem not yet come into its own; there were hundreds of columns of verse – Crashaw; Dryden; Alexander Smith; L. E. L. [Letitia Elizabeth Langdon, whose sentimental poems and novels were popular in the 1830s]; Lydia Sigourney [an American writer of verse who enjoyed great popularity in the mid-nineteenth century]; Fletcher and a purple island; Donne; Marlowe's *Faust*; and Ossian . . . and Rossetti – to name but a few.[10]

As his list shows, the boy's private reading was catholic to a degree. But under the eyes of his robust Classics and English master, W. C. Crofts, he developed a love for Horace, the Romantic poets and the heavyweights of the day: Macaulay, Kingsley, Scott and the two Arnolds – the pedagogue Matthew and the journalist Edwin, whose epic prose-poem on the life of the Buddha, *The Light of Asia*, was a best-seller in 1879 and led Ruddy into a brief flirtation with this Protestant interpretation of Buddhism. According to Beresford, 'Gigger was the apostle of Buddha or Arnold for a span at Westward Ho! and used to declaim very finely certain portions about "om mani padmi Hum" or words to that effect.' For a term he preached reincarnation to his room-mates, although none too seriously, since he built himself a shrine from 'a gas-stove rigged up with a long India rubber tube from the fish-tail gas-burner which led directly to the life-giving sacrament of the cocoa cups'.[11]

Outside Croft's classroom Ruddy's reading was undirected and never subject to the checks and balances that a university education would have imposed, allowing him to absorb the trite alongside the profound. Given his family's and his headmaster's links with the Pre-Raphaelites, it was inevitable that William Morris and the two Rossettis, Dante Gabriel and Christina, should have been enjoyed – until they and the vanguard of the Aesthetic Movement came to be thought of by Ruddy and some of his fellow pupils as suspect, at which point they were dropped in favour of more popular verse. From then on it was the poetry of Robert Browning and Algernon Swinburne which spoke most directly to him: the long dramatic monologues of the first and the seductive power of word and metre of the second. Whatever lines caught Ruddy's imagination were learned off pat, to be declaimed or parodied, half in jest and half in earnest, to receptive audiences in the school study and dormitory.

No less influential were the writings of a number of American poets and writers: Edgar Allan Poe, whose 'tales of the grotesque and arabesque' continued to be popular long after his death in 1849; Henry Longfellow, whose last extended verse epic, *Ultima Thule*, appeared in 1880; Joel Chandler Harris, whose evocation of the American Deep South contained in the first of his Uncle Remus stories, *Uncle Remus, his Songs and Sayings*, was also published in 1880; Charles Leland, whose ponderous *Brietmann Ballads* with their cod-German dialects appealed to Ruddy's adolescent sense of humour; and Bret Harte, whose short stories with such outlandish titles as 'The Outcasts of Poker Flat' and 'The Luck of Roaring Camp' were as much admired and copied by Ruddy as his tragicomic verses. The consequences of this eclectic reading were far-reaching, for when Ruddy began writing his own verse and fiction any subject and every form was acceptable, leading to lapses of taste that Oscar Wilde later characterised as 'superb flashes of vulgarity' from 'a man of talent who drops his aspirates'.[12]

After a difficult first term puberty quite suddenly took hold and, as is so often the case with European children born in the tropics, Ruddy found himself 'physically precocious'. Out of the plump, rounded pupa emerged an angular, whiskered teenager, aggressively impish in manner and appearance. With his short neck, hunched shoulders and slight stoop, Ruddy presented a beetle-like mien, and his features took on that distinctive craggy appearance which his friend Beresford found unnervingly Mongolian: 'So sharp was the set-back from the massive eyebrow ridges that he appeared almost "cave-boy". His lower jaw was massive, protruding and strong; the chin had a deep central cleft or dimple that at once attracted attention.'[13] A new-found strength allied with his growing self-assurance allowed Ruddy to appear 'rather more formidable than he was', and the bullying stopped. This sudden physical change was accompanied by an even more startling growth of intellect, as if within months Ruddy aged mentally as many years. By the age of fourteen he was beginning to look and sound – and write – like a nineteen-year-old. 'Though thoroughly boyish in his pranks,' wrote Major-General Dunsterville of the boy intellectual, 'he was mentally on a par with a middle-aged man, and intellectually superior to most of the grown-ups who had the difficult task of controlling or guiding his early youth.'[14]

Nowhere was this coming of age more dramatically expressed than in Ruddy's transformation into a man of verse. In the late spring of 1878 Lockwood Kipling joined his family in England, granted an extended leave in order to oversee the arts and crafts display in the Indian Hall at the Exposition Universelle in Paris. He took his son with him to Paris and allowed him to do much as he pleased before the two of them joined up with Alice and Trix for a more conventional holiday. The rest of this happy summer was passed at 27 Warwick Gardens in west London, the home of 'three dear ladies': the spinster sister and cousins of a journalist friend of the Kiplings from Bombay, two of them romantic novelists and all three bluestockings.

Within easy walking distance of the Burne-Joneses in Fulham,

Warwick Gardens became thereafter the children's base during their holidays. Here Ruddy found yet another library, and a ready audience for his own literary experiments: 'In my holidays the three ladies listened – it was all I wanted – to anything I had to say. I drew on their books, from *The City of Dreadful Night* which shook me to my unformed core, Mrs Gatty's *Parables from Nature* which I imitated and thought I was original, and scores of others. There were few atrocities of form or metre that I did not perpetrate.'[15] Perhaps because James Thompson had been raised as an orphan in a Glasgow asylum and was an atheist and an alcoholic to boot, his doom-and-gloom-laden poetry held a particular fascination for the adolescent Ruddy. As well as satisfying his schoolboy appetite for the melancholy and the macabre, Thompson's *City of Dreadful Night and Other Poems* provided Ruddy with a rich source of *fin-de-siècle* ideas.

At Warwick Gardens, amid surroundings that were at once literary and old-maidish and initially with both parents at his elbows, what the adult Kipling afterwards described as 'the tide of writing' first set in. Ruddy began to write reams of verse, and when he returned to school in the autumn of 1878 this outpouring continued unabated, much to the puzzlement of his friends. 'I pitied poor Gigger,' wrote his friend Beresford. 'He couldn't help scribbling, so long as it had nothing to do with school-work. He kept spoiling reams – absolute reams, not quires – of cream-laid notepaper for poems; they must have been poems, because the lines were shortish and ended raggedly.' Some of these poems were intended for the *Scribbler*, a self-published magazine which the elder children of the Burne-Jones, Poynter and Morris families assembled from time to time under the editorship of Jenny Morris, daughter of William. But at school Ruddy kept his verse-writing strictly to himself: 'Inspection of the verses inscribed in his Russia-leather, gilt-edged, cream-laid MS. books would not have been at all welcomed . . . The leather-bound books were guarded by a taboo.'[16]

After Alice Kipling's return to India in the late summer of 1880 every letter written by Ruddy contained verses complete or in progress. The three dear ladies and his Aunt Edith Macdonald were similarly privileged, and when Ruddy finally met his parents' Indian confidante Edith Plowden at Warwick Gardens she too became a recipient, the arrangement culminating in the gift of a 'thick school copy-book' filled with this first flowering of juvenile verse. Fearful that she might be missing out, Alice Kipling then wrote to Miss Plowden begging her to copy and post any verses Ruddy had sent her. 'He promised I should have all he did – but he is not sending them,' she complained, 'and as time and distance do their fatal work I am sure his Mother will know less of him than any other woman of his acquaintance.'[17]

However, Alice may well have had another motive in asking for copies of all her son's poems, for in December 1881 she overcame her husband's doubts to have printed in Lahore fifty copies of a set of twenty-three poems under the title of *Schoolboy Lyrics*. Evidently believing that she was acting in Ruddy's best interests, she then dispatched copies unsolicited to a number of public figures, including George Allen in Allahabad and Algernon Swinburne in London – but not to Ruddy, who only saw a copy of *Schoolboy Lyrics* when he joined his parents in Lahore two years later. According to his sister, he was furious that his mother should have 'taken and made use of something he needed and valued, and sulked for two days'.[18]

The pace at which Ruddy's poetry developed was startling. Some months after his return to India Lockwood Kipling wrote to Edith Plowden to say that he had just received a letter from his son in which Ruddy had baldly stated, 'I am writing a poem it begins like this:

> A cry in the silent night
> A white face turned to the wall.
> A pang – and then in the mind of men
> Forgotten! And that is all.[19]

Ruddy completed the poem in Miss Plowden's presence a year later, when he was fourteen. Like so many of his *Schoolboy Lyrics* it was essentially an exercise in style, but reading through these early verses it is possible to see the pastiche and the derivative fall away as the boy-man learns to listen to his own creative impulse and finds his voice. Cynicism is the prevailing note, often put in the mouths of outcastes, such as the world-weary prostitute in 'Overheard', complaining to her customer:

> Took to the street for a life.
>   *Entre nous,*
> It's a terrible uphill strife,
>   Like all professions – too filled.
> And now I'm in lodgings hard by,
>   *Au quatrième,* up in the sky.
> Visit me by and by,
>   They're furnished, but oh – so cold,
> So cold![20]

No less remarkable was Ruddy's determination from the start to be 'Gigadibs the literary man', as his irritated English and Classics teacher labelled him – an ambition evidently shared by his mother. In September 1879 Mrs Mary Dodge, editor of the American *St Nicholas Magazine* for children, received a letter purporting to be from a thirteen-year-old English schoolboy who signed himself 'J. R. Kipling'. The original letter is lost but there are good grounds for supposing that it came not from Ruddy but from a mother eager to promote her son's literary talents. The letter was accompanied by a seven-stanza poem entitled 'The Dusky Crew', celebrating the comradeship of three independent-minded schoolboys and written in a pounding metre disconcertingly reminiscent of Edward Lear's 'Jumblies':

> Our heads were rough, and our hands were black,
>   With the ink-stains' midnight hue;
> We scouted all, both great and small
>   We were a dusky crew;

And each boy's hand was against us raised,
'Gainst me and the Other Two.

We chased the hare from her secret lair,
We roamed the woodlands through;
In parks and grounds far out of bounds
Wandered our dusky crew;
And the keepers swore to see us pass,
Me and the Other Two.[21]

The poem was rejected by Mrs Dodge, who may well have had doubts over its author's claimed age. But it confirms the assessment made by two of Ruddy's fellow pupils outside his circle at USC that he was 'so brilliant and cynical that he was most cordially hated by most of his fellow students'.[22] The fact was that for all his gifts – and, to some degree, because of his gifts – Ruddy could never be one of them, neither at school nor afterwards in India.

Yet the 'col' made Ruddy happy. After the disorder and insecurity of his early childhood the discipline and sense of fair play USC inculcated came as a huge comfort, and consequently he developed an almost uncritical devotion to the school and to the headmaster who had made it work.[23] He learned that society needs rules to avert chaos, and that to be part of a well-ordered society meant abiding by its code. Yet at the same time he became increasingly aware that he was an outsider: he might enjoy the freedom of the observer, the ability to cock a snoot at teachers and other authority figures, but he did not belong. His schoolmates would go on as a 'scattered brotherhood' to enter the military and the other Indian services, whereas he was disqualified from doing so – as much by temperament as by physical inadequacies or social background. They were fully paid-up members of a select community and he was not, and to be part of such a community – whether team, school, club, regiment or class – conferred power and privilege that would always be denied him. He would always remain outside the closed circle looking in, and part of him longed to be admitted to membership, to be one of the pack.

The USC was the first of many institutions that Kipling came to revere and whose approbation he always sought, and it was there that he discovered that a means of gaining this much-desired acceptance was to give public expression to what might be described as the group psyche or mood. Kipling the public poet first made himself known in March 1882, when he was in his sixteenth year. In that month a madman fired a shot at Queen Victoria and missed. 'The school – to put it mildly – is intensely amused,' wrote Ruddy to a friend of his mother's a week after the event. 'I'm afraid we are scarcely loyal and patriotic enough – but anyhow three parts of us laughed and the Democratic quarter seemed to be sorry.'[24] Yet these sentiments did not prevent Ruddy from writing 'Ave Imperatrix': six sonorous verses, set down in the back of a textbook during a French class, hailing the British monarch as 'the greatest as most dear, / Victoria, by God's Grace, our Queen!', and sending greetings from her most loyal of subjects, the boys of United Services College. It was an unashamed paean to British imperialism:

> Such greetings as should come from those
>   Whose fathers faced the Sepoy hordes,
> Or served you in the Russian snows
>   And dying, left their sons their swords.
>
> For we are bred to do your will
>   By land and sea, wherever flies
> The Flag to fight and follow still,
>   And work your empire's destinies.

It was first published in the *United Services College Chronicle* in March 1882, and its patriotic fervour surprised his friends quite as much as its authority astonished his teachers. Beresford, for one, was never convinced and afterwards asserted that 'Ave Imperatrix' was not written out of personal conviction: 'Here was something topical for Gigger to sing about ... His muse did not jib: he brought her to the water, and, behold, she drank. We two, Stalky and I, roared with laughter at the novel tone of the poem and at Gigger's taking on like that.'[25] Beresford was right in thinking that 'Ave Imperatrix' was 'the first finding of the man with the necessary words',[26] but it was equally an early demonstration of the true poet's ability to place himself in any situation and to feel accordingly – what Keats termed 'negative capability'.[27] The poem can also be seen as a response to a rival 'Ave Imperatrix', written a year earlier by one of Ruddy's lesser models, Oscar Wilde. Ruddy read Wilde's version and concluded he could do better, which he did.

Another sphere within which the adolescent Ruddy ran ahead of his peers was in matters of sex. According to the adult Kipling, USC was 'clean with a cleanliness that I have never heard of in any other school'. His friend Dunsterville used the same word and almost the same expression. This absence of sexual activity Kipling ascribed to open dormitories and the headmaster's prophylactic of keeping the boys so active throughout the day that they went to bed dead tired. However, in his fourth year at school his housemaster, Mr Pugh (the hated 'Prout' in the *Stalky* stories), ordered Ruddy – 'with an unreasoning violence that astonished me' – to transfer to another dormitory. Five years later he learned from Dunsterville that it was because he had been suspected of 'impurity and bestiality'. He reacted with fury, writing to Mr Croft swearing revenge: 'I am conscious of a deep and personal hatred against the man which I would give a great deal to satisfy. I knew he thought me a liar but I did not know he suspected me of anything much worse. However, I shall have my consolation. He shall be put into my novel.' Ruddy then went on to claim that at school 'I was not innocent in some respects, as the fish girls of Appledore [the nearby fishing village] could have testified had they chosen.'[28] Some biographers[29] have seen this as a case of Kipling protesting too much. Yet it is clear that Ruddy was regarded by his schoolmates as an authority on the opposite sex,

even if his friend Beresford took the view that his 'vast romantic experience' came from his reading rather than first-hand
knowledge.

Whatever the case, Ruddy considered himself a modern in
the Rossetti mould and at the first opportunity fell romantically
in love. The object of his infatuation was Flo Garrard, whom he
first met under Mrs Holloway's roof while visiting his sister Trix
at Lorne Lodge in the summer of 1880, when he was fourteen
and she sixteen or seventeen. Flo was another of Aunty's young
charges, a grey-eyed, long-haired and ivory-skinned beauty,
described afterwards by Trix as 'like the Princess disguised in
the shepherd's cottage'. The princess showed no interest in
Ruddy the swain, for reasons that only became obvious a
decade later, but Flo's very elusiveness acted as a spur, and all
Ruddy's frustrated, pent-up feelings for her were poured into
his poetry. In October 1880 Lockwood Kipling wrote to Edith
Plowden to say that the latest of his son's verses received was a
love poem. 'They are prettily turned,' he wrote, 'and show that
he has started on a round of spoons which he will follow up till
his death.'

The poem in question was 'The Lesson', concerning the love
of an innocent boy for an older girl so 'womanly-wise' that she
thinks nothing of the meeting which means so much to him.
More love verses followed, of which thirty-two were set down in
one of Ruddy's Russia-leather volumes, entitled *Sundry Phansies
writ by one Kipling*, dated February 1882, and presented by their
author to the object of his affections. One spoke of a princess who
scorned her suitors 'coldly, strangely, and haughtily',[30] another of
'Hot kisses on red lips that burn – / A silence – Then some loving
word'.[31] Many were deeply lugubrious, involving broken-hearted
lovers torn apart by death or fate. The best of the lot, and the most
ambitious yet attempted, was 'The Story of Paul Vaugel', a tale of
a Norman peasant and how he 'took himself an unfortunate [a
prostitute], and maintained her, and how she died, and how he
buried her in the Pol-lourdess [sea coast] and of the evil that came

on him'. It was a dark tale of forbidden love, retribution and guilt set out in sonorous, four-beat iambics that take on an extraordinary dream-like force akin to Coleridge's 'Ancient Mariner' as the narrator carries his dead lover down to the strand and buries her in the dunes:

> Then I piled the sand over face and hair
>   Till I left no whit of the body bare,
> For I felt in the dark lest foot or hand
>   Should be uncovered by the sand.
> And I staked up gorse till my fingers bled,
>   Lest the sheep should pasture over head.
> And I weighted the bushes with boulder clay,
>   And I sat on the dunes and wept till day.
> And a great mist rose from the dim St Lo,
>   And an inland wind on the full tide's flow
> And all night long the sea-mist passed
>   In a thousand shapes before the blast
> And all our past Life shewed to me
>   Till morning broke on the sullen sea.[32]

This was Ruddy on the cusp of turning sixteen, with what he afterwards took to calling his 'Personal Daemon' starting to settle on his shoulder.

In the early autumn of 1880 Alice Kipling rejoined her husband in Lahore. During her absence Lockwood had found somewhere large enough to accommodate their entire family: a square bungalow newly built in the Punjabi style and set in its own compound off the Mozung Road, south of and running parallel to the Upper Mall. Despite being a vast improvement on anything they had known in Bombay, it was not a dwelling in which Alice felt comfortable: 'Our house is very large for two people,' she complained to Edith Plowden after moving in –

we quite rattle about in it – and built on such an inconvenient plan that when we want to go into any of the 14 rooms we have to walk thro the other 13 to get to it. It is ugly too in spite of a wooden floor to the drawing room & papered walls – the rooms being the shape of boxes – and the walls cut up with big doors which take up all the corners. Its only merit is that being new it is clean – but the situation is bad & all the dust of the Mozung Road passes through the house several times a day.[33]

The bungalow came to be known as 'Bikaner House', after the Bikaner desert in Rajasthan. According to Trix, this was because 'my father would never have bullock-gearing fitted to the well – he thought the risk of fever for his young people too great, so the compound grew chiefly dusty *ferash* [date palm] trees with a few flowers round the verandahs'.[34]

A drawing by one of Lockwood's former students, Baga Ram, confirms these descriptions. It shows a whitewashed bungalow with a flat roof, surrounded on all sides by a verandah closed in at each corner to create four extra rooms, its austerity relieved by a series of ornate arches and double pillars. Despite its desertification, Bikaner House was to be the Kiplings' home until Lockwood's retirement in 1893.

Lockwood was now in his element, with two institutions to run of which he was sole master. The Lahore Museum gave full scope to his encyclopaedic knowledge and the Mayo School of Industrial Art allowed him to promote what he now saw as his chief professional duty: the preservation of traditional Indian craftsmanship. 'A charge has been brought against Indian schools of art,' he wrote at this time, 'of seeking to supplant indigenous art by the introduction of European ideas. Their proper function is rather the reverse, so far as style is concerned; and it is the object of the Lahore School to revive crafts now half forgotten.'[35] But Alice had no such cause to keep her busy. With her children gone she had little to fall back on other than the four staples of social life for the memsahib – housekeeping, exercising, entertaining and being entertained – none of which appealed to her. Initially, however, she found herself fully occupied as Lahore prepared to receive the new Viceroy, Lord Ripon.

Lord Lytton's successor was his antithesis in almost every respect, being plump, liberal, middle- rather than upper-class and a convert to Roman Catholicism. Lytton's high-handed and hugely expensive invasion of Afghanistan in 1878, combined with harrowing evidence of the suffering caused by his handling of the recent famines, had contributed to the defeat of Disraeli's government in 1880. His successor William Gladstone had appointed Ripon as Viceroy in the hope that he would break up what Gladstone believed to be a caucus of reactionaries in authority in Calcutta and Simla, and steer India back on the course of reform. As a result, Anglo-India viewed Ripon with suspicion. He was received in Lahore with all due ceremony, but without affection. 'We got rid of the Viceroy two days ago,' wrote Alice to Edith Plowden in mid-November. 'The camps are rolling up & bye & bye the flags and venetian masts will disappear & I shall be able to see what Lahore is really like, which up to this time I have not done, you know, all for we have been going thro'. A procession – a durbar – and nautch party, a big ball, fireworks, theatricals, races – these all ending tragically, Mr Hoare being thrown from his horse & dying of a fractured skull a few hours after the ball, for the decorations of which John toiled like a negro slave.'

But with the celebrations over it was business as usual and, for Alice, a return to boredom: 'I have hardly the patience to describe the doings of the Station, so dreary & uninformed do I find them . . . Take the women all round, they have not brains enough to make such a cutlet as I ate at breakfast this morning & how I am going to exist here god knows.' At this point in the letter its writer breaks off, to pick up her pen a week later: 'This ought to have been posted yesterday & John quite scolded me when I said I had not finished it. You see, I rather broke down as I contemplated things & couldn't pick myself up gracefully . . . I try to find books & papers to read but I feel very much out of it all . . . I long to hear from you when you have seen Trix – I feel the loss of that sweet bright creature even more than I think I should – and I am home sick more than I ever was in my life – I <u>cannot</u> care for this country.'

At the foot of this sad letter is a postscript from Lockwood: 'She certainly does not like India much better than she used to do, but after all, she is very well & the interest she is taking in the arrangement of her room & indeed house generally shows there is nothing very profoundly wrong with her.'[36]

Alice's mother had long suffered from prolonged bouts of melancholia and Alice now began to display the same condition. Her brother Fred was similarly troubled, suggesting a family predisposition towards depression, if not what today would be diagnosed as bipolar disorder, characterised by violent mood swings alternating between acute withdrawal and manic activity, that was inherited by both the Kiplings' children. In the months that followed it was Lockwood who kept in touch with Edith Plowden, maintaining an air of rather desperate jocularity. 'Miss Egerton [daughter of the Lieutenant-Governor of the Punjab] is to be married to Mr Mackworth Young!' he exclaimed in a chatty letter written just before Christmas 1880:

> It is an undreamed of catch, a most tremendous haul. For never, surely, went matrimonial hook into the depths so slenderly baited . . . You remember Dr Dickson – Miss Dallas's widower – well, he is engaged to Miss Coldstream, a grim Scotch lassie, pious as tomb-stone granite, and about as warm, sister of that egregious prig Thunda-pani [cold water, thus Coldstream], late Commissioner of Lahore . . . Going into the museum in the twilight the other day I was aware of a didactically sweet feminine voice chanting or rather reading aloud and there in a secluded place were this couple, the maiden reading from a letter or MS & Dr Dickson's swivel blue eyes wandering wildly with pleasure.

Eight months later Lockwood was writing in much the same vein from Simla: 'There is not a breath of scandal in the whole place and the club's invitations to a masked ball scarcely scandalise anybody, for, like high-caste Brahmins whose incalculate purity nothing can defile, we are immeasurably above all possibility of irony.' He had little to report on Alice's health, other than that she worried constantly about her son: 'He won't write with anything like freedom in his letters and it is not easy to make out his notions . . . Anything you can tell us about Ruddy – whether knowledge, observation or surmise [–] would be above all things welcome. His health worries us – and as to his mental moods we know he is in the troubled waters that beset most young men when they are such very young men.'[37]

Ruddy was now immersed in his unrequited love for Flo Garrard. But he was also troubled about his future, knowing that he could not follow Dunsterville, Beresford and other schoolmates into their military colleges and that his parents could not afford to send him to university. For a period he toyed with what his sister described as 'a fancy to be a doctor'. His Aunt Georgie then arranged for him to visit St Mary's Hospital in Paddington, where a post-mortem proved too much for him. 'Ruddy never described it to me,' wrote Trix. 'All he said was "Oh, Infant" – I had become "Infant" by then, not "Trix" – "Oh, Infant, Mark Twain had a word for it." Dramatic pause. "I believe I threw up my immortal soul."'[38]

It was Crom Price who provided the solution when in June 1881 in a moment of inspiration he proposed to Ruddy that the *United Services College Chronicle*, a six-page periodical which had been started a year or two earlier only to fold for lack of an editor, should be revived. Ruddy at once threw himself into the task: writing most of the copy for the first number, sub-editing it to length, overseeing the typesetting in a small printing shop in nearby Bideford, correcting the proofs and finally overseeing its publication. As an adult Rudyard Kipling afterwards joked about 'how sweet and good and profitable it is – and how nice it looks on the page – to make fun of people in actual print',[39] but as a schoolboy of fifteen and a half Ruddy made a discovery which was little short of a revelation: that there was power in the printed word, and that the means existed whereby he could take control of its printing and thereby gain greater power. In the process he found his vocation: receiving, in the apt words of his first serious biographer, 'the first injection into his veins of the printer's ink that he never again worked out of his system'.[40] His year-long editorship of the *United Services College Chronicle* showed him where his future lay. As soon as the first number had been printed, in midsummer 1881, he wrote to his parents to say that he wished to pursue a career in journalism.

However, Ruddy's parents – his mother, in particular – were equally determined that their son should join them in India when he left school. Initially these two ambitions appeared irreconcilable, because no Anglo-Indian newspaper was going to take on a man who had not thoroughly learned his trade, usually on an English provincial newspaper. Nevertheless, during his annual leave in Simla that late summer Lockwood sought the advice of George Allen, the boxwallah proprietor of the Allahabad *Pioneer*. He talked of his son's experience gained as editor of his school chronicle and no doubt referred Allen to *Schoolboy Lyrics*. The outcome was an offer from Allen to look up the boy when he returned home in the spring, with a view to finding him suitable employment in India when, at eighteen, he left school.

The Kiplings returned to the plains in the autumn buoyed by the thought that both their children would be able to join them in Lahore in the not too distant future. This was little short of a lifeline for Alice, who had given up making any effort to entertain or even to get out of the house. 'I often wonder if this dull depressed woman can be the same she was in England,' she confided to Edith Plowden just before Christmas 1881. And Lockwood's character, too, had changed for the worse: 'He is getting so dreadfully absorbed in things that he is rarely ever the conversational companion he used to be.' Her one consolation was her children, whose companionship would bring 'new life' to them: 'We therefore propose if all be well to have them both – Trixie and Ruddy – out here in two years time & get him newspaper work. We should be together a family <u>square</u> for a few years at any rate, and I think we should be very happy. John would grow younger with his son & daughter by him – a process he sadly needs . . . Ruddy thirsts for a man's life with man's work & if our plans be carried out he will get both when he is eighteen.'[41]

Now that she had something to look forward to, Alice recovered her good humour and her malicious wit. 'Other new young ladies are rather a failure,' she declared in giving a detailed breakdown of Lahore's Cold Weather 'Fishing Fleet' to Edith Plowden:

> Mrs Black's daughter is a dumpy girl who I believe never speaks even when spoken to and we thought her very plain until Mrs Parry Lambert's daughter came and by her transcendent ugliness made Miss Black seem almost beautiful. You remember Major Lambert who is no beauty[;] she is like him but much plainer[;] her eyes are like slits & her mouth a gash. The upper lips do not cover the teeth the nose turns up & the cheeks are large & shapeless. She is short, dumpy & has large hands – altogether she might be an Irish maid of all work in a lodging house. I am told, & can well believe it, that Mrs L is greatly distressed by her daughter's appearance & no wonder.[42]

This was from a letter written in March 1881, when Alice had further reason to be cheerful. George Allen was now in London and if all went well her boy would be coming out to India in eighteen months' time: 'Next spring I hope to go home & return with Ruddy & Trixie, one under each arm, in the cold weather. But for the cursed want of money I should have gone this year.'[43] As it turned out, she had only to wait another five months.

The key to this change of fortune was Allen's acquisition of a second newspaper: the *Civil and Military Gazette*.

When the Kiplings had first arrived in Lahore in 1875 the only local English newspaper was the *Indian Public Opinion*, owned and produced by the eccentric Orientalist and polymath Dr Gottlieb Wilhelm Leitner. After an extraordinary early career during which he had achieved the rank of colonel at the age of fifteen while serving as an interpreter in the Crimean War, Dr Leitner had been appointed Professor of Arabic and subsequently Principal of Lahore's Government College. In the decade since his appointment he had worked tirelessly and often cantankerously for popular education and political reform, believing that the British Government in India had no 'real hold on the people, who in sullen silence felt themselves to be disregarded, and their ancient civilisation despised'. He had also campaigned for Government College to be developed into a university college, which it had duly become in 1870, with Leitner as its Registrar.

To the irritation of the Anglo-Indian community in Lahore, Dr Leitner's *Indian Public Opinion* was stridently liberal, frequently launching attacks on persons and policies its editor considered to be standing in the way of progress. Two years after Lockwood Kipling's arrival in Lahore he became one of the *Indian Public Opinion*'s targets when, in one of his regular columns for the *Pioneer*, he made the mistake of criticising Dr Leitner's campaign to replace English with vernacular languages in schools and colleges in the Punjab. Lockwood had counter-attacked, questioning the way Dr Leitner had secured positions for himself on virtually every educational board in the Punjab and criticising his character. Not unreasonably, this provoked Dr Leitner to respond in kind, his attacks becoming, in Edith Plowden's words, 'more and more virulent', until quite suddenly Dr Leitner sold his paper and left India. He returned to Lahore a year later, by which time the *Indian Public Opinion* had been renamed by its new owners the *Civil and Military Gazette*.

The original *Civil and Military Gazette* had first appeared in 1872 in Simla as a weekly news-sheet, owned by a retired British Army major, George Fenwick, and intended for an exclusive readership of Civilians and army officers. Three years later Fenwick was bought out by two men from the same entrepreneurial mould as George Allen: William Rattigan and James Walker. Rattigan was the elder of the two, the illegitimate son of an illiterate Irish private in the EICo's Ordinance Department, 'country-born' and 'country-bred' – meaning that he was both born and educated in India. After some years in government employ Rattigan had saved up enough money to go to Europe to study law, eventually returning to India to practise in Lahore as a barrister. Walker, too, was, country-born, with a father in the Punjab Police, and had made his money by establishing a *dak* or post-relay system conveying passengers and mail between the railhead at Kalka and Simla. By 1874 he was sufficiently well established to set up the Alliance Bank of Simla, and a year later he and Rattigan formed a partnership to take over the local paper, the *Civil and Military Gazette*.

In 1877, the year in which Lockwood Kipling's dispute with Dr Leitner came to a head, Rattigan and Walker joined with a third partner to buy up two more provincial papers: the *Mofussilite* of Agra and the *Indian Public Opinion* of Lahore. Their new partner was George Allen of the *Pioneer*, whose business interests now included a woollen mill and a tannery in Cawnpore. With the additional funding Allen provided, the three partners closed down the *Mofussilite* and the *Indian Public Opinion* and moved the *Civil and Military Gazette* from Simla into the premises in Lahore previously occupied by the *Indian Public Opinion*. Under Allen's direction they then set about transforming the *CMG*, as it became known, into 'the chief organ of Northern India European opinion',[44] a newspaper that would eschew the dangerous liberalism of Dr Leitner and toe the line taken by its 'big sister' the *Pioneer*.

In pursuance of this policy the *CMG* was first edited by two military men: Major Fenwick, the previous owner, and Colonel Arthur Cory, an Indian Army officer attached to the Adjutant-General's office who had a number of publications to his name, including *Shadows of Coming Events: or The Eastern Menace*. After Cory retired from the Indian Army in late 1877 he became the paper's chief editor and oversaw the relocation of its offices and printing presses from the Mall to two large, thatched bungalows set side by side on the southern side of the Upper Mall, close to the Punjab Club, and little more than a quarter of a mile from Bikaner House in the Mozung Road. Colonel Cory became a friend of the Kiplings and in Simla in the summer of 1881 he, Alice Kipling and George Allen's second wife, Maud, performed together in a series of *tableaux vivants*.

At about this time Cory relinquished the post of editor to a Mr Macdonald, who soon proved to be unsatisfactory. The paper's proprietors concluded that a more experienced journalist was required. Macdonald was offered a subordinate post as sub-editor and refused, moving to Simla to become a special correspondent for the *Times of India* and the *Indian Daily News* – and using their columns to vent his spleen on his former employers and their friends. 'He abuses many people but chiefly me,' Lockwood Kipling complained in a letter to Edith Plowden. 'The sole reason we can think of is that we befriended him and his cleversilly wife as much as we could. His last feat is to describe me as the laziest and most conceited bore he ever knew and Mrs Kipling as the sourest and vainest lady this side Suez! Week after week Calcutta & Bombay are regaled with this kind of thing.'[45]

Macdonald's departure from the *CMG* created vacancies for an editor and an assistant editor. The first post went to twenty-eight-year-old Stephen Wheeler, a dry, humourless professional journalist recruited in England by George Allen, and it was Wheeler who then interviewed sixteen-year-old Rudyard Kipling, apparently without revealing that he had been charged with establishing the boy's suitability as an assistant editor. Wheeler reported back to Allen, now in residence at a grand mansion in London's Prince's Gardens, and Allen then telegraphed out to his partners in Lahore and Simla a message that was brief and to the point: 'Kipling will do.'[46]

Why Allen chose to overlook a sixteen-year-old schoolboy's lack of professional experience is a mystery, but the presumption must be that he thought him worth the risk. Both in *Stalky & Co.* and in *Something of Myself* Kipling asserts that the appointment was made entirely without his knowledge. 'There came a day,' he wrote in his autobiography, 'when he [Cormell Price] told me that a fortnight after the close of the summer holidays of '82, I would go to India to work on a paper in Lahore.' What he omitted to say was that at this time he considered himself engaged to Flo Garrard. He had also discovered the pleasures of London's nightlife beyond the confines of The Grange and Warwick Gardens and had set his mind on studying or tutoring for a year in Germany before settling down to learn his trade on a London newspaper. According to his chum George Beresford, he took the news of his imminent departure to India very badly: 'He had been so completely metropolised, and the faint cobwebs that the distant East had spun about his infantile mind had been so completely swept away, that he looked upon this expedition as rather a wild adventure . . . London, he considered, would be his natural socket, where he thought he fitted in.'[47]

Ruddy wrote to his father hinting that a marriage was in the offing – and received a very sharp reply, pointing out among other things that 'there was a billet all ready and waiting for him with a certain amount of pay attached – a thing not easy to get when one is only sixteen and a half'.[48] But what may have finally settled the business in Ruddy's mind was Flo's ending of their engagement in late May. From this point onwards he accepted his fate and made the best of it. His passionate feelings for Flo gave way to a calmer attachment, one in which his sense of loss and love unrequited could be exploited for his poetry's sake. Five years on he could write in Wildean terms in one of his *Plain Tales from the Hills* that 'one of the most convenient things that a young man can carry about with him at the beginning of his career is an unrequited attachment. It makes him feel important and business-like; and blasé and cynical; and whenever he has a touch of liver, or suffers from want of exercise, he can mourn over his lost love, and be very happy in a tender, twilight fashion.'[49]

In July 1882 he wrote 'A Voyage', clearly intended to be read as a severing of ties. It ends:

> Our galley lamps are bright with hope,
>   Our voices ring across the sea –
> In other lands is wider scope
>   For all our virile energy.
> Let be the past, leave we the quay
>   With firm hands on the tiller rope.[50]

On 20 September 1882 Ruddy boarded the P&O steamer *Brindisi* bound for Bombay by way of the Suez Canal. 'He went thus,' wrote Beresford, 'to the one place in a thousand that provided the stage and the actors that his genius required.'[51]

5

'As a prince entering his kingdom'

LAHORE AND SIMLA, 1882–3

'Come back, Punch-*baba*,' said the *ayah*.
'Come back,' said Meeta, 'and be a *Burra Sahib*.'
'Yes,' said Punch, lifted up in his father's arms to wave good-bye.
'Yes, I will come back, and I will be a *Burra Sahib Bahadur* (a very big man indeed)!'

Rudyard Kipling, 'Baa, Baa, Black Sheep', 1888

When on 18 October 1882 Rudyard Kipling returned to the city of his birth it was, to use his own expression, 'as a prince entering his Kingdom'.[1] He was aged sixteen years and ten months, but onlookers would have judged the compact figure with the pugnacious jaw and thick-lensed spectacles to be at least in his mid-twenties, particularly since the dark moustache he had been allowed to cultivate at school had been joined during the voyage by whiskers. He was also uncommonly sallow-skinned for an Englishman, so much so that it was afterwards put about that he was, in the argot of the time, 'quite eight annas in the rupee' – in other words, half Indian, there being sixteen annas to a rupee.

When Ruddy came ashore he found himself 'moving among sights and smells that made me deliver in the vernacular sentences whose meaning I knew not'.[2] However, the shoreline and skyline of the Bombay of his childhood had altered beyond recognition.

On reclaimed land all along the foreshore the Bombay Port Trust had constructed docks, wharfs and jetties capable of moving huge tonnages of goods and passengers between rail and ship. On 1 January 1880 Princes Dock had been declared open for shipping, which meant steamers now cast anchor alongside a stone jetty and discharged their passengers directly on to dry land. Across the salt marshes beyond the Native Town, factory chimneys had sprouted like mushrooms: the spinning and weaving mills that were about to take on the industrial might of Lancashire. 'Bombay has long been the Liverpool of the East,' went the popular catchphrase of the time. 'Now she is becoming the Manchester also.'

Since the golden years of the American Civil War all sections of the island's population had declined except for its European element, now numbering ten and a half thousand. To cater for the leisure activities of this expanding commercial class a new sort of club had come into being: the Bombay Gymkhana,[3] which in 1875 appropriated a prime section of the Esplanade so that its exclusively white membership could gather to play cricket, hockey, badminton and tennis before adjourning to drink *brandypawnees* on the club's extended verandah. Of more immediate relevance to Ruddy, however, was the fact that the mud-and-lathe shacks of the Sir J. J. School of Art of his childhood had at last been replaced by modern buildings. The 'wigwam' in which he had been born was now a two-storey bungalow with a green-tiled roof and an upstairs verandah. Superintendent Terry had gone and the school was now the domain of his godfather and his father's former colleague, John Griffiths, whose painstaking oil canvases of Indian scenes in the manner of Poynter and Alma-Tadema had failed to win him popular recognition.

There was little to keep the adolescent Ruddy in Bombay so it is highly probable that his next destination was the nearby Victoria Terminus, still incomplete, in time to board the Frontier Mail before its evening departure. As Ruddy journeyed northwards into the Indian *mofussil* or interior, the homeland from which he had been exiled for eleven and a half years began to reclaim him: 'My

English years fell away, nor ever, I think, came back in full strength.'[4]

After a journey of two nights and two days Ruddy arrived in Lahore to what he afterwards claimed was a 'joyous home-coming', but one marred by the discovery that his mother – 'more delightful than all my imaginings and memories' – had published a volume of his love poetry behind his back and was insisting that he shave off his whiskers. He was allotted his own corner of Bikaner House and was given, 'with the solemnity of a marriage-contract', the son of his father's bearer as his personal servant. This

A Muslim servant, possibly Kadir Baksh, J. L. Kipling (National Trust)

was Kadir Baksh, fated to achieve his own immortality by featuring in a number of stories as a faithful but none too bright minion.

By the adult Kipling's account, his return to the bosom of his family came as close to perfect bliss as he or they could have wished for: 'We delighted more in each other's society than in that of strangers.'[5] This unequivocal statement glosses over the fact that it took Ruddy months to come to terms with his new life, Alice Kipling confiding to Edith Plowden in a letter written in February 1883 that her son was 'if possible, less than ever inclined to Lahore itself' and 'at times very trying in his moods – being subject to sudden fits of the blues'.[6]

It was another fourteen months before Trix joined the rest of her family in Lahore and for her, too, Bikaner House became the first real home she had known since her infancy, where she and her brother experienced 'the happiest time of his life – and mine'.[7] Ruddy, she wrote, was initially given a room at the front of the house reached through the dining room, but 'as his work deepened, part of the next room (an entrance hall) was partitioned off to make a writing room for him; he called it his *duftur* [office] in emulation of my Father's big room – and was delighted with it. On the partition above the big Indian dado, with which my Mother beautified it, he inscribed in twisted ornate black and yellow characters, "obviously Chinese to the meanest capacity," as he told me, "RESPECT THE APARTMENTS OF THE GREAT."'[8]

Despite his dislocation and the conflicting emotions that it brought about, Ruddy continued with his verse-writing. The first of his poems which can confidently be ascribed to India is 'A Morning Ride', three galloping stanzas already full of Anglo-Indian argot reflecting the delights of an early morning ride along the banks of the River Ravi. It begins:

> In the hush of the cool, dim dawn when the shades begin to
> retreat;
> And the jackal bolts to his lair at the sound of your horse's
> feet;

'So clever, so fresh and so cynical that he must be young'; Ruddy a year after his return to England, painted in tropical whites by John Collier. He was then aged twenty-five and had suffered the first setback of his career with the publication of *The Light that Failed*, his first non-Indian work. (Bateman's, National Trust)

A coloured postcard of the Apollo Bunder, the traditional landing place before the new docks were built, c.1890. (Charles Allen)

A Mohurrum procession in the bazaar area near the Sir J. J. School of Art; a postcard from the 1890s. (Farooq Issa and Phillips Antiques)

Left: Walkeshwar Temple and Tank, Bombay, 1884; an oil painting by the American artist Edwin Lord Weeks, who made several painting tours of India in the 1880s and 1890s. (Sotheby's)

'Christmas in India'; an idealised image of a British family in India before the children are removed from the servants''promiscuous tendency to worship at the shrine of the *baba-log*', c. 1865. (Mary Evans Picture Library)

Bikaner House in Lahore was home to Ruddy's parents from 1875 to 1893, although he himself only lived there from October 1882 to October 1887. A watercolour painted by one of Lockwood Kipling's pupils, Baga Ram. (Bateman's, Burwash, National Trust)

Lahore from the Fort, showing Ranjit Singh's Samadh, centre left, and the Badshahi Mosque beyond. In the foreground, part of the curved roof of the Naulakha pavilion. Miniature on ivory, painted by a local artist c.1875. (V&A)

A street scene in Lahore by E. L. Weeks. Afghan vendors display their silks to a potential customer as prostitutes look on. According to Kipling many of the girls were young widows forced by custom to take up the profession. (Christie's)

The front of Wazir Khan's mosque with street vendors and beggars; another oil painting by Edwin Lord Weeks, who first visited northern India in 1882. Although contemporaries, there is no record to show that he and Kipling ever met. (Christie's)

A watercolour of Simla by H. B. A. Poulton, drawn in about 1875, showing the church with Jakko Hill in the background. (APAC, BL)

'The Play's the Thing'; Lockwood Kipling's watercolour was probably painted in the hill-station of Dalhousie. Although Ruddy was absent, Trix is shown turning round to speak to her bald-pated father.

(University of Sussex Library Special Collections, courtesy of National Trust)

The Club – 'the whole of my outside world'. A print from Lloyd's *Sketches of Indian Life*, 1890.
(Charles Allen)

'The Last Voyage'; E. L. Weeks's imaginative oil painting of the bathing and burning ghats at Benares. (Art Gallery of Hamilton, Canada)

Mowgli and Bagheera, a dramatic colour print by the twin prodigies Edward Julius and Charles Maurice Detmold; one of sixteen illustrations for *The Jungle Book* commissioned by Macmillans in 1903 when the brothers were aged twenty.

(Courtesy of Simon Brandenburger of Indoislamica.com)

When the great kite preens his wings and calls to his mate in
    the tree
  And the lilac opens her buds ere the sun shall be up to see;
When the trailing rosebush thrills with the sparrow's pent up
    strife,
    Oh! a ride in an Indian dawn, there's no such pleasure in
      life.[9]

Unlike most 'griffs' or newcomers Ruddy had the rare luxury of
being able to 'chum' with his parents in provincial headquarters.
But this was a mixed blessing, since it cushioned him from some
of the realities of Indian life and meant that much of what he did
see was viewed through the filter of his parents' prejudices. Yet the
advantages of living with his parents in a real home were considerable, not least because his duties as *stunt-sahib* or assistant editor
of the *CMG* were onerous and unremitting. 'I represented fifty per
cent of the "editorial staff" of the one daily paper of the Punjab,'
he wrote half a century later, apparently forgetting the paper's sub-
editor and local reporter, W. J. Wilson, one of several locally
recruited Eurasians or working-class Britons who filled subordinate posts on the paper – 'I never worked less than ten hours and
seldom less than fifteen per diem; and as our paper came out in the
evening did not see the midday sun except on Sundays. I had fever
too, regular and persistent, to which I added for a while chronic
dysentery. Yet I discovered that a man can work with a temperature of 104, even though next day he has to ask the office who
wrote the article.'[10]

In reality, Ruddy's office hours usually began at nine and ended
at five, when the paper was ready to go to print. A more accurate
account of his work was set out in a letter written in the *CMG*'s
offices to USC's chaplain, the Reverend George Willes, a month
after Ruddy's arrival. 'I write, so to speak, between the horns of
the gum pot and the scissors,' it begins, then goes on to describe
the scope of his duties:

Some thirty papers go through my hands daily – Hindu papers, scurrilous and abusive beyond anything, local scandal weeklies, philosophical and literary journals written by Babus in the style of Addison. Native Mohummedan, sleepy little publications, all extracts, indigo papers, tea and coffee journals, jute journals and official Gazettes all have to be disembowelled if they are worth it. Moreover I am responsible for every scrap of the paper except the first two pages. That is to say, I bear the blame of correspondents' blunders – it is my duty to correct them – misprints and bad lettering – it is my business to find them out – vulgarities, bad grammar and indecency – we get <u>that</u> sometimes! – have to be looked to carefully and I have a large correspondence all over India with men of all sorts. All local notes come to me and have to be digested, and I must pick up information about approaching polo matches, garden parties, official dinners and dances, to insert in the local column.

For this work his initial monthly remuneration was 150 rupees – the equivalent of £150 per annum – rising to 200 after six months. This was a princely sum for a youth not yet seventeen, and one that was very welcome at Bikaner House. For his work at the Mayo School of Industrial Art Lockwood Kipling earned 800 rupees a month, with a further 100 rupees a month for his curatorship of the museum.

As the *CMG*'s assistant editor Ruddy claimed authority over some 170 proof-readers, clerks, compositors and print-workers whom he could 'bully and hector as I please'.[11] Although the rotary press had been introduced in England a decade earlier, the presses of the *CMG* and *Pioneer* still employed the old-fashioned flat-bed Wharfdale, which printed each double page sheet by sheet, after which the sheets were turned over by hand for printing on the other side. The galleys had first to be set letter by letter from cases of type by compositors who could neither speak nor read English, after which the galley proofs were corrected by Indian and Anglo-Indian proof-readers, often several times over, before being handed over to the European editorial staff for final corrections before being printed as page proofs. Laborious as the process was, it had the great virtue of familiarity, for it was precisely the system Ruddy had used to edit his *United Services College Chronicle*. However, then he had been his own master, whereas now he was very much under the thumb of the paper's 'tetchy and irritable' editor, Stephen Wheeler, the professional journalist hired by George Allen to knock the *CMG* into shape as a modern newspaper.

Ruddy came to hate Wheeler for his bad temper and his determination to keep him tied to 'proof-reading, scissors-and-paste work, and the boiling down of government blue books into summaries for publication'.[12] Right from the start Wheeler had made it clear that Ruddy was to give up all thoughts of creative writing: 'One of the first things a sub editor has to learn is to altogether give up original writing,' he reported to George Willis. 'I have not written three words of original matter beyond reports and reviews since I have joined the staff.' Despite these restrictions, Ruddy kept his temper and held his tongue to a degree which led his father to write admiringly that 'the boy is training for heaven as well as for Editorship'.[13]

The Kiplings mocked Wheeler behind his back as 'the Amber Toad', but afterwards Ruddy had the grace to publicly acknowledge his debt to him: 'My Chief took me in hand, and for three years or so I loathed him. He had to break me in, and I knew nothing . . . the little that I ever acquired of accuracy, the habit of trying at least to verify references, and some knack of sticking to desk-work, I owed wholly to Stephen Wheeler.' Just as usefully, he learned to work at several levels – 'to think out a notion in detail, pack it away in my head, and work on it by snatches in any surroundings'.[14]

Wheeler's tight rein also provided a corrective to the 'select Mutual Admiration Society' of Bikaner House, with its 'forcing-house atmosphere of warm domestic approval, liable to dangerously encourage eccentric growth in Kipling's budding genius'. That, at least, was the opinion of Wheeler's successor as editor of the *CMG*, Kay Robinson, one of the three literary-minded sons of the Reverend Julian Robinson of Allahabad and the first outside the Kipling family circle to recognise both Ruddy's talents and his faults. Much as Robinson deplored Wheeler's failure to give the young Kipling his head, he also believed that by doing so he had kept in check what Robinson considered his chief fault as a writer: 'an excessive self-confidence, a cock-suredness, so to speak, about any phrase or sentiment he may fling to the public being accepted as the mintage of genius'.[15]

Shortly after Ruddy's arrival the college founded through Dr Leitner's endeavours was inaugurated by Lord Ripon as the University of the Punjab, with Leitner assuming an additional post as its Registrar. Although not yet allowed to report on the event for his paper, Ruddy attended as a member of the press and afterwards gave vent to views which mirrored those of his father. 'Just imagine a brown legged son of the east in the red and black gown of an MA as I saw him,' he wrote to Willis. 'The effect is killing. I had an irreverent vision of the Common Room [at USC] in a Muhammaden get up. At the end of the proceeding an excited bard began some Urdu verses composed in Honour of the occasion. It was a tour de force of his own – but I am sorry to say he was suppressed, that is to say, they took him by the shoulders and sat him down again in his chair. Imagine that at Oxford!'[16]

A month later Wheeler's pony jibbed and threw him, leaving him badly concussed and 'quite daft when he tried to talk'. Ruddy had to take over the running of the paper for the next week and acquitted himself well enough to earn the thanks of the *CMG*'s local manager, David Masson. 'He said that "he had the fullest confidence in me",' Ruddy wrote proudly to his old headmaster. 'I have grown at least six inches since then.' And when Wheeler returned to work he acknowledged his assistant's hard work by allowing him to write reviews and editorial notes – 'and this too I am extremely proud of in a small way'.

Ruddy could also report to Crom Price that his father had

presented him with 'a very handsome roan stallion' named Joe, claiming for him a pedigree as late of the 19th Bengal Lancers, a cavalry regiment mounted on Walers imported from New South Wales.[17] In fact, Joe was no more than a pony, which was just as well, for unlike most of his peers Ruddy had not grown up with horses and his poor physical co-ordination ensured that he was frequently unseated in the course of his early-morning rides. But he took his falls in good part, learning that it was no use chasing after Joe or attempting to catch him. 'I wait till he has his back turned and then run away home,' he explained to his Aunt Edith some months after his arrival. 'Presently there is a terrible clatter behind and Joe comes running up trotting his hardest with his reins dangling all anyhow between his feet. I pretend to cut him and turn into the Lawrence gardens to sit down . . . After I have been there a minute or so Joe comes and waits at the back of the seat trying to get me to notice him.'[18] Fortunately for English letters, in May 1883 the Kiplings acquired a 'toy like dog cart', to which Joe was harnessed, giving the pony a 'dissipated and rakish air' and his master a much safer ride between home and work.

In northern India the winter months from late October through to mid-February constituted the Cold Weather, a temperate season of sparkling mornings and warm afternoons during which Anglo-Indians gathered in the large Stations to entertain and be entertained, with garden-parties, burra khanas, *pagal khanas* or picnics, *pagal nautches* or fancy-dress parties, balls, theatricals and every form of sports activity from shooting competitions and tennis tournaments to gymkhanas and polo weeks – although in Lahore the newest craze was for roller-skating on a wooden rink laid in the Montgomery Hall. However, Ruddy was too preoccupied with his work to make much of his first Lahore Cold Weather, which was how his parents wished it to be. After the upsets over Flo Garrard they remained fearful that there was an unbridled side to their son's character associated with his discovery of sex that needed little encouragement to reassert itself. 'I am sure he is better here than anywhere else,' Lockwood Kipling wrote to their confidante Edith Plowden, 'where there are no music-hall ditties to pick up, no young persons to philander about with, and a great many other negatives of the most [un]wholesome description. All that makes Lahore profoundly dull makes it safe for young people.'[19]

The single institution with which Ruddy did become involved was the Punjab Club. One of his father's first actions to help him settle into the Station was to put him up for election as a member, and it is evident that Ruddy savoured the Club's masculine and exclusive air, made all the more precious by his claim to membership being so tenuous. It was, as he wrote in his autobiography, 'the whole of my outside world', and since it was just over the road from the offices of the *CMG* he took to dropping in after the paper had been put to bed, for a drink and a cheroot and perhaps a game of billiards before going home.

As the Club's most junior member he was expected to defer to his elders and no doubt he did so – to begin with. But before very long Ruddy began to gain a reputation for boorish behaviour which continued to be held against him long after his departure from India. Deference never came easily to him and he was, after all, an adolescent with no one of his own age for company, but it is clear that there were times when his behaviour went beyond the bounds. He is said on one occasion to have made disparaging remarks about the Indian Civil Service, on another to have spoken rudely to a visiting colonel, who had to be dissuaded from thrashing him, and on a third occasion to have so irritated a pair of lawyers by repeatedly butting into their conversation that they kicked him down the Club's front steps; he was also said to have a 'caddishly dirty tongue' – all of which suggests that his schooling had failed to dent his capacity for bumptiousness.

However, there may have been good reasons for this insolence, for what Ruddy also discovered at the Club was that he was answerable for whatever appeared in the paper: 'I was almost nightly responsible for my output to visible and often brutally voluble critics at the Club . . . They wanted accuracy and interest, but first of all accuracy.' Before the year was out Ruddy had discovered just how answerable he was.

Shortly before Ruddy's arrival in India Lord Ripon had revoked Lord Lytton's Vernacular Press Act, which had laid the editors of the Indian vernacular papers open to prosecution if they published inflammatory or seditious statements in their pages. This was viewed as pandering to Indian extremism by a large section of the British community, which also opposed Lord Ripon's moves to bring about more self-government at a municipal level. Lockwood Kipling had accurately reflected the resentment felt by many Anglo-Indians towards this well-meaning liberal when he described the advent of Ripon as 'a more terrible calamity than might be thought. We are delivered over into the hands of the Philistines.'[20] He had heard Ripon speak at a public meeting and had come away disgusted at the way he had 'gushed and drivelled' about his 'discovery of India'.[21]

The Anglo-Indian community was spoiling for a grievance and found it when in early February 1883 Sir Courteney Ilbert, the Legal Member on the Viceroy's Council, presented a bill intended to correct an anomaly in the Indian Judicial Code whereby an Indian district magistrate sitting in a court outside the three Presidency cities of Calcutta, Madras and Bombay was disallowed from trying a European brought before him. There were very few Indian covenanted civil servants at this time, but a number of divisions in the Indian *mofussil* had one or two Indian serving magistrates, usually appointed because of their high standing in the local community. Lahore had just one such magistrate in 1883, the much-respected Muhammad Hayat Khan, CSI, who as a young man had served as aide and bodyguard to the great John Nicholson of Delhi fame.[22]

The proposed 'Ilbert Bill' would give power to these few Indian magistrates to sentence Europeans to imprisonment, and for a large section of the British community that was a step too far.[23] In Calcutta the *Englishman* published an anonymous letter which declared: 'What would please our Indian fellow-subjects more than to bully and disgrace a wretched Englishwoman? The higher her husband's station and the greater his responsibility, the greater the delight of his torturer.' The other leading newspapers took their lead from the *Englishman*, among them the *Pi* and the *CMG*. Protest meetings were held and more inflammatory letters were published. In regimental messes there was wild talk of white mutiny, even of secession on American lines, and a tea-planters' plot to kidnap the Viceroy on his way to a tiger shoot was only foiled because his son took his place at the last moment.

In Lahore the Civil Station was as much caught up in the anti-Ilbert hysteria as anywhere else. On 29 March 1883 some unsigned verses appeared in the *CMG* under the title 'A New Departure', reprinted from the *Englishman*. They called Lord Ripon an ass and a 'Brahminee boy' who listened only to the Calcutta *babus*, and whose response when 'India objected' was to flee to Simla. They ended:

> With the tact that belonged to his statiòn,
>   With a suavity solely his own,
> He had set by the ears half a nation
>   And left it – to simmer alone.
> With his maudlin *ma-bap* ['father-mother'; the traditional
>   term for a protector of the poor] legislation,
>   He had played merry Hades and – *flown*.[24]

Although Kipling never publicly acknowledged authorship, he included these verses – the first to be published in India and the first of his political squibs – in a scrapbook of newspaper cuttings of his work published in the *CMG*. They could well have been written jointly by Ruddy and his father, although the seventeen-year-old felt strongly enough over the issue to set out the Anglo-Indian case to Crom Price and declared himself unable to write calmly about the Ilbert Bill: 'Old stagers say that race feeling has never run so high since the Mutiny. If there is a rising, the present Government are directly responsible [–] at least so everyone says.'[25]

Five months later, on 19 November 1883, as the now watered-down Ilbert Bill came up for a Second Reading in Council, the *CMG* carried an editorial calling for it to be passed and declaring further opposition to be 'unreasonable'. Ruddy played no part in the writing of this editorial, but the afternoon before its publication he read it and went directly to Wheeler's office to ask for an explanation for what amounted to a complete change of editorial policy, only to be told that it was '"None of your dam' business".' The following day Ruddy went to the Club as usual and as he entered the dining-room was met by a barrage of hisses: 'I was innocent enough to ask, "What's the joke? Who are they hissing?" "You," said the man at my side. "Your dam' rag has ratted over the Bill."'[26]

As Kipling relates in *Something of Myself*, he was mortified to find himself the object of this abuse, which ended only when the adjutant of their local Volunteer Corps got up and declared that 'the boy's only doing what he's paid to do'. But this remark Ruddy found almost as humiliating as the hissing, because of the truth it contained. 'The adjutant was entirely correct,' he wrote. 'I was a hireling, paid to do what I was paid to do, and – I didn't relish the idea. Someone said kindly: "You damned young ass. Don't you know that your paper has the Government printing-contract?" I *did* know it, but I had never before put two and two together.'

Ruddy had discovered the first of 'many pretty ways by which a Government can put veiled pressure on its employees in a land where every circumstance and relation of a man's life is public property'. The *CMG*'s principal proprietor, George Allen, had too much to lose. Two years earlier he and his main business partner in Cawnpore had won a lucrative government contract to supply boots to the Indian Army and had great hopes of securing further contracts. Furthermore, a significant part of the profits made by his presses in Allahabad and Lahore came from the printing of official government papers, and any direct challenge to the Government could damage the network of high-placed officials he had so carefully built up in Simla. Allen, in sum, put profit before his principles, and in the eyes of his young protégé he became 'the sinner-who-faces-both-ways'.

This revelation of the political realities of the day, combined with the brutal way his fellow members had turned on him at the Club, led Ruddy to think long and hard about the values of his elders. Hitherto he had been too wrapped up in his own cosy world of family and letters to pay much attention to the wider issues of Anglo-Indian life. But with his little world turned upside down he found himself viewing with ever-mounting scepticism the workings of the Government of India and the motives of men he had hitherto held in high regard.

Lord Ripon was never forgiven for his unwitting part in Ruddy's discomfiture. He came to represent all the follies of Gladstonian liberalism, and when he prepared to make a premature departure from India at the end of 1884 Ruddy mocked him in the pages of the *CMG* in another of his unsigned political squibs. In 'Lord Ripon's Reverie' he imagines Ripon brooding on his failures:

> Of the millions that I govern who will wish me back? Not
>> one.
>> Curse the land and all within it. As of old, the papers
>>> scoff –
> Dreary columns of invective, read by stealth at Peterhof.
>> Peterhof, that through the pine-trees overlooks the Simla
>>> hills,
> And the City of Calcutta where they rave against my Bills.
>> There I sketched my swart Utopia, nourishing the Babu's
>>> pride
> On the fairy-tales of Justice – with a leaning to his side.[27]

In May 1883 the Punjab Hot Weather set in with a vengeance. Between sunrise and sunset every door and window was shuttered to keep out the heat, and no foray into direct sunlight was made without the protection of dark glasses and the mushroom-shaped sola topee *de rigueur* at that time. Wheeler went down with a bout of fever and proceeded to Simla to recover, leaving Ruddy once more in charge of the paper. A month later he dashed off a long letter in rhyming couplets to his Aunt Edith on how well he was coping with this first baptism of heat:

> For the heavens are red hot iron and the earth is burning
>   brass,
>   And the river glares in the sun like a torrent of molten glass,
> And the quivering heat haze rises, the pitiless sunlight glows
>   Till my cart reins blister my fingers as my spectacles blister
>   my nose.
> Heat, like a baker's oven that sweats one down to the bone[,]
>   Never such heat, and such health, has your parboiled
>   nephew known.

The letter-in-verse ended on a note of doubtful nostalgia:

> Oh what is 'two hundred a month,' and half year 'rises' to
>   come,
>   To a fellow with hairs in his pen, and lizard-tails in his gum;
> His ink putrescent and loathsome, a paste of corrupting flies,
>   His spectacles dimmed and steamy, and goggles over his
>   eyes.
> 'Oh give me a London *trottoir*, some bywalk damp and
>   muddy,
>   In place of this wholesome heat' is the cry of your washed
>   out
>   Ruddy.[28]

The Hot Weather imagery first deployed in this poem was to be recycled time and again in the many short stories, such as 'At the End of the Passage', which are set in oven-like rooms where a tattered whitewashed punkah can do no more than puddle the hot air as the occupants' lives fall apart.

The *stunt-sahib*'s reward for deputising for his chief was a summons from the banker James Walker, co-proprietor of the *CMG*, to take a month off on full pay and join him as his guest in his summer residence in Simla. In that same month Alice Kipling left for England in order to be with Trix from the start of the summer holidays, while Lockwood stayed on alone in Lahore. It meant that for the first time since his arrival in Lahore nine months earlier Ruddy was off the parental leash – and on his way to Simla, summer capital of British India and already saddled with a reputation for 'frivolity, jealousy and intrigue'[29] for which he himself was afterwards held largely responsible.

Besides serving as the summer capital of both the Government of India and the Government of the Punjab, Simla was also the summer headquarters of the Commander-in-Chief and the various military departments under his authority, as well as other services such as the Police and the Public Works Department. These senior civil and military officers and their wives made up the inner core of Simla's Anglo-Indian population in its summer season and they represented Simla Society, which was as close as British India ever came to having an upper crust. Their presence ought to have made Simla more hidebound than any other any Station in India. But Simla's summer population was further swelled by the presence of large numbers of British wives and their offspring dispatched to the hills to escape the heat of the plains, including a generous sprinkling of unmarried daughters fresh from school in England, the much-maligned 'fishing fleet' come in search of husbands. What this meant was that at the height of summer the British womenfolk in Simla, almost uniquely in India, outnumbered the menfolk several times over – a situation that would have been intolerable but for the presence of significant numbers of male birds of passage influential enough to wangle a fortnight's local leave. These were the 'poodle-fakers', 'danglers' and 'mashers', mostly young and unattached, eager to 'spoon' with a 'grass widow'[30] rooming in one of Simla's many hotels and guest houses. It was this undercurrent of the illicit that gave Simla its peculiar *frisson*.

Simla was also exclusive, because it was hard to reach and almost prohibitively expensive to live in. Perched on one of the lower ranges of the Western Himalayas 170 miles due north of Delhi, it was badly placed for most Anglo-Indians, although conveniently close to Lahore. Even so, Ruddy had first to transport his pony Joe by train to the railhead to Umballa and then transfer to a two-horse *tonga* to Kalka before he could even begin the first stage of the long climb through the Himalayan foothills, with Joe following on behind with his *syce*. It was a journey of delight Ruddy was to make many times, afterwards recalled in almost the last of his many Indian tales, 'Garm – a Hostage' in which Ruddy and his bearer, Kadir Baksh, flee the Hot Weather in the company of his own fox-terrier, Vixen, and a bull-terrier named Garm:

A cool breath from the snow met us about fives miles out of Kalka, and she [Vixen] whined for her coat . . . 'Hi-yi-yi-hi!' sang Vixen as we shot round the curves; 'Toot-toot-toot!' went the driver's bugle at the dangerous places, and 'Yow! Yow!' bayed Garm. Kadir Baksh sat on the front seat and smiled. Even he was glad to get away from the heat of the Plains that stewed in the haze behind us. Now and then we would meet a man we knew going down to his work again, and he would say: 'What's it like below?' and I would shout: 'Hotter than cinders. What's it like up above?' and he would shout back: 'Just perfect!' and away we would go.[31]

Like every European new arrival to Simla, Ruddy spent his first mornings 'calling' – visiting every house where he had hopes of being received to leave his card in a tin receptacle beside the front door. Invitations to call duly followed, which meant that he spent much of his leave on horseback negotiating Simla's precipitous mountainside on roads that were 'just ledges. At first they turned my head a good deal but – in a little I was enabled to canter any how and any where.'[32]

Much of Simla's effervescence was due to the fact that it stood at an elevation of 7000 feet, extending westwards for about a mile and a half along a steep-sided ridge from the deodar-covered mountain peak of Jakko to Prospect Hill, with two knolls in between. On either side of the ridge the ground falls away to create two deep bowls, so that most dwellings have views looking either northwards towards the Himalayan ranges or south towards the Punjab plains. The main thoroughfare was – and still is – the Mall, which runs the length of the ridge and at the Jakko end curls round its southern flank as the Mall Extension. In Kipling's day this was closed to all carriages except that of the Viceroy and Vicereine.

Only at one point does the Mall broaden out to create a patch of open ground, known as the Ridge, scarcely the length and breadth of a football pitch, extending from Christ Church at the foot of Jakko Hill to Scandal Point, where three roads converge. This was the site of Simla's first bazaar, which had sprung up to house the camp-followers accompanying Lord Amherst, the Governor-General, when he made the Simla ridge the site of his summer camp in 1827. There was a single cottage standing before he arrived and half a dozen by the time he left, all simply built in rustic style using local timber, with steep gables and chimneys. It was then decided that Simla ridge should serve as a sanatorium for invalids, land was bought from the local rajas and within a decade more than a hundred summer houses had been constructed along the ridge.

Consciously or not, the English owners of these houses strived to replicate the world they had left behind in a way impossible in the plains – the one concession being the use of corrugated tin for roofing, easy to transport but hard on the ears when it rained. They planted gardens with roses and other conspicuously English flowering shrubs and creepers, and gave their homes and surrounds English names. 'Most of the houses have their peculiar names,' noted the author of *Journal of a Tour of Upper Hindustan* after his visit to Simla in 1839. 'Bearing the most fanciful names are Stirling Castle, Wharncliffe, Annandale Lodge, Oakfield, Eagle Mount, Longwood, Allan Bank, Union Cottage, Primrose Hill, Annandale View, Prospect House, The Crags, Bellevue, Rookwood, Swiss Cottage, Fountain Hall, Daisy Bank, The Hermitage, Blessings, The Briars, Victoria Lodge, Edward's Cot, Morna's Grove, Richmond Villa, Woodbine Cottage, Kenilworth, Abbeyville, Sunnybank, Holly Bank etc.'[33] Most of these cottages were rented out by the season, the rates depending on size and location. Within a quarter of a century the numbers of cottages and guest houses had quadrupled and quadrupled again, following Lord Lawrence's decision to make Simla the summer seat of Government, regardless of the expense involved in moving the entire central administration over 1000 miles twice a year.

Little thought was given to planning until Lord Lytton's first appearance in the summer of 1876. The ever-fastidious Lytton was dismayed to find himself housed in a rented house, Peterhof, which he likened to 'a sort of pigsty'.[34] He immediately called for plans to make Simla fit for an imperial capital, which would mean building a proper Viceregal Lodge and removing the Native bazaars which had grown up on the Ridge at the Mall's eastern end. The opportunity to clear the Mall came when fire swept through Simla's Upper Bazaar, with cholera to follow. 'This fearful visitation,' noted Martin Towelle, the *Civil and Military Gazette*'s local manager and author of *Towelle's Hand Book and Guide to Simla*, 'roused the Municipal Commissioners and the Authorities of Simla to more energetic exertions in endeavouring to cleanse the place of its many impurities.' The eastern end of the Mall was cleared to become the focal point of the Station, forcing 'those who minister to the wants of the glad city – *jhampanis* who pull the pretty rickshaws by night and gamble till the dawn, grocers, oil-sellers, curio-venders, firewood dealers, priests, pickpockets, and native employees of the Government'[35] – to resettle tier upon tier along a series of lower terraces cut into the ridge's steep southern slopes. These became Simla's Middle and Lower Bazaars: 'the crowded rabbit-warren that climbs from the valley to the Town Hall at an angle of forty-five' where Kim's mentor, the Afghan horse-trader Mahbub Ali, rented a room in the house of a cattle-dealer, knowing he could sink out of sight.

When Rudyard Kipling first came to Simla, Lord Lytton's schemes for the town's modernisation had still to be realised. A site had been acquired on the summit of Observatory Hill for the new Viceregal Lodge and the foundations had been laid for a magnificent town hall to rise from the ashes of the Upper Bazaar, incorporating a small theatre, library, Masonic hall, public hall, ballroom, police station and an armoury for Simla's volunteer Rifle Corps, only for the work to be put on ice on Lord Ripon's orders. This meant that the Ridge resembled a building site, so that the promenade known as the *hawa khana* or the 'eating of the air' held every afternoon between half-past four and seven now took place at the top end of the Mall Extension, running south along Jakko Hill's western flank from the Church to Chota Simla or Little Simla. For two and a half hours every day this one-mile stretch of road was thronged with promenaders, gentlemen on horseback and ladies in their *jampans*, clumsy-looking sedan chairs on wheels which required the services of four *jampanis*, and were about to be superseded by the very latest importation from Japan, *ginrickshas*, swiftly Anglo-Indianised into 'rickshaws'. It was here that Ruddy was first introduced to Simla society, although in his case society with a small 's'.

Simla Society with a capital 's' revolved around three *lat sahibs*: the Viceroy, otherwise known as the *Mulki Lat Sahib* or Lord of All the Land; the Commander-in-Chief – the *Jungi Lat Sahib* or Lord Of War; and the Lieutenant-Governor of the Punjab – the *Punjab Lat Sahib*. Of the three, only the last had an official residence worthy of his position: Barnes Court, a sprawling mock-Tudor building set in forty-six acres of land in Chota Simla. The other two had to make do with temporary accommodation, and in the summer of '83 the C-in-C found himself in the humiliating position of having to vacate Woodville, located above Barnes Court on the sunny side of Jakko, and move to the less attractive property Snowden, also on Jakko Hill but on its northern flank. The reason for this enforced move was that Woodville was one of a number of Simla properties recently acquired by James Walker and his Alliance Bank of Simla.

The head office of the Alliance Bank of Simla was at Kelvin Grove, which also doubled as James Walker's private residence, and it was here that Ruddy spent his first summer leave. Sited on the upper side of the Mall Extension just south of Combermere Bridge, Kelvin Grove was ideally placed to put Ruddy at the centre of Simla's main amusements. Of these, by far and away the most important in Ruddy's eyes was Benmore, a property owned by a German musician, Herr Felix von Goldstein, who had been imported to Simla by Lord Lytton as his bandmaster and had stayed put. After securing Benmore for himself von Goldstein had converted it into an entertainment centre, advertised in 1877 as '"Benmore" with its new and handsome Concert Room, and Stage, available for Theatrical Performances, Balls, Parties, Musical and other Entertainments'. The concert room and stage could be hired for private functions for fifty rupees, with an additional twenty-five rupees for the adjoining drawing room and hall, and a further thirty-two rupees for the supper room. When 'rinking' became fashionable in the late 1870s a roller-skating rink was added, which makes Rudyard Kipling's homage to Benmore in 'The Lovers' Litany' more understandable, if rather less romantic:[36]

> Eyes of blue – the Simla Hills
>   Silvered with the moonlight hoar;
> Pleading of the waltz that thrills,
>   Dies and echoes round Benmore.
> *'Mabel'*, *'Officers'*, *'Goodbye'*,
>   Glamour, wine, and witchery –
> On my soul's sincerity,
>   *'Love like ours can never die!'*[37]

During that first summer the short ride between Kelvin Grove and Benmore and back again was one that Ruddy made many times over. Returning from late-night revelries at Benmore he had always to pass Simla's earliest cemetery, the Old Burial Ground, which lay just out of sight below a bend in the road. This became the subject of two early meditations in prose and verse, written within days of each other. The first drew the attention of Ruddy's Simla readership to the fact that close by a favourite trysting place for lovers was this forgotten cemetery – 'a short tumble backwards, in fact, from the white railings – you come suddenly upon a relic of old Simla neglected and forgotten, as are most old things in India'.[38] The idea of Simla's forgotten dead was then used to chilling effect in the poem 'Possibilities':

> Ay, lay him 'neath the Simla pine –
> A fortnight fully to be missed:
> Behold, we lose our fourth at whist
> A chair is vacant where we dine.[39]

The poet imagines the unlamented dead listening to the sounds of music wafting across from Benmore and mocking the living they have left behind.

A better-known landmark on the Mall Extension was the bandstand, heralding the beginning of Simla's shops and hotels, beginning with the Rockcliffe and Lowrie's Hotel, where bachelors and other hopefuls stayed during their brief visits. Then came Combermere Bridge and the beginnings of Upper Bazaar, fronted by a row of two-storey buildings that included Combermere House, containing Meakins & Co., purveyors of 'celebrated beers and porters', and Moore's the milliners, offering 'the latest Parisian trimmed millinery, the newest styles in Untrimmed Felt and Straw Hats, French Flowers and Feathers in great variety, Bonnet silks etc., its dress department being under the entire management of Mrs Craymer'. Next door to Combermere House was Regent House, 'where are located the establishments of Messrs Richards and Co., Thacker, Spink and Co., and the renowned restaurant of Peliti'. The last-named was Signor F. Peliti, Calcutta's favourite confectioner and ice-cream maker, first brought to Simla by Lord Lytton along with the French chef Monsieur Bansard. Both men had subsequently gone into business in Simla as restaurateurs and hoteliers, and Peliti's had become the fashionable place of rendezvous, where ladies gathered on the restaurant terrace to exchange gossip and pleasantries with their cakes and ices.

Immediately below Peliti's were the Assembly Hall and the Billiard Room, as well as the Station Press building – the last of particular interest to Ruddy because it housed the local offices of his newspaper. Here Ruddy must have called on his arrival to pay his respects to George Allen's right-hand man in Simla, Howard Hensman. As much a diplomat as a journalist, Hensman was the *Pioneer*'s officiating editor in Allahabad and its special correspondent in Simla. He had made his name as a correspondent in the recent Afghan War and, by learning to play his cards in both the figurative and the metaphorical sense, had become the confidant and sometime mouthpiece of anyone who mattered, including the outgoing Viceroy, Lord Ripon, and the present Commander-in-Chief, Major-General Sir Donald Stewart. According to Kipling, Hensman was a 'power in the land' who played whist with 'Great Ones, who gave him special news'.[40]

What must also have impressed Ruddy on his arrival in Simla was that Kelvin Grove stood at the very gates of the United Services Club, exclusive to members of the 'Civil and Military'. Despite its shabby buildings, the Club could claim to be the most important meeting place in India, for, as one of its members explained, it was where he 'met every day the great men of India . . . I would hear what the Viceroy thought or what he had said, would be told who were the coming men, and sometimes would listen to opinions on the Ilbert Bill and on Lord Ripon's scheme for Local Self-Government.'[41] However, the Club was open only to the ruling caste. Ruddy's host James Walker was Simla's leading banker, co-proprietor of the two most successful newspapers in the country, a generous benefactor to the town and first Chairman of Simla's newly formed Municipal Committee. Like his business partner George Allen, Walker had many friends in the ICS and Army. Yet both men were inadmissible for membership of the United Services Club, and so excluded from Simla's inner circle. Allen, it was reported, gave '*le beau monde* in Simla picnics, presents, balls and fetes' and 'panted for social and political advancement', yet was snubbed at every turn: 'Indian [Anglo-Indian] Society, though quite ready to eat his excellent dinners, drink his expensive wines, and accept his costly presents, would not fraternise with anyone who had been in trade. In this respect it is far more "select" than royalty.'[42]

Ruddy could not have failed to note the social vulnerability of his two main proprietors and the degree to which it reduced his own horizons. It may explain why the only woman he is known to have set his cap at during his first season in Simla was a Miss O'Meara, the daughter of a dentist, albeit a well-known one who had drawn the teeth of the Amir of Afghanistan.

Simla Society was no less rigid in the way it shunned those of its own kind who broke the rules, of whom the most notorious at this time was Allan Octavian Hume, late of the Bengal Civil Service, a man 'of exceptional ability and brain power' but 'not free from the eccentricity which sometimes accompanies genius'.[43] Hume had considerable private means and owned one of Simla's oldest properties, Rothney Castle, standing on the lower slopes of Jakko between Snowden and Christ Church, on which he spent huge sums to accommodate a library of ornithological books and a vast collection of stuffed birds, eggs, nests and trophies numbering in excess of 100,000 specimens. He had laboured for eight years as Secretary of Revenue, Agriculture and Commerce until his progressive views on land reform and indentured labour proved too much for Lord Lytton, who had him demoted in a manner described by the *Pioneer* as 'an act of the grossest jobbery'. Ejected from Simla on Lytton's orders and directed to take up a minor revenue post in Allahabad, he had there fallen under the spell of

Madame Blavatsky, co-founder of the Theosophical Society and newly arrived from America. Hume and A. P. Sinnett, the *Pioneer*'s editor, had subsequently become Madame Blavatsky's most ardent advocates.

After Lord Lytton's departure in 1880 Hume had returned to Simla to complete his *magnum opus*, *The Game Birds of India, Burma and Ceylon*, only to find that one of his servants had sold the fruit of twenty years' work in the bazaar for kindling. The disaster led him to redirect his formidable energies towards the building of a charity hospital to serve Simla's Indian poor – and to the promotion of Madame Blavatsky's Secret Doctrine as conveyed to her by spirit adepts from Inner Tibet known as the Mahatmas. In 1881 Hume invited Madame Blavatsky to stay at Rothney Castle, where she presided over a series of seances and occult manifestations, duly written up by A. P. Sinnett in the *Pioneer*, which divided Simla into those who fell under her spell and those who saw her as a charlatan. Among the latter was Lockwood Kipling, who after attending one of her seances concluded that she was 'one of the most interesting and unscrupulous imposters he had ever met'.[44] A more outspoken sceptic was the Civilian Sir Edward Buck, who had succeeded Hume as Secretary of Revenue, Agriculture and Commerce and was no friend of his. At a dinner party at Rothney Castle he confronted Mrs Blavatsky and exposed her as a fraud, at which point public opinion in Simla turned against her – and against her local champion Allan Octavian Hume.

According to Rudyard Kipling's autobiography, the Blavatsky episode 'devastated the *Pioneer*'. Sinnett had used the paper to promote Madame Blavatsky with ever-increasing stridency, and had joined forces with Hume to form the Simla Eclectic Society, a liberal body seeking to improve relations between Indians and Englishmen. These actions eventually led George Allen to dismiss him and install a safer pair of hands, in the person of Howard Hensman.[45] Hume, however, remained utterly convinced by Madame Blavatsky until the moment early in 1883 when he compared her handwriting with that of the chief Mahatma 'Koot

Hoomi', whose astral letters fluttered down from the ceiling during seances, and found them to be identical. At this point the scales fell from Hume's eyes, and he abandoned Theosophy for politics. In March 1883 he published an open letter to the graduates of Calcutta University calling on them to organise and work towards political reform, a rallying cry which led directly to the setting up of the Indian National Congress.

After the Blavatsky episode Hume and Allen became the bitterest of enemies, Allen using the editorial pages of the *Pioneer* and the *Civil and Military Gazette* to undermine Hume and the causes he promoted. 'I much fear that we shall have The Pioneer against us,' wrote Hume to Lord Ripon in January 1883. 'Allen is of the worst type of educated Englishmen, sneering at all things native and natives generally . . . always guided by the opinions of a clique of civilians who were uncompromising despots, who wanted and want to keep the people for ever in the cradle.'[46] Courageous as he was, Hume was also his own worst enemy, losing friends as fast as he made them. 'Mr Hume,' observed Sir Edward Buck's nephew in his classic history, *Simla Past and Present*, 'was essentially a man of hobbies, and whatever hobby he took up was ridden well and hard.'

Three other Simla property owners were to play a significant part in the Kipling story over the next few years. The most distinguished was the Bengal Civil Servant Sir William W. Hunter, owner of Stirling Castle, one of the oldest and best-sited of Simla's homes, perched on the wooded summit of Elysium Hill. Hunter was a prodigious worker, the author of numerous Government surveys and statistical compendiums but also a historian of note and a minor novelist. Sir Courteney Ilbert had stayed at Elysium Hill as Hunter's guest in the summer of 1882 while preparing his notorious Bill and was again a guest the following summer when Ruddy first came to Simla – which may help to explain why Hunter subsequently became the butt of a number of Ruddy's early political squibs.

The second figure was less respected than feared: Horace Goad,

son of one of Simla's pioneer settlers, whose judicious land pur-
chases in the 1850s and 1860s had made him Simla's foremost
landlord, with thirty-three large properties to his name. A police
officer by profession, Goad was spoken of in Ruddy's day as the
cleverest policeman in the North-Western Provinces. According
to one of his contemporaries, 'His extraordinary knowledge of the
native language and customs, combined with a genius for dis-
guising himself, rendered him a terror to all evil-doers within his
jurisdiction . . . Even the ayahs regarded him as a man to hold in
awe; indeed many of the little ones they tended were quieted by
the threat of being handed over to "Goad Sahib" unless they
behaved as good children on the Mall.'[47] Together with Forjett of
Bombay, Goad forms part of the composite policeman
Strickland, who is 'feared and respected by the natives from the
Ghor Kathri to the Jamma Masjid; and is supposed to have the gift
of invisibility and executive control over many Devils'.[48]

The third Simla figure must have excited Ruddy's interest the
moment he first stepped into his jewellery and curio shop on
the Mall: A. M. Jacob, a man of mystery in appearance and
antecedents. Jacob's private residence, Belvedere, was sited unfash-
ionably below Lakka Bazaar on the road to Elysium Hill, but it was
the scene of many tea and dinner parties, one or more of which
Ruddy may well have attended as the Walkers' guest.

Very little was known about Mr Jacob's early life other than that
he had arrived in Simla in 1871 with money. He was believed to
be an Armenian Jew who had been sold as a child-slave to an
Ottoman pasha before securing his freedom to become a clerk at
the court of India's wealthiest prince, the Nizam of Hyderabad.
There he had entered into Hyderabad's jewellery trade, eventually
gaining a clientele that included the wealthiest maharajas in India.
His learning and his charm, combined with the aura of mystery[49]
that he seemed always to convey, had enabled him to prosper. He
dressed and behaved like an ascetic, yet both his shop and his house
were piled with precious objects of every description, all of which
made him an obvious subject of speculation – and inspiration.

In September 1879 a young journalist working on an up-country newspaper entered Mr Jacob's curio shop in the Simla Mall and found himself transported 'into the subterranean chambers whither the wicked magician sent Aladdin in quest of the lamp'. The owner of the shop spoke English 'like a fellow from Balliol' and had a presence that immediately overwhelmed the journalist, who found himself in thrall to eyes that had 'a depth of life and vital light in them that told of the pent up force of a hundred generations of Persian magii'. This was not Rudyard Kipling but a young American named Francis Marion Crawford, employed by the *Indian Herald* of Allahabad. He later went home to America, where he turned his encounter with Mr Jacob into a work of fiction. *Mr Isaacs: A Tale of Modern India* was published in Britain in 1883, so it is reasonable to suppose that Simla's Station Library – hon. sec. Mr James Walker – was in possession of a copy by June of that year.

The real Alexander Jacob remained a Simla landmark for almost a quarter of a century. But his luck deserted him in 1890 when he purchased on behalf of the Nizam of Hyderabad the largest and most expensive diamond of the age, known then as the Imperial and today as the Jacob Diamond, weighing 184.5 carats. It cost Jacob 4,600,000 rupees, of which the Nizam advanced half before reneging on the deal. Jacob's increasingly desperate attempts to recover the rest of the money embarrassed the Government of India, and pressure was applied to get him to drop his claim. He refused, and in 1891 what became known as the Imperial Diamond Case was heard in the Calcutta High Court over fifty-seven days. Although Jacob finally won his case against the Nizam, the costs ruined him and in 1892 he was forced to sell his home and his shop in Simla and retire to Bombay, a broken man.

Besides his starring role in *Mr Isaacs*, Alexander Jacob appeared as 'Mr Emanuel' in Colonel Newnham Davies's novel *Jadoo*, published in 1898, and as 'Mr Lucanster' in Mrs Flora Annie Steele's *Voices of the Night*, published in 1900 – by which time he had secured literary immortality as 'Lurgan Sahib' in Rudyard Kipling's *Kim*.

In mid-August, after a month of 'exceeding delight' and 'a round of picnics, dances, theatricals and so on' at which he claimed to have 'flirted with the bottled up energy of a year on my lips',[50] Ruddy returned to Lahore and his desk in the offices of the *CMG*. With the Rains in full spate, he wrote a thank-you letter to Mrs Lizzie Walker in Simla in the form of thirteen quatrains, the first of his many ditties from the Hills. It reads in part:

> No longer by the *Jhampan*'s side
>   I frisk along the crowded Mall
> From half past four till even fall,
>   Or by Peliti's take my ride.
>
> No longer through the stately pines
>   The soft Hill breezes come and go,
> No longer in the dusk below
>   The merry *Rickshaw*'s lantern shines.
>
> For Jakko's woods are far away
>   And, in the place of Combermere,
> Across the muddy *chick* [slatted screen] I hear
>   The rain that 'raineth every day'.[51]

6

'The seething city'

LAHORE AND THE FAMILY SQUARE, 1883–4

> Unkempt, unclean, athwart the mist
>   The seething city looms.
> In place of Putney's golden gorse
>   The sickly *babul* [thorny mimosa] blooms.
>
> Rudyard Kipling, 'The Moon of Other Days', first
> published in the *Pioneer*, 16 December 1884

When Ruddy returned to Lahore in mid-August 1883 it was to an empty bungalow. Lockwood Kipling had taken his place in Simla and was intending to proceed afterwards to Calcutta to set up the Punjab's contribution to an international exhibition to be held in December. Alice Kipling was not due back in India with Trix until the end of the year. So for the next four months Ruddy found himself 'alone, like a hermit crab'[1] in Lahore. 'There are 9 men and 2 ladies in the Station and most of these are going away,' he wrote to his Aunt Edith, referring to that section of the Anglo-Indian population which constituted Lahore Society. 'The dullness,' he added, 'is something hideous after the bustle of Simla.' During the day he had plenty of work to keep his mind occupied, but the lack of company in the evenings very soon got to him and he took to dining every night in the Club, returning to Bikaner House only to sleep: 'At five go to the empty house,' he wrote of his out-of-office-hours routine, 'to load cartridges and shoot parrots from my hammock in the garden for an hour, then afternoon tea and a ride to the [Montgomery] hall, where we sit (9 of us) around drinking strange iced drinks and feeling bored. Then home again to change for dinner at the Club, which is a terribly dull ceremony. Then a game of billiards or whist and back to bed.'[2]

To fill his leisure hours Ruddy began to study for the Indian Army's Lower Standard Urdu exam, employing a *munshi* or Native language teacher to come to his bungalow for an hour before he took his morning ride. He also took up polo, and enlisted as a private soldier in B Company of the 1st Punjab Volunteer Rifle Corps, part of the auxiliary force formed in the wake of the Mutiny to ensure that Europeans in up-country Stations were never again caught unprepared as they had been in '57. Ruddy's chief, Stephen Wheeler, went down with another bout of sickness and he was again in sole charge of the paper, during which time he took the opportunity to sit in on an adultery case being heard *in camera* in the courts, involving a British barrister and the wife of the proprietor of the Lahore Livery Stables. Having sat through every word he then exercised his editorial judgement by refusing to publish the details – 'to the intense indignation of the two Lahore ladies'.

He wrote 'reassuring fibs' in the wake of the second successive failure of the Rains to save the *kharif* crops sown in May and June, and grumbled to Crom Price by letter that he found himself 'hard pressed at times for a really original lie'.[3]

In mid-November he sent 'some specimens of the stuff I write daily' to Mr Crofts asking him to 'pass sentence'.[4] The cuttings included an account of the Dassera Festival celebrated by Lahore's Hindu minority in October, on which he had reported in a tone of amused disdain. 'Sita,' he had told his readers, 'uncomfortably astride a broad-backed wicker-work bull, supported by an uneasy Rama, buried in tinsel . . . was a spectacle more comic than imposing . . . It may occur to some, that a city, which has had an Oriental College, teaching Oriental poetry, in its midst for many years, might have acquired a taste for more interesting and popular manifestations.'[5] His proprietors evidently appreciated his efforts, for at the end of the year Ruddy was appointed a special correspondent and awarded an extra £7 a month.

As Lahore's full quota of Europeans returned to their posts Ruddy's social life picked up. He attended rehearsals for a production by the Lahore Amateurs of *Plot and Passion*, a melodrama by two well-known Anglo-Indian writers, John Lang and Tom Taylor, and acquitted himself well in the part of Desmarets, head of the secret police in Napoleon's Paris. The first performance, on 20 December, resulted in a glowing review in the *CMG*, in which Ruddy described himself as the 'hero of the evening'. But his acting was also admired by others, one of whom was Berthold Ribbentrop of the Indian Forest Service, who urged him to 'drop newspapering' and take to the stage. Some years later Ruddy returned the compliment in casting Ribbentrop in his first Mowgli story, 'In the Rukh', as the 'gigantic German' Muller, 'head of the Woods and Forests of all India' and a man of great perception.[6]

A further performance of *Plot and Passion* took place on Christmas Day and was surely a memorable occasion for Ruddy, since both his parents and his fifteen-year-old sister were present in the audience: Lockwood was back from the Calcutta Exhibition and Alice had just arrived from Bombay with Trix. 'When my sister came out . . . our cup was filled to the brim,' wrote Rudyard Kipling of their reunion. 'Not only were we happy, but we knew it.'[7] And Trix thought likewise: 'I really believe the happiest time of his life – and mine – was when we lived together after I came out to Lahore.'[8]

It was only a year and three months since Ruddy had seen his sister, but in that time she had grown into a young woman, petite and fragile-looking but delightfully pretty. In what is now an incomplete letter to his Aunt Edith, written towards the end of January 1884, Ruddy described how he and his sister felt free 'to "frivol" like babies and the parents are delighted to think us so'. Their sibling closeness extended to their writing. According to Trix, the two of them always talked over whatever they were working on, to the extent that she could 'recognise "something of myself" in his writing – in *Departmental Ditties* especially', although 'there was never any Charles-and-Mary-Lamb or Dorothy-and-William-Wordsworth nonsense about us'. In her old age Trix clung to what may well have been no more than a conceit, that much of her brother's writing was a 'family affair' to which all four members contributed: 'If we all had our rights the longest and most admired part of "On Greenhow Hill" would be signed J. L. K. and sundry verses A. M. K. In those simple days "Bags I" made a copyright – and the family square "pooled" their work even as No. 5 study in Stalky did their impots [schoolboy slang for imposed punishments].'[9] What is rather more credible is Trix's claim that her mother did her best to steer Ruddy over what he could or should write about their sex: 'Mother and I used to drop severely on things his women said in *Plain Tales*. "No, Ruddy, no! Not that." "But it's true." "Never mind; there are lots of things that are true that we never mention."'[10]

As well as trading ideas, Ruddy also took great delight in teaching Trix to ride, going out with her nearly every morning before work:

This morning she and I went into the open and trotted back as hard as we could come (T. bumped a good deal but that is only natural). If you could have seen her with the colour in her cheeks, her hair down and blowing about in the wind, and the hat jammed at the back of the head you would have seen her at her loveliest – and that's a tall order. We are all spoiling the maiden sadly – but she won't spoil easily and brightens up the domestic shanty like a 'Swan's incandescent' [Swan match].[11]

Included in this same letter to Edith Macdonald was a recent cutting from the *CMG* in the form of a parody of Lewis Carroll's 'The Walrus and the Carpenter' that began:

> The Stranger and the Resident
> Were strolling down the Mall;

> The former jumped at times to see
>   The merry bullets fall.
> 'If this goes on for long,' he said,
>   'Expect a funeral.'

The verses had been written in response to a complaint from the Director of Public Instruction that a shot fired from the 1st Punjab Volunteers' rifle range in the Lawrence Gardens had ploughed into the ground at his feet as he passed the *CMG*'s offices on his morning constitutional. 'I need only explain,' wrote Ruddy to his aunt, 'that I too was once nearly shot while riding down the Mall, and the "Poet's mind" was, consequently, vexed by the "shallow wit" of volunteers who could miss a mark at two hundred yards and nearly hit a man at two thousand.' Afterwards ignored by its author, 'A Beleaguered City' was the first Rudyard Kipling poem to be published in the *CMG*,[12] its appearance in print being all the sweeter for having been slipped in under Wheeler's nose under the pseudonym of 'Blank Cartridge'.

The volunteers whose loose shooting had inspired Ruddy's poem were from the same battalion which Ruddy had joined only months earlier, but already he had lost the taste for amateur soldiering. 'No one ever saw him on parade,' complained his company commander, Colonel H. R. Goulding, who had eventually to write to Ruddy demanding the repayment of the capitation grant paid to all volunteers – which was promptly done, accompanied by a letter 'frankly admitting the justice of the penalty and expressing regret for neglect of duty'.[13]

Two days after the publication of Ruddy's 'A Beleaguered City' in January 1884 the *CMG* ran the verdict of a murder trial at the Punjab High Court involving a British Army private, William Day, who had quarrelled with another soldier and then shot him as he slept. A number of military murders and subsequent executions took place during Kipling's years in India, but this was the only one where he saw the accused face to face and witnessed the passing of a sentence of death – and it left its mark. On 26 September that same year the *CMG* carried a report of an incident at Multan in which three drunken soldiers from the Manchester Regiment had fired on passers-by, killing an Indian. Three days later 'The Story of Tommy' appeared in the *CMG* under the signature of 'E. M.' In six terse stanzas it told the tale of Tommy, 'aged twenty and drunk in his cot', who shoots the slumbering *punkah-wallah* on a hot night and duly suffers the extreme penalty:

> Waited a couple of weeks, while the padris [*sic: padres*] came
>> and harangued,
>> Then, in Central Jail, Tommy, aged twenty, was hanged.[14]

'The Story of Tommy' is one of the many unsigned or pseudonymous verses pasted by Rudyard Kipling into his Lahore scrapbook but never publicly acknowledged or collected, which is a puzzle since it is another milestone. One year on and a third military murder was given extensive newspaper coverage, although this time it was *CMG*'s sister paper, the *Pioneer*, which reported it – and with a twist that made it unusually macabre. The victim was Lance-Sergeant William Carmody of the 1st Battalion of the Leicestershire Regiment, his killer Private George Flaxman. What was remarkable about the murder was that Flaxman was one of a group of disgruntled soldiers who had drawn cards to decide who should kill their sergeant. Flaxman had drawn the ace of spades and then shot Carmody as he sat in his tent drinking a cup of tea.[15] He was duly found guilty of murder at a general court martial. Because of the circumstances of the card-cutting a plea for leniency was entered, but it was rejected by the Commander-in-Chief, General Sir Frederick Roberts, and on 10 January 1887 Private Flaxman was put through the awful ritual of a military execution, involving a full parade on the Lucknow *maidan*, the forming of troops in an open square and the condemned man marching to the scaffold behind a military band and a coffin on a gun-carriage drawn by two bullocks.

'The Band struck up with the Dead March in Saul which sent

a thrill through every living soul on that parade ground,' wrote one of the condemned man's comrades:

> He marched with a firm step and his head slightly bent . . . When he got to the scaffold he halted and ran up the steps as if he was the executioner and not the condemned man . . . Then a native ran up the steps and placed the rope around his neck. Now he was not aware that the native was going to hang him, but anyhow he must have smelt him, for he said, 'go away, you black.' The native then drew the bolt and he was no more. After hanging a few minutes the black cloth that covered the grave was removed, and all the troops marched past him. He hung with his head on one side and there was blood on the coat, he looked an awful sight.[16]

Kipling's masterpiece 'Danny Deever' did not appear in print until February 1890,[17] but those grim verses were almost certainly sketched out in the weeks following Private Flaxman's hanging in Lucknow on 10 January 1887. As a child Ruddy had heard his Macdonald grandmother sing a traditional English verse ballad in the form of a dramatic duologue, with a question in one line and an answer in the next:

> 'Pray where are you going, child?' said Meet-on-the-road.
> 'To school, sir, to school, sir,' said Child-as-it-stood.
> 'What have you in that basket?' said Meet-on-the-road.
> 'Some pudding, sir, some pudding, sir,' said Child-as-it-
>   stood.[18]

For 'Danny Deever' Ruddy reworked those well-remembered lines with a 'combination of heavy beat and variation of pace' that gave the poem 'a unity of movement which enhances the horror of the occasion'.[19] It was the work of a poet at one with his craft:

> 'What are the bugles blowin' for?' said Files-on-Parade.

'To turn you out, to turn you out,' the Colour-Sergeant
     said.
'What makes you look so white, so white?' said Files-on-
     Parade.
'I'm dreadin' what I've got to watch,' the Colour-Sergeant
     said.

The story unfolds through the questions put by the frightened
recruit, Files-on-Parade, and the replies of his superior, the Colour-
Sergeant, who tries to shield him from the awfulness of what is
happening until finally both have to face the truth:

'What's that so black agin the sun?' said Files-on-Parade.
     'It's Danny fighting 'ard for life,' the Colour-Sergeant said.
'What's that that whimpers over'ead? said Files-on-Parade.
     'It's Danny's soul that's passin' now,' the Colour-Sergeant
          said.

Ruddy's triumph on the boards over Christmas had given him
a taste for amateur theatricals, and when the Lahore Amateurs
decided to stage a production of W. S. Gilbert's poetical whimsy
The Palace of Truth at Easter he threw himself into the part of
Chrysal, a court poet in love with a lady-in-waiting called Palmis,
played by a Miss Coxen, daughter of a military officer. A 'very
sudden indisposition' meant that Ruddy missed the play's two performances in mid-April, but this did not prevent him from falling
for Miss Coxen and writing to her after she left Lahore in June. At
the same time he continued to maintain the illusion that he and Flo
Garrard still had a romantic understanding, despite receiving a letter
from her in July in which she again made it plain that she had no
feelings for him.

The eighteen-year-old had by now grown tired of the company
he was forced to keep outside Bikaner House. 'There is no society in India as we understand the word,' was how he put it when
he came to write about the narrowness of Station life:

There are no books, no pictures, no conversations worth listen-ing to for recreation's sake. Every man is in some service or other, has a hard day's work to do, and has very little inclination to do anything but sleep at the end of it . . . All the older men *invariably* talk about their own work or pay or prospects when two or three gather together; and the younger men, if in the army, talk of their horses. In a country where every Englishman owns at least one horse, this is natural but monotonous. No one talks lightly and amusingly as in England . . . They don't seem to realise any of the beauties of life – perhaps they haven't time.[20]

The only people outside his home with whom Ruddy could iden-tify were the junior officers of the army regiments quartered at Mian Mir. They had more leisure time than the civilians, so they tended to organise most of the local sporting activities and to entertain more generously. Soon after his arrival in Lahore Ruddy had been invited to dine in the officers' messes of the two British Army Regiments stationed at Mian Mir, represented at this time by the East Lancashire Regiment and units of the Royal Artillery. The junior subalterns of these two units were only a year or two older than he, and invited Ruddy to dine with them when they commanded the detachment on guard duty at Lahore Fort. This led to 'ghostly dinners . . . all among marble-inlaid, empty apartments of dead Queens, or under the domes of old tombs, meals began with the regulation thirty grains of quinine in the sherry, and ended – as Allah pleased!'[21] One such evening in February 1884 inspired the poem 'On Fort Duty', in which a bored artillery subaltern laments being stuck on fort duty beside the pestilent Ravi when he could be up on the Frontier where 'the passes ring with rifles / And the noise of Afghan raids'.[22]

In that same month Ruddy was given a first opportunity to explore beyond the confines of the Station when he received an invitation, 'couched in flowery English and flowerier Persian', from an Afghan tribal chief in Lahore city. Greatly intrigued, he allowed himself to be led on his horse into the heart of the city. His host turned out to be a political hostage from the recent Afghan War who evidently believed that pressure on the government from the *CMG* could end his exile. To reinforce his case he presented Ruddy with a large bundle of currency notes, which were returned to him with the remark that English sahibs did not take bribes. The Afghan's response was to produce 'a Cashmeri girl that Moore [Thomas Moore, author of *Lalla Rookh*] might have raved over'. If Ruddy's account of the business to his Aunt Edith is to be believed, the girl was beautiful, 'but I didn't quite see how she was to be introduced into an English household like ours'. Having rejected this second offer, he was then prevented from leaving the room, causing him to 'sweat big drops'.

However, it turned out that the Afghan had a bigger and better bribe to offer, in the form of 'two bay Arabs, one grey Kathiawar

'*Sulaiman Khel Horse-dealers*', J. L. Kipling (*National Trust*)

mare, and four perfect little Hazara country breds', from which he was told to take his pick of any three. After spurning this third temptation as vehemently as before Ruddy returned to his horse, only to find hidden under the saddle 'a little bag of uncut diamonds and big greasy emeralds', which he threw 'through one of the windows of the upper storey'.[23] No doubt Edith Macdonald read the tale with the pinch of salt it probably deserved.

A more credible tale of bribery followed six weeks later, after Ruddy had won his spurs as the *CMG*'s special correspondent by reporting on Lord Ripon's viceregal visit to Patiala, a princely state on the edge of the Punjab plains south of Simla. Patiala's wealthy Sikh rulers had already acquired a reputation for conspicuous profligacy, to which Ruddy's dispatches, published in four instalments in late March, added colourful detail. As a guest of the maharaja he was allowed to explore every corner of the palace other than the *zanana* housing the ruler's wives and concubines, and had taken full advantage. 'However much I wrote,' he told his Aunt Edith, 'I couldn't describe the jewels, the champagne, treachery, intrigue, princely hospitality, elephants, four-in-hands etc. I came across . . . You may say what you like about the decadence of India, but, in a purely native state you see what a blaze of jewels and colour India must have been.'[24]

At the close of his visit Ruddy found a thousand rupees hidden in a *dauli* or presentation basket of fruit and nuts, which he returned, only to discover that two rival reporters also covering the event had happily pocketed their bribes, having received twice as much as he had. He took his revenge by being first with the news, riding through the night to the nearest railway station on a borrowed horse, 'covering the 32 miles in a trifle less than two and a half hours and getting my letter into the paper next day – much to the disgust of the other men'.[25] This 'starlight ride' was to provide the material for one of the few credible passages of *The Naulahka*, written six years later in collaboration with Wolcott Balestier, when the novella's hero Tarvin sets out for Chittor 'under the last of the setting moon, the fields silver-white with the opium poppy, or dark with sugar-cane', riding through the night across 'a vast level plain flanked by hills of soft outline – a plain that in the dim light seemed as level as the sea'.[26]

Having proved his usefulness as a reporter Ruddy was now regularly assigned to cover local events. His early experience on the *United Services College Chronicle* had already taught him to set down in his notebook exactly what was said and seen. But Ruddy also brought to his reporting a determination to 'get to grips' with his subject that bordered on the compulsive. His early admirer Kay Robinson was particularly struck by some satirical verses of his which mocked a famous British cavalry regiment in India for its timidity in making the Umballa steeplechase course safer than need be. Its lines were 'filled with such technicalities of racing and stable jargon that old steeplechasers went humming them all over every station in Upper India, and swearing that "it was the best thing ever written in English". . . What impressed me was that a sporting "vet", who had lived in the pigskin almost all his life, should have gone wandering about the Lahore Club, asking people "where the youngster picks it up?"' Robinson put it down to a 'marvellous faculty for assimilating local colour without apparent effort'[27] – which takes no account of the hard graft which Ruddy put into understanding his material. Other observers of Kipling at work have left accounts of the way he worried at a subject like a terrier with a bone, not leaving off until the working of every nut, bolt and flange of its machinery was understood, along with every technical term, nuance, phrase and piece of slang that went with it.

This rigorous investigation and note-taking also supplied Ruddy with a natural framing device for many of the two hundred or so short stories he wrote in India: that of the reporter who purports to reproduce verbatim what has been told him, as copied down in his notebook. There are early tales where it is impossible to tell if what appears on the printed page is fact or fiction, particularly when the story takes the form of a rambling monologue, seemingly reproduced as heard, word for word. 'When I comes to a gentleman and says, "Look here! You give me a drink," and that gentleman says, "No, I won't neither; you've 'ad too much," am I angry? No! What I says is . . .'[28] So opens 'Mister Anthony Dawking', which deals with one of Ruddy's favourite low-life subjects: the European loafer, almost always an ex-soldier who has fallen on hard times and taken to drink, staggering from one Station to another, scrounging off the Native population until he dies alone and unlamented. This and other tales may have been worked into fiction, but their credibility comes from scrupulously observed fact.

In late April 1884, as midday temperatures once more climbed above ninety degrees and the Punjab prepared to be 'ringed by a circle of fire', Trix went down with her first bout of fever, which her brother took as 'a not too delicate hint to Mrs Kipling to take her daughter to Dalhousie as soon as may be'. All the signs pointed to an unhealthy Hot Weather to come. 'Measles and typhoid and small pox among the natives in April are pretty certain to grow unpleasant in July and August,' wrote Ruddy to his Aunt Edith on 28 April. 'There has been a case of sporadic cholera already . . . It is funny to watch the progress of the disease. It begins like an [military] engagement with dropping shots, falling no one knows where and gradually settling down into a steady roll – a death roll if you please.'

In early May the two Alices left Lahore for Dalhousie in the Kangra Hills, the closest hill-station to Lahore, the least fashionable and the least expensive – a prime consideration for a family still beset by financial worries. The women's departure left their men free to take up the bachelor life: 'a collarless, cuffless, bootless paradise of tobacco, unpunctuality, and sloth'.[29] The lowering of sartorial standards extended to the Club. 'Men grew careless,' wrote Kipling in his autobiography, 'till at last our conscience-stricken Secretary, himself an offender, would fetch us up with a jerk, and forbid us dining in little more than singlet and riding breeches.' It was this image of untidy summer undress that Ruddy's second Chief, Kay Robinson, afterwards evoked in portraying his assistant as a rather comic figure so focused on his work as to be careless of his appearance:

White cotton trousers and a thin vest constituted his office attire, and by the day's end he was spotted all over like a Dalmatian dog. He had a habit of dipping his pen frequently and deep into the ink-pot, and as all his movements were abrupt, almost jerky, the ink used to fly . . . Driving or sometimes walking home to breakfast in his light attire plentifully besprinkled with ink, his spectacled face peeping out under an enormous, mushroom-shaped pith hat, Kipling was a quaint-looking object.[30]

That this ink-spattered figure was no figment of Robinson's imagination is confirmed by an account gathered some decades later from an elderly Sikh named Nikka Singh who had looked after the newspaper's library and who remembered Ruddy as the *kharab misaij sab siyahi* or 'bad-tempered inky sahib' who insisted that his inkpot should always be kept filled to the brim: 'To interrupt him, so Nikka Singh would say, was to see a book or a paperweight flying through the air.'[31]

The departure of the Kipling women gave Ruddy the opportunity to work out of hours at the *CMG*. With the help of the paper's printer, J. M. Chalmers, he set in type a selection of poems that he and Trix had decided to publish together in one volume under the title of *Echoes*, to consist of twenty parodies of Ruddy's favourite English poets written by him in England, with a further eight poems from Trix. His original plan was to have everything printed and bound by the end of June but, whether by intent or not, the sheets were still at the press when his father left for Dalhousie in the third week of July to begin his annual three months' leave. Indeed, it seems that Lockwood had originally planned to go at the *end* of the month, but was persuaded by his son to go early and take an extra ten days' holiday as 'privilege leave'.

Only when his father had left Lahore did Ruddy add more verses to the book, thereby evading the communal vetting process of Bikaner House. As Rudyard Kipling himself hinted in his autobiography, the usefulness of the Family Square as a creative writing workshop went only so far. 'Here the Mother was at hand,' he wrote of Alice Kipling's interest in his poetry, 'with now and then some shrivelling comment that infuriated me.' With his parents gone Ruddy felt free to add a new set of verses, some of which he had sketched out in an article entitled 'Music for the Middle-Aged', published in the *CMG* on 21 June 1884 under the name of 'Jacob Cavendish, M.A.' These new verses were cynical to a degree, mostly on the theme of matrimonial betrayal, among them a parody of a popular drawing-room ballad of the period that began, 'In the gloaming, oh my darling'. Ruddy's version cut to the quick:

> In the spring time, oh my husband,
>   When the heat is rising fast,
> When the coolie softly pulling
>   Puddles but a burning blast,
> When the skies are lurid yellow,
> When our rooms are 'ninety-three',
>   It were best to leave you, ducky –
> Rough on you, but best for me.

Even more disquieting was the nursery rhyme which the 'nursing mothers of Anglo-India' were advised to sing to their babes:

> I had a little husband
>   Who gave me all his pay.
> I left him for Mussoorie,
>   A hundred miles away.
>
> I dragged my little husband's name
>   Through heaps of social mire,
> And joined him in October,
>   As good as you'd desire.

The inspiration for these ballads of infidelity and betrayal was not hard to find, for every day Ruddy had to cut and paste the several pages of advertisements that appeared in the paper. Both the *CMG* and the *Pioneer* ran personal columns which carried notices advertising such items for sale as polo ponies, bay Waler geldings, Swiss cottage tents, barouches or express rifles, often accompanied by the subheading 'owner going Home'. Another popular category was 'Houses to let for Season', which gave details of cottages available to rent at one or other of the Himalayan hill-stations. However, a third category was for miscellaneous notices under the heading of 'New Advertisements', within which were to be found a breathtaking number of private messages whose intent was all too clear – and which must have been pored over daily in messes and clubs in every Civil Station and cantonment in Upper India. Two examples selected more or less at random from one issue of the *CMG* will suffice:

> Darling, your letter safely received, write fully as promised, nothing to fear from my quarter. I will not write to you without your permission, G. B.

> Hope you will enjoy your ten days at F——h, from the 22nd with your old pal, do not forget your make up box, after which sing "Ask nothing more of me."[32]

These personal advertisements show that adultery was alive and flourishing in British India in the 1880s.

The Hot Weather of '84 was more harsh than that of '83. Again Ruddy began by treating it as a trial of strength and delighted in his capacity to rise to the double challenge, for Stephen Wheeler had once more made an early departure for the hills, suffering from fever and 'ulcer of the cornea'. In early June Ruddy wrote to his Aunt Edith bragging of the hardships – and how well he was surmounting them:

A two mile ride with the thermometer at 122° has skinned my
nose, and the iron of my giglamps has burnt a blue horse-shoe
over the bridge of it, but there are times when Life is really
worth living . . . It's curious to note how the weather trains one
down. Just now I am 8 st. 5 lbs. And the Pater chaffs me about
my slimness. He calls it 'leanness' which is vulgar. I prefer to
consider it hard condition . . . The beauty of Lahore in the hot
weather is that you can carry on as you will and there is no one
to say 'don't'.

Together with some subalterns from Mian Mir Ruddy rode out
late one evening into a dust storm and came home 'singing and
shouting along the deserted roads like children out for a holiday'.[33]
He and they also hosted an intimate moonlight picnic in Lahore's
Shalimar Gardens, eighty neglected acres of what had been
Emperor Shah Jehan's once famous pleasure garden – 'great sheets
of still water, inlaid marble colonnades, and carved marble couches
at the edge, thick trees and lime bushes and acres of night bloom-
ing flowers that scented the whole air . . . We just sat around and
talked and then the women began to sing naturally and without
pressing and the voices came across the water like the voices of spirits.'[34] These two events were afterwards merged to provide the
setting for 'False Dawn', in which the unfortunate Saumarez accidentally proposes to the wrong sister in the Shalimar Gardens
during a dust storm. 'Moonlight picnics,' declares the narrator in
a quintessentially Kiplingesque passage, 'are useful just at the very
end of the season, before all the girls go away to the Hills. They
lead to understandings, and should be encouraged by chaperones
especially those whose girls look sweetest in riding-habits. I knew
a case once. But that is another story.'[35]

But as the heat continued to build, the isolation of the bungalow became increasingly hard to bear and Ruddy's resolve began
to weaken. 'Alone in the big dark house my eyes began their old
tricks again,' he confessed to Edith Macdonald. 'I was so utterly
unstrung (you'd be as bad if you sweated twenty four hours a day

for three weeks on end) that they bothered me a good deal. I could only avoid the shadows by going sixteen hours grind a day at office.'[36] Fearing that he was about to suffer a physical and mental collapse similar to that experienced at Christmas 1876, Ruddy became increasingly unnerved.

By the end of June conditions for the few remaining Europeans on the Station had become all but intolerable. At the Club 'sudden causeless hates flared up between friends and died down like straw fires; old grievances were recalled and brooded over aloud; the complaint book bristled with accusations and inventions'. Back in the bungalow there was 'the taste of fever in one's mouth, and the buzz of quinine in one's ears; the temper frayed by heat to break-ing-point but for sanity's sake held back from the break; the descending darkness of intolerable dusks; and the [no] less sup-portable dawns of fierce, stale heat'. One solution tried and abandoned was to drag the bed from room to room in search of less heated air, another to sleep on the bungalow's flat roof, 'with the waterman to throw half-skinfuls of water on one's parched carcase'. A third was to leave the bungalow altogether and walk, and it was this option that Ruddy now began to follow with increasing fre-quency: 'Often the night got into my head . . . and I would wander till dawn in all manner of odd places – liquor shops, gambling- and opium-dens, which are not a bit mysterious, wayside entertain-ments such as puppet-shows, native dances; or in and about the narrow gullies under the Mosque of Wazir Khan.'

What Ruddy discovered on these night prowls was that 'much of real Indian life goes on in the hot-weather nights', and that as a newspaperman he was invested with a kind of invisibility denied other sahibs: 'Having no position to consider, and my trade enforc-ing it, I could move at will in the fourth dimension . . . Sometimes, the Police would challenge, but I knew most of their officers, and many folk in some quarters knew me as the son of my Father, which in the East more than anywhere else is useful. Otherwise, the word "Newspaper" sufficed; though I did not supply my paper with many accounts of these prowls.'[37]

These night walks first began in the summer of '84 and the three and a half months during which Ruddy had sole occupancy of Bikaner House – although these months were not consecutive. At the start of August the 'Amber Toad' returned from his sick leave, leaving Ruddy free to take off to Dalhousie for a four-week break. 'For one blessed month I am become a child again,' he wrote to his Aunt Edith midway through his leave. Despite incessant rain 'we four have been very happy. In the daytime it is my business to go awalking or ariding when the weather permits; to play hop scotch with Mr Kipling; to shoot with an air gun at a target, drink bottled beer (a thing impossible in the plains) and to write poems – at the rate of one a day.'[38]

This is one of a number of the surviving letters to Edith Macdonald which are incomplete, suggesting a family censor at work, and since Ruddy had arrived in Dalhousie bringing with him the first printed copies of *Echoes* it seems reasonable to speculate that in this instance the lost page carried some reference to his family's reaction to his additional verses. Ruddy mailed copies of *Echoes* to family members and friends in England, each with a flattering dedication added to the fly leaf, and no doubt his parents' copies (which no longer survive) were as sweetened with compliments as the others, but it is hard to believe that Alice in particular could have been anything but dismayed by her son's public harping about a wife who escapes to the hills to cheat on her 'little husband' in the plains. Could Ruddy have been trying to make a point? At least one biographer has suggested that both Ruddy's parents had eyes for the opposite sex, but evidence of actual impropriety is scant. It does seem odd, however, that the first book of poetry Rudyard Kipling assembled and published by his own hand should not get so much as a mention in *Something of Myself*.

What is equally curious is the first verse inscribed in a copy of *Echoes* sent to Mrs Tavernor Perry, a woman who had become something of a confidante to Ruddy in London a year earlier. 'Who is the Public I write for?' he asks,

Men 'neath an Indian sky
  Cynical, seedy and dry [?]
Are these then the people I write for?
  No, not I.[39]

Echoes failed to impress its Anglo-Indian readership, the *Indian Review* going so far as to declare that some of the verses it contained 'ought never to have been published at all'. However, literary London did take some note. A review in the *World* magazine called it 'a clever little book' and singled out for praise the 'Nursery Rhymes for Little Anglo-Indians'.

Ruddy returned to Lahore at the start of September to find Wheeler down with another of his bouts of ill-health and the editor's desk filled by one of the *Pioneer's* assistant editors from Allahabad, Mr Macdonald. He took advantage of the Amber Toad's absence to place in the *CMG* his first sustained piece of fiction to be published in India, again under the pseudonym of 'Jacob Cavendish, M.A.' Written in the cod-archaic language of Daniel Defoe, 'The Tragedy of Crusoe, C. S.' purports to be the diary of Mr Crusoe of the Punjab Civil Service, who returns from the Hills without Mrs Crusoe and finds that without her controlling presence his man Friday can turn his life into a living hell within the space of a week. 'Found this morning that I had but one clean shirt,' runs part of Crusoe's entry for the sixth day: 'Now I know I had twelve when I left my wife, so askt of Friday – who walks as though the ground was air under him – what had become of all my gear. At this he wept for ten minutes (over mine only towel) and prayed me to send him to prison since I had blackt his face this far.'[40]

'The Tragedy of Crusoe, C. S.' drew heavily on a vein of Anglo-Indian satire made popular by George Aberigh-Mackay, G. H. Keene and others, but there was an undercurrent of desperation beneath the humour, enough to hint that all was not well with its author. Within days of its publication Ruddy went down with what his older self termed a 'break down', brought on by 'straight overwork, plus fever and dysentery'.[41] Ruddy had always had a morbid fear of dirt and disease. Even in his days as editor of the *United Services College Chronicle* he had proclaimed himself 'death on drains and water-supply' and in Lahore he had missed no opportunity to write up anything that touched on the city's sanitation. Back in May he had been greatly disturbed when one of the office orderlies at the *CMG* was struck down by what was said to be cholera. 'The Abominable has come into the station,' he had written. 'I saw her knock a man down. He died in a trifle under two hours.'[42]

But Ruddy had been even more perturbed when he returned from Dalhousie in September to find that the typhoid had spread to the Civil Lines, affecting eleven out of the seventy adults on the Station: 'The men sat up with the men and the women with the women. We lost four of our invalids and thought we had done well. Otherwise, men and women dropped where they stood. Hence our custom of looking up anyone who did not appear in our daily gatherings.' This stiff-lipped account of the outbreak set down in *Something of Myself* carries no hint of the fears that assailed the eighteen-year-old every evening when he retired to his bungalow, not just the night horrors but a real terror of *cholera morbus*, the killer that struck seemingly at will and was still believed by the best medical men of the time to be 'a poison, which may be transmitted from adjacent places through the air'.[43] Hence Kipling's view of cholera as 'manifestly a breath of the Devil that could kill all on one side of a barrack-room and spare the others'. Something of the fear he felt was caught in two early poems written over this period: 'The Moon of Other Days', in which he talks of a 'seething city . . . unkept, unclean';[44] and 'The City of the Heart', in which he imagines himself riding through the streets 'in the hush of a hopeless night' and finding himself surrounded by a pack of pi-dogs, a 'yelping, yellow crew' which he can only keep in check 'with the dog-whip of Work and Fact'.[45]

In the middle of the night of 16 September Ruddy was woken by violent stomach spasms. He tried to find his medicines in the dark and failed, and began calling out for his manservant, Kadir Baksh:

> When I had dug up my man he lit a lamp and took a look at me and straightway bolted out of the house. That made me fancy that I must have got a touch of the 'sickness that destroyeth in the noonday' as distinguished from the other article and I poured myself a stiff dose of chlorodyne and sat down to await the march of events and pray for the morning. I had hardly rolled on the floor however before my man turned up for the second time with a naked oil lamp, a little bottle and a queer-looking weapon in his hand. The fellow had brought me opium and a pipe all complete.

Believing that he had nothing to lose, Ruddy took the pipe and began to smoke it: 'Presently I felt the cramps in my legs dying out and my tummy more settled and a minute or two later it seemed to me that I fell through the floor. When I woke up I found my man waiting at the bed side where he had put me, with a glass of warm milk and a stupendous grin.' Although Ruddy felt well enough to go to work, Macdonald told him afterwards that he 'came into the office with every sign of advanced intoxication'. Ruddy promptly sent an account of this incident to his Aunt Edith, which he closed with a tribute to Kadir Baksh: 'You may guess how grateful I am to him for his prompt action. He vows and declares that I was going to have a touch of the sickness that is loose in our City now. Whether he is right or wrong I know not but . . . no woman could have tended me more carefully than he through those three terrible hours between eleven and two.'[46]

This was Ruddy's only publicly acknowledged experience of opium-taking, but by his own admission it was combined with 'a stiff dose of chlorodyne', which was itself a mixture of opium in alcoholic solution, tincture of cannabis and chloroform. There is convincing evidence that this double dose hit him with the force of a revelation.[47] In modern parlance, it 'blew his mind', opening the doors of his unconscious hitherto kept tight shut and causing him to lose some of his fearfulness. His letters[48] show that from this time on he continued to rely on opiates, in the form of opium, morphine and *bhang* or Indian hemp medicinally taken, to get him through Lahore's hot summer nights – nights of real horror which, as he confessed in *Something of Myself*, he came to dread more and more with each passing year and 'cowered in my soul as it [the Hot Weather] returned'. This drug-taking was by no means as shocking then as it might appear today: heat-induced 'night terrors' were recognised as a medical condition by such authorities as the Surgeon-General of India and routinely treated with bromide of potassium and Dr Collis-Browne's Chlorodyne, patented in 1871. A well-known side-effect of this treatment was hallucination, never more lucidly described than in a quite extraordinary piece of writing that appeared unsigned in the *CMG* on 7 August 1885 under the title of 'De Profundis', complete with bravura passages that an habitual user could instantly recognise as 'tripping' – and a 'bad trip' at that. 'Here you are alone,' runs one of these passages,

> utterly alone on the verge of a waste of moonlit sand, stretching away to the horizon. Hundreds and thousands of miles away lies a small silver pool, not bigger than a splash of rain water. A stone is dropped into its bosom, and, as the circles spread, the puddle widens into a devouring, placid sea, advancing in mathematically straight ridges across the sand. The silver lines broaden from east to west, and rush up with inconceivable rapidity to the level of your eyes. You shudder and attempt to fly.

After being swallowed by mountains and pursued by rivers, the 'you' who recounts these hallucinations finds himself on a wayside railway station amid burning sands awaiting the train that will bear him away from his pain:

> At length it comes. Showing first as a tiny speck on the polished burning metals, nearer, nearer, nearer, in a reverberating

crescendo, till it halts hotter even than the mid-day sun, a mon-
ster of winking brasswork and roaring fires. From the foot-plate,
where he has hidden himself until now, leaps off a royal Bengal
tiger with yellow eye balls and open jaws, and as he springs at
your throat, the masterless train flies away out of your reach, and
disappears as rapidly as it came.

The nightmare ends at dawn with the 'first deep draught of iced
water that Kurim Buksh – taught by experience – brings with *chota
hazree* ['little breakfast', usually a cup of tea]'.

Ruddy's involuntary drug-taking begun in mid-September
brought a new dimension to his thinking. The transformation can
be seen in a letter written to his cousin Margaret Burne-Jones, now
aged eighteen, who over the course of the next year was to
become his closest confidante, one referring to the other as the
'Wop of Asia' and the other hitting back with 'Wop of Albion'. In
one paragraph Ruddy sums up for her his received opinion of
Indian culture:

> If you knew in what inconceivable filth of mind the people of
> India were brought up from their cradle; if you realised the
> views – or one tenth of the views – they hold about women and
> their absolute incapacity for speaking the truth as we understand
> it – the immeasurable gulf that lies between the two races in all
> things[,] you would see how it comes to pass that the
> Englishman is prone to despise the natives – (I <u>must</u> use that mis-
> leading term for brevity's sake) – and how, except in the matter
> of trade, to have little or nothing in common with him. Now
> this is a wholly wrong attitude of mind but it's one that a Briton
> who washes, and don't take bribes, and who thinks of other
> things besides intrigue and seduction most naturally falls into.
> <u>When he does</u> – goodbye to his chances of understanding the
> people of the land.

But Ruddy had also recognised that as long as he continued to think like that and hide behind the purdah of the Civil Station and its moral values he could never cross the racial divide: 'Underneath our excellent administrative system; under the piles of reports and statistics; the thousands of troops; the doctors; and the civilians [ICS] runs wholly untouched and unaffected the life of the people of the land – a life as full of impossibilities and wonders as the Arabian nights . . . immediately outside of our own English life, is the dark and crooked and fantastic, and wicked, and awe inspiring life of the "native".'

To understand this 'dark' India and conquer one's fear of it meant putting one's prejudices to one side and reaching out. In Ruddy's own words, he had to 'penetrate into it' – and by the end of the year he could report to the 'Wop of Albion' that he was putting what he had learned from this penetration into the pages of a novel, to be entitled *Mother Maturin*: 'Heaven send that she may grow into a full blown novel before I die – My experiences of course are only a queer jumble of opium dens, night houses, night strolls with natives; evenings spent in their company in their own homes (in the men's quarter of course) and the long yarns that my native friends spin me, and one or two queer things I've come across in my own office's experience. The result of it all has been to interest me immensely and keenly in the people.'[49]

This growing interest in Indian India was further whetted by Ruddy's reading of a new novel, *Lalun the Beragun, or The Battle of Panipat: A Legend of Hindoostan*, published in Bombay earlier in 1884 by one Mirza Moorad Alee Beg 'Gaekwaree', a Native of Bhavanagar princely state. It was thought to be the first-ever novel written in English by a Muslim, and gave its readers a far more convincing glimpse into the lives of Indian Muslims than that conjured up by the author of *Lalla Rookh* and other British writers; for Ruddy it provided an invaluable source of information. Quite soon – and how soon has still to be determined – it became known that Mirza Moorad Alee Beg was a fraud: no Indian but an English clergyman's son who had converted to Islam while working for the Maharaja of Bhavnagar, only to then become a Theosophist after meeting Madame Blavatsky in Bombay. Following Madame Blavatsky's public exposure in 1882–3 the unfortunate Moorad Alee Beg had suffered a mental breakdown, conceiving a hatred of her so violent that he had to be confined, and eventually dying insane.

Exactly when Ruddy first heard of Moorad Alee Beg's true antecedents is uncertain, but he had only to read the book's introduction to learn that its author had suffered a series of misfortunes in life which had taken him to the very edge of despair. That reading appears to have preceded the episode of the night cramps and the opium-and-chlorodyne binge on the night of 16 September.

Ten days later, on 26 September, a short story entitled 'The Gate of the Hundred Sorrows' appeared in the *CMG*, under the byline of 'The Janitor', who opens the tale by declaring that 'This is no work of mine. My friend, Gabral Misquitta, the half-caste, spoke it all, between moonset and morning, six weeks before he died; and I took it down from his mouth as he answered my questions.' A rambling monologue follows, as Misquitta describes his life as an opium addict, centred on the opium den of the title, sited 'between the Coppersmith's Gully and the pipe-stem seller's quarter, within a hundred yards, too, as the crow flies, of the Mosque of Wazir Khan'. As Misquitta describes the regulars who gather to smoke the 'Black Smoke' he explains how he became an addict, how it destroys all who partake of it and how he awaits his own end with an addict's fatalism. Misquitta's underworld is filled with grotesques, yet entirely believable. So completely has Kipling entered his poppy-fuddled head that the distinguished English literary critic Andrew Lang was led to declare that as an expression of drug-induced writing the tale 'defeats de Quincey on his own ground'.[50]

Mid to late September 1884 marked Ruddy's literary coming of age. The publication of 'The Gate of the Hundred Sorrows' in the *CMG* on 26 September was sandwiched between his cutting verses on the departing Viceroy, 'Lord Ripon's Reverie', published on 15 September, and 'The Story of Tommy' on 29 September. They constitute a turning point in Rudyard Kipling's creative life: the moment when the young writer throws off the protective carapace grown during his English exile and with it his dependency on English literary models – including his need for the security of the Family Square, which for all its Pre-Raphaelite modishness was deeply conventional.

T. S. Eliot once wrote that 'some forms of illness are extremely favourable, not only to religious illumination, but to artistic and literary composition', and he could well have cited Rudyard Kipling as a classic case. A combination of circumstances – overwork, a lonely bungalow and the night terrors, an involuntary drug-taking, a horror of rampant disease and, at the back of it all, a lurking fear that he might be going mad – had combined within the cauldron of a hot September night to break down the inhibitions of an eighteen-year-old, freeing him to speak more directly from within himself. It did not mean that he abandoned his former self, far from it. Rather it gave voice to another aspect of his personality, long suppressed: that of his Bombay childhood, when he had moved freely between worlds as a child of many parts.

With that rediscovery his imagination sloughed off the inhibitions holding it in check, leaving him free to write with a facility and a versatility that at times became positively Mozartian in its brio and industry. 'I chuckle a good deal over the week's work,' was how Ruddy concluded his letter to his Aunt Edith on 17 September, 'and am meditating a whole series of fresh assaults . . . But Lord! Lord! What vanity is this. Here am I, just helped by my servant out of something exceedingly unpleasant to say no more, and with my head still ringing like a bell from the fumes of that infernal opium, plotting and planning and crowing on my own dunghill as though I were one of the immortals.'[51]

7

'The Oldest Land'

THE PUNJAB AND SIMLA, 1885

A stone's throw out on either hand
  From that well ordered road we tread,
And all the world is wild and strange:
  Churel and ghoul and *Djinn* and sprite
Shall bear us company tonight,
  For we have reached the Oldest Land
Wherein the Powers of Darkness range.

Verse heading to 'In the House of Suddhoo', first published
in the Civil and Military Gazette, 30 April 1886

In December 1884 Lord Ripon left India a disappointed man, acclaimed by crowds of Bengalis in Calcutta but reviled by the bulk of the Anglo-Indian community. His successor was the fifty-eight-year-old Anglo-Irish aristocrat Frederick Blackwood, 3rd Earl of Dufferin and Clandeboye, ex-Eton and Christ Church, witty, urbane to the point of caricature and a man of letters, as befitting a descendant of Sheridan on his mother's side. 'Charming in manner,' was how one of his senior political staff later described him, 'no shyness or awkwardness, a touch of blarney, a quick temper, a slight or more than slight lisp, and a very decided will.'[1] Besides terms as Governor-General of Canada and Ambassador in Turkey, Lord Dufferin had served under Palmerston as Under-Secretary for India, so that he came to India well-versed and not altogether surprised to find the country 'divided into two camps with Natives and Anglo-Indians yelping at each other across a ditch'.[2] Yet he was well received by the British community. 'If Lord Dufferin had not come,' wrote Lockwood Kipling to Edith Plowden, 'I think poor Anglo-India would have gone crazy with vexation and apprehension but we have no end of confidence in the new man.'[3]

The commencement of the Dufferin viceroyalty marked an upturn in the fortunes of the Kiplings. During his visit to Calcutta the year before Lockwood Kipling had been taken up by the Duke of Connaught, the third son of Queen Victoria and newly appointed to the post of Divisional Commander at Meerut. Lockwood gave the Duchess of Connaught advice on collecting Indian brassware, and his enthusiastic advocacy of traditional Indian craftsmanship led the Connaughts to become patrons of his work. In December 1884 the Connaughts visited Lahore, where, after touring the workshops of the Mayo School of Industrial Art they placed an order for the decoration of a billiard room and a smoking room in their home at Bagshot Park in Surrey, both rooms to be panelled throughout in wood carved in traditional eighteenth-century Punjabi style. This was a most prestigious contract and a formidable one, requiring more than five hundred panels, mouldings and other fixtures that would take four years to complete. Combined with the Government of the Punjab's decision to entrust him with the design for a new building to house the Punjab Museum, it confirmed Lockwood Kipling as the leading British authority on Indian arts and crafts. The Duchess of Connaught also put him in touch with the administrator-poet Sir Alfred Lyall, now Lieutenant-Governor of the North-Western Provinces, and together they founded a new magazine, the *Journal of Indian Art*, with Lockwood as its editor.

Things were also beginning to go well for the younger Kipling. In November 1884 Ruddy had submitted two poems to the *Pioneer*: 'The Moon of Other Days' and 'To the Unknown Goddess'. Both were published pseudonymously, and to his great joy he received in payment one gold *mohur*, a Mughal coin then worth about sixteen rupees, and a note from George Allen offering to publish in the *Pioneer* 'anything I might choose to send'.[4] He responded with 'In the Spring Time', a bitter-sweet poem written as an Indian homage to Robert Browning's famous lamentation of the Englishman in exile, 'Home Thoughts from Abroad':

My garden blazes brightly with the rose-bush and the peach,
  And the *köil* sings among them in the *siris* by the well,
From the creeper-covered trellis comes the squirrel's
    clattering speech,
  And the blue jay screams and flutters where the cheery *Sat-bhai* dwell.
But the rose has lost its fragrance and the *köil's* note is
    strange, –
  I am sick of all this splendour, sick of blossom-burdened
    bough –
Give me back the leafless woodlands where the winds of
    spring-time range,
  Give me back one day in England, for it's Spring in
    England now!
In the pines the winds are waking; o'er the brown fields
    blowing chill;
  From the furrow of the ploughshare comes the scent of
    fresh-turned loam;
And the hawk nests in the cliffside, and the jackdaw in the
    hill,
  And my heart is back in England mid the sights and sounds
    of home.
But the 'garland of the sacrifice' this wealth of rose and peach
    is;
  Ah! *köil*, little *köil*, singing on the *siris* bough,
In my eyes the knell of exile your ceaseless bell-like speech
    is –
  Can *you* tell me aught of England, or of Spring in England
    now?[5]

Lyrical and confident in metre, 'In the Spring Time' was arguably the best thing he had written since 'Ave Imperatrix'.

Ruddy had now entered his nineteenth year, and since his discovery of Lahore's dark side he had begun to follow a more independent way of life. By happy chance, a diary left behind in the *CMG*'s offices when he moved on to Allahabad was later found and preserved,[6] allowing a rare glimpse into the private life that Kipling afterwards worked so hard to erase from the record. It runs from mid-December 1884 through to early October 1885 and was intended to be a working diary, most of the entries being limited to details of work in progress and remarks of the sort expected of a hard-working journalist trying to fit in his own creative writing. The very first entry, dated 8 December 1884, begins: 'Mem. to finish handsomely the 'Village of the dead' which was taken in hand three days ago.' Over the next weeks the progress of this work is noted and charted:

> *Saturday 10 January*: Wrote three scraps . . . and did seriously take in hand – having a spare hour at three, my City of the Dead – wh. may be some use eventually.
> *Thursday 15 January*: A bad day and a worse headache . . . so fell back on the Village of the Dead and Among the Houhnyms and did something to each.
> *Saturday 17 January*: Wrote scrap on attempted assassination of Munquldass Nathoobhoy . . . Also my Village of the Dead.

By 23 January 1885 'Village of the Dead' had become 'The Strange Ride of Morrowbie etc.', clarified a day later with the entry: 'Did a lot to Morrowbie Jukes who is beginning to look well.' So the story continued to take shape, each entry showing that 'Morrowbie Jukes' was written in snatched breaks between official duties at the office.

What the diary entries make clear is that much of Ruddy's creative writing was now taking place away from the eyes of his family – and that his taste for night explorations whetted the previous summer had further developed, with the city of Lahore providing rich material for copy. 'Dug up a couple of opium dens in the city,' runs one telling diary entry. 'Queer night altogether. Suddhu is his name.' Suddhu duly became 'Suddhoo', the tale of a white-haired old man who owns a two-storey house near the Taksali Gate and rents out rooms to two Kashmiri courtesans, Azizun and Janoo. All three are characters in a tale of *grand guignol* in which they and the English sahib who narrates it witness a terrifying act of magic in a darkened room.[7] Written at this same period was a poem submitted to the *Calcutta Review* – the first to be printed in India giving his full name as author. Written in blank verse, 'The Vision of Hamid Ali'[8] has obvious links with 'The Gate of the Hundred Sorrows' in that it has a narrator and involves drug-taking, although now the narrator is a Muslim cleric, a *moulvie*, and the drug *ganja*, Indian hemp dried for smoking. Three habitual hashish smokers are gathered late at night in the company of Azizun, Pearl of Courtesans, dreaming of the future glories of Islam when one of them, Hamid Ali, breaks out of his stupor to tell the narrator to set down his vision, in which he foresees the destruction of Islam and all the world's great religions. It is just one of a score of verses written in 1885–6 afterwards repudiated by their author.

On Saturday 7 March Ruddy noted in his diary: 'The idea of "Mother Maturin" dawned on me today.' He would write a great Indian novel – but about an India unknown to his peers. It would 'deal with the unutterable horrors of lower-class Eurasian and native life as they exist outside the reports', it would be 'not one bit nice or proper'[9] and it would be set in Lahore: 'The yard-wide gullies into which the moonlight cannot struggle are full of mystery, stories of life and death and intrigue of which we, the Mall abiding, open-windowed, purdah-less English know nothing and believe less.' In the hands of the right man, 'our City, from the Taksali to the Delhi Gate, and from the wrestling-ground to the Badami Bagh, would yield a store of novels'.[10] By the spring of 1885 Ruddy had no doubts as to who that man would be.

But before Ruddy could make any real headway on *Mother Maturin* he was called to take on his most important assignment to date. The Amir of Afghanistan was to meet the Viceroy at Rawalpindi in the northern Punjab. It would be a grand state occasion, which Ruddy was to attend and report on. Over the previous months the *CMG* had carried a series of lively on-the-scene reports written by its assistant editor which had left the paper's proprietors in no doubt that the boy had a talent for vivid reporting that could be used to greater advantage. Accordingly, on Monday 9 March Ruddy received his orders: to proceed with all speed to the Afghan frontier at Peshawar to await the coming of the Amir.

The Rawalpindi Durbar was the most significant political gathering to be held in India since Lord Lytton's Imperial Assembly of 1877, and no effort was to be spared to ensure that Amir Abdur Rahman was left in no doubt as to his importance to Britain as an ally against Russia – and of the military might of the British Raj. A tented town was laid down outside Rawalpindi on the lines of the earlier Delhi model: Viceroy's Camp at the centre, lesser camps for the visiting Amir, the Commander-in-Chief, the Lieutenant-Governor of the Punjab, various local princes and other dignitaries. But what the organisers could not plan for was the spectacularly foul weather, with days of heavy rain which turned the camp into a quagmire and made a nonsense of the carefully drawn up programme of events. It meant that after a long, bumpy ride in an open *tikka gharri* Ruddy arrived at Peshawar soaked, battered and bruised, his hat cut to bits by hailstones.

The Civil Station was so crowded with visitors that Ruddy was forced to share accommodation in a *dak* bungalow or rest house with a motley assortment of down-at-heel journalists and a hard-drinking loafer. To cheer himself up he went for an evening stroll in Peshawar town, to find himself confronted by scenes which he likened to Dante's *Inferno*. The streets were crammed with pack animals and their drivers, together producing a rank stench 'the

Two Waziri tribesmen, J. L. Kipling (National Trust)

most offensive in the world'. Even more disquietingly, the city's
inhabitants scowled and spat at him as he strolled through the
bazaar. Their hostility unnerved him and he exacted his revenge
by declaring Peshawar to be a 'vast human menagerie' populated
by bestial creatures:

Faces of dogs, swine, weazles, and goats, all the more hideous for being set on human bodies, and lighted with human intelligence . . . all giving the onlooker the impression of wild beasts held back from murder and violence, and chafing against restraint. The impression *may* be wrong; and the Peshawari the most innocent creature on earth, in spite of history's verdict upon him; but not unless thin lips, scowling brows, deep set vulpine eyes and lineaments stamped with every brute passion known to man, go for nothing. Women of course are invisible in the streets, but here and there instead, some nameless and shameless boy in girl's clothes with long braided hair and jewellry – the centre of a crowd of admirers. As night draws on, the throng of ignoble heads becomes denser and the reek of unwashed humanity steaming under the rain, ranker and more insupportable.[11]

Two days later Ruddy's dislike for the local Pathan and Afghan tribesmen was reinforced when he was stoned by a boy as he made his way on foot to Jamrood, the great mud fortress at the foot of the Khyber Pass. The incident might have been forgotten but for the fact that when he arrived back at the Station that evening he ran into a military patrol and found himself staring down the barrels of two loaded carbines. No one had told him that a curfew existed in Peshawar's Civil Lines which came into effect as soon as darkness fell. The fright was over in a moment – but four years on he found himself admitting that he still sweated whenever he thought about it.[12] When he next wrote to his old schoolmate Lionel Dunsterville the stone-throwing boy had become a knife-wielding Afghan whose attack he had foiled by heaving rocks at him[13] – and by the time he came to write his autobiography more than fifty years on the two incidents had merged into one to become a pot-shot fired at him by an Afghan sniper in the Khyber Pass.

After keeping his reception committee waiting and watching at the foot of the Khyber, Amir Abdur Rahman finally made his appearance, and on 30 March the focus shifted to Rawalpindi. The continuing bad weather forced the cancellation of a grand procession of elephants and a day of military manoeuvres, but for the sake of Government *izzat* or prestige it was decided that the planned review should go ahead, despite the mud. The concluding march-past was intended to impress the Amir with a show of armed might as magnificent as only the British military could make it – and it had much the same effect on the youngest and probably the most sceptical of the reporters present:

When twenty thousand men march past in a straight line for two hours, in the presence of the men who will have to make the history of the next four years, the occasion is of anything but ordinary importance; and it is only fair, therefore, to record how superbly the whole function went off . . . Red, khaki, green, buff, maroon coats and facings – an infinity of booted feet coming down and taking up, with the exactness of a machine – thousands of pipe-clayed pouches swinging in the same direction, and all with the same impetus, dazzle the eyes, and produce on the mind, the impression of some interminable nightmare. Finally, one loses all idea that the living waves in front are composed of men. It has no will, no individuality – nothing, it seems, save the power of moving forward in a mathematically straight line to the end of time.

After the infantry come the cavalry, shaking the earth as they came on, to be followed by the artillery, with its horse-drawn batteries passing the grey-clad figure of the Amir on the saluting dais in perfect alignment: 'The Field and Horse batteries go past as one gun. A little thickened and blurred in the outlines, as if seen through a mist, but nevertheless one gun. How it's done, the civilian's mind cannot tell. To all appearance, the driver of the nearer wheeler lays the stock of his whip lightly on the withers of the off wheeler – and there you are, with about six inches between axle and axle, as level as though all six guns have been planed across the muzzles, jammed into a gauge and left there.'[14]

It was an unforgettable spectacle that Ruddy was to revisit in the short story 'Servants of the Queen', and the accompanying poem, 'Parade Song of the Camp-Animals', published in *The Jungle Book*. But his abiding memory was of the marching feet. In the three weeks leading up to the review he had dispatched eleven lengthy articles to the paper, written in extremely trying conditions, so that by the time he came to write his two-column special on the review he was exhausted almost to the point of collapse. 'Phantasm of hundreds of thousand of legs all moving together have stopped my sleep altogether,' he wrote in his diary that same night, Tuesday 7 April. 'Top of head hot and eyes are beginning to trouble me.' The phantasm stayed with him. It inspired the beat of marching feet which gives 'Danny Deever' its relentless pace, and it was reanimated many years later in the mesmeric tramp-tramp-tramp to his poem 'Boots'.[15]

Once the talks and ceremonials were over and the Amir escorted back over the border, the Dufferins descended on Lahore with their royal guests the Connaughts. As always, no effort had been spared to present the city *en fête*, leaving Lady Dufferin with the impression that everything was covered in roses: 'One drives through hedges of them,' she wrote in her journal, 'and there are great bushes, and arches, and trees covered in them; it seems to me to be a real city of gardens.'[16] An address at the railway station was followed by a durbar in Montgomery Hall and then a little sight-seeing, concluding with a visit to the Mayo School of Industrial Art. Here Lady Dufferin noted that 'the only uncommon sight was a row of juvenile carpenters, about eight years of age, learning their trade. They begin with carving, and they sit on the floor as only an Oriental can sit, working away with a chisel and a hammer on a sort of wooden copy-book and using their toes almost as much as their hands.' The visit provided an opportunity for Lockwood and Alice Kipling to be introduced to the Dufferins by the Duke of Connaught, and to be noticed.

From Lahore the Dufferins and the Connaughts proceeded directly to Simla, where the Vicereine, the formidable Hariot Lady

Dufferin, likened their accommodation at Peterhof to Noah's Ark balanced on Mount Ararat. 'Altogether it is the funniest place!' she wrote in her journal. 'But I do feel that it is very unfit for a Viceregal establishment. At the back of the house you have about a yard to spare before you tumble down the precipice, and in front there is just room for one tennis court before you go over another. The ADCs are all slipping off the hill in various little bungalows, and go through most perilous adventures to come to dinner.' Simla itself seemed little better: 'Walking, riding, driving, all seem to me to be indulged in at the risk to one's life . . . I never saw a place so cramped in every way out of doors.'[17]

However, the Blackwoods were made of stern stuff and with their two eldest daughters, Lady Nelly and Lady Rachel, they lost no time in setting the pace for the Simla Season, with an exhausting round of *burra khanas*, state balls, 'fancy' adult balls, children's fancy balls, dances, evening receptions, garden parties, gymkhanas and *pagal khanas* or 'fools' dinners' – the Indian term for picnics, for who else but fools would deliberately eat food out on a hillside when they had homes to eat in. By the end of the Season in mid-October the Dufferins had played host to more than fifty functions in the cramped confines of Peterhof and had attended four times that number as guests. In his political role as *Mulki Lat Sahib*, Lord Dufferin was equally commanding, establishing himself as much by his charm as his authority, so that during his four-year term of office British India underwent one of those periods that was afterwards looked back on as a golden age. Among the many who fell under his spell was Walter Lawrence, a friend of the Kiplings from Lahore, in his capacity as a junior under-secretary to Government, who afterwards remembered Dufferin as 'a consummate whip', presiding over 'the best team of Indian administrators ever brought together' and winning the hearts of all who served under him by 'his power of making each think that his one object was to have a good talk with him'. In Lawrence's eyes, Simla under Dufferin was transformed into 'the brightest, wittiest, most refined community I ever knew'.[18] And it was precisely this community that Rudyard Kipling now put under the microscope.

As his reward for his recent exertions on behalf of the *CMG* Ruddy was granted a month's early leave, with the additional bonus of a temporary appointment as the paper's Simla correspondent for the summer – four and a half months in Elysium! The only drawback was James Walker's insistence that he must learn to waltz, which he considered an essential requirement for all Simla correspondents. Hitherto Ruddy had resisted all efforts by his family to teach him, believing himself too clumsy. Now, as his father put it in a letter to Edith Plowden, 'what we at home couldn't persuade him to like, became a duty . . . and he has gone in for it very heartily . . . and being determined to do it well, bids fair to be a very good dancer'.[19]

Much of Ruddy's month of leave was spent in the company of a newly-married friend from the Punjab Public Works Department and his bride on what was then termed a hill tour and would now be called pony-trekking. Their route took them north-east through the Himalayan ranges towards Tibet. Three days out of Simla the track dropped steeply into the Sutlej Valley at Kotgarh, where they stayed in a cottage belonging to a mission school run by a lone European missionary, with a congregation of local hill-women whose younger members struck Ruddy as pretty enough to make him wish 'to be Padre in these parts'. One of their number was duly worked into what became the first of his *Plain Tales from the Hills*, as 'Lispeth',[20] the tragic story of a local beauty baptised by the Chaplain of Kotgarh, who finds an English traveller collapsed in the hills, nurses him back to health and falls in love with him. After assuring Lispeth that he will come back to marry her, the Englishman goes off to hunt butterflies in Assam, and after three months she realises that he and the missionaries have lied to her, whereupon she renounces her faith and goes back to her own kind.

Like most of Kipling's stories, it contained more than a grain of hard truth, for there was such a woman from the Kotgarh mission.

She became the *bibi* or kept woman of an officer in a Gurkha regiment and bore two children by him, both removed to England. After her death she was found to have written a will leaving all her worldly goods to 'Johnnie Baba' and 'Willie Baba'. The Simla authorities set out to trace the two boys and found one farming sheep in Australia and the other captaining a sailing ship off the coast of Florida.[21]

By 10 May Ruddy was back in Simla and staying by himself in an out-of-the-way cottage. 'Nothing to be done there,' he noted in his diary, adding in subsequent daily entries, 'Loafed and began to count the days to getting in collar,' and 'More loafing . . . Must wait like Micawber for something to turn up.' While he waited he wrote up an account of his trek to Kotgarh and observed a troupe of langurs, long-tailed monkeys with black faces surrounded by a fringe of silvery whiskers, which daily invaded his cottage. The monkeys became the first subject of his 'Simla Notes' for the *CMG*: 'The hillside is alive with their clamour, and presently they assemble in force on the lawn tennis court; despatching a deputation to warn me that the babies are tired and want fruit. It is impossible to explain to the deputation, that the sayings and doings of their descendants are of much greater importance than theirs.'[22] The troupe's leader showed unusual boldness, stealing a pair of hairbrushes from Ruddy's dressing table, and duly became the hero of 'Collar-Wallah and the Poison-Stick', a long-forgotten children's story which features both the Simla langurs and the trek to Kotgarh.[23]

May ended with an invitation to attend a state ball at Peterhof to celebrate the Queen's Birthday. This was the climax of 'Simla Week', which traditionally marked the official start of the Simla Season. Sixteen of the most important guests sat down with the Dufferins in their dining-room, another forty-eight dined in the ballroom and a larger number of the less privileged gathered in a *shamiana* or marquee erected on the lawn, including the *CMG*'s Simla correspondent. 'As all the guests were in uniform,' noted Lady Dufferin in her journal, 'it was very pretty and very gay for an official performance.' But Ruddy was not in uniform and he did not enjoy himself. 'Went with scar on cheek painted up to the Eyes,' he wrote in his diary. 'Felt an abject worm and think looked it.' Three months earlier he had been stung in the face by what he thought was an ant, causing his cheek to develop a nasty sore which his father described somewhat callously as a 'grievous blotch . . . appearing and disappearing as he revolves, like the red bull's eye of a light house'.[24] On the following day, with his cheek so inflamed and swollen that he was unable to work, he had been seen by Dr Lawrie at the Lahore Hospital and treated with cocaine for a nasty case of 'Lahore sore'. This was probably leishmaniasis, caused by a parasite carried by the female sandfly, its symptoms being fever, weight loss and an enlarged spleen. Although it is occasionally fatal, most cases heal spontaneously, as did Rudyard Kipling's, but not before causing him discomfort and embarrassment throughout the summer.

In June Alice Kipling and Trix arrived in Simla for the summer, taking a small cottage named North Bank, one of several belonging to the Civilian Sir Edward Buck. Trix thought Sir Edward a 'vague clever creature' but he was one of Simla's inner circle, acting as *éminence grise* to Lord Dufferin as Secretary to the Viceroy's Council, and he was a powerful and useful friend. The Kiplings were now gratified to find themselves on Peterhof's much-prized 'free list', containing the names of those automatically invited to whatever social functions the Viceroy and Vicereine chose to hold. Whether it was Sir Edward Buck or the Connaughts who initiated the Kiplings' elevation, it was helped along by Alice Kipling, whose boldness caught the attention of the Viceroy, who thereafter 'took such opportunities as offered of conversing with her', leading to 'heartburning among some of the titled ladies'. Lord Dufferin's declaration that 'dullness and Mrs Kipling cannot exist in the same room'[25] swiftly went the rounds of the Simla salons, as did Alice's response when challenged by a female acquaintance over the length of her conversation with the Viceroy: 'Yes, my dear, and it was as broad as it was long.'[26] The consequence was that Alice Kipling came to be regarded as a Simla wit and as someone whose company was to be sought, resulting in what Trix termed 'many pleasant invitations'.

Where the mother led the daughter followed, so that Trix too came to be seen as a delightfully clever young woman, for all that she turned seventeen only that June. A contemporary of Ruddy's at USC who joined him in India after completing his military training afterwards recalled how popular was Mrs Kipling and how her daughter 'Beatrice' had 'inherited most of her mother's wit and skill' – so much so that as a junior subaltern he had found her intimidating. 'Looking back after all these years,' he wrote in 1941, 'it seems to me that I, uncouth youth that I was, felt rather shy in the company of this brilliant, witty girl.'[27] But when Lockwood Kipling joined the two women later in the season he observed how Trix's 'radiant, merry look' had the greatest effect not on Simla's eligible bachelors but on his own age group: 'It is they [–] to whom the beaming grin of happy youth is only a memory – who admire her most.'[28] What was even more vexing for Trix was the ease with which her mother, at forty-nine, filled her dance cards while she remained a wallflower. It prompted her to set down her woes in verse and when, in early July, Ruddy joined the two ladies in their rented cottage, brother and sister at once put their heads together to write 'My Rival'. Published in the *Pioneer* on 8 July under the signature of 'Girofte', it is the lament of a young lady of seventeen who finds herself overshadowed by a rival twice her age – her mother:

> I go to concert, party, ball –
>   What profit is in these?
> I sit alone against the wall
>   And strive to look at ease.
> The incense that is mine by right
>   They burn before Her shrine;
> And that's because I'm seventeen
>   And She is forty-nine.

Wherever she goes and whatever she does, it is always the same story:

> The young men come, the young men go,
>   Each pink and white and neat,
> She's older than their mothers, but
>   They grovel at Her feet.
> They walk beside Her 'rickshaw wheels –
>   None ever walk by mine;
> And that's because I'm seventeen
>   And She is forty-nine.

Trix always maintained that it was she who wrote 'My Rival', but it was her brother who transformed it into a classic of light verse. And there was, of course, another unspoken reason why Trix failed to secure dance partners, which was that unmarried daughters 'came out' in the Simla Season expressly to find marriage partners. An unmarried man who danced with a single woman more than once was making a public statement, and if he was subsequently seen walking beside her rickshaw along the Mall or taking an ice with her at Peliti's it was assumed that an understanding would soon be arrived at, with an engagement to follow. But Trix was not, to put it bluntly, a catch. Her family were not paid-up members of Simla Society, even if judged worthy of mixing with it. Lockwood Kipling's position and salary were published annually in *Thacker's Directory* and the Civil Lists for all the world to see, and because British India was the 'land of the open door' – in a quite literal sense, with curtains instead of doors – all the world knew that his daughter had neither position nor provision. It followed that Trix's dance cards were filled mainly by married men, well aware that no impropriety was allowed where unmarried girls were concerned. Small wonder that Trix took to calling Simla 'looking-glass land'.

Yet Trix was too pretty to go through a Simla season without someone falling for her and by October her father had been driven to comment on how popular with subalterns he had become: 'They didn't use to walk by the side of my pony for a mile at a time, nor did they put on a certain propitiatory air, nor were they careful to slip in an occasional "Sir".' As for Trix, 'her brightness and enjoyment are so striking, even when she is limited to the society of her ancient parents, and she makes so much of the very few and very <u>cutcha</u> girl friends she has here, that I cannot help – tho' I think it somewhat imbecile – echoing her longings for the impossible'.[29] Presumably by 'impossible' Lockwood meant a good match, but his reference to '<u>cutcha</u> girls', meaning the exact opposite of '*pukka*', shows how far Trix still had to go in finding acceptance among the daughters of her parents' friends in Simla Society.

Ruddy had initially moved into North Bank to be with his mother and sister, but when his father joined them for his annual leave at the start of August he took the opportunity to return to his former haunt, James Walker's Kelvin Grove. He needed his privacy, for at North Bank he had made the mistake of showing the two Alices what he had written of his Anglo-Indian novel *Mother Maturin*, now extending to 237 foolscap pages. One had thought it 'nasty' and the other 'awfully horrid', but he was determined to push on with it. 'It is an unfailing delight to me,' he confided to his Aunt Edith, 'and I'm just in that pleasant stage where the characters are living with me always.'[30]

As the *CMG*'s Simla correspondent Ruddy was expected to provide weekly reports on the summer capital's activities, leavening the latest political developments with social tittle-tattle. This he did with a will, in his first column waxing lyrical on the newly installed 'plate-glass boards' in the ballroom at Benmore – 'ample, smooth, springy and cool, the very beau ideal of a dancing room . . . For the first time this season, it has been possible to twirl from the first to the last waltz, without being violently lacerated by military spurs, or hopelessly entangled in feminine trains.' An important advance was made on the dance floor with the Dufferins' introduction of the mazurka, although with mixed results: 'It was possible to see how sadly His Excellency's example has borne fruit. Two or three couples spun round to the measure of the dizzying *deux temps* (there will be two or three hundred before the season is over).' As part of his duties Ruddy attended and duly reported on Simla's Monday Pops and Bachelor's Balls, when groups of single men clubbed together to hire Benmore's ballroom for an evening and invited subscriptions. He reviewed the local theatricals and made rude remarks about Allan Octavian Hume, classifying him as a shrike or butcher bird: 'Originally of a blood thirsty and carnivorous disposition, it had killed 64,000 smaller birds and sucked 18,500 eggs . . . Now, however, it had learned a "more perfect way", and lives exclusively on *dhall* [lentils] and rice, which had not improved either the temper or the plumage of the bird.' He wrote about Simla's drains and found them wanting, and he wrote about 'the Simla baby . . . fearfully and wonderfully spoilt . . . amenable to no law save hunger',[31] ancestor to 'Tods' and 'Wee Willie Winkie'.

The spare room vacated at North Bank had now been turned into a studio where Lockwood held drawing classes for a select clientele that included the two Dufferin daughters. The Viceroy dropped in from time to time, and on one of these occasions met Ruddy and complimented him on his verses – which suggests that Alice had been at work with a copy of *Echoes*. Disarmed by the Viceroy's charm, Ruddy confided in his diary that 'His Excellency [is] an Angel of the first order'.[32]

By the end of July the sore on Ruddy's face was sufficiently healed for him to risk having his photograph taken in a Simla studio. He was reassured that his blemishes would be touched out (as indeed they were; see cover photograph), but feared that 'the sunken brands and red tracings' would leave him scarred for life. He had now been in post as the *CMG*'s Simla correspondent for nearly three months and had become thoroughly disenchanted with the constant round of entertainments, even to the extent of wishing himself back in Lahore. 'I will tell you a secret,' he informed his Aunt Edith in a letter. 'The best way to sicken a youth of frivolity is to pitch him neck and crop into the thick of it on the under-standing that he is to write descriptive matter about each dance, frivol etc. Were it not for my love of waltzing I should abominate the whole business. As it is, the dullest of dull things is to be *chroniqueur* of a Gay Season in the hills.'[33]

His diary entries for his last fortnight at Kelvin Grove suggest that sex was very much on his mind. The room next to him was occupied by a military surgeon known as 'Banjo' Hayes and his wife, whose noisy lovemaking got on his nerves. 'Wish they wouldn't put married couple next door to me with one ½ [inch] plank between,' he jotted in his diary on 1 August. 'Saps one's morality.' The next night was just as bad: 'Same complaint. This is ghastly.' However, on the following evening he attended a Monday Pop at Benmore with a Mrs Hogan and twenty-four hours later was able to report in his diary: 'My own affair entirely. A wet day but deuced satisfactory.' This ambiguous entry was fol-lowed a day later by a second, written in a very different mood: 'Begin to think I've been a fool but ain't certain. Out for a ride round Jakko. Weather vile.' Finally, on 16 August he could write: 'This day I left Simla for Lahore. It was a pleasant three and a half months and taught me much.'[34]

Two days later Ruddy was back in the real world. 'Hell!' he wrote in his diary. '94 in the verandah at four in the morning. Went to office wanting to kill someone.' And on the following day: 'Worse. A blazing day. Took up the reins and went ahead. Dined with the Kers.' The day after that: 'Too savage to swear. Not a soul worth looking at in the Station. Dined with Levett Yeats and laughed. Mem. Must really make my diary a working one. Went home and thought a good deal.' By the fourth day of his return, Friday 21 August, he had had enough. That night he closed his diary entry with two sentences: 'Usual philander in Gardens. Home to count the risks of my resolution.'

Even a cursory reading of this precious diary shows that its author had developed a private life in Lahore that he wished to keep private. Scattered throughout are coded remarks suggesting mysterious contacts and assignations, usually in the form of Latin words and symbols. On Friday 6 February 1885 his entry concludes with two cryptic sentences: 'Mem. eris cum Ⅎ Thursd. Ⅎ a bundobast. My tack is to lie low and wait.' *Bundobast* means an 'arrangement' and the Latin translates as 'Remember you will be with', suggesting that an assignation has been arranged for Thursday with the person identified by the Ⅎ symbol. On the Thursday in question, 12 February, the diary entry ends: 'W.R.W.M.Ⅎ. – a thoroughly satisfactory conclusion.' Two weeks later a further mysterious assignation took place, this time at a site identified as the Shahdera Gardens, an expanse of 'rose-burdened gardens' and acres of decaying Mughal tombs on the banks of the River Ravi much favoured by the younger members of the Station for picnics and romantic assignations. The diary entry on that date ends with a series of indecipherable letters and symbols followed by the remark: 'Jam! on toast.' A week later Ruddy is back in the Shahdera Gardens and his diary entry reads: 'Shadera xxx where found opportunity for another note. There's something wrong there.'

Ruddy's next recorded visit to the Shahdera Gardens was on 21 August after his return from Simla; the 'usual philander' that ended with him returning home to 'count the risks'. What these 'risks' were can be deduced from the diary entries that follow. On Monday 24 August the entire entry is restricted to three words: 'Club. work. anticipation.' On Tuesday the entry is a little longer: 'I wonder! Work of sorts. [indecipherable] and gardens.' On Wednesday longer still: 'Gardens and talk to T. Young. He is sanguine and hopeful. I also. More anticipation.' By Thursday, the tension seems to have gone: 'First period probation over. Mind easier. Now to look about me.'[35]

The only 'T. Young' listed in *Thacker's Directory* as resident in Lahore in 1885 is Civil Surgeon L. T. Young, Professor of Chemistry and *materia medica* at the Lahore Medical School, newly arrived in the Punjab. It is a fair assumption that Ruddy's philandering in the Shahdera Gardens had led him to fear that he might have caught a venereal disease, that he avoided going to the family doctor, Dr Lawrie, and instead sought professional advice from Civil Surgeon Young – and was subsequently relieved to learn that he was uninfected.[36]

From notes left with Lord Birkenhead it is clear that others on the Station knew of Ruddy's night excursions, and did not approve. The priggish Louis Dane of the Indian Political Service was serving in the Punjab Secretariat at this time and afterwards joined with his close friend Francis Younghusband to damn Kipling as a cad who not only acted 'above his station' but let the side down with his roamings in Lahore city, where 'everyone thought he was going for a mucker with the harlotries therein'.[37] That Ruddy did indeed go for a 'mucker' is clear from his letters: in one he writes of being no more capable of abandoning his writing than he can 'put aside the occasional woman which is good for health and the softening of ferocious manners';[38] in another he writes, in reference to the plight of Indian widows, that 'My experience of "widdies" [widows] is extensive and peculiar. The virgin widow takes to prostitution in seventy five cases out of a hundred – 'cos she can't remarry.'[39]

Even though the worst of the Hot Weather was over, his isolation again got to Ruddy, as he admitted in a candid letter to his cousin Margaret Burne-Jones, the 'Wop of Albion'. She too had literary ambitions, and over the course of a series of letters exchanged that late summer and autumn these two developed a relationship so close that Ruddy felt able to tell her that she was 'only one shade less dear to me than my own sister'. In late September Ruddy wrote to Margaret of lonely nights at Bikaner House filled with 'noises and whispers, and sighs and groans and chuckles from headachy dawn to delirious dusk' – and hinting at his own sexual frustration. In the same letter he revealed how he had spent 'one weary weary night on the great minar of the mosque of Wazir Khan, looking down upon the heat tortured city of Lahore and seventy thousand men and women sleeping in the moonlight; and did I not write a description of my night's vigil and christen it "The City of Dreadful Night".'[40]

The night-walk had taken him across the Mall and northwards through the Civil Lines to the Delhi Gate and thence into the city to Wazir Khan's mosque, laying the ground for one of the most atmospheric passages of writing ever to come from his pen:

> Straight as a bar of polished steel ran the road to the City of Dreadful Night; and on either side of the road lay corpses disposed on beds in fantastic attitudes – one hundred and seventy bodies of men. Some shrouded all in white with bound-up mouths; some naked and black as ebony in the strong light; and one – that lay face upwards with dropped jaw, far away from the others – silvery white and ashen gray . . . They lie – some face downwards, arms folded, in the dust; some with clasped hands flung up above their heads; some curled up dog-wise; some thrown like limp gunny-bags over the side of the grain carts; and some bowed with their brows on their knees in the full glare of the Moon.

As the narrator enters the city by the Delhi Gate he is met by 'a stifling hot blast . . . a compound of all evil savours, animal and vegetable, that a walled city can brew in a day and a night.' But he presses on, to enter the open square in front of the mosque of Wazir Khan, crowded with more corpse-like sleepers, through which he picks his way to the foot of the staircase leading to the top of one of the mosque's *minars*, from which the calls to prayer are sounded. He steps over the sleeping janitor and climbs up the corkscrew stairs until at last he can turn and look down on the sleeping city:

> The pitiless Moon shows it all. Shows, too, the plains outside the city, and here and there a hand's-breadth of the Ravee without the walls. Shows lastly, a splash of glittering silver on a house-top almost directly below the mosque Minar. Some poor soul has risen to throw a jar of water over his fevered body; the tinkle of the falling water strikes faintly on the ear. Two or three

other men, in far-off corners of the City of Dreadful Night, follow his example, and the water flashes like heliographic signals. A small cloud passes over the face of the Moon, and the city and its inhabitants – clear drawn in black and white before – fade into masses of black and deeper black. Still the unrestful noise continues, the sigh of a great city overwhelmed with the heat, and of a people seeking in vain for rest.

The narrator's vigil is interrupted by the arrival of the *muezzin* to make the midnight call to prayer:

A bull-like roar – a magnificent bass thunder – tells that he has reached the top of the Minar. They must hear the cry to the banks of the shrunken Ravee itself! Even across the courtyard it is almost overpowering. The cloud drifts by and shows him outlined in black against the sky, hands laid upon his ears, and broad chest heaving with the play of his lungs – 'Allah ho Akbar'; then a pause while another *Muezzin* somewhere in the direction of the Golden Temple takes up the call – 'Allah ho Akbar'. Again and again; four times in all; and from the bedsteads a dozen men have risen up already – 'I bear witness that there is no God but God.' What a splendid cry it is, the proclamation of the creed that brings men out of their beds by scores at midnight! Once again he thunders through the same phrase, shaking with the vehemence of his own voice; and then, far and near, the night air rings with 'Mahomed is the Prophet of God.' It is as though he were flinging his defiance to the far-off horizon, where the summer lightning plays and leaps like a bared sword. Every Muezzin in the city is in full cry, and some men on the rooftops are beginning to kneel. A long pause precedes the last cry, 'La ilaha Illallah,' and the silence closes up on it, as the ram on the head of a cotton-bale.

The call of the muezzin acts like the breaking of a spell and the sleepers awake like the dead rising from their tombs. The narrator continues his vigil until just before the dawn call to prayer, but as he crosses the square before the mosque he is asked to make way for a woman's corpse being taken down to the burning-ghat. A bystander explains, '"She died at midnight from the heat." So the city was of Death as well as Night after all.'

By the end of October the Family Square was once more reunited in Lahore. Lockwood Kipling had at once to concentrate on the 'detestable business'[41] of assembling a collection of Punjab ware and an accompanying catalogue for a forthcoming Indo-Colonial Exhibition. His wife and children, however, were in high spirits as they worked together on a joint enterprise: a supplement to the *CMG*, entitled *Quartette*, to be sent out to all subscribers as a Christmas supplement, its contents consisting of poems and stories written by 'Four Anglo-Indian Writers'. Ruddy had put the proposal to James Walker during his stay in Kelvin Grove and permission had been given to use the *CMG*'s presses and staff. But Stephen Wheeler had not been consulted, and his response was to have nothing to do with the project. Lockwood also refused to help, on the grounds that he was far too busy, and as a result his contribution was limited to four very feeble stories he had written while recovering from his typhoid attack ten years earlier. Both Alice and Trix contributed poems, with Trix also providing a short story about a shipboard haunting which her brother thought 'a neat bit o' work'. However, the bulk of the copy came from Ruddy: five poems and three short stories, of which two were more ambitious than anything he had hitherto written.

The printing of *Quartette* consumed Ruddy's every spare moment for the better part of six weeks. Set after set of the 124 pages of proofs came back from the *CMG*'s typesetters riddled with errors, and time and again the head printer, Ram Dass, had to be cajoled into resetting them. 'If Quartette comes out without a howling misprint in every other line it will be by the blessing of Providence alone,' Ruddy wrote to his cousin Margaret. 'Imagine 513 mistakes in one galley of five pages! The family seem to be rather amused than afflicted by "those absurd misprints" but it's anything but fun for me.' As the deadline of 15 December came and went, it became obvious that the only way to get the book printed in time for Christmas was by bullying and bribing the *CMG*'s labour force into working long past their agreed overtime hours.

The printing of *Quartette* was finally completed at five in the morning on 18 December. At ten the previous evening Ruddy had gone home, leaving the paper's Scottish foreman, Chalmers, to supervise the final print run and the binding. He had returned at midnight to find the workmen on the verge of mutiny. By allowing them to bring in their hookahs and smoke ten at a time, and supplying the tobacco himself, Ruddy brought the men back to work. 'What a mad night it was,' he told the Wop of Albion:

> About two o'clock something went wrong with the title page <u>again</u> and the impression went bad. Got that corrected and kept on. And the lights bobbed, and the native tobacco stank; and I smoked many cheroots; and Chalmers tramped up and down the shifts; and I tramped and read proofs and Ram Dass was heartened a second time with the bottle and it grew colder and wetter and more dismal and the clock struck five. Then was Quartette born and we laid her aside reverently and departed into the dark each our several ways.[42]

Wheeler's revenge was to forbid his assistant to take up an invitation from the Walkers to join them on a tour of Rajputana and Central India. Not that Ruddy minded too much. He knew that the two longer stories contained in *Quartette* were something out of the ordinary – and critical opinion has subsequently judged him right. Both are tales of the supernatural after the manner of Edgar Allan Poe, but a cut above Poe in that they leave us guessing as to how much of each tale is a real haunting and how much the figment of a fevered imagination. The one that had come most easily from his pen was 'The Phantom 'Rickshaw', begun that summer in Simla and finished on his return to Lahore. In his autobiography Rudyard Kipling states that it was in the writing of this story that his 'Personal Daemon' first came to him 'when I sat bewildered among other notions, and said: "Take this and no other." I obeyed and was rewarded . . . Some of it was weak, much of it was bad and out of key; but it was my first serious attempt to think in another man's skin.'

The 'skin' in question belongs to a sick man, Jack Pansay of the Bengal Civil Service, who is persuaded by his doctor that it will ease his mind if he writes out 'the whole affair' from beginning to end. A dramatic monologue in the manner of Gabral Misquitta in 'The Gate of the Hundred Sorrows' follows as Pansay relates to his doctor how he turned his back on his married lover, Mrs Keith Wessington, and how she wreaked her revenge. Having terminated the affair, Pansay had fallen in love with Miss Kitty Mannering, causing Mrs Wessington to die of a broken heart. A year later Pansay returns to Simla to resume his courtship of Kitty, but as he rides out past Combermere Bridge with Kitty laughing by his side he hears his name called and sees a rickshaw drawn by four jampanis dressed in Mrs Wessington's familiar livery of black and white. Inside is Mrs Wessington, 'golden head bowed on her breast'. From then on every time he takes Kitty out for a ride he meets the ghost in her rickshaw crying, 'It's a mistake, a hideous mistake.' His friends think him mad and Kitty breaks off the engagement. With his life in ruins, he meets his dead lover face to face and discovers that he has left the reality of his world and has entered hers:

Mrs Wessington spoke and I walked with her from the Sanjowlie road to the turning below the Commander-in-Chief's house as I might walk by the side of any living woman's 'rickshaw, deep in conversation . . . There had been a garden-party at the Commander-in-Chief's, and we two joined the crowd of homeward-bound folk. As I saw them then it seemed that *they* were the shadows – impalpable, fantastic shadows – that divided for Mrs Wessington's 'rickshaw to pass through.

The second of the two stories was 'The Strange Ride of Morrowbie Jukes', an even more disturbing tale. Again, it is told in the first person – by Morrowbie Jukes, a civil engineer, whose work has taken him far out into a wilderness of sand. His story starts with 'a slight attack of fever'. It is a full moon and the baying of pariah dogs drives Jukes so frantic that he rides out after one particularly large beast with a hog-spear. But his horse slides down an unexpectedly steep slope of sand into a large pit, from which he is unable to extricate himself. He finds himself trapped among a colony of outcastes, victims of cholera and other diseases cast into the pit. Instead of acknowledging him as a sahib, they greet his appearance with derision and mock him. Their leader is an educated Brahmin named Gunga Dass, a *babu* of the sort that Rudyard Kipling most despised, who tells Jukes that 'We are now Republic', and that he must abide by *their* rules, not his. But their rules amount to anarchy, for 'the living dead men had thrown behind them every canon of the world which had cast them out', and Jukes has to fight not only to stay alive but also to preserve his identity as 'a representative of the dominant race'. Just when all seems lost he is saved by the appearance of Dunnoo, the dog-boy, the least of his servants, who has tracked him down and brought a rope with him.

'The Strange Ride of Morrowbie Jukes' can be read as a straightforward horror story in the manner of Poe's 'The Pit and the Pendulum', or as a tale of hallucination brought on by a combination of isolation and fever. But it is also the ultimate Anglo-Indian nightmare, in which roles are reversed and the ruler becomes the ruled, helpless under the tyranny of the Bengali *babu*, who for all his trappings of Western civilisation will plunge India back into the darkness and disorder of its past. From his diary notes we know 'Morrowbie Jukes' was written over a period when Ruddy was just beginning to lose his fear of the predominantly Muslim city of Lahore – but not, it seems, of the Hindu minority of the sort he encountered daily in the law courts and the university, men whose studies of Western models of government had made them ask why those same models could not be applied to India.

Even as copies of the *CMG*'s Christmas supplement were being read and enjoyed up and down the land, a small gathering was taking place in Bombay. Held over the last four days of December 1885, it was attended by seventy-two delegates drawn from all over India and chiefly inspired by three of the Kiplings' *bêtes noires*: Madame Blavatsky, Allan Octavian Hume and Lord Ripon. The delegates declared themselves to be an Indian National Congress, and one of their first published resolutions was that this body should form 'the germ of a Native Parliament' that would constitute within a few years 'an unanswerable reply to the assertion that India is still wholly unfit for any form of representative institution'.

8

'In vigil or toil or ease'

THE PLAINS AND THE HILLS, 1886

Was there aught I did not share
  In vigil or toil or ease,
One joy or woe I did not know,
  Dear hearts across the seas?

From the dedicatory verses to the English edition of
Departmental Ditties, first published in Lahore, 1886

The year 1886 began with a 'New Year's present to the Queen' in the form of the annexation of Burma, achieved with deceptive ease and few casualties, but among them Lieutenant R. A. T. Dury, who had been a year above Ruddy at United Services College. The news of his death in action led Ruddy to comment in a letter to Lionel Dunsterville, 'Did you see that poor Durey [*sic*] was killed by those swine? There's £1,800 worth of education gone to smash and a good fellow with it.'[1] Ruddy had himself asked to be allowed to cover the Burma campaign as the *Civil and Military Gazette*'s special correspondent, but can hardly have been surprised by Stephen Wheeler's answer.

Despite this news Ruddy began his twentieth year in the best of spirits. *Quartette* was being received by the Indian press with 'all manner of sweet and gushing things', a reviewer in the *Bombay Gazette* going so far as to compare 'The Strange Ride of Morrowbie Jukes' to the work of Wilkie Collins. The editor of the *Englishman* was begging for more of his verse to print, and Sir

Auckland Colvin, the Financial Member of the Supreme Council, wrote to congratulate him on his 'wit and delicate humour' after the *CMG* printed Ruddy's poetical squib 'The Rupaiyat of Omar Kal'vin', attacking his financial policies.[2] In fact, the only two persons who did not seem to appreciate Ruddy's literary progress were his chief and his father. Lockwood Kipling was becoming increasingly concerned by the direction in which his son's writing was taking him and the reputation he was gaining in consequence, concerns he expressed in a letter to Margaret Burne-Jones written on 31 January. Its tone helps to explain why Ruddy was so eager to break away from Bikaner House. 'It is of less than no use snarling at Ruddy,' Lockwood declared:

> I was (personally) sorry that <u>Quartette</u> came out, but he had set himself to it so eagerly one didn't like to baulk him. Also I hoped someone would rap his knuckles for the unwholesomeness of the Phantom 'Risha . . . But the Indian Press has given him only praise and his knuckles await a rapping. I am too near, too little of a judge and too personally interested in his eager, vivid life to do much; but anything from you or his Aunt would sink deep . . . So the truest kindness is to speak and spare not.[3]

But if Lockwood expected Ruddy's closest confidante to use her influence to get him to abandon his 'vulgar smartness' he was to be disappointed; the Wop of Albion wisely left the Wop of Asia to write as he thought fit.

Ruddy had other reasons for feeling cheerful: his 'screw' had been increased to 500 rupees a month; he had been reunited with his old school friend Lionel Dunsterville, on his way to join his regiment in Rawalpindi; and he had met a young woman with 'the face of an angel, the voice of a dove and the step of the fawn',[4] going so far as to attend church for the first time in four years. The object of his affections was the 'dark-eyed' Miss Duke, daughter of a clergyman – according to Lockwood Kipling, 'an awful military Chaplain at Mian Mir, who, I am told, preaches impossible sermons . . . The boy for two Sundays has driven five miles to attend Mian Mir Church!'[5] The romance with the clergyman's daughter never got as far as a third Sunday. At an afternoon tea-dance Trix introduced Miss Duke to her brother and after one dance he had had enough, his explanation being that she had 'the breath of the tomb . . . When she leant and whispered something to me I could have fainted.'

Two weeks later a more solid reason for cheerfulness was pro-vided by the visit to Lahore of a journalist from the *Pioneer*'s offices in Allahabad: thirty-one-year-old Kay Robinson, India-born son of George Allen's old partner in Allahabad, the Reverend Julian Robinson, and younger brother of Phil Robinson, the well-known writer of the *Indian Garden* series. After a schooling at Cheltenham and several years in Fleet Street Kay Robinson had followed his elder brother's footsteps by returning to his parents' home in Allahabad to work on the *Pi*. Some Latin verses of his had appeared in the paper under the initials 'K. R.' and shortly afterwards Kay had received a good-humoured letter from Ruddy telling him that he was being complimented on the other's verses. A correspon-dence had begun and in mid-February Kay Robinson took some leave and came to stay at Bikaner House for four days.

It was a visit with consequences. Someone – almost certainly Wheeler – had complained to Allen that the *CMG*'s assistant editor was not pulling his weight, was averse to routine and disliked working on the 'scraps' used to fill the page. Allen had then writ-ten a stiff letter to Ruddy, who had kept uncharacteristically silent: 'I sat tight, he [Allen] being a full mouthed man and one of the [newspaper's] owners to boot.'[6] So Robinson may well have come to Lahore with orders to find out how things stood with the *CMG* and its editorial staff. He challenged Ruddy directly with the charge of slacking and received a furious denial, reiterated in a letter:

The whole settlement and routine of the old rag from the end of the leader to the beginning of the advertisements is in my hands and mine only: my respected chief contributing a blue pencil mark now and then and a healthy snarl just to soothe me. The telegrams also and such scraps as I or my father write are my share likewise; and these things call me to office half one hour before, and let me out, always three-quarters, sometimes one hour behind, my chief. My Sabbath is enlivened by the official visits of the printer and my evenings after dinner are made merry by his demands. So much for the routine of which I am averse.

He went on to answer Wheeler's charge that his 'skits' were being written in office hours: 'The rhymed rubbish and the stuff like "Section 420. I. P. C." [the original title under which 'In the House of Suddhoo' was published] is written out of office for my own personal amusement (I don't play tennis or whist or ride and my driving is no pleasure to me) and then – O my friend – is damned as a waste of time and only put in with a running lecture on the sinfulness of writing such stuff.'[7]

Robinson had come to Lahore expecting to find an aesthete and was initially disappointed by the uncouth appearance of his correspondent: 'his juvenile appearance . . . his stoop . . . his heavy eyebrows, his spectacles, and his sallow Anglo-Indian complexion . . . his jerky speech and abrupt movements'. After ten minutes' conversation, however, Robinson's first impressions were forgotten. The two men very quickly discovered that they had much more in common than a love of literature. Ruddy thought Robinson 'a nice youth and a merry [one]',[8] while Robinson, for his part, found Ruddy 'the best of company, bubbling over with delightful humour'.

Robinson returned to Allahabad convinced that the younger Kipling was a great writer in the making and a hard-working one at that, afterwards declaring in print that 'if you want to find a man who will cheerfully do the work of three men, you should catch a young genius . . . The amount of stuff that Kipling got through in the day was indeed wonderful.' He appears to have passed these sentiments on to Allen – and to Ruddy, too, telling the latter that his talents were lost on British India, where his readership was 'either too preoccupied with dry-as-dust official business, or too devoted to the frivolities of life to regard literature as anything better than a vehicle for the conveyance of ponderous statistics, or a means of embroidering the accounts of polo matches.'[9] He urged him to go to England, where he would 'win real fame, and possibly wealth'.[10]

Ruddy was hugely flattered – 'you ought to know better at your time o' life than to knock a youngster off his legs in this way' – but at twenty the idea of making his way in England did not appeal to him. 'My home's out here,' he wrote back. 'My people are out here; all the friends etc. I know are out here and all the interests I have are out here. Why should I go home[?] Any fool can put up rhymes and the market is full of boys who could undersell me as soon as I put foot in it.' Besides, he was greatly indebted to his employers, believing that the 'personal and purely professional gratitude' he owed Allen, Walker and Rattigan gave them the right to his services 'for as long a time in fact as they may choose to retain them'. And he had another reason for wishing to make his future in India:

I am deeply interested in the queer ways and works of the people of the land. I hunt and rummage among 'em; knowing Lahore City – that wonderful, dirty, mysterious ant hill – blindfold and wandering through it like Haroun Al-Raschid in search of strange things . . . I'm in love with the country and would sooner write about her than anything else. Wherefore let us depart our several ways in amity. You to Fleet Street (where I shall come when I die if I'm good) and I to my own place where I find heat and smells of oil and spices, and puffs of temple incense, and sweat, and darkness, and dirt and lust and cruelty, and, above all, things wonderful and fascinating innumerable.[11]

Gone was the suspicion and hostility that had characterised Ruddy's initial response to the local Punjabi culture, and in its place was an open-hearted infatuation that spoke volumes. Six months earlier Ruddy had shared a train carriage with an Urdu-speaking Pathan magistrate from Peshawar, an encounter which had forced him to revise his earlier judgements on the Afghan people. The Pathan had explained that their two peoples would always think and act differently because they followed different ethical codes: 'God made us different – you and I, your fathers and my fathers. For one thing, we do not have the same notions of honesty and of speaking the truth . . . You come and judge us by your own standard of morality – that morality which is the outcome of your climate and your education and your tradition . . . Who are we to have your morals, or you to have ours?' They had eaten together and when the time had come for them to continue their respective journeys on separate trains the two had parted as friends, but in the knowledge that their peoples had little in common and would always go their own ways. 'God made us – East and West – widely different,' Ruddy had concluded. 'Literally and metaphorically, we were standing upon different platforms; and parallel straight lines as everybody does not know, are lines in the same plane which being continued to all eternity will never meet.'[12]

The exchange foreshadows the philosophy contained in 'The Ballad of East and West', published three years later, which contains perhaps the most quoted and most misunderstood lines Kipling ever wrote: 'Oh, East is East, and West is West, and never the twain shall meet.' The 'Ballad' drew on the true story of Harry Lumsden, founding father of the renowned Corps of Guides Cavalry and Infantry, and his dealings with one of his more difficult early recruits, Dilawar Khan. It is a celebration of two strong men, one English and one Afghan, its message that mutual respect *can* overcome cultural differences, for 'there is neither East nor West, Border, nor Breed, nor Birth, / When two strong men stand face to face, though they come from the ends of the earth!'[13]

Ruddy's reappraisal of the Afghan character had continued after his return to Lahore. In early January 1886 he spent an entire Sunday exploring Lahore's Sultan Sarai – 'that huge open

The Afghan caravansarai, Lahore, J. L. Kipling (Beast and Man)

square . . . surrounded with arched cloisters, where the camel and horse caravans put up on their return from Central Asia'. His initial contact was an Afghan horse-trader named Aslam Khan, known throughout the Punjab for having 'sold more racing and polo ponies to subalterns than any other man in history'.[14] But Aslam Khan then passed Ruddy on to one of his compatriots from Kabul: 'not much over six foot high; wore a jet-black beard, clean *postheen* [fur-lined Afghan coat]; fancifully embroidered Bokhara belt and pouches; looked like a hero of medieval romance'.[15] The burly Afghan took to the bespectacled little *topi-wallah*, and from then on Ruddy and the Kabuli met whenever the latter was passing through Lahore. 'I remember one long-limbed Pathan,' Kay Robinson was afterwards to write, 'indescribably filthy, but with magnificent mien and features – Mahbab Ali, I think was his name – who regarded Kipling as a man apart from other "Sahibs". After each of his wanderings across the unexplored fringes of Afghanistan, where his restless spirit of adventure led him, Mahbab Ali always used to turn up, travel stained, dirtier and more majestic than ever, for confidential colloquy with "Kuppeling Sahib", his "friend".' Robinson was rather in awe of Mahbab Ali, but not so Ruddy: 'I have seen Kipling in his cotton clothes and great mushroom hat, and Mahbab Ali's towering, tur-baned and loose-robed figure, walking together in earnest and confidential colloquy, the queerest contrast that friendship, even in India . . . but Mahbab Ali, peace to his bones, was only one link in the strange chain of associations Kipling rivetted round himself in India.'[16]

It should be noted that Robinson's description of Mahbab Ali appeared in print long before *Kim* was published – a reminder that the Afghan horse-trader 'Mahbub Ali', the most rounded and sympathetic character in the novel after 'Kim' himself and his Tibetan lama, was drawn from life – as indeed was the courtesan Ruddy named 'Lalun, the Pearl', the delightful, devious courte-san in 'On the City Wall', who plies her trade from a little house on Lahore's city wall which looks out across the sandbanks of the Ravi River and the walls of Lahore's Fort. Ruddy took her name from Mirza Moorad Alee Beg's novel *Lalun the Beragun*, but he clearly based her on a city prostitute known to him, and when he returned briefly to Lahore some five years later he made a point of looking out the house where she had lived. References to women prostitutes in two letters written at this time (quoted in the previous chapter) show that Ruddy was now on intimate terms with the city's street women. This intimacy led to a surprising outcome: in February 1886 Ruddy wrote a leader in the paper 'on infant marriage and enforced marriage', and from this time onward the injustices inflicted on Native women by their menfolk became a pet hobby-horse that he rode with ever-increasing vigour.

This growing intimacy with Lahore and its denizens extended to the city's dominant religion: Islam. When Ruddy heard that one of the office *chaprassis* or messengers was planning to attend the city's annual Chiragan Fair, a 'festival of lamps' held in the Shalimar Gardens to honour a local Muslim saint, he asked him to be his guide. 'Nearly every body's *khitmatgar* [butler] and bearer was there,' Ruddy afterwards observed, and it seemed to be rubbed into you that the people who make up our *nauker-log* [servant-people] have the manners and instincts of gentlemen away from their service and on their own ground. Humiliating thing to confess of course; but I fancy it's true. My friend the *chaprassi* will be '*O-chaprassi-idher ao*' [Chaprassi, come here] in another twelve hours and my bondslave for six rupees per mensem as is right and proper and just. But I saw another side of his character on the day he piloted me through the packed tumult of the Chiragan fair of 1886.[17]

Muslims at prayer, J. L. Kipling (National Trust)

From then on Ruddy showed himself to be favourably disposed towards Muslims and Islam in India, even to the extent of writing admiringly of a Wahhabi prisoner in a chain gang, most probably encountered at Lahore railway station while he was being transferred to the Punjab Central Jail behind Lawrence Gardens and the racecourse. The Wahhabis had a long history of anti-British violence and the fomenting of tribal jihads on the North-West Frontier, and were viewed by the authorities as dangerous fanatics. But if Ruddy's verses entitled 'From the Masjid-Al-Aqsa of Sayyid Ahmed (Wahabi)' are to be taken at face value, he had questioned the prisoner at length, and came away greatly moved by the Wahhabi's devotion:

> So I submitted myself to the limits of rapture –
>> Bound by this man we had bound, amid captives his
>> capture –
> Till he returned me to earth and the visions departed;
>> But on him be the Peace and the Blessing; for he was great-
>> hearted.[18]

Nothing better illustrates Ruddy's changed attitude than the 'scrap' he slipped into the *CMG* in early September that same year. In January he had puzzled in the paper over a household servant sentenced to three months' imprisonment for stealing a cricket ball, wondering 'what in the name of everything incongruous can a bearer want with a cricket-ball?'[19] He supplied an answer of sorts in 'The Story of Muhammad Din', which begins with the narrator's *khitmatgar* asking if he has any use for the chipped polo ball on his mantelpiece, which his little son wants to play with. The next day the narrator comes back from the office earlier than usual and surprises the little boy in his room. The boy, Muhammad Din, is given permission to play in his garden and thereafter the two exchange grave *salaams* whenever they meet. This goes on for some months, until one day there is no Muhammad Din to greet the narrator on his return home. He makes enquiries and learns that the boy has fever. A doctor is summoned but departs with the comment that 'They have no stamina, these brats,' and the boy dies. Kipling closes his story with a series of terse, simple sentences, devoid of emotion, making the ending all the more powerful.

'The Story of Muhammad Din'[20] was the third written of the stories that later went into *Plain Tales from the Hills*, 'The Gate of the Hundred Sorrows' and 'In the House of Suddhoo' being the first and second.

On 5 April 1886 Ruddy was initiated as a Freemason in the Lodge Hope and Perseverance, No. 782, at Lahore. What attracted him was Freemasonry's emphasis on universal brotherhood: in a country riven by caste and race, Lodge Hope and Perseverance was neutral territory, where Indians and English met as equals. 'I was entered by a member of the Bramo Samaj [a reformist Hindu movement], passed by a Mohammaden and raised by an Englishman,' he wrote in a letter to *The Times*. 'Our Tyler was an Indian Jew. We met, of course, on the level, and the only differ-ence anyone would notice was that at our banquets some of the Brethren, who were debarred by caste rules from eating food not ceremonially prepared, sat by empty plates.'[21]

In contrast to his dismal record of attendance as a Punjab Volunteer, Ruddy was a regular attender at every monthly meet-ing and acted conscientiously as the Lodge's secretary for a year. He also researched the subject of Freemasonry well enough to be able to present papers to his brother Masons on the 'Origins of the Craft' and 'Some Remarks on Popular Views of Freemasonry', and he took the opportunity to attend meetings at the Military Lodge at Mian Mir, from whose rolls he purloined the names of two fellow Masons: Surgeon-Captain Terence Mulvaney and Lieutenant Learoyd of the Royal Artillery. The older Kipling is said to have declared that Freemasonry was the closest thing to a reli-gion that he knew.[22] Raised as a non-believer, Ruddy nevertheless had a strong religious impulse which Freemasonry satisfied by providing a spiritual centre ground, a sanctuary from which he could emerge as he pleased to explore the plethora of creeds about him. His ballad 'The Mother Lodge' is a tribute to the fellowship he found in Lahore's Lodge Hope and Perseverance and the lodge he joined subsequently when he moved to Allahabad. In the opening verse all the local European trades are listed, in the next all the Lodge's Indian Brothers. 'There ain't such things as infidels,' asserts the poem's soldier narrator, going on to describe how at their monthly meetings the Brothers often end up discussing their respective religions late into the night:

> So man on man got talkin',
>   An' not a Brother stirred
> Till mornin' waked the parrots
>   An' that dam' brain-fever-bird;
> We'd say 'twas 'ighly curious,
>   An' we'd all ride 'ome to bed
> With Mohammed, God, an' Shiva
>   Changin' pickets in our 'ead.[23]

Freemasonry looms large in some of the best of Kipling's fiction. That stirring tale of trickery and derring-do in the mountain fastnesses beyond Afghanistan, 'The Man Who Would Be King', is stuffed with Brother Masons, Masonic talk and Masonic imagery, as is *Kim* to a less obvious degree. In both these major works the 'Craft' is represented by men who can hardly be regarded as shining examples of Freemasonry: the two loafers 'Dravot' and 'Peachey' in 'The Man Who Would Be King', and in *Kim* ex-colour sergeant 'Kimball O'Hara' of the Mavericks, deceased, who leaves his son little else besides a Masonic certificate, a birth certificate and his own name.

That little boy, of course, is Kim, who may have had his origins in a white adolescent boy who for a period in the late 1870s and early 1880s was a familiar figure in the Anarkali bazaar area, where the Mayo School of Industrial Art and the Lahore Museum were located. He was the son of a clerk for the Punjab Government Secretariat, identified only by the first letter of his surname, B——, a retired British soldier who had married a local Indian woman and died after having had several children by her. According to Colonel Goulding, the man who commanded the company of Punjab Volunteers of which Ruddy was briefly a member, the widow and her children 'lived in the bazaar near Kapurthala House where young B—— reigned supreme . . . He was to be seen driving a *tikka gharri* owned by an Indian who had married one of his sisters . . . Hatless and barefooted, with the cunning of a street Arab, this boy roamed about at will, and anything he did not know about bazaar and serai life was not worth knowing . . . The market crossing, where the Zamzammah then stood, was one of his favourite haunts.'[24] At the risk of spoiling a good story, it should be added that a more literacy source for Kim is the Meerut lawyer John Lang's novel *Who Was the Child?*, published in 1859, the child in question being the orphaned son of a sergeant of the 13th Regiment of Foot, raised by Indians and restored to European society after being identified by his signet ring.

At the start of May 1886 Alice and Trix Kipling departed for Simla, as usual, Lockwood following on a month later, so that once more Ruddy was alone to enjoy what he described as the 'desolate freedom of the wild ass' until his own leave began in July. Again the Hot Weather did its worst and by mid-June he was complaining to Margaret Burne-Jones of being 'nearly crazy' for lack of sleep, and of having to be 'hypodermically syringed' with morphine by the doctor. He had been suffering nightmares ever since reporting on a fatality at the Lahore High School, where the roof had collapsed killing three boys as they slept. Since visiting the scene of the tragedy he had been haunted by what he had seen and heard and smelt: 'A view . . . of the three swathed figures in the cots, the sound of the midwives who had laid them out, whispering together, and the smell – the death smell of carbolic acid . . . If I'd been a convicted murderer I couldn't have been more persistently followed by those things on the beds.' The 'washers of the dead' afterwards reappeared in 'Without Benefit of Clergy' and the awful sounds of their ministrations in 'At the End of the Passage', in which the narrator has to stand by as a dead man is prepared for burial.

What saved Ruddy from 'the horror of a great darkness' was a book: Walter Besant's *All in a Garden Fair*. Biographers have puzzled over why a reading and rereading of this mediocre novel should have been regarded by Kipling as an act of 'salvation' that kept him sane. The answer can only be that Ruddy identified with its hero, a young man trying to make his way as a writer in London. The book gave him hope by allowing him to believe that through his own efforts he could make a career for himself outside India and that what Kay Robinson had said to him only months earlier was indeed possible: his future lay not in India among his own people, but in London.

Just as Ruddy was reading his way out of his Hot Weather crisis he received a letter from a friend whom he identified to Margaret Burne-Jones as 'only eight and twenty, a brother journalist from the Northwest', telling him of his feelings for Trix and asking if he thought his case was hopeless. Ruddy had always been fiercely protective of his sister and ever since her arrival in India had fretted about the prospect of her being removed from his care. 'You being a mere woman,' he had written earlier to Margaret, 'can't understand my intense anxiety about the maiden and my jealous care lest she should show signs of being "touched in the heart".' Now he was outraged: 'Personally I liked the man – would have even gone so far as to back his bill for him [–] but that didn't prevent me from sitting down and sending him a brief and courteous epistle of an exceedingly unpleasant nature. Unofficially of course I was sorry for him because I knew how he'd feel but, officially and as a Brother, I was at some pains to thoroughly sit upon and end him.' He went on to ask the Wop of Albion not to let on to Trix or his parents what he had done, revealing that he had acted as much for his own sake as for his sister's: 'You can't realise how savage one feels at a thing of this kind – an attempt to smash the Family Square and the child barely eighteen too! If after my lucid reasoning he chooses to write to the Parents and get their verdict he has only himself to thank for what follows. I shall declare war against him to the knife.'[25]

A rather different view of this episode was provided by Trix herself a decade after her brother's death: 'There was a man who wanted to marry me – a lifelong friend of Ruddy's – and he kept on writing me letters. I took one of them to Ruddy one day and said, "Here's Herbert again; what *am* I to do?" Ruddy shifted his pipe to the other side of his mouth and said, "Shoot the brute!" That was all the help I got from *him*.'[26] Trix might have chosen to identify her suitor as 'Herbert', but there is little doubt that he was none other than Ruddy's best friend in India and his most supportive admirer, Kay Robinson.[27]

The pacification of Upper Burma, so successfully occupied the previous November, was now failing to proceed according to plan. Resistance took the form of ambush and sniping, with officers as prime targets. In early June the *CMG* ran a report that a Lieutenant J. E. O. Armstrong of the Hampshire Regiment and another officer had been shot by unseen snipers as they took an evening stroll outside Mandalay's Fort Sagaing. Ruddy's first response was 'The Grave of the Hundred Dead', which begins:

> A Snider squibbed in the jungle,
>   Somebody laughed and fled,
> And the men of the First Shikaris
>   Picked up their Subaltern dead,
> With a big blue mark in his forehead
> And the back blown out of his head.[28]

Further reflection led Ruddy back to his first reaction to the news of Dury's death seven months earlier and his remark about '£1,800 worth of education gone to smash', which he expanded into the six acerbic verses of 'Arithmetic on the Frontier'. Three decades before Wilfred Owen, Kipling turns on their head his beloved Horace's lines about how sweet and proper it is to die for one's country. 'A great and glorious thing it is,' his poem opens, 'To learn, for seven years or so, / The Lord knows what of that and this, / Ere reckoned fit to face the Foe.' The scene shifts to India's North-West Frontier, where the crude *jezail* flintlock and the curved *tulwar* are the weapons of choice, and the verses go on to expound on the awful ease with which the product of an expensive education can be blown away by a few grains of crude saltpetre:

> A scrimmage in a Border Station –
>   A canter down some dark defile –
> Two thousand pounds of education
>   Drops to a ten-rupee *jezail* –
> The Crammer's boast, the Squadron's pride,
>   Shot like a rabbit in a ride![29]

Despite having been the odd man out at United Services College, Ruddy had always felt a close affinity with his former schoolmates. In India he was almost pathetically keen to keep in touch with those who had gone into the British or Indian Armies. During the Rawalpindi Durbar he had met and dined with seventeen USC old boys, and had afterwards maintained a close watch on their movements, detailed in every letter sent to 'Uncle Crom' or to other teachers at USC. 'Maxwell goes to Burmah with his regiment,' runs part of one such list from 1886. 'Molesworth has died of typhoid fever at Cherat near Peshawur . . . Ranken has been ordered off to Burmah to join the transport there. "Toby" Fitzgerald and "Nelly" Gordon are at Umballa with the Queen's Bays. Dunsterville in the Murree Hills with the 107th is reported to be spending his time "gardening".'[30]

Having been schooled among their kind Ruddy identified with the junior officers in the Indian Army and the British Army in India. He derived a great deal of pleasure from dining in their company in the regimental messes at Mian Mir and delighted in joining in the after-dinner ragging, rowdy games, sing-songs and other arcane rituals that were part of mess life. The jolly marching song 'Bang upon the Bass Drum', celebrating the Army's achievements in the late Afghan War, became a lifelong favourite of his – as did a popular mess song which told the tale of a young officer who, when 'he first came to land / On this hot and burning strand / As a valet he engaged a mild Hindoo'.[31] This 'dusky son of sin' is named 'Gunga Deen' and he cheats his master at every opportunity. Yet for all his shortcomings 'Gunga Deen' earns his master's respect and affection – as, indeed, he does in Rudyard Kipling's rewrite, 'Gunga Din', which retains the original metre but transforms the servant into a *bheesti* or water-carrier who dies heroically on the battlefield after bringing succour to a wounded Tommy, thus earning his unqualified admiration as 'a better man than I am'. Popular as 'Gunga Din' subsequently became as a *Barrack-Room Ballad*, it is a rare instance of Kipling failing to do his source justice, for the real-life water-carrier on whom his verses are based was an Indian officer of the Corps of Guides named Jumma who in the mid-1850s was cashiered for having lied to shield a superior officer. Unable to continue as a soldier in the regiment that was his life, Jumma re-enlisted as a *bheesti* and in that humble capacity served with the Guides throughout the famous siege of Delhi in 1857, carrying his leather water sack under fire to wherever it was most needed. For its gallantry the corps was collectively awarded the Order of Merit, but the men conferred and voted that the medal should go to Jumma alone, since he had shown more courage than any soldier.

Given Kipling's subsequent reputation as a vivisectionist of his own kind, it is curious to find that, when it came to writing about the British officer caste in India, his supposed detachment all too often dissolved into sentimentality. Whether from a sense of his own physical inadequacy or a desire to belong, in India Ruddy displayed an admiration for the subaltern type bordering on hero-worship, exemplified by his portrait of the young Bobby Wicks in the short story 'Only a Subaltern'. When his regiment is stricken by cholera, Bobby does all he can to keep up the spirits of his men, nursing the sick and the dying until he too catches the disease and dies, greatly mourned by his men as a 'bloomin' hangel'.[32] Bobby Wicks is simply too good to be true. An Army officer,

Ruddy wanted to believe, was 'set up, and trimmed and taut', and he walked 'as though he owned himself'. He did not 'spout hashed libraries' – as Ruddy himself did – 'or think the next man's thought'.[33]

Thankfully this uncritical view of the military did not extend to the lower ranks, known at that time as Common Soldiers. Since 1857 every large Station in India had had its detachment of British Army troops, usually quartered in barracks sited, like Mian Mir, far enough away from the Civil Lines to be out of sight but close enough to be on hand in an emergency. When Ruddy first came to Lahore the British Army element of the garrison at Mian Mir was made up of the 2nd Battalion of the Royal Northumberland Fusiliers supported by a detachment of the Royal Artillery. The former were stationed in Mian Mir cantonment from 1882 to 1887 and were afterwards affectionately regarded by Rudyard Kipling as 'my first and best beloved Battalion'.[34] Initially Ruddy's contact with these two units was confined to their officers. Opportunities for meeting the men they commanded were few, since most of Lahore, including the Native city and the railway refreshment rooms, was out of bounds to Common Soldiers.

Before coming out to India Ruddy's only knowledge of the ordinary soldier had derived from his contacts with USC's 'school sergeants', first a 'rich, full-flavoured Irishman' named Kearney, then his replacement, Sergeant-Major Schofield, known to the boys as 'Foxy', an energetic down-to-earth cockney who had travelled the world and who made the schoolboy Gigger 'the recipient of wonderful confidences'.[35] In Lahore Ruddy's first recorded encounter was as he was being driven home in a *tikka gharri* on the evening of St George's Day 1885, when he was accosted by a drunken Fusilier wearing roses in his sun helmet. Ruddy smuggled the man back to barracks under the nose of an officer and soon afterwards requested permission to interview some of the men for his newspaper. This led to a meeting in the Sergeants' Mess with Colour-Sergeant John Fraser, who escorted the journalist to the canteen of 'H' Company and hovered in the background as Ruddy questioned a number of the men: 'By chance I found a suitable knot of men,' wrote Fraser afterwards, 'in the shape of 8 or 10 "boozing chums" who belonged to the musketry fatigue party, headed by Cpl MacNamara. I did my best to give them an idea of what Mr Kipling wanted, warning them not to give themselves away by misstatements and so on, and I left them.' Further interviews with these 'boozing chums' followed, with Ruddy paying for the drinks, allowing Fraser to claim in later years that the garrulous, hard-bitten Irish corporal MacNamara was the original for Kipling's 'Mulvaney'.[36]

What further stimulated Ruddy's interest in the British soldier was a book he reviewed for his paper: Nathaniel Bancroft's *From Recruit to Staff Sergeant*, the autobiography of a retired British soldier living in Simla. Bancroft had fought as a boy soldier with the Bengal Horse Artillery through the Sikh Wars of the 1840s and his graphic account of the horrors of battle made a great impression on his reviewer – in particular, an incident at the battle of Ferozeshah in which his mounted battery had been torn to bits by cannon fire, afterwards recreated by Kipling in the ballad 'Snarleyow'.[37] According to Bancroft, three quarters of the soldiers serving with the Bengal Horse Artillery were Irishmen, among them one Gunner Terence O'Shaughnessy, a fount of wisdom on all things but especially women. In his autobiography Bancroft did his best to transliterate their thick spoken brogue on to the printed page, as in the sentence 'Av ye think it's me wud be openin' me gob to sing in the Orderly Room and the Major in it – not to spake of 'erself – av coorse.' To the discomfort of modern readers, Ruddy immediately took to Bancroft's Irish rendering, first applying it in print in one of the most forgettable of his verses, 'A Levéety in the Plains', a view of the Queen's Birthday Levée held at Government House on the evening of 24 May 1886, as seen by an Irish private on duty:

> There was music brayin' an' punkahs swayin',
> An' men displayin' their uniform;

An' the native ginthry [gentry] they thronged the inthry
    [entry];
  An' oh, by Jabers! 'twas powerful warm![38]

To begin with Ruddy played the stock figures of Tommy Atkins and his Irish equivalent for light relief. However, in June 1886 the *CMG* reported the death from heat apoplexy of a number of British soldiers at the Mian Mir cantonment, and Ruddy took note. 'Three soldiers died in Cantonments last night,' he reported to the Wop of Albion in a letter he had been writing on and off since early May. 'They have been having a funeral nearly every day for a fortnight. But Tommy is <u>so</u> careless. He drinks heavy beer and sleeps at once after a full flesh meal and dies naturally.' Ruddy then went on to describe a scene he had recently witnessed while spending the evening with the subaltern commanding the guard picket on duty at Fort Lahore: 'I'd been round before but never on a night like this. It was pitchy black, choking hot with a blinding dust storm out. Fort Lahore is wickedly hot always as I've learned to my cost before now. I went into the main guard at midnight (it marked 97° in the guardroom verandah) and I saw by the lamp light every man jack of the guard stripped as near be <u>sitting up</u>. They daren't lie down for the lives of them in heat like that. It meant apoplexy.' The infernal scene in the guardroom stayed with him to become the setting for 'With the Main Guard', one of the tales concerning the *Soldiers Three*: the Irishman Terence Mulvaney, the cockney Stanley Ortheris and the Yorkshireman Jack Learoyd.

This glimpse of the harsh realities of a soldier's life in India led Ruddy to look harder at the 'single men in barracks' and the conditions under which they served, and the more he learned of their stultifyingly constrained lives the more serious his treatment grew. Mulvaney, Ortheris and Learoyd are first encountered fully formed in the refreshment room at Umballa Station, as they and the journalist narrator are changing trains: 'I supplied the beer. The tale was cheap at a gallon and a half.' The three became 'The Three Musketeers', published in the *CMG* in March 1887, the first of eighteen stories involving the three privates of 'B' Company of the 'Ould' Regiment. Four more *Soldiers Three* stories followed in quick succession, all lightweight by comparison with those that came later, summarised by their author as 'how the three most cruelly treated a Member of Parliament ["The Three Musketeers"]; how Ortheris went mad for a space ["The Madness of Private Ortheris"]; how Mulvaney and some friends took the town of Lungtungpen ["The Taking of Lungtungpen"]; and how little Jhansi McKenna helped the regiment when it was smitten with cholera ["A Daughter of the Regiment"]'.[39]

Lightweight or not, the *Soldiers Three* tales had the great advantage of novelty, for no writer hitherto had thought the lives of ordinary British soldiers worth writing about. In the early tales one or other of the three comrades provides the peg upon which the actual story itself is hung, but as their author grows in authority the tales become darker, the very best of them as harsh and remorseless as any Greek tragedy. 'The horror, the confusion, and the separation of the murderer from his comrades were all over before I came,' begins the narrator of the opening passage of 'Love-o'-Women':

> There remained only on the barrack-square the blood of man calling from the ground. The hot sun had dried it to a dusky goldbeater-skin film, cracked lozenge-wise by the heat; and as the wind rose, each lozenge, rising a little, curled up at the edges as if it were a dumb tongue. Then a heavier gust blew all away down wind in grains of dark coloured dust. It was too hot to stand in the sunshine before breakfast. The men were in barracks talking the matter over. A knot of soldiers' wives stood by one of the entrances to the married quarters, while inside a woman shrieked and raved with wicked filthy words.[40]

In July 1886 Ruddy joined his family in Simla for his month's leave, bringing with him a surprise gift in the form of another new publication. Once again he had taken advantage of their absence to assemble a new body of verse: eleven satires concerning the running of civil and military affairs which he termed 'departmental ditties', and a further fifteen verses on a variety of themes. Some had appeared in the *Pioneer* or the *CMG* over the previous six months but a significant number were hitherto unpublished, including 'Arithmetic on the Frontier'. This time the printing had proceeded without a hitch, which was all the more remarkable because each sheet, printed on one side of the paper only, had been trimmed into a narrow oblong folio before being bound and stitched with the other pages and then enclosed within brown paper covers so as to resemble a government-issue docket. On the cover was stamped in bold letters 'DEPARTMENTAL DITTIES AND OTHER VERSES', and where the address might be was handwritten in ink 'To: all heads of Departments and all Anglo-Indians', the sender's address being given as 'Rudyard Kipling Assistant Department of Public Journalism Lahore District'. Finally, each slim volume was tied up in the pink ribbon known throughout India as 'red tape'.

The verses within were prefaced by a 'General Summary' suggesting that modern man was in no way different from his ape ancestors and just as self-seeking. What followed was equally sardonic, detailing the follies of the Civil and Military and their spouses, nearly all on the make in one form or another, from 'that snowy-haired lothario Lieutenant-General Bangs' to Jack Barrett's wife, who arranged for her husband to be transferred to Quetta, 'that very healthy post', where he quickly 'gave up the ghost', thereby allowing her to marry her lover.

In both form and content *Departmental Ditties* was a brilliant wheeze, and it was received in Simla with laughter and a great deal of gossiping over the identities of those mocked in one squib or another. 'This queer demi-official docket turned out very successfully,' Lockwood Kipling was able to write, as he posted a copy to Margaret Burne-Jones. 'A new edition is coming out & he [Ruddy] had the satisfaction of hearing all sorts of complimentary things. Lord Dufferin, who frequently comes into our sketching room, professed to be greatly struck by the uncommon combination of satire with grace and delicacy, also what he calls the boy's "infallible ear" for rhythm & cadence.'[41]

Besides printing his own work Ruddy had also undertaken his own promotion: 'I took reply-postcards, printed the news of the birth of the book on one side, the blank order-form on the other, and posted them up and down the Empire from Aden to Singapore and from Quetta to Colombo. The money came back in poor but honest rupees, and was transferred from the publisher, my left-hand pocket, direct to the author, my right-hand pocket.'[42] What is today an extremely rare first edition of five hundred copies sold out within days. 'There arose a demand for a new edition,' wrote the author, 'and this time I exchanged the pleasure of taking in money over the counter for that of seeing a real publisher's imprint on the title page.' Bearing the imprint of the Calcutta publishers Thacker, Spink and Co., this second edition was more conventional in appearance but it carried more poems and it sold even better, so that a third and fourth edition had to be rushed into print, each now carrying the name of the author in bold type.

One new ditty was particularly warmly received, for it touched on a raw Anglo-Indian nerve: 'Pagett, MP' tells of the visit to India of a British Parliamentarian who has all the answers to India's problems and thinks the Anglo-Indian community has it easy. Finally losing his patience with his visitor, his host the narrator tricks him into staying on into the Hot Weather until Pagett finally cracks and flees. He ends:

And I laughed as I drove from the station, but the mirth died
     out on my lips
   As I thought of the fools like Pagett who write of their
     'Eastern trips',
And the sneers of the travelled idiots who duly misgovern the
     land,
   And I prayed to the Lord to deliver another one into my
     hand.

'Pagett, MP' was based on the Liberal parliamentarian and temperance reformer William Sproston Caine, who had come out to India at the recommendation of Allan Octavian Hume.

The Family Square in Simla, as seen by J. L. Kipling (National Trust)

In Simla the Kiplings had taken a tiny cottage called The Dingle, so cramped that when Ruddy joined them he found himself having to share the dining table with his father as a writing desk. However, his parents were in the best of spirits. Alice was now back in the element she loved best, with Lord Dufferin among the several male admirers who regularly dropped in to enjoy her conversation. Lockwood, too, had his own circle of admirers, centred on his 'Ladies' Sketching Club' which met in a studio in Barnes Court and was attended by Lady Helen Blackwood, eldest of the Dufferins' five daughters, and the two daughters of the Lieutenant-Governor of the Punjab. All doors were now opened to them, and when the Dufferins gave a fancy-dress ball at which all were required to wear costumes made of calico, Lockwood found his skills greatly in demand.

The Viceroy's Calico Ball was the much-talked-about occasion when Trix, observed seated by herself by Lord Dufferin and asked why she was not dancing, replied: 'Well, sir, you see I am quite young. I am only eighteen. Perhaps when I am forty I shall get some partners.'[43] The Viceroy at once asked her to dance and Trix's reputation as both an 'ice maiden' and a wit was established. But for Trix herself the evening was a disaster since her only dancing partners were Sir Courteney Ilbert, three other senior married men and, of course, the Viceroy, dressed as an Arab.

All this changed with the arrival in Simla of the Dufferins' son and heir, Archibald James Leofric Temple Blackwood, Viscount Clandeboye, who in late July joined his regiment in India and proceeded very soon afterwards to Simla – at which point the published journals of Lady Dufferin become uncharacteristically vague. Despite his title, his commission in a smart cavalry regiment and his twenty-three years, young Lord Clandeboye seems to have passed through India with scarcely a ripple – except for the rumour of a romantic attachment to Miss Kipling. If Trix's account is to be believed, he pursued her and proposed, was rejected and duly returned to his regiment, where he promptly went down with a bout of typhoid which brought his mother hurrying down from Simla to his sickbed.

Finding his style cramped at The Dingle, Ruddy very soon moved in with the Walkers at Kelvin Grove, as he had in previous summers. Here he had his own circle of friends, chiefly made up of young bloods drawn from the military, among them Captain Ian Hamilton, who had distinguished himself in the Afghan War and had been rewarded by General Sir Frederick Roberts by being taken on as his ADC. Hamilton had just got back from Burma, where he had seized the opportunity to loot a gilded Buddha statue while his chief's back was turned. 'At that time I was in constant touch with Rudyard Kipling,' wrote Hamilton of the summer of 1886. 'Every Sunday I lunched with him . . . and one way or another hardly a day passed when I did not see him.'

Despite his army background Hamilton wrote poetry, and his younger brother, the artist Vereker Hamilton, had contacts in

London's literary world. At Ruddy's request he wrote to his brother about 'a young fellow . . . who had a pretty talent for writing and was anxious to publish something in England'. A manuscript of a short story followed which Vereker Hamilton showed first to the poet and critic Andrew Lang and then the novelist William Sharp. Lang dismissed the work out of hand, remarking that he would 'gladly give Ian a fiver if he had never been the means of my reading this poisonous stuff', while Sharp's reaction was even more negative: 'I would strongly recommend your brother's friend instantly to burn this detestable piece of work . . . I would like to hazard a guess that the writer in question is very young and that he will die mad before he has reached the age of thirty.'[44] After two editors of literary magazines had also turned it down Vereker Hamilton was forced to return the manuscript unpublished.

The manuscript in question was the disturbing tale 'The Mark of the Beast', which tells the story of Fleete, who, like Pagett, MP, knows nothing of Indian ways, gets drunk at the Club and desecrates a Hindu temple by stubbing out his cigar on an image of the god Hanuman. The temple priest bites him, leaving a livid mark on his breast, and soon Fleete begins to behave like a wolf, howling and chewing raw meat. Only after the policeman Strickland has intervened to force the priest to remove his curse does Fleete return to normal. When eventually published in England in 1891 'The Mark of the Beast'[45] was declared by a critic writing in the *Spectator* to be 'loathsome' and showing 'Mr Kipling at his very worst'. Other critics were equally hostile, but the story went on to become a great hit at the Grand Guignol theatre in Paris. As a tale of horror it outstrips Kipling's 'The Strange Ride of Morrowbie Jukes', and was probably written at that same dark period in the summer of 1884 when the author teetered on the verge of a nervous breakdown.

The two groups of military aides who attended the Commander-in-Chief and the Viceroy were natural rivals and formed opposing camps, one led by Ian Hamilton and the other by Lord Dufferin's Military Secretary, the dashing Old Etonian Major Lord William

Leslie de la Poer Beresford, VC, who was in almost every sense larger than life. 'Lord Bill' had served a succession of Viceroys ever since 1875 and was said to have 'raised the office of Military Secretary to a science, and himself from an official into an institution'.[46] Bolstered by a private fortune, which allowed him to keep a very comfortable salon and a string of racehorses and polo ponies, he ran Simla's outdoor events from the front, boasting 'a record of eight broken collar-bones, four concussions of the brain, and contusions innumerable'.[47] But for all his gallantry and charm, 'Lord Bill' was a bachelor born and almost forty, and it was Ian Hamilton, with age and good looks on his side, who led Simla's younger set.

And if Captain Hamilton was regarded as Simla's leading beau, then the belle of that season of '86 was undoubtedly the beautiful Miss Jean Muir, said to be 'the loveliest woman who ever came east of Suez', and widely assumed to be about to be claimed by a visiting prince of the Austro-Hungarian empire, Prince Louis Esterházy. 'How I used to watch for "Miss Muir" on the Mall, or at dances,' wrote Trix of this gilded couple. 'Of course in 1886 we were all on the alert, hoping that dull-faced Prince Louis would not be the favoured one.' Trix's hopes were answered when Ian Hamilton claimed Miss Muir for himself, leaping dramatically through a paper hoop and sweeping her off her feet at a cotillion given by the Dufferins. He then proceeded to woo her furiously and in secret for a fortnight – until found out by Sir Frederick Roberts. Livid that his aide had disobeyed his command to remain at his beck and call at all times, the Commander-in-Chief ordered Hamilton to leave Simla within the hour. This cruelly broken-off romance prompted Ruddy to write a double-edged set of verses, 'An Old Song', which reflect the delights and tensions of that summer:

> So long as Death 'twixt dance and dance
>   Chills best and bravest blood
> And drops the reckless rider down
>   The rotten, rain-soaked *khud* [mountainside],
> So long as rumours from the North

Make loving wives afraid,
So long as Burma takes the boy
And typhoid kills the maid,
If you love me as I love you
What knife can cut our love in two?[48]

For Ruddy himself the young and eligible beauties of Simla appeared to hold no charms, perhaps because he knew them to be far beyond his reach. Instead, he joined the large circle of admirers who professed themselves to be in thrall to the seemingly ageless beauty of Mrs Parry-Lambert, wife of a major in the Public Works Department, whom he immortalised as 'Venus Annodomini' – 'as immutable as the Hills. But not quite so green.' Another of Mrs Parry-Lambert's swains that summer was a young subaltern of the Corps of Guides named George Younghusband. According to Ian Hamilton, Younghusband became infatuated with her and 'since his face was a looking-glass and his forehead an open book, by reason of his innocence, his brothers-in-arms made life a burden to him and embittered his naturally sweet disposition'. But then Mrs Parry-Lambert was joined in Simla by her eighteen-year-old daughter, as plain as her mother was beautiful. In Kipling's telling, George Younghusband becomes 'Very Young Gayerson', who is joined in Simla by his father, 'Young Gayerson', at which point he discovers that his father was himself an admirer of the 'Venus Annodomini' in his youth and that she has an eighteen-year-old daughter – whereupon he abruptly leaves for the plains. 'Probably I was the only person in Simla who did not know who "Very Young Gayerson" was,' wrote George Younghusband in his autobiography. 'It was only years later that the secret was revealed to me.'[49] It may explain why he and his brother Francis were afterwards so hostile to Kipling.

In subsequent Simla seasons it became something of a parlour game to try to work out who exactly was who among the leading characters created by Rudyard Kipling. It was generally agreed that Strickland, the policeman of many disguises who makes his first appearance in the pages of the *CMG* in April 1887 as 'Miss

Youghal's Syce' and is fleshed out thereafter in a number of *Plain Tales*, could only be based on Horace Goad, and that 'Venus Annodomini' was mostly Mrs Parry-Lambert. However, the main subject of speculation was always the identity of the delightful, dangerous woman who was 'clever, witty, brilliant and sparkling beyond most of her kind; but possessed of many devils of malice and mischievousness'.[50] Her name was 'Mrs Hauksbee' and she slipped fully formed out of the pages of the *CMG* on 17 November 1886, going on to make a further nine appearances over the next fourteen years.[51] Everyone had their own theories as to who the real Mrs Hauksbee might be, George Younghusband remembering that the 'entrancing' older woman whom he and his friends had identified as the model for 'Mrs Hauksbee' was mortified to hear of it, until it was suggested to her that Kipling 'must have taken all the best parts of the character from you, and the rest from other people'.

No doubt there were wise heads in Simla ready to point out that a strong candidate for Mrs Hauksbee was 'Mrs Vereker' in Judge Cunningham's *Chronicles of Dustypore*, published in 1877. There is equally a case for arguing that something of Alice Kipling went into her making, just as there is for believing that an element of Lockwood Kipling went into the all-wise Strickland. But if any single person inspired Mrs Hauksbee it could only have been a forty-year-old, round-faced, full-lipped and rather dumpy little woman who liked to parade up and down the Simla Mall dressed in yellow and black in misguided tribute to her husband's corps, popularly known as the 'Yellow Boys'. She was Mrs Isabella Burton, wife of a major of Skinner's Horse, whose main attraction to a young man half her age was that she was both a flirt and a bluestocking but, above all, a woman of the world, possessing 'the wisdom of the Serpent, the logical coherence of the Man, the fearlessness of the Child, and the triple intuition of the Woman'. By modern standards Mrs Burton was not promiscuous, but she delighted in surrounding herself with ardent young men whom she could amuse, manipulate, tease and educate all at the same time – a woman determined, in the words of her fictional alter ego, 'to act, dance, ride, frivol, talk scandal, dine out, and appropriate the legitimate captives of any woman I choose, until I d-r-r-r-op'.[52] Ruddy had first met Mrs Burton when his mother had drawn him into Simla's busy amateur-theatrical scene the previous summer. A year later their renewed acquaintance blossomed to the point where she became Ruddy's 'guide, philosopher and friend',[53] particularly in matters pertaining to female sexual mores.

Whether it was because they represented a maternal aspect of womanhood that Ruddy craved but failed to find in his mother or because their sexual confidence allowed him to engage with them to a degree forbidden with other women, he was drawn to older married women like Mrs Burton as a bee to nectar. And when he came to write about them as a distinct Anglo-Indian species he did so with an honesty that acknowledged their many strengths:

> Women of forty to fifty and upwards . . . are the Lillie Langtrys of India . . . They have more individuality than English women. They know more of life, death, sickness and trouble than English women, I think; and this makes them broader in their views . . . I admit that their 'belles' startle one rather. They would be out of consideration in a small country town in England. As a general rule, only the older women try to be 'fast', and their fastness is very modified; but it lasts for many years.[54]

All in all, Simla in July–August 1886 was a heady brew for a young man of twenty to imbibe, and when Ruddy returned to Lahore in mid-August his head was swimming with ideas, one of which was to write a series of glimpses of Simla life for his paper. Almost the first of these was 'Three and – an Extra', in which the reader is first introduced to 'Mrs Hauksbee'. Over the next four months another four stories appeared in which this devious, bitchy, worldly-wise schemer played some part, establishing Mrs Hauksbee as one of the most engaging female characters in English fiction.

To Ruddy's great satisfaction Stephen Wheeler had retreated to England for five months' sick leave, and his desk was occupied by

Kay Robinson. What Ruddy termed a 'joyous reign' now began, for Robinson was under instructions from George Allen to 'put sparkle' into the *CMG*, and did so with an enthusiasm that was infectious. 'Between the two of us we've been making the Civil and Military Gazette hum,' wrote Ruddy to his Aunt Edith in early December, as Robinson's brief period in office drew to a close. 'They say the paper is immensely improved under the new direction. We certainly have freshened things up all round and cut down expenses simply because we used to write the greater part of our paper ourselves . . . Robinson gave me absolutely free hand and consulted me about questions of "views" and "lines" and "policies" so that in his Consulship I got a greater insight into the higher workings of a paper than ever before.'[55]

As well as being more directly involved in the running of the paper Ruddy also had a lot more fun working alongside an editor who was 'in every way congenial and bright and witty . . . and [with] a shameful levity of disposition'. There were evenings when the two of them went rat-hunting with their terriers through the paper's offices and when they decorated the walls with large drawings of themselves carrying out Allen's instructions to put sparkle into the paper. Like his elder brother Phil Robinson, Kay was a keen naturalist and adopted an office mascot in the form of a crow picked up injured in the road, which was tamed and given its own column in the paper within which to comment 'upon politics and things in general'. However, Robinson's greatest contribution to Ruddy's well-being was his introduction of the 'turnover', which he had discovered earlier while working in London for the *Globe* newspaper. This consisted of a feature of approximately two and a half thousand words which filled one column, usually in the middle spread of the paper, and then continued over on to the next page for a further half-column. It was perfect for Ruddy's Simla tales, and from November onwards the turnover became an established weekly feature of the paper, so that when Wheeler reappeared in December and reclaimed his office it was a case of *fait accompli*. The turnover stayed and the stories kept coming, week on week.

At Christmas that year two seasonal poems appeared in the *Pioneer*, one signed 'K. R.', the other 'R. K.', both entitled 'Christmas in India'. The first was conventionally sentimental, the second characteristically sardonic:

High noon behind the tamarisks – the sun is hot above us –
  As at Home the Christmas Day is breaking wan.
They will drink our healths at dinner – those who tell us how
    they love us,
  And forget us till another year be gone![56]

Printed side by side, the two poems celebrated a fellowship of like minds – which makes Ruddy's continuing hostility towards Robinson in the matter of his sister's affections all the more perplexing. It is clear from Trix's remarks that Robinson wrote to her after being warned off by Ruddy and that it was on his advice – 'Shoot the brute!' – that she gave him no further encouragement. By the standards of the day their age difference was hardly an impediment to marriage, so Ruddy evidently had other objections. Whatever these were, in the light of what befell Trix they were misplaced. Not a word or note survives to show if Ruddy ever felt remorse or had second thoughts, but there was to be a curious parallel some years later when he found himself in love with the sister of his best friend – and fled the scene.

At the end of the year the Family Square celebrated the attainment of Ruddy's majority, and with it the news that Lockwood Kipling was to be appointed to the Order of the Indian Empire as a Commander (CIE). Public recognition had come to both father and son, and, in the case of the son, literally so. 'I have made a mark,' wrote Ruddy to his Aunt Edith. 'Everyone in the sets I know, has read or heard about the Departmental Ditties and strangers in trains, and hotels and all manner of out of the way places come up to me and say nice things. Also – last proof of notoriety – people turn their heads and look and ask to be introduced to me when I dance or dine in strange places beyond my district.'[57] At twenty-one he was known among his own people.

9

'Forty foolish yarns'

From Lahore to Allahabad, 1887–8

Between the gum pot and the shears,
  The weapons of my grimy trade,
In divers moods and various years
  These forty foolish yarns were made.

Rudyard Kipling, from the inscription in his presentation copy of
Plain Tales from the Hills to Mrs Edmonia Hill, 1888

Only seven Rudyard Kipling letters have survived from 1887, of which three are business letters addressed to the Calcutta publisher Thacker, Spink and Co. In the first, written in February, he asks for a price quotation for the printing of a book of no more than 130 pages containing twenty-four short stories, to be called *Punjab People Brown and White.*[1] In the second, dating from mid-June, he states that the projected book is now to be called *Plain Tales from the Hills* and will be made up of thirty-nine stories 'of Simla and the plains'.[2]

The four private letters are all addressed to older married women, three of them to Mrs Isabella Burton, the spirited 'Mrs Hauksbee' figure whose acquaintance Ruddy again renewed in Simla in the summer of '87 when they rehearsed and performed together in a play at the Gaiety Theatre. The letters hint at sexual advances on his part and rebuffs on hers. In the first Ruddy asks permission to dedicate his forthcoming book to Mrs Burton: 'If I put on the title page, sans initials or anything, just this much, "To

235

the wittiest woman in India I dedicate this book" will you, as they say in the offices, "initial and pass as correct?"'[3]

When *Plain Tales from the Hills* was finally published in January 1888 it consisted of thirty-two stories selected from the more than seventy which had previously appeared in the *CMG*, as well as another eight previously unpublished. These last show that Ruddy's decision to wait until he had forty good stories written was a wise one, and not simply because another Simla leave had given him more grist for the mill. Four of the eight escaped the censors of the Family Square and had their roots in Ruddy's fifth and last Lahore Hot Weather.

'Thrown Away' tells the story of a young officer who is too sensitive to survive the realities of India and is driven to blow out his brains with his revolver. The narrator and one of the man's brother officers conspire together to concoct 'a big, written lie . . . to soothe the Boy's people at Home', making it appear that he has died of cholera. 'The Madness of Private Ortheris' also deals with acute depression, in this case that of Private Ortheris of the *Soldiers Three*, driven half mad by homesickness and boredom. 'What must I do to get out o' this 'ere a-Hell?' he cries desperately, leading his two friends to join with the narrator in a scheme to bring him back to his senses.

The third story of the four, 'Beyond the Pale', is even darker, being 'the story of a man who wilfully stepped beyond the safe limits of decent everyday society, and paid heavily for it'. This is Trejago, an Englishman who 'took too deep an interest in native life; but he will never do so again'. Trejago likes to wander through Lahore's back streets and has gained a great knowledge of Indian lore in the process. One evening he comes upon a dead end in a dark gully and he hears a laugh from behind a grated window. He flirts with the unseen woman and next day receives a coded message, which he correctly interprets as coming from an Indian widow who seeks him as a lover. He responds and a month of illicit visits follows. By day Trejago goes through the routine of office work and puts on his best suit to call on the ladies of the Station, but every night he conceals himself under an 'evil-smelling *boorka*' and enters the sleeping city to find 'endless delight' with his lover, the teenage widow Bisesa, 'fairer than bar-gold in the Mint' but 'ignorant as a bird'. In the 'narrow dark Gully where the sun never came and where the buffaloes wallowed in the blue slime' Trejago finds passion unlike anything he has known or will ever know in the ordered, sunlit world of the Civil Lines. He swears he loves Bisesa more than anyone else in the world, but she tells him he has been seen walking with a memsahib by the bandstand. She is unable to understand that this means nothing to Trejago, and to his bemusement breaks off the relationship. After three weeks without a sign from Bisesa, Trejago returns to the gully and raps at her grated window as of old: 'There was a young moon, and one stream of light fell down into Amir Nath's Gully, and struck the grating which was drawn away as he knocked. From the dark black Bisesa held out her arms into the moonlight. Both hands had been cut off at the wrists, and the stumps were nearly healed.' A hidden assailant lunges at Trejago with something sharp and wounds him in the groin. The grating is closed and he is left alone in the blackness of the gully.

The structure of the tale is unusual for the young Kipling in that he dispenses with a narrator and instead opens with what appears to be a moral: 'A man should, whatever happens, keep to his own caste, race, and breed. Let the White go to the White and the Black to the Black' – lines frequently taken at face value. But this is Rudyard Kipling the story-teller articulating the censorious views of British India, for he goes on to show that his sympathies lie with the lovers who have dared to cross the racial divide and who are punished for it. Like the lovers Héloïse and Abélard, Trejago and Bisesa have dared to break society's bounds and suffer the consequences, in Trejago's case with a symbolic castration.

The fourth story appeared last in Ruddy's ordering of his forty published *Plain Tales* and is arguably the weakest. 'To Be Filed for Reference' is about McIntosh Jellaludin, one of those European loafers whose fuddled, drink-soaked lives held such a fascination for

Ruddy precisely because they had abandoned social constraints and had struck out into the 'fourth dimension'. McIntosh Jellaludin's surname marks him out as a convert to Islam, but his particular tragedy is that he was once a scholar and a gentleman. Despite being filthy drunk most of the time he befriends the narrator and tells him that he proposes to bequeath him a manuscript of a novel he has written – 'the materials of a new Inferno' – which will make the narrator famous. The loafer duly dies of pneumonia and his Native wife hands the narrator a bundle of papers 'all numbered and covered with fine cramped writing'. The policeman Strickland helps the narrator sort them out and declares the writer to have been either 'an extreme liar or a most wonderful person. He thought the former. One of these days you may be able to judge for yourselves.' Only then do we learn that McIntosh Jellaludin's master work is entitled 'The Book of Mother Maturin'. The story is nothing less than an advertisement for the great novel of Lahore low-life that Ruddy had been writing on and off for almost two years.

At the start of the Hot Weather of '87 Alice Lockwood and Trix went up to Simla ahead of their menfolk as usual. It was now widely known that the Kiplings were on intimate terms with the Dufferins, and one consequence was that Trix was besieged with suitors, again headed by Archie, Lord Clandeboye, whose regiment had now returned to England but who had remained behind as an additional ADC to his father. Clandeboye now proposed for a second time, and was again turned down. 'He suggested that though I didn't think him up to much it might amuse me to be a countess,' wrote Trix witheringly of her suitor. '"Too expensive," I said and he explained at length in his stodgy schoolboy way that though of course I should have to be "presented [at Court] at my marriage", my wedding dress with a train of family lace would be A.1. and a small tiara that belonged to his beautiful Granny would suit me far more than the "fender full of shamrocks Mother sports" [Lady Dufferin's tiara].' Lord Clandeboye's first proposal had remained a secret between the two of them but this second rejection was evidently too much for him and he complained to his parents. One reacted with approval, the other with indignation: 'Though Lord D. loved me for my good sense,' commented Trix, 'Lady D. never forgave me, and she had always been so nice to me before. Of course a penniless daughter-in-law was the last thing she wished for, but she said openly that she had always thought me a really sweet and charming girl – but – if her "splendid Arch" was not good enough for me – she gave me up.'[4]

Simla Society being what it was, it soon became known that Lord Dufferin had personally approached Alice Kipling and asked her to remove her daughter from Simla, whereupon Alice had replied indignantly that it was his son who should go – which he did. Small wonder that when Lady Dufferin's journals were published after her return to Ireland in 1889 her account of the first half of the Simla Season from late April to the end of July was limited to eleven entries and just one reference to her eldest son: 'Archie played polo before breakfast.' The affair led to a *froideur* between the Dufferins and the Kiplings, which Ruddy's subsequent public poems attacking various policies of Lord Dufferin's government can have done little to ease.

But there was one aspect of the Dufferin Viceroyalty of which Ruddy heartily approved: Lady Dufferin's decision to make a cause of the low status of women in Indian society and the lack of medical facilities for them. In June 1885 she had announced the formation of the Countess of Dufferin's Fund for Supplying Medical Aid to the Women of India and then set about securing contributions. Hariot Lady Dufferin had, according to Ruddy, a 'most baleful and malevolent glare due to short sight' and this, combined with a forceful character and the exploitation to the hilt of her privileged position, produced results. Indian maharajas and other wealthy notables vied with one another to demonstrate their loyalty, and the happy outcome was the provision of Lady Dufferin hospitals, dispensaries and medical training schools for women up and down the land. Ruddy lent his support, for nothing engaged his ire more than what he saw as the hypocrisy of the Indian intelligentsia in demanding political rights for themselves while refusing to grant human rights to their womenfolk. 'We might wait till

Doomsday till the Bengalis educated their native women,' he wrote in one of his letters to the Wop of Albion:

> Meanwhile they are rotting in the zenanas, for sheer want of medical attendance; English docs you know aren't allowed to see a zenana woman in her last agonies ... Same with 'widow remarriage'. Thank Goodness you haven't any notion of the horrors of enforced widowhood out here. The agitation is as old as the hills but our progressive Aryan brother, the Oxford BA who'll eat with you, ride with you and talk to your wife won't dare to fly in the face of his 'custom'.

Ruddy saw it as his duty to fight this humbug, and developed two potent weapons for doing so, in his on-the-spot reporting and his public verse: 'People won't stir quickly for abstracts of reports. Go down and look at the place yourself and write all you know on the running pen. Serve hot and something is sure to come of it ... If prose doesn't go home hack out some verses with a lilting refrain that will take and catch the public ear and you have helped scotch a snake.'[5] Here was a stratagem of which Ruddy the polemicist became the supreme proponent, first tested in India and subsequently applied to great effect in London in the 1890s.

One example of snake-scotching verses hacked out with a lilting refrain was published in the *CMG* in mid-February 1887 to mark the laying of the foundation stone of the Lady Aitchison Hospital for Women in Lahore, paid for through the Lady Dufferin Fund. The verses called for continuing support for Lady Dufferin's Fund but also demanded that Indian menfolk play their part:

> The Wisdom of the West is theirs – our schools are free to all.
>   The strength of all the West is theirs, to prop them lest they
>   fall;
> And men may say what things they please, and none dare stay
>   their tongue.
>   But who has spoken out for these – the women and the young?[6]

Such public verses now became an established feature in both the *CMG* in Lahore and the *Pioneer* in Allahabad, and it comes as a surprise to find how many of these were attacks on the Government of India for its failure to fulfil its duty as protector of the Indian poor. One of the most remarkable was written in response to the numerous public celebrations and events staged to mark Queen Victoria's Golden Jubilee. Published in the *CMG* in May 1887 and given a metre which matches the plod of the ox at the plough or the wheel over the well, 'What the People Said' suggests that the Queen-Empress and her Empire mean nothing to the vast bulk of the Indian populace:

> By the well, where the bullocks go
>   Silent and blind and slow –
> By the field, where the young corn dies
>   In the face of the sultry skies,
> They have heard, as the dull earth hears
>   The voice of the wind of the hour,
> The sound of the Great Queen's voice:
>   'My God hath given me years,
> 'Hath granted dominion and power:
>   'And I bid you, O Land, rejoice.'

But India's peasants are concerned only with their crops and the harvest. The poem closes:

> And the Ploughman settled the share
>   More deep in the sun-dried clod:
> 'Mogul, Mahratta, and *Mlech* [foreign barbarian]
>   from the North,
>   'And White Queen over the Seas –
> 'God raiseth them up and driveth them forth
>   'As the dust of the ploughshare flies in the breeze;
> 'But the wheat and the cattle are all in my care,
>   'And the rest is the will of God.'[7]

AND THE PLOUGHMAN SETTLED THE SHARE

MORE DEEP IN THE SUN-DRIED CLOD:

THE WHEAT AND THE CATTLE ARE ALL MY CARE.

AND THE REST IS THE WILL OF GOD.

Rudyard Kipling.

J. L. Kipling's drawing inspired by his son's verses (National Trust)

These verses anticipate and rehearse Kipling's more famous meditation on Empire set down in 'Recessional' a decade later, marking the Queen's Diamond Jubilee of 1897.

Ruddy joined his family in Simla in mid-August to find a theatrical revival under way. On 30 May the Gaiety Theatre in the new Town Hall had opened with a play performed by the Simla Amateur Dramatic Club, the A. D. C., whose membership was largely military staff officers and their wives, led by the ubiquitous Lord William Beresford. Three months later a rival theatre opened in the Commander-in-Chief's refurbished ballroom at Snowden, with a gala performance in aid of Lady Roberts's own charity,

'Homes in the Hills', set up to improve the nursing facilities in British military sanatoriums. The evening consisted of a burlesque of *Lucia di Lammermoor* in which the Kiplings were very much to the fore, Ruddy providing a verse prologue and Trix delivering it dressed fetchingly in a nurse's uniform. Some weeks later the Kiplings and the Burtons were involved in a production of Sardou's popular French farce *A Scrap of Paper* at the Gaiety, with Major Burton playing the leading role of Count Prosper Couramont, Isabella Burton Susanne de Ruseville and Ruddy her lover Brisemouche. The Dufferins put in an appearance, the Viceroy afterwards writing to his eldest daughter Lady Helen that he had found Ruddy's performance 'too horrid and vulgar' and Lady Dufferin making it clear in her journal entry that they had 'felt obliged just to look in' only because a Member of Council was in the cast.

On 11 June Trix turned nineteen. Her enhanced status and what Kay Robinson called her 'statuesque beauty' now ensured that she had more admirers than she could ever have wished for. By one account,[8] she rejected no fewer than four proposals of marriage, and by late summer was sufficiently worn down by the persistence of a fifth suitor to accept him. The successful beau was twenty-nine-year-old Captain Jack Fleming of the Survey of India, a dull and gloomy Scot whose charms were not readily apparent to the rest of Trix's family, and particularly not to Ruddy, who called him an 'objectionable cuss'. Trix herself seemed to be unconvinced and after less than three months broke off the engagement 'on the grounds of incompatibility of temper', only to relent to the extent of giving Fleming permission to write to her. To Ruddy this was a case of misplaced pity and he returned to Lahore at the end of his month's leave filled with foreboding: 'In respect to Jack Fleming I do not care one straw . . . but . . . my faith in my sister's excellent judgement . . . is a little shaken. There was no compulsion, and there was ample time to choose . . . For my little maiden I have nothing but sympathy because she is very sorry and upset in her poor little mind.'[9]

Ruddy returned to Lahore knowing also that his days there were numbered, for it had been decided that his talents could be put to better use in Allahabad. Wheeler had now gone, judged by Allen and his co-proprietors on the *CMG* to be incapable of maintaining the 'sparkle' that Kay Robinson had brought to the paper. His editorial chair was now taken by Robinson, and a new man had been hired to work as his assistant.

So it came about that in mid-November 1887 Ruddy packed his bags and papers, and said goodbye to family and friends – and to the now familiar mosque, minaret and tomb-strewn landscape of the Punjab that he had come to know and love. From the Land of the Five Rivers he and his bearer Kadir Baksh journeyed six hundred miles by train to the Doab, the Land of the Two Rivers, and to Allahabad, capital of the North-Western Provinces and Oude.

Two years earlier Lady Dufferin had noted in her journal that 'Allahabad is very uninteresting; there is nothing at all to see'. She was right as far as the Civil Station went, but wrong in thinking that Indian Allahabad had nothing to offer.

Despite its Muslim name, Allahabad was very much a Hindu city, revered for centuries as Prayag, the confluence of three sacred rivers, of which only two, the Ganges and the Jumna, were visible to the naked eye. Consequently it was one of four holy places which every Hindu was expected to visit in his lifetime, ideally at the height of the spring festival of Magh Mela, when many thousands of devotees assembled to bathe from the sand spit where the two rivers converged. Like Lahore, its most dominant feature was the Fort, built by the Great Mughal Akbar to command the two rivers. But despite its strategic importance Allahabad had never achieved the greatness of Lahore. After being ceded to the East India Company in 1801 it had served as a staging post on the Grand Trunk Road linking Delhi to Bengal, but had never been thought important enough to merit a garrison of British troops. Consequently there was no British corps present when in June 1857 the sepoys of the 6th Bengal Native Infantry mutinied and killed their officers before torching the bungalows of the Civil Station.

Ten days later Colonel Neill retook the town with the European Madras Fusiliers and set about exacting revenge, setting fire to the Native bazaar and suburbs and shooting down all who tried to escape the flames. Four tribunals had then sat in summary judgement, executing at least as many innocent persons as guilty, so that when General Havelock brought the rest of the army into Allahabad some days later he saw corpses hanging from every tree as the 'fresh fruits of rebellion'. According to the British historian Sir John Kaye, 'six thousand beings had been thus summarily disposed of and launched into eternity'.[10] Allahabad's Muslim community bore the brunt of this punishment, and from that time onward the Native population was ninety per cent Hindu. In November 1858 British Crown rule was proclaimed in Allahabad and the town became the capital of the North-Western Provinces and Oude, usually known as the NWP.

The rebuilt town that Ruddy saw when he climbed down from his train carriage had been shaped around these tragic events, with the new Civil Lines being laid over the ruins of the Native Town. The new railway line, built parallel to the Grand Trunk Road, effectively divided Allahabad into two: the Station on the north side, the bazaars and Native Town on the south. 'To the immediate front of the railway lies the Civil Station,' explained G. H. Keene in his *Handbook for Visitors*, written in 1875. 'It contains a number of wide streets . . . laid out in building sites, now mostly occupied with houses, and crossing each other at right angles like those of a modern city in the United States. These roads are all well planted with teak and other timber trees, and each bears the name of some person of local or imperial celebrity. Thus, parallel with the City Road runs the Queen's Road and Albert Road, while transversely run Canning and Elgin Roads.'

At the heart of the Station was the *maidan*, which became Alfred Park after the visit of a lesser heir to the British throne, and at its northern end a district known officially as Colonelganj, and unofficially as *Lalkurtiganj* or 'Redjacket town' – not on account of the barracks which had formerly stood there but because of its military brothels, where the women wore red blouses as the mark of their calling. Here, wrote Keene, 'a large and handsome pile of adapted Saracenic architecture is being raised for the use of the new Central College, to be known by the name of an ex-Lieutenant-Governor Sir William Muir. Still further on is the Government House.'[11] Two months before Ruddy's arrival in Allahabad Lord Dufferin's Council had passed an act incorporating Muir College as Allahabad University, with the power to confer degrees in the Faculties of Arts and Law.

Keene's *Handbook* makes no reference to the district abutting Colonelganj to the north and east and just over the road from the University. By 1887 this had become known as Allenganj, or 'Allen Town', dominated by the offices and printing works of George Allen's Pioneer Press, the biggest private employer in Allahabad, with a workforce of six hundred. After the 1857 Mutiny a political decision had been made to move the capital of the NWP from Agra to Allahabad and to keep the latter free of modern industrial development – not for environmental reasons but in order to ensure that 'the turbulent natives' of Cawnpore, 110 miles upriver and the scene of the appalling massacres of 1857, were 'absorbed in industrial concerns and . . . tamed to such an extent as to help us to consolidate our Empire in India'. One of the principal beneficiaries of this 'politico-industrial experiment'[12] had been George Allen, who had set up a leather works and tannery in Cawnpore which he enlarged in 1884 with the help of an enormous loan authorised by Sir Auckland Colvin, then the Financial Secretary. A month after Ruddy's move to Allahabad Allen's close ties with central Government were further strengthened when Colvin became Lieutenant-Governor of the NWP and moved into Government House, right across the road from the Pioneer Press, which was itself little more than a stone's throw from No. 1 Bund Road, where George and Maud Allen lived in a palatial bungalow overlooking the sand flats of the River Ganges.

No. 1 Bund Road was where Ruddy was put up for his first weeks in Allahabad, and where he found himself 'like a rabbit in

a strange warren'[13] as Allen pondered on how best to employ his
protégé's talents. The *Pi* already had two assistant editors in post
so Allen decided to make Ruddy a special correspondent, but
with the additional responsibility of editing a new weekly. Some
years earlier he had founded *Allen's Weekly Mail*, printed in London
and containing all the latest news from India. This was now to
be revived in Allahabad as the *Week's News*, made up of 'a re-hash
of news and views' taken from the main newspaper together with
an extra page devoted to fiction. However, the *Week's News* was
not to commence publication until the start of the New Year, and
in the meantime Ruddy was sent off to gather new material in
the field.

'Since November last I have been a vagabond on the face of the
earth,' Ruddy wrote to the Wop of Albion in late January 1888.
'Did I tell you how the Pioneer took me over and bade me go out
for a month into Rajputana – the home of a hundred thousand legends?' Rajputana stood at the very heart of India, a region made up
of a score of Native states ruled by maharajas and rajas, great and
small, permitted to govern or misgovern according to their own
traditions provided they did not step too far out of line. Ruddy
had been anxious to explore the territory ever since Wheeler had
forbidden him to accompany the Walkers on their tour the year
before. Beginning at the old Mughal capital of Agra, he journeyed
by train to Jaipur and Udaipur, then by hired tonga to the ancient
Rajput citadel of Chittor, before doubling back by train to visit the
desert principalities of Jodhpur and Bikaner. As he criss-crossed
Rajputana he mailed a series of dispatches to Allahabad that
appeared in the *Pioneer* under the title of 'Letters of Marque'.
Reading these neglected dispatches today, one is reminded that the
fresh perspective Kipling brought to his fiction served him equally
well as a travel writer.

Apart from the brief foray up to Peshawar and the Khyber made
when he was a callow youth of nineteen this was Ruddy's first
opportunity to fend for himself in unknown country and he
returned thoroughly pleased with himself. 'Was there anything like

that dissolute tramp through some of the loveliest and oldest places upon the face of the earth?' he asked his favourite cousin:

> I railed and rode and drove and tramped and slept in King's palaces or under the stars themselves and saw panthers killed and heard tigers roar in the hills, and for six days had no white face with me, and explored dead cities desolate these three hundred years, and came to stately Residencies [where British Political Agents attached to the local rulers were quartered] where I feasted in fine linen and came to desolate wayside stations where I slept with natives upon the cotton bales and clean forgot that there was a newspapery telegraphic world without. Oh it was a good and clean life and I saw and heard all sorts and conditions of men and they told me the stories of their lives, black and white and brown alike, and I filled three notebooks and walked 'with death and morning on the silver horns' [Tennyson, *The Princess*].[14]

Only at one point on his tour did Ruddy's confidence falter: as he explored the vast Rajput fortress of Chittor, where the ruins of the ancestral home of the oldest of the Hindu warrior clans crown the summit of an enormous rock bluff. Three mass immolations of Rajput women, each accompanied by the slaughter of their menfolk, had cast their shadows over Chittor, and Ruddy was all too aware of the site's grim past. After clambering down the cliff face in search of a spring known as the *Gau-Mukh* or 'Cow's Mouth', he entered a dark watery recess where the air 'was thick with the sick smell of stale incense' and came upon a rock-cut pool fed by water pouring from a shapeless stone gargoyle and 'oozing between the edges of the steps and welling up from the stone slabs of the terrace'. Here he was confronted by a Shaivite shrine in the form of a phallic stone lingam – 'the loathsome Emblem of Creation'. Ruddy must surely have encountered this popular expression of Hindu worship before, but the overtly sexual nature of the scene and its setting now overwhelmed him. 'It seemed,' he wrote, 'as though the descent had led the Englishman, firstly, two thousand years away from his own century, and secondly, into a trap, and that he would fall off the polished stones into the stinking tank, or that the Gau-Mukh would continue to pour water placidly until the tank rose up and swamped him, or that some of the stone slabs would fall forward and crush him flat.' Overcome by 'an apprehension of great evil', Ruddy fled the scene, stumbling over the smooth, worn rocks to get away: 'He felt their sliminess through his boot-soles. It was as though he was treading on the soft, oiled skin of a Hindu . . . He did not care to look behind him, where stood the reminder that he was not better than the beasts that would perish.'

Despite this horror, which lends itself to all sorts of Freudian interpretations, Ruddy felt compelled to return to Chittor that same evening, to explore by moonlight the abandoned citadel, with its crumbling redoubts and its marbled palaces of kings and queens, inhabited only by jackals and monkeys. Although he later visited the palace-fortress of Amber, abandoned when the new city of Jaipur was built in the eighteenth century, it was the older and infinitely more charged bastion of Hindu civilisation at Chittor that remained fixed in his memory. At the time he wrote that he would never try to describe what he saw there by moonlight for fear of insulting 'a scene as lovely, wild, and unmatchable as any that mortal eyes have been privileged to rest upon', but five years later he conjured up that same memory to depict the ruined palace known as 'Cold Lairs' of his *Jungle Books*.

The tour of Rajputana led inevitably to encounters with fellow travellers which he also put to good account, most notably the European loafers met in railway refreshment rooms or wayside dak-bungalows – 'a genial, blasphemous, blustering crew, and pre-eminent even in a land of liars'. One particular encounter involved two Freemasons, whose mode of communicating with each other was so bizarre that he promptly wrote about it to his cousin Margaret. 'The message was perfectly unintelligible to me,' he wrote:

My brother [Freemason] gave me this message and I went up and northwards from the Western side of India till I came to a junction on the edge of the desert and was set out of the train at five on a bitterly cold winter's morning with all the stars blazing overhead and a wind fit to cut you in two blowing off the sands. The Calcutta train . . . came in and a man in one of the carriages opened a window and looked out sleepily . . . I went towards the window and behold, it was the man I was told to find; for he also (doesn't this sound mad) was a brother of mine. I bent over him and gave the message and he said sleepily: 'Thanks, I know what it means. You needn't repeat it. Tha'anks.' Then I went away and the Calcutta train went off to Bombay and I set out into the desert on my journey . . . Wasn't it odd and out of this world?[15]

When Ruddy got back to Allahabad just before Christmas 1887 he was startled to see the railway station bookstall advertising his name and coupling it with that of Bret Harte, one of the American authors he most admired. The *Pioneer* was promoting him as the author of a series of 'Anglo-Indian Studies' to be carried in the new *Week's News*, which would also run stories from Harte and other well-known writers. Ruddy's response was to go to Allen armed with a proof copy of *Plain Tales from the Hills* and point out that he could dispense with Harte, since he himself could supply all the fiction required, and at half the price. Allen duly gave him his head – but must have wondered if he had done the right thing when he read the first short story published in the *Week's News*. 'A Wayside Comedy' tells of the hell on earth brought about in the tiny up-country Station of Kashima when its two memsahibs – Mrs Boulte, 'who hated her husband with the hate of a woman who has met with nothing but kindness from her mate, and, in the teeth of this kindness, has done him a great wrong', and Mrs Vansuythen, who 'knows and is deeply sorry for the evil she has done to Kashima' – both commit adultery with the same man. By the standards of the day it was a deeply immoral tale, made all the more shocking by the amoral ending, for the punishment of the guilty parties is to remain trapped in the 'rat-pit' of Kashima and to have to pretend that all is well.

'A Wayside Comedy' seems to have been written as an act of revenge, evolving out of the supposed infatuation of Mrs Isabella Burton with a senior political officer notorious for his 'poodle-faking', Sir Lepel Griffin, brilliant and arrogant and already targeted by Ruddy in one of his milder Simla stories, 'Wressley of the Foreign Office'. Since Ruddy had feelings for Mrs Burton, he must have observed these two carrying on behind Major Burton's back in Simla that summer with considerable disgust. Immediately after its publication in the *Week's News* he sent a copy of 'A Wayside Comedy' to Mrs Burton, declaring himself pleased by its 'economy of implication'. To his dismay, Mrs Burton replied that she and her husband had decided to leave India for good, with the hint that the move was to save their marriage. Ruddy's response was to reprint in the *Week's News* a short story which had appeared earlier as a turnover in the *CMG* and was in many respects a preliminary sketch for 'A Wayside Comedy', with adultery and its corrupting consequences as its central theme. This prototype version, 'The Hill of Illusion', had so shocked Alice Kipling when she was shown it in draft form that she had tried to ban it with the remark, 'Never you do that again.' But now Ruddy's mother saw the same unpleasant story reproduced in an even more offensive form. Her response was to write her son a reproachful letter telling him, 'It's clever and subtle and all that and I see the morality of it but, O my boy, how do you know it? Don't tell me about "guessing in the dark". It's an insult to your old Mother's intelligence. If Mrs Hauksbee enlightened you I'm not sorry that she has gone home.'[16]

Ruddy's next step was to write to Mrs Burton to tell her that he had 'fallen in love with an American woman' who was 'everything that is beautiful and fascinating'.[17] No doubt he did it to wound, but he had indeed discovered a replacement for Mrs Burton in Mrs Edmonia Hill, the thirty-year-old daughter of an American Methodist college principal and wife of Professor Alex Hill. A meteorologist by profession and an Ulsterman, Alex Hill had come out to India in 1879 to join his brother as a teacher at the Muir College and was now Professor of Physical Sciences at Allahabad University. Ruddy had met the Hills at a dinner party given by the Allens soon after his arrival and had been bowled over by Edmonia Hill's outgoing nature, which he thought quintessentially American. She was another of those free-spirited matrons who gave as good as they got, but intellectually a cut above others of that type that Ruddy had previously got to know in India – and a great deal more sympathetic.

The Hills occupied Belvidere House – in Mrs Hill's words, 'a famous old bungalow, standing since Mutiny days when nearly every other house was destroyed' – a dilapidated single-storey house with a thatched roof which stood in its own overgrown garden just across the road from the *Pioneer* offices. The couple were accessible and welcoming, and although Edmonia Hill was not particularly attractive, even by Anglo-Indian standards, and stood several inches taller than Ruddy, she had an open countenance not unlike Alice Kipling's, with dark eyes and hair and a sympathetic smile. More importantly, she enjoyed literary talk and, with no children of her own and no family in India, she had time on her hands. Ruddy was immediately drawn to her and she, too, was greatly taken by this exuberant young man, describing him to her sister Caroline in the United States as looking 'about forty, as he is beginning to be bald, but . . . in reality just twenty-two. He was animation itself, telling his stories admirably, so that those about him were kept in gales of laughter.'[18]

Ruddy was by now back with the Allens at No. 1 Bund Road, and finding it increasingly stressful to have George Allen breathing down his neck day and night: 'The *Pioneer* lived under the eye of its chief proprietor,' he wrote of this period. 'It is true I owed him my chance in life, but when one has been second in command of even a third-class cruiser, one does not care to have one's Admiral permanently moored at a cable's length. His love for his paper, which his single genius had created, led him sometimes to "give the boys a hand." On those hectic days (for he added and subtracted to the last minute) we were relieved when the issue caught the down-country mail.'[19] Ruddy had also discovered that social life in Allahabad was stultifying by comparison with Lahore. The Station was top-heavy with 'large-bore officials, and of a respectability all new'[20] and lacked the 'frontier' spirit that was part of Lahore's slightly raffish charm. The same went for the Club, where, according to a contemporary, Ruddy refused to play tennis, billiards or poker and kept himself to himself, so much so that he gained the nickname of 'Muskrat' because he was 'quiet and shy, rather going about the fringe of things and not seeking to make much of a splash'.[21] He maintained this same air of aloofness in the office, causing some resentment among his colleagues. 'Kipling seemed to do little work in the office, and certainly no sub-editing,' was how one of the *Pioneer*'s assistant editors of the time remembered him. 'Most of his time was spent in the *Pioneer*'s library, and it was when I passed through the room on occasion that he looked up from his book and I became conscious of an ominous glint that made me wonder whether this exceedingly amiable youngster could not be a trifle disagreeable without any grave provocation.'[22]

Ruddy's inveterate scruffiness also marked him out. Another journalist on the *Pioneer* afterwards recalled that his first impression of Rudyard Kipling was 'distinctly unfavourable – a small bespectacled youth, blotchy, with startlingly bushy eyebrows – the worst tailored Englishman I had encountered since I left old England's shores, with not an inch of clothes that seemed to fit him'.[23] All this helps to explain why late one night when Ruddy was staying over at the Club three bold and probably inebriated fellow members crept into his room intending to give him a ragging: 'They were almost alongside the bed when suddenly Kipling awoke. "Who's there?" he yelled. A scuttering from in the darkness was the only reply. Suddenly, to the terror of the practical jokers, Kipling whipped out a service revolver from beneath his pillow and fired into the darkness. The room was emptied in a couple of seconds.'[24]

What is striking about these recollections from acquaintances rather than friends or family is that in almost every instance they tell of a young man who kept to himself and chose his own company. Ruddy had begun a process of withdrawal that he was to continue for the rest of his life, socialising only on his own terms, keeping the company of an ever-diminishing circle of trusted friends, guarding his privacy with ever-increasing vigilance.

One trusted friend was the Frenchman Émile Édouard Moreau, the earliest of Kipling's admirers to recognise the commercial potential of his work. Moreau was based in Allahabad and a senior partner of the firm of A. H. Wheeler and Co., which had bookstalls on all the major railway stations in northern India, and it was he who came up with the idea of marketing the stories as part of an 'Indian Railway Library': a series of slim, soft-cover volumes to be sold to railway travellers at one rupee each. Each volume would contain half a dozen or so of the tales already published in the *CMG* and the *Week's News*, assembled by themes. Moreover, Moreau felt confident enough to propose that Wheeler's should not only bear the cost of publication of six volumes but also pay a £200 sterling advance to their author, with further royalties to follow after 1500 copies had been sold. It was a very generous offer that Ruddy was quick to accept. A contract was duly drawn up under which the first volume would be published in the late autumn and the rest at monthly intervals thereafter.

A second round of travels began at the start of 1888. This time Ruddy journeyed eastwards, with Benares as his first stop. The outcome of his visit to this most sacred of Hindu cities was 'The Bride's Progress', published in the *Pioneer* a month later. Purporting to be a humorous account of the visit of a newly married English couple to 'the city of monstrous creeds', it allowed Ruddy to give free rein to his anti-Hindu prejudice. As they make their way down to the city's famous riverside *ghats*, the honeymooners feel increasingly threatened from all sides by 'the symbols of a brutal cult . . . Hanuman, red, shameless, and smeared with oil, leaped and leered upon the walls above stolid, black, stone bulls, knee-deep in yellow flowers. The bells clamoured from unseen temples, and half-naked men with evil eyes rushed out of dark places.' When they emerge into the open air beside the river the bride is horrified to see corpses burning on the steps below and pariah dogs gnawing at half-burned human limbs. She and her husband struggle back through the sunless lanes where 'at every turn lewd gods grinned and mouthed at her, the still air was clogged with thick odours and the reek of rotten marigold flowers, and disease stood blind and naked before the sun ... The walls dripped filth, the pavement sweated filth, and the contagion of uncleanliness walked among the worshippers.' Unable to see beyond the dirt, the bride turns to her husband and asks indignantly, '"Why don't these horrid people clean the place out?" "I don't know," said the Bridegroom, "I suppose their religion forbids it."'

The English couple flee Benares early next morning, and as they leave the city they hear the call to prayer of the muezzin, reasserting the supremacy of monotheism: 'In the silence a voice thundered far above their heads: "*I bear witness that there is no God but God.*" It was the mullah proclaiming the Oneness of God in the city of the Million Manifestations. The call rang across the sleeping city and far over the river, and be sure that the mullah abated nothing of the defiance of his cry for that he looked down upon a sea of temples and smelt the incense of a hundred Hindu shrines.'

Some literary critics have interpreted this story as a satire against globetrotting tourists, but the fact is that Kipling's writing of this period is suffused with anti-Hindu rhetoric; the sentiments expressed in 'The Bride's Progress' are too heartfelt to be anything other than a true reflection of his views. His prejudice is also laced with the fears of disease and of sexual intimacy that Ruddy had evidenced elsewhere in his earlier writing. This may explain why he afterwards suppressed the story. 'My life had lain among Muslims, and a man leans one way or other according to his first service'[25] was how Rudyard Kipling afterwards explained his antipathy towards Hinduism and Hindus. Islam he could relate to, but never Hinduism, as he made clear when he reviewed an English translation of the Sanskrit epic *Mahabharata* in terms that echoed

Macaulay's notorious denunciation of Hindu culture contained in his *Minute on Education* of 1837: 'Boars like purple mountains, maidens with lotos feet and the gait of she elephants, giants with removable and renewable heads and bodies accommodating as the stomach of the sea-cucumber, are scattered broadcast through its pages. The high thoughts, the noble sentiments, the outcomes of human genius . . . are few and far between.'[26]

From Benares Ruddy continued to Bengal, where he inspected coalfields and railway workshops before moving on to Calcutta. Here he professed himself to be hugely shocked to discover a city of squalor, permeated throughout by the stench of drains: 'the big Calcutta stink . . . sickly . . . indescribable'. He had once before drawn a memorable parallel with James Thompson's 'The City of Dreadful Night' in describing Lahore by night, and he now reapplied that same Gothic metaphor to Calcutta, a city with all the outward trappings of modern living but filled with 'the essence of corruption' from which there was no escape. 'Where is the criminal,' he demanded, 'who is to be hanged for the stench that runs up and down Writers' Building staircases; for the rubbish heaps in the Chitpore Road; for the sickly savour of Chowringhi; for the dirty little tanks at the back of Belvedere; for the street full of small-pox; for the reeking gharri-stand outside the Great Eastern [Hotel] . . . and for a hundred other things?' And because the city was now governed by a locally elected municipal council, Ruddy found someone to blame in the Indian membership of the Calcutta Municipal Board – 'men of the breed born in and raised off this surfeited muckheap!'

He visited the debating chamber of the Bengal Legislative Council and there had all his prejudices against both English liberals and Bengali intellectuals confirmed when he heard one of the latter quote John Stuart Mill. 'It is Our own fault,' Ruddy duly protested. 'We taught him what was constitutional and what was unconstitutional in the days when Calcutta smelt. It smells still, but We must listen to all he has to say about the plurality of votes and the threshing of wind and the weaving of ropes of sand . . . They want shovels, not sentiments, in this part of the world.'[27]

This deeply unpleasant attack on Calcutta and its Bengali inhabitants extended over seven articles, afterwards republished under the title of *The City of Dreadful Night and Other Places.* The heading of the last chapter, 'Deeper and Deeper Still', is an allusion to Dante's *Inferno.* Calcutta is depicted as a hell on earth and Kipling sees himself as a modern Dante, touring one circle of hell after another, albeit with a police escort rather than Virgil.

Ruddy was still in Calcutta when it was announced that Lord Dufferin was to end early his term of office as Viceroy and would be leaving India at the end of the year. Dufferin's lukewarm support for the nascent Indian National Congress had been enough to raise Ruddy's hackles but he still greatly admired Lady Dufferin for her advocacy of Indian women's rights, and he responded to the news by writing 'The Song of the Women', thanking her on behalf of Indian women 'in darkness by her hand set free'.[28] Ruddy's reward was a letter of thanks, a volume of Lord Dufferin's poetry and a photograph of Lady Dufferin complete with 'tiara, pink sash and scowl'. 'Wah! Wah!' noted Ruddy. 'They'll be making me Poet Laureat [*sic*] of Peterhoff [*sic*] next!'[29]

In late April 1888 Ruddy was ordered to return to 'the old rag' to deputise for Kay Robinson, who had taken a month's leave and gone to Darjeeling. For the first week he had the company of his father but Lockwood then left for England to oversee the installation of the panelling commissioned by the Duke of Connaught for Bagshot Park. Ruddy then moved into the Club and tried to make the best of it, professing to Edmonia Hill that he was cheered to be back among 'the savage, boastful, arrogant, hot headed men of the North . . . I am rejoiced to be among the men I understand again. They are not saints but I like them and they pretend to like me.'[30] Among them was a 'snaky locked and vulture eyed' Pathan whose proud demeanour inspired Ruddy to work up a report of a frontier murder case in the *CMG* into 'Dray Wara Yow Dee', a short story in which an Afridi tribesman explains how he has beheaded his wife caught in the act of adultery, and why he cannot rest until he has tracked down and killed the other partner in the act. Edmonia Hill found the tale violent beyond comprehension, but to Ruddy it made perfect sense. 'What is your Law to me?' Kipling has his Afghan explain. 'Do the kites of Ali Masjid forbear because the carrion lies under the shadow of the Ghor Kuttri? The matter lies across the Border. It shall finish where God pleases. Here, in my country, or in Hell.'[31]

But as the old realities of Lahore in May began to kick in once more, so too did Ruddy's depression. 'I have returned to the old, wearying, Godless futile life at a club,' he wrote to Mrs Hill. 'Same men, same talk, same billiards – all *connu* and triple *connu* and . . . I could almost swear I had never been away.'[32] Again the heat made it impossible to get a good night's sleep and the night terrors returned – terrors symbolised by the krait which he *knew* lay curled under his bed at night, waiting to strike should he put so much as a hand or toe out from under his sheets. On 19 May Ruddy placed an unsigned turnover in the *CMG* entitled 'Till the Day Break', another of his soliloquies about heat and mental collapse. 'Curious idea – a man's bellowing,' he writes in one paragraph. 'It would be amusing for a punkah-coolie to hear a Sahib bellowing and to know that the Sahib could do nothing, and so to fan that Sahib from this world to the next – if there is one; the punkah-stroke answering the last beat of the pulse just like the relentless tick, tick, tick, of the watch under the pillow.'

As he had done in earlier times of crisis Ruddy kept himself sane by writing: political squibs in verse for the *Pioneer*, stories for the *Week's News* and so many turnovers for his own paper that he had to resort to pseudonyms. The best of his writing from this torrent of work are portraits of Indians at the bottom of the social pile: the sweeper Mowgi in 'The Great Census', who uses his wits to get ahead; the money-lending Marwari twins Ram Dass and Durga Dass in 'Gemini'; the Indian lovers in 'Through the Fire' who die together in a suicide pact; and Little Tobrah in the story of that name who kills his blind sister in a time of famine as an act of mercy. But there is also a deal of bad writing, including an extraordinarily mean-spirited attack on the Bengal civilian Sir William Hunter, who had recently retired from India after years of distinguished service. Hunter's crime was to show support for the Indian National Congress, for which he was branded a hypocrite seeking political advancement in Ruddy's poem 'To the Address of W. W. H.', printed in the *Pioneer* on 1 June. What Ruddy may not have known was that only weeks earlier Hunter had gone out of his way to talk to the editor of a London magazine about publishing some of Ruddy's poems. His restrained rebuke must surely have cut Ruddy to the quick. 'It is to be regretted,' he wrote to Ruddy in July, 'that you devote to clever trifles of this sort talents which are capable of much better things. They practically fix your standard at that of the gymkhana and the mess-room.'[33] Before the end of the year Hunter had written a review of *Departmental Ditties* for the *Academy* which could well be accounted the most important notice Rudyard Kipling ever received. 'Perhaps this young poet is the destined man,' Hunter declared, 'who will make that nobler Anglo-Indian world known as it really is . . . His serious poems seem to me the ones most full of promise. Taken as a whole his book gives hope of a new literary star of no mean magnitude rising in the East.'[34]

When not writing verse or fiction Ruddy passed the hours scribbling long, rambling and increasingly personal letters to Mrs Edmonia Hill. He had now lost the Wop of Albion as a confidante following Margaret Burne-Jones's engagement to Jack Mackail, a scholar of Balliol, and Mrs Isabella Burton had to all intents stopped replying to his letters, so it was Mrs Hill who now became the principal recipient. Night after night he retired to his room at the Club to pour his heart out to her in letters that were part literary, part gossip and part confession. Ruddy confided to Mrs Hill that he was desperately in love with a 'Maiden Peerless' who lived 'far far away'. In letter after letter he agonised at length over what her feelings for him might be and how he should proceed: the Maiden only writes to him infrequently, and when she does her letters are never 'lengthy outpourings'; how can he find out what she thinks, and should he force the issue? 'Tell me how I can tell my Lady to write to me more than she does,' he asks plaintively at one point. 'Again and again I come back to the old question: "Does she know what her power is over me?" My own pride has kept me from writing to her point blank: "For pity's sake write – if it is only a line to let me know that you are still under the same sky as I."'[35] But then Ruddy does force the issue, apparently writing to his beloved 'in the bitterness of my heart', and he immediately regrets it. Again he begs Mrs Hill to advise him on what he should do, apologising as he does so for his 'ravings'. 'Is that vanity to assume she does care a little?' he asks. 'I suppose I shall never know until the end whether she does or whether she does not . . . In your opinion is it worth while for a man to change the whole tenor of his life and his views – whatever they may have been – for the future of a girl's sake?'

The letters have led to a lot of speculation over the identity of Ruddy's 'Dark Lady'. In the absence of any further evidence the most plausible explanation is that she was Ruddy's first love Flo Garrard and that he still clung to the hope that she had some feelings for him, as well as indulging in what he himself called 'building castles in the air at a rate that would disgrace a Clapham Jerry-builder'.[36] Nevertheless, his outpourings had the effect of drawing him much closer to Edmonia Hill, who became his comforter in a way that was maternal without ever being censorious or judgemental. In doing so Edmonia Hill came to fill that void in his life which Ruddy's mother must have ached to close, but which his distrust and her temperament had made it impossible that she should.

The letters have also to be seen as a companion piece to what was Ruddy's major preoccupation during those six weeks in Lahore: the completion of a *conte* or playlet in eight scenes entitled *The Story of the Gadsbys*, inspired by the writings by a popular *fin-de-siècle* French novelist.[37] He had started work on the *Gadsbys* just before setting out for Lahore and when it was done he convinced himself it was the best thing he had ever written: a sophisticated dissection of an Anglo-Indian marriage, nominally for the stage but intended to be read between the lines.

The Story of the Gadsbys opens with the moustachioed masher Captain Gadsby of the Pink Hussars laying siege to Mrs Threecourt, who has 'the worn smile of sixteen seasons, the worse for exchange' – until he notices her virginal daughter Minnie. Three weeks later Gadsby proposes to Minnie and ends a loveless liaison with a Mrs Herriot. Gadsby duly marries Minnie and after an idyllic honeymoon in the hills they face the reality of married life in the plains. When Minnie nearly dies of fever Gadsby is forced to choose between his wife and the army career he loves. He resigns his commission, taking what the author of the play clearly regards as the coward's way out.

It was a while before Ruddy realised that *The Story of the Gadsbys* was a disaster. Whether out of mental exhaustion or from lack of understanding, Ruddy had failed to give expression to the deeper human emotions except in terms that were trite and sentimental. Only the sexually predatory Mrs Threecourt and Mrs Herriot come to life as characters. His Minnie is not so much a person as an ideal, in very much the same way as the 'Maiden Peerless' of his letters appears to be an idealised fantasy of the real Flo Garrard. 'I had an experience,' he admitted afterwards in his autobiography, 'which, in my innocence, I mistook for the genuine motions of my Daemon . . . My pen took charge and I, greatly admiring, watched it write for me far into the nights.'[38] The only literary merit in the *Gadsbys* is to be found in the verses of the closing 'Envoi', with its memorable refrain of 'He travels the fastest who travels alone'. They summarise the play's message that marriage is an obstacle to a man's fulfilment as a man, which suggests that the play's author had very ambivalent feelings about love and marriage.

What should have been a month of 'acting' in Lahore became six weeks as Kay Robinson delayed his return from his leave. He had, it seems, gone to Darjeeling for an assignation with a woman, and to Ruddy's indignation it was this 'strong attraction' that had kept him there beyond the period of his leave. He eventually turned up at Lahore on 12 June, and on the following day Ruddy set off for the hills – although not to Simla, where his mother and sister were, but to Mussoorie, to spend a week with Edmonia and Alex Hill.

Mussoorie was where the Hills habitually took their summer leave. They knew the place intimately, and it is reasonable to assume that they introduced Ruddy to Charlie Wilson, the wealthiest man in Mussoorie and owner of several properties in the area, including the Hotel Charleville, where Ruddy stayed.

The episode back in December of the two Freemasons on the train had given Ruddy a starting point for a tale involving a pair of English loafers with a thirst for adventure who set out to seek their fortunes in the Indian hinterland. There were plenty of examples of European freebooters on the sub-continent whose real-life adventures Ruddy could draw on, ranging from the naval deserter George Thomas, who had ruled over part of the Punjab in the last decade of the eighteenth century, to the American mercenary Josiah Harlan, who had carved out a kingdom for himself in Afghanistan in the late 1830s. But in Mussoorie Ruddy was presented with a much more recent case: that of Charlie Wilson's father, the legendary Frederick Wilson, also known as Rajah Wilson or as *Pahari* Wilson, the 'Mountain-man'.

Described by a contemporary as 'a sort of superior "European loafer" . . . whose skill as a hunter enabled him to earn more than a livelihood', Rajah Wilson was widely believed to be a British soldier who had deserted at the time of the First Afghan War. In fact, he had served in India at that time but after being invalided home to England had returned to India to seek his fortune. According to his obituary notice which the *Pioneer* carried on 6 August 1883: 'He started from Calcutta, armed with five rupees and a gun, on his long march to the Himalayas, accomplishing it successfully. There, amid the scenes he loved with passion to the last, he lived for many years by the sale of what he shot, and finally embarked on timber contracts in the forest with which he was so familiar, until he amassed a considerable fortune . . . Though wholly self-educated, he added to the lore of the sportsman and the naturalist contributions full of bright imagination and literary grace.' What the obituary failed to say was that Wilson had forced himself at gunpoint on the local population of the Upper Gangotri valley, deep in the Himalayan ranges north of Mussoorie, and by the 1850s had become to all intents the local ruler, minting his own coins, taking wives and concubines from the local community and building himself a magnificent summer palace of deodar wood, hidden away in a high mountain valley beyond the Central Himalayan Range. Initially Wilson had made his living as a hunter but in the 1860s he had turned to logging the great deodar and sal forests of the foothills to supply timber for the railways, and by 1877 'had made so much money that it is currently believed in Masuri . . . that he was worth more than £150,000'.[39]

The *Pioneer* obituary also omitted any mention of the tragedy that had clouded the last years of Wilson's life, revolving around his two younger sons, Nathaniel and Henry, whom he had left to 'rule' his mountain estate while he retired with his youngest wife to Mussoorie's premier property, Astley Hall. According to local legend, Nathaniel, the elder and wilder of the two brothers, persuaded the more malleable Henry to join him in kidnapping two high-caste local women at gunpoint and carrying them back to their mountain palace. The scandal was on the point of being resolved by negotiation when Nathaniel went mad and began taking pot-shots at anyone who approached, killing some pilgrims. He was eventually seized while in a drunken stupor, and both he and his brother were then expelled from their mountain kingdom. One version of the story ends with Nathaniel Wilson dying insane as a prisoner of the Maharaja of Tehri-Garhwal, but a more plausible account has him being caught up in a flash-flood soon after his expulsion, and drowning.[40]

Here was a story to stir the imagination, and whether Ruddy got it direct from Charlie Wilson or at third hand, he left Mussoorie for Simla knowing that *his* two Freemason loafers would do as

Rajah Wilson had, and carve out a kingdom for themselves in the mountains. But a more remote location than Tehri–Garhwal was required, and the story itself had to be more than a mere tale of high adventure.

10

'Who travels the fastest'

SIMLA, ALLAHABAD AND AN ENDING, 1888–9

One may fall, but he falls by himself –
    Falls by himself, with himself to blame;
One may attain, and to him is the pelf,
    Loot of the city in gold or fame:
Plunder of earth shall be all his own
    Who travels the fastest, and travels alone.

Rudyard Kipling, 'L'Envoi', from *The Story of the Gadsbys*, 1888

June–July 1888 marked Ruddy's last visit to Simla, and the least enjoyable. Simla now appeared to him as 'a land of ghosts'. Herr von Goldstein's pleasure dome of Benmore had been sold to the Punjab Government and was in the process of being turned into a Secretariat office. The days of 'glamour, wine and witchery' had gone. Despite having 'the ordered felicity of our domestic life to content me, and our queer brutal interchange of thought and work to enjoy', Ruddy felt so alienated that both mother and sister were driven to comment. 'It is owned that I am no longer own-able and only a visitor in the land,' he wrote to Edmonia Hill soon after his arrival. 'The Mother says that it is so and the Sister too and their eyes see far. "You belong to yourself" says the Mother and the Maiden says: "You don't belong to us at any rate."'

The main reason for this discontent was that Ruddy now *knew* he had to leave India for the sake of his career. 'I must – must get away,'[1] he informed Edmonia. His mind was set on what he called 'the Scheme', which was to leave India and make a career for himself in London, initially as a journalist before becoming a full-time writer.

George Allen was also to blame, for he had decided to spend the summer at Mashobra, seven miles east of Simla, together with his second wife, Maud, and their growing family. To Ruddy's 'extreme disgust', Allen ordered him to take over the weekly Simla letter which his mother had been writing for the *Pioneer*, ignoring the fact that his protégé was supposed to be on leave. Then within days came news that in Allahabad George Chesney, the editor of the *Pioneer*, was seriously ill with smallpox and his assistant Park also seedy – and that in Lahore Kay Robinson was down with acute dysentery. Allen held what Ruddy termed a 'tiffin-of-war', at which it was decided that his political correspondent, Howard Hensman, should leave at once to take over the paper in Allahabad and that Ruddy should take Hensman's place in Simla. 'I must put my shoulder to the wheel,' Ruddy wrote to Edmonia Hill. '"We'll give you more leave in September or October," says Allen. "Can't afford it," says I, and once I quit Simla I am sure as nails that I don't go back . . . I am more than ever set in my determination to go home and quit the *Pi* (but this is a confidence most particular). The leading paper in India is an excellent thing but there are many things better in the world and I must strike out and find them.'[2]

With Robinson's recovery the editorial crisis was partially resolved, but Ruddy remained deeply enmeshed in Allen's schemes and became increasingly resentful: 'Allen is reiterating his promises about giving me compensatory leave later on. I don't want it and won't take it . . . I explained to him this morning that I am neither "fish, flesh, fowl nor good red herring" where I am – neither working nor on leave, and that I want to get away to some place where I can work.'

Ruddy also had a family crisis to deal with, involving Trix, who while out picnicking among the pine woods at Mashobra had confessed that her rejected suitor from the previous summer, the gloomy Captain Jack Fleming, was once more calling on her and had again begged her to marry him:

> She talked to me and told me as much about it as a woman would ever tell a man and at last the blessed tears came to her relief and she cried all among the pine-needles while I lacked words that could give her any comfort. Then she pointed out, half crying and half laughing, the uselessness of the beauty of the forest . . . So we agreed that never since the world began was there any sorrow like to her sorrow and hunted for raspberries till the tears were dried and our fingers blue red, and we began to steal from each other's vines and throw pine-cones at each other's heads as it was in the very early days. But somehow the fooling was not amusing and when Trix collapsed on a rock and said: 'Oh how miserable I am!' I felt that we could not play at being babies any more.[3]

With his father absent and his mother down with an imagined attack of diphtheria, Ruddy felt obliged to step in. He ordered Fleming to stay away from their rented cottage – but to no avail; a fortnight later he had to admit defeat:

> 'Only let him see me,' said the Maiden, 'try not to hate him so and then – if there is another quarrel it will all be over – indeed it will.' The Mother said: 'Let them see each other and get to understand each other and perhaps they won't care so much' . . . So I trotted out and caught him and explained that while I hated him as much as ever (poor brute, he was _so_ humble) I liked my sister's peace of mind more and consequently he wasn't to stay at the Club making a gibbering baboon of himself but to come down and see the maiden now and again . . . I always thought that the maid was so wise and sensible. But she said to me: 'In these things I'm no wiser than anyone else – and I care for him ever so much.' I give it up.[4]

Two weeks on and Trix and Jack Fleming were once more engaged, leading her father in England to speculate, all too accurately, on their future prospects of happiness. 'I can only hope with all my heart the child is right,' he wrote to Edith Plowden in late August, 'and that she will not one day when it is too late find her Fleming but a thin pasture, and sigh for other fields . . . He is in the Survey & his record is good – a model young man: Scotch and possessing all the virtues; but to me somewhat austere; not caring for books nor for many things for which our Trix cares intensely.'[5] Right though he was to suggest that the pair were unmatched, Lockwood Kipling quite overlooked the fact that ever since Trix had joined them in Lahore in January 1884 she had lived in close quarters with her mother, a woman whose temperament was every bit as uneven as her own.

Trix was to publish in 1891 a novel under the not entirely anonymous pseudonym of 'Beatrix Grange' entitled *The Heart of a Maid*. Set in British India, it is full of remarks about marriage as a matter of convenience rather than love, with the narrator asserting that 'half the hasty, ill-assorted marriages that take place [in India] have for a cause the fact that the girl is not happy at home'. The maid of the title is 'May' and between May and her mother there is 'very little sympathy, a result probably of their never having lived together until the girl was eighteen. When mother and daughter – comparative strangers, having scarcely met since the latter's early childhood – are put to the test of living together, without the links of custom to bind them, disagreement, even constant quarrelling, is too often the result.' In May's case, two years of living with her mother are enough 'to convince a not very strong-minded girl that marriage was the only career to look forward to'. In Trix's case it was four and a half years.

In late July 1888, with six months of his curtailed term of office left to complete, Lord Dufferin moved into the completed Viceregal Lodge. It was the first residence in Simla to be equipped with electric light, and when the first Viceregal ball was held there it was observed that the ladies' gowns, so bewitching by lamp- and candle-light, now appeared distinctly shabby. The event scarcely gained a mention in the *Pioneer*'s weekly Simla letter, its writer having more pressing concerns on his mind. The most immediate of these was the progress of the first of A. H. Wheeler and Co.'s Indian Railway Library volumes. It was to be entitled *Soldiers Three*, consisting of five already published tales of 'the lives and adventures of my esteemed friends and sometime allies Privates Mulvaney, Ortheris, and Learoyd', together with two more serious stories as yet unpublished: 'With the Main Guard' and 'Black Jack'.

Ruddy had by now secured a promise from George Allen that if he did leave India Allen would retain him as the *Pioneer*'s special correspondent in England. This was enough for him to believe that he had the financial security he needed to seek his fortune in London. 'I go home next year with a new book or two under my arm to make my place,' he wrote to Edmonia Hill. 'As soon as I am fixed up with the regular papers to take my work, [with] a lien on the *Pioneer* for English letters which ought to be a sure prop of £200 a year, I shall rest content to be forgotten by all the sets . . . and to live my life in my own way.' He had plans to revisit some of the country scenes where he had known happiness as a child, including 'the whole of North Devon that I used to know and love,' but then he would settle in London – 'above all, rattling London with some place to go to every night if one cares to . . . to dive into London and break with all the folks I know. If all goes well I shall marry there'.[6]

Whether deliberately or unconsciously, Ruddy now set about burning his bridges. 'Simla always makes me savage,' he wrote to his confidante in Allahabad, 'and this year more than any other of my five seasons.' He treated with contempt Miss Parry-Lambert, the unlovely daughter of the lovely 'Venus Annodomini', to whom he was reported to be engaged; he made fun of the lovely Miss Gussie Tweddell, whom his mother thought just the sort of girl he should marry, but who was unwise enough to show him some verses she had written; he was brutal to the 'gigantic' Mrs Beauclare, who had 'a notion that India is improperly governed', taking her out in a rickshaw to 'an unfrequented path of surpassing vileness' and encouraging her to walk, so that 'in half an hour her boots were cut to pieces, [and] she was blowing like a grampus'; and he was even more brutal to Mrs Napier, who believed herself to be a rival to Mrs Hauksbee, calling her the bigger liar of the two because she was the elder. He also offended the Allens, penning a 'slightly acid' review of a play in which Mrs Maud Allen played the leading role and making no effort to disguise from his employer his determination to get away from India as soon as possible. 'All of this is black treachery to Allen,' he wrote to Edmonia Hill, 'who wishes me to live and die in his service. "Journalism" sez he and, inferentially, "me for your Lord God Almighty." "Literature" sez I and, though this does not concern him, "a divinity of my own choosing."'[7]

Praises from the highest in the land failed to move Ruddy or to curb his appetite for political baiting. One afternoon as he rode down the Mall he was joined by the Commander-in-Chief, General Sir Frederick 'Bobs' Roberts, who asked him what the British troops in India thought about 'their accommodation, entertainment-rooms and the like'. Coming from the second most powerful man in India this was a remarkable compliment, and almost half a century later Kipling described the exchange as 'the proudest moment of my young life'.[8] But this was not how he felt at the time, for Sir Frederick and Lady Roberts were disliked by many of the younger members of the Simla set, chiefly on account of their imperious ways. On 31 August the *Pioneer* ran an editorial suggesting, 'cautiously as a terrier drawing up to a porcupine', that Sir Frederick Roberts's position left him in control of a 'vast patronage' which was open to abuse – a polite hint that he was indulging in nepotism in making military appointments. This left the door open for Ruddy to write one of his political squibs, which appeared in the paper on the following day under the title of 'A Job Lot', with an additional sub-title of 'NOT to be sung in Snowden Theatre'. The verses spoke openly of nepotism, 'that too notorious vice', ending with a hard-hitting, four-line chorus:

> We've heard it before, but we'll drink once more,
>   While the Army sniffs and sobs
> For Bobs its pride, who has lately died,
>   And is now succeeded by Jobs.

This was well over the mark and, as Kipling afterwards admitted in his autobiography, caused a great deal of anger: 'I don't think Lord Roberts was pleased with it, but I know he was not half so annoyed as my chief proprietor.' But as if this offence was not enough, Ruddy then compounded it by writing a second set of verses that further displeased the Commander-in-Chief, as well as angering the departing Viceroy. 'One Viceroy Resigns' purports to be the thoughts of Lord Dufferin in the form of an extended late-night reverie in which he broods over what advice he might give the incoming Viceroy, Lord Lansdowne. It is a sombre meditation in the free style of Robert Browning, full of arresting passages as the Viceroy seeks to put his disillusionment into words: 'You'll never plumb the Oriental mind, /And if you did it isn't worth the toil.'[9] It was not the thoughts put into his head that had raised the Viceroy's temperature, however, but the invasion of his privacy. He had confided to an inner circle of friends in Simla that he proposed to publish some poems written by his mother, Helen, Countess of Gifford, to whose memory he was devoted. Ruddy referred to this in his poem, which led Lord Dufferin to accuse Alice Kipling of betraying a confidence. In fact, it was the scheming Mrs Napier, whose sour 'Mrs Riever' character can be glimpsed in half a dozen of the Simla tales. But Alice was forced to write the most grovelling of apologies on her son's behalf, explaining that she and her husband had been 'grieved to note from time to time offences . . . which no cleverness, nor even genius itself, can excuse. His youth and inexperience of the world in which he does <u>not</u> live, are I feel sure the explanation of what no one regrets more keenly than do his parents.'[10] Despite Alice's assurances that 'the parody will not be republished', it was, reappearing in a revised edition of

Departmental Ditties in 1890, albeit with the offending lines about the Viceroy's mother omitted.

If Ruddy's obstreperousness was intended to bring an end to the state of limbo in which he had been suspended since arriving in Simla, his tactics succeeded. Following the publication of 'A Job Lot' he was ordered to return to Allahabad, his proprietor having conceded that it was indeed time for his star employee to move on. 'I fancy my owners thought me safer on the road than in the chair,' he afterwards wrote. 'My proprietor at Allahabad had his own game to play (it brought him his well-deserved knighthood in due course) and, to some extent, my vagaries might have embarrassed him.'[11] Having already agreed that Ruddy could leave India at some time in the following year, Allen now had to accept that it would be best for all parties if he departed sooner rather than later.

When Ruddy returned in Allahabad in late September 1888 it was not to the Allens but to his new hosts, Alex and Edmonia Hill. His room at No. 1, The Bund had been taken by Howard Hensman, acting for George Chesney at the helm of the *Pioneer*. The Hills offered to have him, and Ruddy accepted with alacrity. At Belvidere House he was given 'the Blue room for his study, and the guest room with the big four poster mahogany bed'.[12]

Here he was able to enjoy the comforts of a family home unencumbered with family tensions, but the greatest blessing was to have the daily companionship of Edmonia Hill and her remarkably tolerant husband. 'You shouldn't have taken me in, dear people, and showed me what a happy home is like,' Ruddy wrote tellingly to them soon after moving in – the Hills themselves having left Allahabad on a tour of the Satpura Hills in the Central Provinces, where Professor Hill had secondary duties to perform as a Government meteorologist. 'Never was a graceless boy in thicker clover,' he added. 'I fare sumptuously on egg soup, cunning stews, roast fowl with all the liver and plantain fritters followed by coffee set upon a table handy to the blue couch, the reading lamp gently moderated thereover and my noble soul cased

in yellow slippers . . . The servants take a wicked delight in pressing beer upon me.'[13]

Quite apart from the company, Belvidere House had the inestimable advantage of being surrounded on all sides by an expanse
of overgrown garden. Ruddy could breakfast every morning on
the front verandah under a thatched roof supported by red sand-
stone pillars and look out from his study window over a garden
abounding in tuberoses, balsams, sunflowers and passion flowers,
with blue jays and parrots screaming in the date palms.[14] Despite
the snakes in the garden, it was as close to his childhood home in
Bombay as he could hope to find, afterwards evoked in 'Rikki-
Tikki-Tavi', the tale of the mongoose who protects the little
English boy Teddy from the two cobras Nag and Nagaina.

In the event, Ruddy's sojourn at Belvidere House was very
brief – scarcely more than four months all told – and his time spent
in the Hills' company briefer still. He was now determined to
leave India before the next Hot Weather, and his thoughts were
increasingly focused on how he might make his way as a writer in
London. In June the *Saturday Review* had called him 'a born story-
teller and a man of humour into the bargain' and in September Sir
William Hunter's essay had appeared in the *Academy*. Buoyed up
by these notices, he wrote to all the literary contacts he knew,
including his former editor Stephen Wheeler, now working for
the *St James's Gazette* and whom he believed responsible for
another favourable notice of *Departmental Ditties* which had
appeared in that paper. He also wrote to literary figures he
admired, including Walter Besant, whose novel *All in a Garden Fair*
had made such a powerful impression on him a year earlier. Besant
had helped set up the Society of Authors, founded with the
express purpose of encouraging young writers and establishing
international rules for copyright, so he was an obvious name to
turn to for support.

To say that Ruddy now experienced a renewal of creative energy
is no exaggeration, except that the bout of activity which now
began was of a different order from the episodes of almost frantic

writing that had accompanied his Hot Weather crises. Now it was as if he was working against a deadline which required that every idea and scrap of plot which he carried in his head should be set down on paper before he left India. It was at Belvidere House that Ruddy poured out the quasi-autobiographical story of the 'House of Desolation' at Southsea in 'Baa, Baa, Black Sheep'. According to Edmonia Hill, the circumstances were that George Allen wanted a Christmas story that would fill a whole sheet of the *Week's News*. Ruddy brooded for a while and then sat down to write. 'It was pitiful,' Mrs Hill afterwards wrote, 'to see Kipling living over the experience, pouring out his soul in the story . . . When he was writing this he was a sorry guest, as he was in a towering rage at the recollection of those days.'[15] According to Trix, the published story came as a very unwelcome Christmas present to their parents. As she told it to her brother's first biographer, and as he subsequently reported it, 'They tried to make Trix say it was all exaggerated and untrue, but even to comfort them she could not pretend that they had ever been happy [at Southsea].'[16] This public airing of the family's dirty linen inevitably widened the gap now growing between Ruddy and his parents.

Over the next four months Ruddy completed some of the best of his Indian tales, the most undervalued being 'The Drums of the Fore and Aft', whose unlikely protagonists are two foul-mouthed drummer-boys, Jakin and Lew: 'When not looked after, they smoked and drank. They swore habitually after the manner of the barrack-room; and they fought religiously once a week. Jakin had sprung from some London gutter and may or may not have passed through Dr Barnardo's hands ere he arrived at the dignity of a drummer-boy. Lew could remember nothing but the regiment and the delight of listening to the band from his earliest years.' The story only takes off when the boys' regiment, nicknamed the 'Fore and Aft', is ordered to Afghanistan to reinforce the troops already engaged in the Second Afghan War. Its ranks are largely made up of untried men, and the realities of frontier warfare come as a shock to them:

At the end of their third march they were disagreeably surprised by the arrival in their camp of a hammered iron slug which, fired from a steady rest at seven hundred yards, flicked out the brains of a private seated by the fire . . . At every march, the hidden enemy became bolder and the Regiment writhed and twisted under attacks it could not avenge. The crowning triumph was a sudden night-rush ending in the cutting of many tent-ropes, the collapse of the sodden canvas, and a glorious knifing of the men who struggled and kicked below. It was a great deed, neatly carried out, and it shook the already shaken nerves of the Fore and Aft . . . Sullen, discontented, cold, savage, sick, with their uniforms dulled and unclean, the Fore and Aft joined their Brigade.

When the regiment finally meets the Afghans in open battle the ferocity of the enemy's charge takes the men by surprise and panic spreads through the ranks. The men turn and run, leaving the two drummer-boys behind. Tipsy on rum stolen from a soldier's canteen, Jakin and Lew can think of nothing better to do than to start playing 'British Grenadiers' on fife and drum. They are soon shot down but their action shames their comrades and they regroup and counter-attack, with 'the curses of their officers in their ears, and in their hearts the shame of open shame'. Fortunately for the regiment, the war correspondent attached to the brigade misses the action and their cowardice goes unreported.

In writing 'The Drums of the Fore and Aft' Kipling combined three episodes of Indian military history: an incident from the days of Clive involving two Indian drummer-boys recounted in Orme's *Military Transactions of the British Nation in Indostan*; the battle of Ahmed Khel in the Second Afghan War, where Mulvaney's supposed 'ould regiment' (the 59th Foot, afterwards the East Lancashire Regiment) suffered a momentary panic; and the Black Mountain Campaign of 1888, in which his old friends from Mian Mir, the Northumberland Fusiliers, were involved. The details of battle, so scrupulously observed, came from Ruddy's questioning of Howard Hensman and other veterans of the Second Afghan War – such as two army officers met at a dinner party in Allahabad. 'After dinner Kipling directed the conversation to the last Afghan War,' recalled a barrister friend. 'The way in which he extracted the information he wanted to know of the two officers made me understand how he was able to write with such detail on subjects on which he had no personal knowledge.'[17] A further source from Allahabad tells of Ruddy 'loafing about [army] Canteens, persuading soldiers to sit and talk to him while he supplied them with all the beer their thirsty souls demanded'.[18]

Yet none of this can fully explain how Kipling came to write with such authority on the psychology of military discipline, courage and cowardice as he does in 'The Drums of the Fore and Aft'. 'Cursed with the rudiments of an imagination,' Kipling writes of Tommy Atkins,

> this young man is suddenly introduced to an enemy who in eastern lands is always ugly, generally tall and hairy, and frequently noisy. If he looks to the right and the left and sees old soldiers – men of twelve years' service, who, he knows, know what they are about – taking a charge, rush, or demonstration without embarrassment, he is consoled and applies his shoulder to the butt of his rifle with a stout heart . . . But, on the other hand, if he sees only men of his own term of service, turning white and playing with their triggers and saying: 'What the Hell's up now?' while the Company Commanders are sweating into their sword-hilts and shouting: 'Front rank, fix bayonets. Steady there – steady! Sight for three hundred – no, for five! Lie down, all! Steady! Front rank kneel!' and so forth, he becomes unhappy, and grows acutely miserable when he hears a comrade turn over with the rattle of fire-irons falling into the fender, and the grunt of a pole-axed ox. If he can be moved about a little and allowed to watch the effect of his own fire on the enemy he feels merrier, and may be then worked up to the blind passion of fighting, which is, contrary to general belief, controlled by

a chilly Devil and shakes men like ague. If he is not moved about, and begins to feel cold at the pit of the stomach, and in that crisis is badly mauled and hears orders that were never given, he will break, and he will break badly, and of all things under the light of the sun there is nothing more terrible than a broken British regiment.[19]

Part of the answer was that Kipling had learned his craft so well as to be able to fool the reader, as the magician fools his audience into believing an illusion to be real. But along with that craftsmanship there is also heightened perception. Just as Charles Darwin's acute observation of the finches on the Galapagos Islands enabled him to draw conclusions about the evolution of species, so Kipling's scarcely less rigorous study of the British soldier in India led him to a greater understanding of human behaviour.

Imagine Jakin and Lew surviving the Second Afghan War and growing into adulthood, only to be discharged from the army for drunkenness or insubordination to become wandering loafers and you have the two heroes of the second of Ruddy's three valedictory stories. Too long to fit into the *CMG* or the *Week's News*, and too good to be cut to fit, 'The Man Who Would Be King' was written in bursts between July and November 1888. It opens with the journalist-narrator being accosted by a European loafer and Freemason, Peachey Carnehan, on a train journey and asked to deliver a message to a brother mason, Daniel Dravot, in a manner almost exactly as described in Ruddy's letter to his cousin Margaret. Six months later the two ne'er-do-wells turn up at the narrator's office with a scheme to set themselves up as rulers of their own kingdom. They have made enquiries and have located the ideal country. 'We have decided that there is only one place now in the world that two strong men can *Sar-a-whack*,' Carnehan tells the narrator:

They call it Kafiristan. By my reckoning it's the top right-hand corner of Afghanistan, not more than three hundred miles from

Peshawar. They have two-and-thirty heathen idols there, and we'll be the thirty-third and thirty-fourth . . . We shall go to those parts and say to any King we find – 'D'you want to vanquish your foes?' and we will show him how to drill men; for that we know better than anything else. Then we will subvert that King and seize his Throne and establish a Dy-nasty.

Kafiristan was a mysterious country inhabited by heathen *kafirs*, first penetrated in 1883 by Captain William MacNair of the Survey of India and a subordinate, Syed Shah, who was one of the explorer-spies trained by the Survey of India to covertly map the countries beyond British India's northern borders. MacNair and 'the Syed' had travelled in disguise and at great risk of their lives, with MacNair growing a beard and darkening his skin with a 'solution of caustic and walnut juice' in order to present himself as a Muslim *hakim* or doctor. Even if Ruddy had failed to get hold of a copy of MacNair's *Confidential Report*, printed at the Survey of India's headquarters in 1885, he was bound to have read the account of his journey subsequently published in the *Proceedings of the Royal Geographical Society*. Remote and mysterious, Kafiristan provided the perfect setting for the most ambitious and most accessible work of fiction written by Rudyard Kipling in India.

Three years after Carnehan and Dravot's visit the narrator is working late in his office, waiting for a final item of news to be wired in, when a 'rag-wrapped, whining cripple' appears at the doorway and declares himself to be Carnehan returned: '"I've come back," he repeated; "and I was King of Kafiristan – me and Dravot – crowned kings we was!"' Carnehan then recounts how he and Dravot entered Kafiristan disguised as a Muslim mullah and servant, and succeeded in establishing themselves as joint rulers by a combination of courage and guile, exploiting their knowledge of Freemasonry to fool the local tribesmen into believing them to be gods. Initially Carnehan and Dravot are presented as figures of fun, but as the story unfolds they are transformed into tragic heroes: men of action whose ambition sets them apart, only to be brought down by the fatal flaw of the classic hero – in this instance Dravot's desire to take a wife for himself from his subjects. By doing so Dravot reveals himself to be all too human; their subjects turn against them, and their empire-building ends in disaster. Only Carnehan lives to tell the tale, which he brings to a climax with a macabre *coup de théâtre*:

> He fumbled in the mass of rags round his bent waist; brought out a black horsehair bag embroidered with silver thread, and shook therefrom on to my table – the dried, withered head of Daniel Dravot! The morning sun that had long been paling the lamps struck the red beard and blind sunken eyes; struck, too, a heavy circlet of gold studded with raw turquoises, that Carnehan placed tenderly on the battered head.
>
> 'You be'old now,' said Carnehan, 'the Emperor in his 'abit as he lived – the King of Kafiristan with his crown upon his head. Poor old Daniel that was a monarch once.'

'The Man Who Would Be King' can be enjoyed as a tale of derring-do with a suitably blood-curdling climax, but it can also be read as an allegory on the romance and folly of empire-building, modelled on the British conquest of India. The two loafers may be rogues, but so was Clive of India; what they further have in common and what sets them apart from other men is their ambition. 'We have decided that India isn't big enough for such as us,' explains Davot to the narrator. 'We are not little men, and there is nothing that we are afraid of except drink, and we have signed a contract on that.' He and Carnehan have sworn to govern according to a set of rules, and when they become kings of Kafiristan, they duly set about establishing a government on British lines by taking a census, establishing land rights and setting up a bureaucracy. But then Dravot breaks their 'contrack', the fatal consequences of which Carnehan describes as 'our Fifty-Seven', by which he means the Indian Mutiny of 1857, provoked as much by British interference with local custom as by naked imperialism. Just as the

East India Company forfeited the right to rule over India by breaking its 'contrack' with the Indian people in 1857, so by abandoning
the rules of non-interference do Carnehan and Dravot lose their
thrones.

The last of the three stories was 'On the City Wall', with its tale
of Lalun, beautiful as a pearl and 'a member of the most ancient
profession in the world'. It is a multi-layered story that brings
together everything Ruddy had learned about Lahore, from his
night-time explorations of the city to his first-hand experiences of
reporting on the annual Muslim festival of Mohurram and the
inter-communal rioting that almost invariably accompanied it.
The story of an anti-British conspiracy, into which the narrator is
unwittingly drawn because of his attraction to Lalun, is not hugely
convincing; what stands out is Kipling's sympathetic portrayal of
Lalun and her circle of admirers. Lalun herself, with all her charms
and her songs and her unsurpassed knowledge of the 'hearts of
men, and the heart of the City', may well be the odalisque beloved
of Orientalists, but she is also a prime mover in the conspiracy,
both seductive and controlling. Her devotees are drawn from all
faiths and all levels, the most ardent being the troubled young
court pleader Wali Dad, who believes he has lost his identity as a
result of his mission education. 'I am not a Muslim,' he protests.
'I am a Product – a Demnition Product. That I owe to you and
yours: that I cannot make an end to my sentence without quoting from your authors.' So Wali Dad wastes his life paying court to
Lalun, constantly mourning 'the shattered hopes of his youth . . .
the country of which he despaired, or the creed in which he had
lost faith'. He is just the kind of English-educated, politicised type
of Indian that Ruddy most despised, but instead of turning him
into the butt of his prejudices, he portrays his plight with enormous sensitivity, so that Wali Dad becomes almost as fully rounded
a character as Lalun.

Unknown to the narrator-journalist, Lalun and Wali Dad are
involved in a plot to free an elderly rebel from the Lahore Fort,
where he has been imprisoned for many years. The Shia festival of

Mohurram is always a time of tension in the city, when the ancient enmity between Hindus and Muslims comes to a head. The prisoner in the Fort is to be sprung under cover of the ensuing violence. Unaware of the plotting, the narrator–journalist turns up unannounced at Lalun's salon, which he finds full of strangers, including 'a fat person in black, with a gold *pince-nez*' – a seditious babu type who is the brains behind the plot. Wali Dad draws the narrator away by taking him out to watch what he mocks as a disgraceful exhibition of superstition: the gilt and painted-paper *taziyas* representing the tombs of the martyred saints Hassan and Hussain being carried in procession through the streets. As the *taziya* processions enter the city the tension mounts:

> The drums were beating afresh, the crowd were howling '*Ya Hasan! Ya Hussain!*' and beating their breasts, the brass bands were playing their loudest, and at every corner where space allowed, Muhammadan preachers were telling the lamentable story of the death of the Martyrs. It was impossible to move except with the crowd, for the streets were not more than twenty feet wide. In the Hindu quarters the shutters of all the shops were up and cross-barred. As the first *tazia*, a gorgeous erection ten feet high, was borne aloft on the shoulders of a score of stout men into the semi-darkness of the Gully of the Horsemen, a brickbat crashed through its talc and tinsel sides.

The cry goes up that the Hindus are dishonouring the faith and fighting breaks out in half a dozen places across the city. The police move in but are powerless to stop the mobs surging through the streets. Hitherto Wali Dad has watched the proceedings with the eye of a cynic but now he too gets caught up in the fervour and plunges into the thick of the fighting. The narrator rides back to Lalun's house by the city wall, where he helps her pull an old man out of the ditch surrounding the Fort. She then asks him to do her a special favour by escorting the old man across the city. Quite unaware that he is the rebel from the Fort, the narrator leads him through the lines of British troops to hand him over to the fat gentleman with the gold *pince-nez*. The narrator returns to Lalun's door to find Wali Dad transformed: 'He was sobbing hysterically and his arms flapped like the wings of a goose. It was Wali Dad, Agnostic and Unbeliever, shoeless, turbanless, and frothing at the mouth, the flesh of his chest bruised and bleeding from the vehemence with which he had smitten himself. A broken torch-handle lay by his side, and his quivering lips murmured, "*Ya Hasan! Ya Hussain!*" as I stooped low over him.'

'On the City Wall' is replete with ironies, one of which is that, once freed, the old rebel finds that India has moved on and has no place for him and his vision of liberating India with the sword: 'He went to the young men, but the glamour of his name had passed away, and they were entering native regiments or Government offices, and Khem Singh could give them neither pension, decorations, nor influence – nothing but a glorious death with the back to the mouth of a gun.' So he gives up and returns to imprisonment in the Fort. The narrator, too, is finally made aware of the extent to which he has been a pawn in a game played entirely over his head. Having unwittingly participated in a conspiracy against his own people, he must remain silent or face ruin. At an early stage of the game Lalun has joked that his role is to be that of vizier at her court, and at the end he has to acknowledge that is what he has become: counsellor to a queen of courtesans.

In all three stories the leading characters are outsiders and low-lifers: two foul-mouthed barrack-rats; two ex-Army loafers; a prostitute and an Anglicised Muslim who has lost his faith. All are dreamers and losers, who nevertheless achieve the status of heroes because they chance everything; even when they lose, they do so gloriously. The three stories constitute a second milestone in Ruddy's literary life. There were plenty of Simla tales, plains tales and *Soldiers Three* stories still to come, many of them as frivolous as any that had gone before, but in the nine months that had passed since he had left Lahore Ruddy's outlook on life had undergone a radical transformation. In growing older and wiser he had

John Lockwood Kipling and Alice Macdonald; the engaged couple looking pensive, photographed in Wolverhampton in early 1865 shortly before their wedding. (University of Sussex Library Special Collections, courtesy of National Trust)

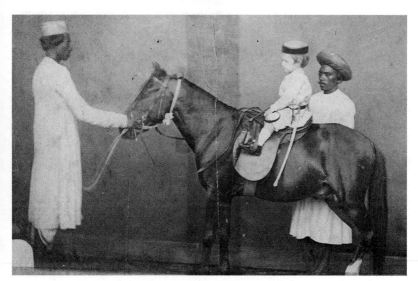

The *chota sahib* mounted; probably taken in a Bombay studio when Ruddy was aged three or four. One of the Indians is a Muslim, the other a Hindu Pathare Prabhu.

(University of Sussex Library Special Collections, courtesy of National Trust)

'A sturdy little boy not quite six'; Ruddy at about the time he entered 'The House of Desolation' at Southsea in 1871.

(University of Sussex Library Special Collections, courtesy of National Trust)

The budding poet; Ruddy in the throes of puberty at fourteen at the United Services College, Westward Ho!

(University of Sussex Library Special Collections, courtesy of National Trust)

'Gigger knows his way about'; Stalky and Co at USC, Westward Ho! George Beresford's drawing shows Beresford ('M'Turk'), Kipling ('Beetle') and Dunsterville ('Stalky'), with Pugh ('Prout'), the headmaster Cormell Price ('the Head'), and the English and Classics master Crofts ('King').

(Kipling Society)

Ruddy and the Pater, Simla 1883; Ruddy at seventeen and enjoying his first leave in Simla before returning to the heat of the plains.
(University of Sussex Library Special Collections, courtesy of National Trust)

'Kipling will do'; Ruddy's patron George Allen, chief proprietor of the Allahabad *Pioneer* and part-owner of the *Civil and Military Gazette*, painted in old age.
(Col. Mike Allen)

The Civil and Military Gazette offices in 1885. A sketch based on a photograph, from the papers of 'A Hustling American' who wrote to the *Kipling Journal* in 1930: 'Mr Kipling is leaning against the pillar on the left. A man named Wilson may be in the group. He had been a corporal in the 9th Lancers – a very smart fellow who was employed in the office as a draughtsman for maps etc. He used to take Rudyard Kipling sometimes to a sergeants' mess.' (Kipling Society)

Kim's gun zam-zammah outside the old museum, before it was moved to its present site outside the new Lahore Museum, postcard c. 1890. (Charles Allen)

Simla Ridge, with the Lower Bazaar and the newly completed Town Hall, seen from just above James Walker's House 'Kelvin Grove' on the slopes of Jakko, c. 1888.

(From the album of Lt. Col. C. L. Harvey, APAC, BL)

Trix at eighteen, mounted on 'Yorick',
Lahore 1886. (Miss Helen Macdonald and Mrs Lorna Lee)

Trix in evening dress with fan, Simla 1888.
(Carpenter Kipling Collection, Library of Congress)

Trix's jilted suitor Kay Robinson, with his wife and children on the lawn of their house in
Lahore. The photograph was taken in the early 1890s after Ruddy had left India.

(Robinson Album, APAC, BL)

A rare copy of *The Phantom 'Rickshaw*, published in 1889 as the fifth in the Indian Railway Series. Although the Mayo School of Art is credited all the covers were the work of Lockwood Kipling. (BL)

The *lat sahib* off duty: Lord and Lady Dufferin, together with their five children and members of their staff at Peterhof, probably photographed in the summer of 1887. Trix Kipling's twice-jilted suitor Archie, Lord Clandeboye, is seated on the far right. Lord 'Bill' Beresford stands with arms folded nearby.

Ruddy seated in his open carriage known as the 'the pig and whistle', outside Belvidere, Allahabad, 1889. (Carpenter Kipling Collection, Library of Congress)

Mrs Edmonia Hill seated on the aerial root of a banyan tree in the grounds of Belvidere, Allahabad, 1889. (Carpenter Kipling Collection, Library of Congress)

Carrie Balestier, aged twenty-seven, a studio photograph taken in Brattleboro, Vermont, before she and her sister Josephine came to join their brother Wolcott in London in 1889.

'The Infant Buddha': Lockwood Kipling's pencil drawing of a stone figure in the Lahore Museum, which he passed on to his son.

'O best beloved': Ruddy with Josephine in a pushchair, 1896.

become more serious and reflective. A growing identification with the common man, whether in the guise of a British Tommy, an Afghan horse-dealer or a Jat peasant farmer, had been accompanied by an increased antipathy towards those he perceived as their exploiters, British and Indian – not the virile men of action who sweated it out in the district or on the frontier but those who sat behind desks in headquarters or on committees, writing reports or manifestos and tying themselves and others in red tape. Perhaps there was an element of self-loathing here, for what were these last but men like himself: thinkers and intellectuals, physically inadequate either by breeding or through soft living, who lived by the pen rather than the sword or the ploughshare?

Ruddy's last two political squibs written in India were both directed at men and institutions he despised. Published in the same month, October 1888, they represent the two faces of the Kipling coin, the one a sneer at the native press for its presumption in criticising Lord Dufferin's viceroyalty, the other an attack on a Government Commission which had delivered a report on the conditions of the Indian peasantry and found no cause for concern, despite the fact that several regions of India were experiencing drought and famine. This last allowed Ruddy to expound his view that the *Pax Britannica*, for all its proclaimed achievements, had done nothing for the ordinary Indian:

> His speech is of mortgaged bedding,
>   On his kine he borrows yet,
> At his heart is his daughter's wedding,
>   And his eyes foreknowledge of debt.
> He eats and hath indigestion,
>   He toils and he may not stop;
> His life is a long-drawn question
>   Between a crop and a crop.[20]

These same concerns about the nature of good government and the fitness of those who wish to govern can be seen in two short stories begun in Ruddy's last months in India but subsequently completed and published in England: 'The Enlightenment of Pagett, MP',[21] and 'The Head of the District',[22] both written with the intention of educating the English public as to the true state of affairs in India.

The visiting Parliamentarian Pagett had already made an appearance in Kipling's writing as the 'fluent liar' Pagett, MP, in the poem of that name. In 'The Enlightenment of Pagett, MP' the same man embarks on a fact-finding tour of British India but has the good fortune to encounter an old school chum who is now a

THE APPLAUSE OF LISTENING

SENATES TO COMMAND

Gray.

MEMBER OF PARLIAMENT COLLECTING

INDIAN FACTS & FIGURES

The Enlightenment of Pagett MP, J. L. Kipling (National Trust)

Deputy Commissioner. His friend Orde soon puts him right by producing a string of local witnesses who each in turn profess loyalty only for their own caste or racial group and hatred for the rest. 'Pride of race, which also means race-hatred, is the plague and curse of India and it spreads far,' he explains. To keep India's racial and caste divisions in check requires a strong and impartial government, which the Indian National Congress will never be able to provide.

The other story, 'The Head of the District', is less polemical but no less prejudiced against the babu and the Bengali intellectual.

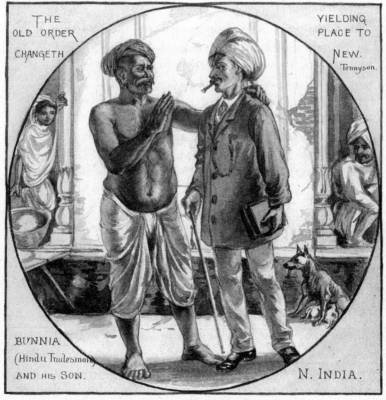

J. L. Kipling reflecting his son's anti-babu prejudices (National Trust)

The British head of a District on the North-West Frontier dies of fever and, despite his pleas for a strong man who can command the respect of the volatile local tribesmen, is replaced by a well-educated Bengali, Grish Chunder De. When word of the appointment gets out, law and order break down, and the Bengali's brother is murdered by the tribesmen. Grish Chunder De cannot cope and his British deputy has to step in to restore order. Both stories carry the same message: Indians are unfit to rule themselves, and only Britain can provide the firm hand that India requires.

Today both stories leave a bad taste in the mouth, but they had a specific context: the decision of the Indian National Congress to hold its fourth annual conference in Allahabad at the end of December 1888. Initially the *Pioneer's* response had been to declare the body an irrelevance. However, this time there were twelve hundred delegates in attendance, drawn from all over India, and the movement could no longer be ignored. The *Pioneer* was now the leading mouthpiece of those Anglo-Indians determined to preserve the political status quo in India. Under George Allen's direction the paper waged an unrelenting campaign against the Indian National Congress, one in which the young Rudyard Kipling more than punched his weight. Always conscious of the debt he owed his chief proprietor, Ruddy was more than happy to do his bit, having convinced himself that the Indian National Congress was a Hindu-dominated political party made up of men disqualified by breeding, religion, history and education from ruling over the Indian masses – in marked contrast to the Muslims, in his view 'the most masterful and powerful minority in the country', possessing strength of character, strong moral convictions based on their religion, and a long history as the traditional rulers of India. In Allahabad Ruddy had found a champion of the Muslim cause in Sir Syed Ahmad Khan, founder of the progressive Alighar Muslim University, and he had come to share the Muslim leader's fears that if the Indian National Congress ever came to power, the voices of India's Muslim minority would cease to be heard.

On 1 January 1889, two days after the conclusion of the Indian National Congress conference, the *Pioneer* carried an article entitled 'A Study of the Congress by an Eye-Witness', unsigned but unquestionably the work of its most waspish writer. The report dismissed the conference as a *putli nautch* or puppet show, mocked the delegates as unrepresentative and referred to the presence of a number of 'half-castes', including one 'brown Captain'. This was unmistakably a reference to Captain Andrew Hearsey, the natural son by an Indian *bibi* of the late General Sir John Hearsey, famous as the man who had ridden down and disarmed Mangal Pandey, the first sepoy mutineer of 1857. Captain Hearsey had taken the courageous step of publicly supporting the Congress movement. However, he was notoriously short-tempered, and when he read the report in the *Pi* he stormed into the editor's bungalow and proceeded to thrash George Chesney with a horsewhip. The office staff came to Chesney's rescue and Hearsey was thrown out of the building. He was then charged with assault, brought before the city magistrate and sentenced to a month's imprisonment in Naini Tal jail.

Ruddy followed these events from the sidelines, reacting to Hearsey's punishment with uncharitable delight but knowing also that he was partly to blame and fearful of the consequences. 'The Native Press,' he wrote in a note to Edmonia Hill, 'is pointing out with great glee that I, and not Mr Chesney[,] ought to have been whacked by Hearsey. Hall tells me that the same gentleman is now in Naini [jail] maturing plans that shall sweep the *Pi* off the face of the earth.'[23] As Ruddy feared, Captain Hearsey was not the sort of man to let things lie and on his release he sued Chesney, as editor of the *Pioneer*, for defamation. At this point George Allen stepped in, declaring that it was he and no one else who had written the offending article. He also initiated a cross-action against Hearsey, which led to both cases being dropped. However, the furore effectively resolved the issue of when Ruddy should quit India: it was to be in weeks rather than months.

The Hearsey scandal came at a bad time for Ruddy, for in mid-January a fever which Edmonia Hill had been nursing since the start of the year suddenly flared up into what the doctor diagnosed as cerebral malaria, followed by pleurisy. A nurse had to be brought in and Ruddy moved out to the Club, from where he dispatched a stream of letters to Belvidere House, addressing Edmonia Hill no longer as 'Mrs Hill' but as 'My Lady'. For a week Edmonia Hill was 'deathly sick' and 'babbling like an idiot' and it was another five before she was strong enough to receive visitors. Her illness happened to coincide with an outbreak of smallpox in the station and the combination of events was almost too much for Ruddy to bear. 'The last month,' he wrote in mid-February, 'has been to me one long stretch of "fever an' ague" coupled with violent sickness and mental depression, yea even to the verge of hanging myself. It was never bad enough to spoil my work or at least stop it but it put me "down in a gulf of black despair". . . I wrote you two letters that were so gloomy, and suicidal in their tendencies that I tore 'em up.'

This confession was written not to Mrs Hill but to Ruddy's cousin Margaret Burne-Jones. It had been a year since he had last written to her and although he could no longer address her as 'Wop' or speak as freely as before, he still felt the need to unburden himself. 'It nearly broke me,' he confessed:

> You don't know how awful it is to have a brilliant clever American woman in whose house you have lived, becoming for the time being insane. Except for the joy of her recovery, and the deep delight in proving the doctor wrong, I wouldn't go through the past six weeks for all under Heaven . . . She's hysterical and captious and exacting beyond belief but these little incidents are cheap at the price. She can do anything she darn well pleases so long as she keeps her head.

What Ruddy also revealed in the same letter was that the date of his departure from India was now fixed. The Hills had decided that Edmonia needed a long sea voyage to recover her health and were therefore going to go home to America by easy stages by way of

Burma, Singapore, Hong Kong and Japan – and they had invited Ruddy to join them. In a week's time he would go to Lahore to say goodbye to his parents, and three weeks later would join the Hills on the quayside in Calcutta:

> On the 9th of next month the bows of my steamer ought to be pointing for Rangoon . . . I've got about a thousand pounds of my own and the *Pi* will take a series of letters on my wanderings. Further they will guarantee me £100 a year for the sister paper, the *Civil and Military Gazette*, and at the end of two years claim first refusal of my services at enhanced rates if I don't wish to stay on in England. Also the royalty of my *Plain Tales* is bringing me in £300 a year . . . My other books are all about the country and are selling like smoke . . . Anyway I ought to be in blue water a month after this and if I have time to stay over a steamer or two I shall go up to Mandalay the capital of our new Burma and see all the old schoolfellows I can.

Even though Ruddy looked forward to seeing his mother again – 'I confess that I should like to feel her arms round me once more before I go' – he was eager to bring the 'tyranny' of India to an end, 'for I am practically fifteen years older than my age – broken down, bitter, and un[?] . . . It has taken the bulk of my top-hair off and I am as bald as a coot: or I shall be soon: and the gray hairs (don't laugh) have begun to come on my temples whence I pluck them in disgust.'

And yet, for all the hardships, he was proud of what he had achieved in his six and a half years in India:

> As your grandfather said: 'Lord what things I lie here and remember!' I've had a good time. I've tasted success and the beauty of money, I've mixed with fighters and statesmen, administrators and women who control them all, and 'much have I seen, cities and men'. It was vivid and lively, and gloomy and savage. I've tried to get to know folk from the barrack room

and the brothel, to the Ballroom and the Viceroy's Council and I have in a little measure succeeded. My training has been extensive and peculiar and now I'm going to come home by long wanderings to see how it will work.[24]

A week later Ruddy bade farewell to the proprietor of the *Pioneer* and his staff. As a parting gift, George Allen gave Ruddy six months' pay in lieu of notice. Although relieved to see him go, he had no doubts as to the twenty-three-year-old's literary talent and was canny enough to ensure that he continued to write for him. But not everyone on the paper thought as Allen did. William Dare, managing director of the *Pioneer*, told Ruddy: 'Take it from me, you'll never be worth more than four hundred rupees a month to anyone.'[25]

On 21 February Ruddy and his bearer Kadir Baksh were reunited with their respective families in Lahore, and Ruddy's relations with his parents, which had been strained for some months, were restored. 'I can hardly tell you how pleased I am to find the Fambly looking so well,' he wrote to Edmonia Hill. 'The Pater is a young and frivolous lad by comparison with the weighed-down man I left behind me. The Mother is stronger than I have known her for years, and the child radiant in the hope of Jack's approaching return.' Trix and Jack Fleming were to be married in the summer and Ruddy had no great desire to witness their wedding, grumbling to Mrs Hill that Fleming had 'hung her about with jewellry from pearl necklaces to curb-chain bangles and one – two – three engagement rings! I walked round and round her till she grew dizzy asking: "Where did you get this" and the invariable answer was: "Oh, Jack gave that to me, ages ago. Didn't you know?" I didn't but perceive now that there is a steady undercurrent of Jack flowing through the house.'

What was much more to Ruddy's liking was to find himself greeted as a friend by all and sundry in Lahore, and to have a stream of 'horsedealers, clerks (we don't keep babus in these parts), carpenters, coach-builders, and a whole horde of chaprassis and low folk' turning up on the verandah to pay their respects. He called in at the offices of the *CMG* and found his old friend Kay Robinson fit and hearty, but uncommunicative. Ruddy had recently learned that the woman Robinson had taken to Darjeeling the previous May was in fact his newly married wife, but when he raised the subject Robinson refused to enlighten him: 'I didn't pursue the topic as it did not seem to delight him.'

It was now the kite-flying season in the Punjab, and one morning father and son joined the local population in the streets of the Mozung District to try their hands at this most deceptive of sports, for every kite string was limed with ground glass so that it might cut through the string of other kites. ''Tis a most fascinating game and mysterious withal,' he told Edmonia Hill. 'You don't see and cannot tell who your antagonist is. He may be a quarter of a mile away and the spoils of battle fall to a third person equally unknown to you both. Very much like life isn't it. I am very delighted with the new pastime and this morning cut away a big white butterfly kite that deliberately challenged me and flew across a high belt of trees to catch me.'[26]

Shortly before his departure Ruddy called in again at the 'old Rag' to say goodbye to Kay Robinson. Now he learned a little more about Robinson's marriage: 'Kay really is married but, being by nature a brute, he keeps his wife in Amritsar and doesn't tell people up here.' For reasons unknown but which may have been linked to his wife's background Robinson was unwilling to have her with him in Lahore. 'This is not nice,' was Ruddy's response. 'Seems to me that if a man becomes possessed of a wife, no matter by what strange and accidental means, it is his duty to see that she ranks with him. His own pride ought to make him jam her down the throat of society.' The newspaper had recently moved into new premises, so that all that remained of Ruddy's old office was 'the chair and table where I had sweated through those long hot nights . . . It all seemed so strange and so distant.'[27]

On 3 March Ruddy handed over to his parents for safe keeping the tin box containing the manuscript of *Mother Maturin* – 'the novel that is always being written and yet gets no furrader'.[28] His motives for leaving behind what was supposed to be his great Indian novel remain unexplained. He then bade farewell to his parents and his sister, to his beloved terrier Vixen and to Kadir Baksh and the other family servants at Bikaner House, and was driven by his father in the family trap to the railway station in time to catch the evening train. Two mornings later he alighted briefly at the station platform at Allahabad, where he saw the Hills into their railway compartment and said goodbye to his old employer George Allen. After a further night in the train he and the Hills arrived in Calcutta, where on 7 March Ruddy sold the copyright of his six Indian Railway Library books to A. H. Wheeler and Co. for £200 and a four per cent royalty on all sales.[29] Two days later the three travellers boarded the SS *Madura*, bound for Rangoon.

II

'Life and Death ... and Love and Fate'

> 'And what,' said Gobind one Sunday evening, 'is your honoured craft, and by what manner of means earn you your daily bread?'
> 'I am,' said I, 'a *kerani* – one who writes with a pen and paper, not being in the service of Government ... I write on all matters that lie within my understanding, and many that do not. But chiefly I write of Life and Death, and men and women, and Love and Fate according to the measure of my ability, telling the tale through the mouths of one, two or more people.'
>
> Rudyard Kipling, Preface to *Life's Handicap;*
> *Being Stories of Mine Own People,* 1891

On 4 October 1889 Ruddy landed in Liverpool, accompanied by Mrs Edmonia Hill, on whom he doted, and her younger sister, Carrie Taylor, whom he professed to love. Seven months of travelling had taken him across two-thirds of the globe and had engendered a stream of jaunty articles for the *Pioneer* and the *CMG*. In Burma he had been charmed by the forwardness of the women, who had looked 'at all the world between the eyes'; in Singapore, struck by the energy of the Chinese as compared to the Indians; in Japan, uncertain whether to class the Japanese as sahibs or Natives. From San Francisco he had continued his sight-seeing alone while Alex and Edmonia Hill went on ahead to visit their families, and the further he had travelled eastwards across the

North American continent the stronger had grown his conviction that egalitarian America presented a model for the future in which the composite 'Anglo-American-German-Jew' would be 'the Man of the Future'. 'Here are Americans,' he had enthused to his Anglo-Indian readers, 'men ruling themselves by themselves and for themselves and their wives and their children – in peace, order and decency.'

Ruddy had also found much to admire in American womanhood: 'They are clever: they can talk . . . they are self-possessed without parting with any tenderness.'[1] Indeed, so enamoured did he become of this new model woman that after two idyllic weeks spent among Edmonia Hill's strait-laced Methodist family in Beaver, North Pennsylvania, he fell romantically in love – both with her sister Carrie, a 'full-statured woman with the imperial eyes and the mouth of eloquence', and with the 'absolutely fresh, wholesome, sweet life'[2] she represented. By the end of August Ruddy and Carrie Taylor had become unofficially engaged, the only obstacle to a public engagement being Professor Taylor's qualms about Ruddy's religious affiliations. When the time came for Ruddy to begin the last stage of his travels and return to England, both sisters chose to accompany him. This curious arrangement came about because Professor Hill had gone on ahead to resume his teaching duties at Allahabad, leaving Edmonia to follow at a more leisurely pace together with her sister, who had agreed to join her in India as a companion.

During his progress across the Pacific and America Ruddy had received further intimations of literary success: a pirated American edition of *Plain Tales from the Hills* displayed in a bookshop in Yokohama; requests for interviews from no fewer than four reporters when he disembarked at San Francisco; a month later, news of a 'splendid review' of *Soldiers Three* in the *Spectator*, together with a fan letter from the essayist and critic John Addington Symonds also praising *Soldiers Three*; finally, in September, favourable reviews of *In Black and White* and *Wee Willie Winkie* in the *World* and the *Saturday Review*, the latter describing their author as 'a new writer, new to the English as distinct from the Anglo-Indian public. He is so clever, so fresh, and so cynical that he must be young.' There had also been a memorable put-down from the New York publishers Harper and Brothers when the firm's head, Henry Harper, turned Ruddy away with the remark: 'Young man, this house is devoted to the production of literature.'[3]

After revisiting his Aunt Georgie and her family at The Grange, the Three Dear Ladies in Warwick Gardens – now very old – and the lesser Macdonald aunts and uncles living in London, Ruddy set about finding lodgings in the West End with the help of the Taylor sisters and a male Taylor cousin who had come along in the role of a chaperone. They settled on a suite of unfurnished rooms on the fifth floor of Embankment Chambers, 19 Villiers Street, between the Strand and the Thames, which they then set about furnishing in as exotic a style as Ruddy could afford. The location was a district 'primitive and passionate in its habits and popula-tion' – in plainer terms, infested with prostitutes and brothels – and was probably chosen because of its close proximity to the *Pioneer*'s London offices in the Strand.

In the hurly-burly of London the *tendresse* that Ruddy and Carrie Taylor had evidently felt for each in the pastoral landscape of northern Pennsylvania began to wane, and a point must surely have been reached when all three parties became aware that Ruddy cared much more for Edmonia than he did for Carrie – and that the unmarried sister's role was essentially that of a stalk-ing-horse. On 25 October Ruddy and the Taylor cousin saw the two sisters off at the Royal Albert Docks. It was an awkward part-ing for all and an agonising one for Ruddy, as he continued to keep up the pretence that it was Carrie who had his affections. 'Verily dear people,' he wrote to both sisters after returning to his rooms that evening. 'When your faces had gone into white blobs and the last twirl of Mrs Hill's boa was indistinct (or else there was something in my eyes) my empty tummy heaved within me and there fell upon me a fine and gilt edged misery.' But as he continued to write his letter became increasingly directed at Edmonia alone:

> I wasn't half so wretched when I went away by myself 7 years ago [i.e. from England to India in 1882]. Nor indeed was there so much reason, for you have made my life happy and delightful for two years – given me help, sympathy, encouragement and council [*sic*] and a host of things of which it is easy to think but not so easy to write down in black and white . . . I'm miserable and a perfectly illogical soul within is crying out 'Come back to me, come back to me!' as tho' I were a little child. I believe I am and a deed fool too. But you go on and have a good time and take care o' Miss Taylor who is going to take care of you and remember that I am always and always
>
> Your Ruddy.[4]

In the weeks that followed Ruddy wrote to both sisters, but his long, chatty letters to Edmonia were in marked contrast to those he sent Carrie, which were short and stilted, for all his protestations of undying love. One letter stands out, written to Carrie on 9 December apparently in response to a request from her father that he clarify his religious beliefs. In it Ruddy set out his credo:

> Chiefly I believe in the existence of a personal God to whom we are personally responsible for wrong doing . . . I disbelieve directly in eternal punishment . . . I disbelieve in an eternal reward. As regards the mystery of the Trinity and the Doctrine of Redemption I regard them most reverently but cannot give them implicit belief . . . Summarized it comes to <u>I believe in God the Father Almighty maker of Heaven and Earth and in one filled with His spirit who did voluntarily die in the belief that the human race would be spiritually bettered thereby</u> . . . I believe[,] having seen and studied eight or nine creeds[,] in Justification by work rather than faith, and most assuredly do I believe in retribution both here and hereafter for wrong doing,

as I believe in a reward, here and hereafter for obedience to the Law. There! You have got from me what no living soul has ever done before.[5]

Not even for her 'sweet sake', Ruddy told Carrie, would he perjure himself on the question of his faith, and as if to emphasise how differently he thought from her Ruddy then went on to declare that there was something else that worried him even more than her questioning his beliefs: 'You wrote, Mademoiselle, some stuff – not to put too fine a point upon it – some ABJECT DRIVELLING ROT – LUNACY – BOSH – ! on the subject of All in a Garden Fair and your views about poets and sympathy, culled from the pages of Walter Besant. You fear and then again, you didn't know as to how and so forth . . .' It was a none-too-kind way of saying that the two of them were incompatible.

This was Ruddy's penultimate letter to Carrie Taylor and almost the last of his many letters to Edmonia Hill. With his letter of 9 December Ruddy had effectively sabotaged his relationship with Carrie Taylor and, in doing so, his relationship with Edmonia Hill.

Embankment Chambers had the inestimable advantage of being directly opposite Gatti's Musical Hall, built into the foundations of Charing Cross Railway Station, and it had Harris the 'Sausage King' on the ground floor, where he could dine on quantities of sausage and mash for tuppence. This became Ruddy's home for the next twenty-two months; a period when success came to him 'as a flood' and which he afterwards looked back upon as 'a dream, in which it seemed that I could push down walls, walk through ramparts and stride across rivers'.[6]

Entrance to Gatti's was to be had for fourpence, to include a pewter tankard of beer or porter, and Ruddy became a music hall regular, enjoying 'the smoke, the roar and the good fellowship of relaxed humanity', often in the company of 'an elderly but upright barmaid . . . deeply and dispassionately versed in all knowledge of evil as she had watched it across the zinc she was always swabbing off'. After the staid entertainments of the Gaiety Theatre, Benmore and Montgomery Hall, the vibrancy and the sheer vulgarity of London's music halls were a revelation, and Ruddy plunged deep into what he saw as their 'basic and basaltic truths' which 'opened a new world to me and filled me with fresh thoughts'. After one such visit on 15 November he lay in bed all morning ruminating before rising to set down a very personal account of the music hall for his Anglo-Indian readers. It ended:

> That night, as I looked across the sea of tossing billycocks and rocking bonnets – as I heard them give tongue, not once, but four times, their eyes sparkling, their mouths twisted with the taste of pleasure – I felt I had secured Perfect Felicity . . . The chorus bubbled up again and again throughout the evening, and a Red-coat in the gallery insisted on singing solos about 'a swine in the poultry line' . . . and the pewters began to fly, and afterwards the dark street was vocal with various versions of what the girl had really told the soldier, and I went to bed murmuring: 'I have found my Destiny'.[7]

The outcome was 'the first of some verses called *Barrack-Room Ballads*, which I showed to Henley of the *Scots*, later *National Observer*, who wanted more'. As Kipling tells it in *Something of Myself*, W. E. Henley, a flamboyant, larger-than-life character with a wooden leg who inspired Robert Louis Stevenson's pirate 'Long John Silver', was the man who first brought his work to public attention in London. But that was not quite how it happened, for if any single person deserved that accolade it was Ruddy's former *bête noire*, the 'Amber Toad'.

Unknown to Ruddy, his letter to Stephen Wheeler written the previous December asking him to promote his Indian Railway Library volumes in the *St James's Gazette* had paid off, for the editor, Stephen Low, had been so struck by *Soldiers Three* that he had talked of a new talent which had 'dawned on the eastern horizon', as great as Charles Dickens and possibly greater. 'I got

Wheeler to put me in touch with Kipling on his arrival in London,' wrote Low some years later,

> and one morning there walked into my office a short, dark, young man with a bowler hat, a rather shabby tweed overcoat, an emphatic voice, a charming smile, and behind the spectacles the brightest eyes I had ever seen. He told me that he had to make his way in English literature, and intended to do it . . . I suggested that he might like to keep his pot boiling by writing sketches and short stories for the *St James's*, which suggestion he willingly accepted.

Low took the twenty-three-year-old out to lunch in Fleet Street and encouraged him to talk – 'and he talked in those days with the same abandon and energy as he wrote. One after another of the lunchers laid down knife and fork to listen to him, and presently he had half the room for his audience.' The outcome was an offer of 'permanent engagement' on the *St James's Gazette* which Ruddy turned down, politely and in verse. It was agreed instead that he would contribute fiction and verse to Low's newspaper on a freelance basis. 'A day or two later he sent me a contribution,' wrote Low, 'the first piece from Kipling's pen published in England.'[8] Kipling afterwards repudiated the self-referential poem 'The Comet of the Season', published on 21 November 1889, but the style is unmistakably his.

Hard on the heels of this first piece of luck came a second, also with an Indian connection, in the person of Mowbray Morris, painter and art critic. Morris had briefly worked for the *Pioneer* in Allahabad as an art editor before returning to London to become editor of *Macmillan's Magazine*, a monthly linked to the publishing house of Macmillan. At George Allen's request, Morris invited Ruddy to call on him on his arrival in London and was astonished to learn he was not yet twenty-four. 'He took from me,' wrote Kipling, 'an Indian tale and some verses, which latter he wisely edited a little. They were both published in the same number of the *Magazine* – one signed by my name and the other "Yussuf" [Joseph, Kipling's other Christian name].'9

The verses were 'The Ballad of the King's Mercy', a lilting tale of Afghan cruelty as exercised by the same ruler whose reception by the Viceroy in Rawalpindi Ruddy had witnessed as a cub reporter: 'Abdhur Rahman, the Durani Chief, of him is the story told. / His mercy fills the Khyber hills – his grace is manifold.' The short story was 'The Incarnation of Krishna Mulvaney', twelfth of the eighteen *Soldiers Three* stories, in which a drunken Mulvaney is carried insensible in a decorated palanquin into a temple in Benares, where he revives to find himself being worshipped as a Hindu god. Morris thought Mulvaney 'too drunk' for his readers' conservative tastes and asked for some thirty lines to be cut, and as the two discussed the changes over a cigar in Macmillan's offices in Covent Garden, Ruddy produced a second 'border ballad', which he claimed to have finished that morning at breakfast. This was 'The Ballad of East and West', with its famously misread opening couplet: 'Oh, East is East and West is West, and never the twain shall never meet, / Till Earth and Sky stand presently at God's great Judgement Seat.' The poem was pronounced by Mowbray Morris to be 'dee [damned] fine', and when it appeared in the December issue of *Macmillan's Magazine* the public response confirmed the accuracy of his judgement. A third border ballad, coming hard on the heels of the first two, made it abundantly clear that here was no flash in the pan. This was 'The Ballad of the King's Jest', with its jingling account of the laden *kafilas* or camel caravans crossing into India:

> When spring-time flushes the desert grass
>   Our kafilas wind through the Khyber Pass.
> Lean are the camels but fat the frails,
>   Light are the purses but heavy the bales,
> As the snowbound trade of the North comes down
>   To the market square of Peshawur town.

No less phenomenal was the speed with which Ruddy was welcomed into London's literary fold. Heading the list of eminent men of letters eager to make his acquaintance was the Scot Andrew Lang, the most prolific writer of his generation as poet, novelist, critic, anthropologist, historian, folklorist and much more besides. Lang had been following Ruddy's writing ever since being introduced to his early work by Vereker Hamilton, the artist brother of Ruddy's military friend Ian Hamilton, and soon after his arrival in London he took him to the Savile Club – a meeting place for writers, editors and publishers. Here Ruddy dined in the company of Thomas Hardy and his hero Walter Besant. Lang subsequently persuaded the publishing house of Sampson Low to buy the English rights to the six volumes of Wheeler's Indian Railway Library, and Besant introduced Ruddy to his literary agent, Alexander (A. P.) Watt, who took him on at once and urged him to 'Hurry up your novel and become rich'.[10] Watt's acumen, particularly in handling his authors' syndication rights, transformed Ruddy's financial position – so much so that within nine months Lockwood Kipling was marvelling at his son's popularity: 'Owing to the recent development & organising of journalism, syndicates & what not, each new book is more portentous, more widespread and more voluminous in print than the last and it will literally be true that in one year this youngster will have had more said about his work, over a wider extent of the world's surface, than some of the greatest of England's writers in their whole lives.'[11]

Through membership of the Savile Ruddy came to know virtually every established writer of the day, of whom only one, Henry Rider Haggard, proved sufficiently like-minded for them to remain close friends into old age. Although Ruddy afterwards wrote of the 'kindness and toleration' shown to him at the Savile, he was no more at ease there than he had been at the Allahabad Club – and for the same reason: that he did not feel himself to be one of their number. 'London is a vile place,' he wrote to Edmonia Hill in early November. 'Anstey [Thomas Anstey Guthrie, humorist] and Haggard and Lang and Co. are pressing on me the wisdom of identifying myself with some "set", while the long-haired literati of the Savile Club are swearing that I "invented" my soldier talk in Soldiers Three. Seeing that not one of these critters has been within earshot of a barrack, I am naturally wrath. But this is only the beginning of the lark. You'll see some savage criticisms of my work before spring.'[12]

Advised by Besant to 'keep out of the dog fight', Ruddy did just that. 'It seemed best to stand clear of it all,' he wrote of his refusal to integrate with his fellow writers, adding that in consequence, 'My acquaintance with my contemporaries [in literature] has from first to last been very limited.'[13] He had expected to find London's men of letters as committed to their craft as he was, and was profoundly disappointed by what he saw as their lack of professionalism: 'Had they been newspaper men in a hurry, I should have understood; but the gentlemen were presented to me as Priests and Pontiffs. And the generality of them seemed to have followed other trades – in banks or offices – before coming to the Ink; whereas I was free born. It was pure snobbism on my part, but it served to keep me inside myself.'[14] Kipling's use of the terms 'Priests and Pontiffs' is revealing. He viewed his literary contemporaries as the English equivalent of India's Brahmins, the Hindu high caste of priests and intellectuals. It was not a caste he could identify with.

Given Ruddy's fondness for older women, it comes as no surprise to find him neglecting the Savile in favour of the salon of the romantic novelist, hostess and forty-three-year-old widow Mrs Lucy Clifford. Ruddy's sister Trix was later to describe Mrs Clifford as 'a warm-hearted widow with thick lips', but she was just the sort of matronly type with whom Ruddy felt most at ease and he admired her practical, no-nonsense attitude to her work. She gave him sound professional advice and he became a frequent visitor to her house in Paddington. The friendship led to an introduction to Mrs Clifford's publishers, Macmillan, and an invitation to dine with George Macmillan, the junior partner in the family firm, that ended badly when Mrs Macmillan told Ruddy that

'India was fit to govern itself and that "we in England" (the ultra liberal idiots always speak of "we") are very much in earnest about putting things right there.' This was red-rag stuff, and Ruddy responded with what he termed 'engaging frankness' by telling Mrs Macmillan that she was suffering from hysteria because 'you haven't got enough to divert your mind'.[15] The encounter helped fuel a growing suspicion in Ruddy's mind that publishers were bent on enriching themselves at the expense of their authors, and he became as wary of them as he was of his literary peers. Nevertheless, he came to an accommodation with Macmillan and it was they who afterwards became the publishers of his collected fiction and verse in Britain, just as *Macmillan's Magazine* became the leading British outlet for his short stories.

Before November was out a stream of editors and publishers were knocking uninvited on his door. An extended letter to Edmonia Hill in the form of a journal with daily entries from 3 to 25 December tells its own story. 'A business day,' begins part of the entry for 23 December,

first with Thacker Spink about P.T.s [*Plain Tales from the Hills*] and royalties . . . Sampson Low and Co. were republishing Soldiers Three and the work w'd be in the market after ten days. As the 4th edition of the D. D. [*Departmental Ditties*] (£50 worth of new poems added) will be out in a fortnight I shall begin the new year a little better than I had hoped . . . The provincial papers including the Manchester Courier are beginning to ask "Who is Mr Rudyard Kipling?". . . I received a letter from one journal – no you shan't know the name; it made me blush – asking for an interview. I said NO awful loud and strong. Monday also brought me a letter from James Payne [editor of the *Cornhill Magazine*] demanding short stories for the Cornhill. I sent the chit on to my agents who will settle the terms. My system is simple – the shorter the yarn the longer the price. And I get it. Wah! Wah!

This immediate recognition gave Ruddy the confidence to believe that he could 'smash Arnold [author of the best-selling *Light of Asia*] into his own lights of Asia yet', and that his means of doing so would be the great Indian novel. He wrote to his parents in Lahore asking them to send him the manuscript of *Mother Maturin*, and in the meantime he set about revising and adding to the trunkload of unpublished material and unfinished scraps that had accompanied him on his travels. These included a number of soldier songs and verses which he had tried and failed to sell to Thacker, Spink and Co. a year earlier under the title of *Barrack-Room Ballads and Other Verses*. Now a new format for these military verses began to take shape in his mind, arising out of his discovery of the London music hall, and he set about reworking them by giving them the voice of the cockney in uniform, Tommy Atkins.

Determined to strike out on his own, Ruddy kept his aunts and his cousins at a distance. He would have been welcome at The Grange, but chose to spend his first Christmas back in London alone in his chambers. 'There are five million people in London this night,' he ended his Christmas letter to Edmonia Hill, 'and saving those who starve I don't think there is one more heartsick or thoroughly wretched than that "rising young author" known to you as − Ruddy.'[16] No doubt part of the reason for his heartsickness came from his spurning of Carrie Taylor, but he was also becoming increasingly disillusioned with the consequences of his sudden rise to fame. On his twenty-fourth birthday, 30 December, he was invited to tea by a society hostess and found himself being 'shown off to a lot of people', including three titled personages who backed him into a corner 'and stood over me pouring melted compliments into my throat, one after the other. And through it all I kept thinking to myself: "Unless it happened that I was the fashion of the moment − to be treated like a purple monkey on a yellow stick for just as long as I amuse you, you'd let me die of want on your doorsteps." So they would, but now, it's "O dear Mr Kipling <u>please</u> come as often as you can and we'll talk".'[17] His alienation found expression in the verses of 'In Partibus', promptly

dispatched to both Lahore and Allahabad, in which he bemoaned
the fact that he was now forced to

> Consort with long-haired things
>   In velvet collar-rolls,
> Who talk about the Aims of Art,
>   And 'theories' and 'goals',
> And moo and coo with womenfolk
>   About their blessed souls.[18]

Isolated, disillusioned and almost as much oppressed by
London's winter fogs as he had been by Lahore's summer heat,
Ruddy sank into another of his depressions. 'I have broken up,' was
how he put it to Edmonia Hill in a letter overflowing with self-
pity. 'My head has given out and I am forbidden work and I am
to go away somewhere. This is the third time it has happened . . .
but this time is the completest. I do not want, even if I deserved,
your pity. I must go on alone now till the end of time. I can do
nothing to save myself from breaking up now and again . . . I am
physically in perfect health but I can neither work nor think nor
read.'[19]

Written at the end of January 1890, this was the last intimate
letter Ruddy ever sent to Edmonia Hill.[20] Both it and his last letter
to Carrie Taylor on 2 January 1890 are incomplete, suggesting that
Mrs Hill found the offending sections too painful or too private
for further scrutiny. Since Rudyard Kipling and his wife between
them subsequently destroyed every letter that Edmonia Hill wrote
to him in his youth, we can hardly begin to know what she thought
or felt about him apart from what can gathered from his surviving
letters. It seems extremely unlikely that she ever let her feelings go
to the extent of becoming Ruddy's lover, but it is obvious that
for the space of two years they were very close. After the rupture
Edmonia continued to follow his career, and of course she kept
Ruddy's letters until after his death.

As in Lahore, Ruddy's depression was accompanied by a bloody-minded mood which led him to respond to a judicial committee report clearing the Irish nationalist Charles Parnell of links with Fenian terrorism by reworking some old verses into a bitter diatribe against Gladstonian liberalism. The verses were rejected by *The Times* and the *Fortnightly Review* and Ruddy put them to one side – at which point W. E. Henley, poet, dramatist, true-blue Tory and editor of the *Scots Observer*, made his appearance.

Popular legend has Henley receiving the manuscript of 'Danny Deever' by an unknown hand and hopping up and down on his wooden leg whooping 'in an ecstasy of delight' before he was halfway through reading it. But in fact Henley had first come across Ruddy's work two years earlier when his brother-in-law, a chief officer on board the P&O steamer SS *Lycia*, sent him a copy of *Departmental Ditties*. He had taken note, and when he heard of the author's arrival in London had asked to meet him. If Henley danced anywhere on his wooden leg it was at Embankment Chambers, where he was taken by a nephew of the eminent biographer Leslie Stephen. Here he was shown 'Danny Deever' and 'Fuzzy Wuzzy', the earliest of Ruddy's *Barrack-Room Ballads* – and the rejected anti-Government squib 'Cleared!', allegedly rescued from Ruddy's wastebasket.

Henley prided himself on his ability to spot up-and-coming talent, and he was delighted to meet a young author whose political views accorded with his own 'organic loathing of Mr Gladstone and all Liberalism'.[21] He immediately published 'Cleared!' and the *Barrack-Room Ballads* followed week on week: first 'Danny Deever' in February; then 'Tommy', 'Fuzzy-Wuzzy', 'Oonts' and 'Loot', all in March. A further fourteen ballads appeared at weekly or fortnightly intervals thereafter, among them 'The Widow at Windsor', 'Gunga Din', 'Gentlemen-Rankers', 'Ford o' Kabul', 'Snarleyow' and 'Mandalay' – the last a reversal of the several exile's laments Ruddy had written in India as the retired soldier, sick of the 'blasted Henglish drizzle' and of 'wastin' leather on these gritty pavin'-stones', looks back on the India he has left behind:

> Ship me somewheres East of Suez, where the best is like the
>   worst,
>   Where there aren't no ten commandments an' a man can
>   raise a thirst.
>   For the temple bells are callin', an' it's there that I would be –
>   By the old Moulmein Pagoda, lookin' lazy at the sea.

A similar mood of alienation can be found in 'Tommy', with its disquieting truth that the British public held the British common soldier in contempt – until such time as his services were needed:

> I went into a public 'ouse to get a pint o'beer,
>   The publican 'e up an' sez, 'We serve no red-coats here.'
>   The girls be'ind the bar they laughed an' giggled fit to die,
>   I outs into the street again an' to myself sez I:
>   O it's Tommy this, an' Tommy that, an' 'Tommy, go away';
>   But it's 'Thank you, Mister Atkins', when the band begins
>   to play.

The shock-value of 'Danny Deever', 'Tommy' and the best of the *Barrack-Room Ballads* has faded over the years – and the rest have not aged well. 'Mandalay' now sounds almost maudlin, Kipling's cockneyfication seems contrived and the racial insensitivities contained in such poems as 'Gunga Din', 'Loot' and 'Fuzzy-Wuzzy' are embarrassing, even when taken in context, which is Kipling giving voice to the Victorian working man. For all his talk of 'niggers', the cockney soldier admires the water-carrier 'Gunga Din' and the spiky-haired warriors of the Sudan. As a member of a supremely successful nation he looks down on them, but as a fellow soldier he salutes them: 'So 'ere's to you, Fuzzy-Wuzzy, at your 'ome in the Soudan, / You're a pore benighted 'eathen but a first-class fightin' man.' What is also overlooked today is the degree to which the *Barrack-Room Ballads* challenged British social taboos, just as *Departmental Ditties* had done with the Anglo-Indian

community. In 'The Ladies' the cockney soldier speaks unblush-
ingly of the various women he has enjoyed while on overseas
service:

I've taken my fun where I've found it;
　I've rogued an' I've ranged in my time;
I've 'ad my pick o' sweet'earts,
　An' four o' the lot was prime.
One was an 'arf-caste widow,
　One was a woman at Prome,
One was the wife of a *jemadar-sais* [Indian military groom]
　An' one is a girl at 'ome.

He then goes into details about his four lovers, ending each verse
with 'And I learned about women from her'. His conclusion is
that 'the more you have known of the others / The less you will
settle for one', ending with one of the most quotable of the
Kipling aphorisms still in circulation: 'For the Colonel's Lady an'
Judy O'Grady / Are sisters under their skins!' This was not at all
a common sentiment in the drawing rooms of Chelsea and
Kensington in 1890.

The *Barrack-Room Ballads* were eminently memorable,
quotable and singable, and there can have been few among those
who read or heard them that spring and summer of 1890 who did
not recognise that a new genre of popular poetry had arrived, or
who did not agree with *The Times* that their author was 'a bright,
clever and versatile writer, who knows he has caught the public
taste'. On 25 March 1890, with only the first four of the *Barrack-
Room Ballads* published, *The Times* paid Ruddy the signal honour
of an entire leading article devoted to his work. It compared the
best of his short stories to those of Guy de Maupassant and praised
him as 'the discoverer, as far as India is concerned, of "Tommy
Atkins" as a hero of realistic romance'. It also wondered if Kipling
possessed the necessary 'staying power' to last the course.

Kipling was right to honour Henley as 'a jewel of an editor', but he also owed a great deal to the marketing skills of his literary agent, Alexander Watt. The fact that 'Danny Deever' had been published in the *Scots Observer* did not prevent it from appearing in the *Week's News* in India and the *New York Tribune* in the United States. The same applied to his fiction, which now began appearing in different magazines on both sides of the Atlantic. These early magazine publications included a number of short stories that were masterpieces of the genre, all drawing their inspiration from India. They included 'At the End of the Passage', in which a man dies of terror arising from a combination of isolation, heat and insomnia; two military love stories – 'The Courting of Dinah Shadd' and 'On Greenhow Hill'– widely regarded as among the finest of the *Soldiers Three* tales; and a third love story, 'Without Benefit of Clergy', set in Lahore. The last tells of John Holden's doomed love for his beloved Ameera, a sixteen-year-old Muslim girl. Holden buys Ameera from her mother and sets her up as his *bibi* in a house in the city, where he visits her in secret. Theirs is a forbidden love and, despite Holden's best efforts to bridge the cultural divide, both he and she come to understand that it is doomed. A child is born, upon whom both parents dote, only to be snatched away 'as many things are taken away in India – suddenly and without warning'. Their shared grief draws the lovers closer together, until Ameera too is struck down with cholera, dying in Holden's arms. 'There are not many happinesses so complete as those that are snatched under the shadow of the sword,' Kipling writes of the lovers trapped in a city gripped by cholera:

The city below them was locked up in its own torments. Sulphur fires blazed in the streets; the conches of the Hindu temples screamed and bellowed, for the gods were inattentive in those days. There was a service in the great Mahomedan shrine, and the call to prayer from the minarets was almost unceasing. They heard the wailing in the houses of the dead, and once the shriek of the mother who had lost a child and was calling for its return. In the grey dawn they saw the dead borne out through the city gates, each litter with its own little knot of mourners. Wherefore they kissed each other and shivered.

Twelve of the best of these dark tales were collected and published as *Life's Handicap; Being Stories of Mine Own People*, together with a dedication to Kay Robinson acknowledging Ruddy's indebtedness to him and the time they spent together on the *Civil and Military Gazette* in Lahore. Published within months of each other on both sides of the Atlantic, *Barrack-Room Ballads* and *Life's Handicap* were the literary equivalent of giving the reading public both barrels. They made the name of Kipling famous as far away as Australia, confirming the judgement of the commentator in the *Weekly Times* that 'even if he were twice that age [of twenty-four] his talents would be remarkable; but as matters stand they look something akin to genius'.[22] The novelist Henry James had no qualms about using the same word, declaring Rudyard Kipling to be 'the most complete man of genius' he had ever known.

In February 1890 Trix passed through London with her husband Jack Fleming, invalided home after contracting malaria in Burma. She visited her brother in his chambers and was dismayed to find him suffering recurrent bouts of fever and dysentery, and very low in spirits. Having broken off his engagement with Carrie Taylor and in the process lost his beloved Edmonia Hill, he had now become re-entangled with his first love, Flo Garrard. Flo had by this time graduated from the Slade School of Art and had moved to Paris to continue her art studies, but while on a visit to London had bumped into Ruddy in the street. Again she had given him no encouragement, but the encounter had been enough to reignite all his old feelings and he was once more pining for her. His unhappiness pitched Ruddy into making his first serious miscalculation as a writer since *The Story of the Gadsbys*. He threw himself into writing a novel about a young artist, Dick Heldar, who comes to London to make his fortune and suffers from his unrequited love for an art student, Maisie, whom he has known since childhood, when the pair of them suffered together at a seaside lodging house run by a cruel housekeeper. But Maisie is more interested in her art than in him, so Dick abandons London to become a war-artist in Egypt and the Sudan. After several years in exile he returns to London, where he accidentally meets his love again.

But with the novel half-written Ruddy suffered another of his breakdowns. He telegraphed to Lahore the terse message 'Genesis 45:9', which his parents had no trouble in interpreting as an appeal to follow the command of Joseph to 'come down unto me: tarry not'. They had already received Trix's report, and they lost no time in coming home. There was leave owing to Lockwood and they could now afford to travel, since Trix was no longer a financial burden and the success of the commission for the Duke of Connaught had led to a further royal command to install a Durbar Room at Queen Victoria's residence at Osborne House 'in the Indian manner'. His parents' arrival in London in early May lifted Ruddy's spirits and he felt sufficiently emboldened to go to Paris with the intention of proposing to Flo. Nothing came of it. As Trix saw the situation, 'Flo was naturally cold, and she wanted to live her own life and paint her very ineffective little pictures.' But this was unkind, for no one guessed then that Ruddy's failure to win Flo Garrard's heart had much more to do with her sexual orientation than with any failings on his part or heartlessness on hers. Nevertheless, Ruddy returned to London deeply dejected, a state which even the company of his father and a visit to Uncle Crom and United Services College failed to lighten.

Flo's rejection continued to fester over the summer. Writing to Edith Plowden from the London flat they had rented, Lockwood Kipling described his son as going through 'tribulation'. No doubt it was partly for this reason that Lockwood took to staying over at Ruddy's chambers, sleeping on the couch in his study. It allowed the two of them to work together with a new intimacy, Lockwood providing the Yorkshire details for the latest *Soldiers Three* story, 'On Greenhow Hill', and much else besides. But the one area where Lockwood could do nothing but look on helplessly was in his son's writing of *The Light That Failed* – 'a story he went at in a sort of fury that lasted for a long time'.[23]

Whatever Ruddy's original intentions, his novel now became an outlet for the rage and pain he felt, so that what had been intended as a romance became a rant against cheating publishers, effete literary types and women who refused to conform to men's idealised images of them. *The Light That Failed* was first published in the United States in *Lippincott's Monthly Magazine* in February 1891. In this American version Maisie finally warms to Dick Heldar when they meet again after his exile, and all ends happily. But when the novel was published in England two months later it had an additional chapter and was prefaced with the author's untruthful remark that 'This is the story of *The Light That Failed* as it was originally conceived by the writer.' In this second, bleaker version Maisie knows that Dick wants her to love him but she doesn't understand 'what that feeling means'. When they meet again Dick pleads with her to come back East with him: 'You'll see for yourself what colour means, and we'll find out together what love means.' But Maisie again rejects him, and Dick eventually goes to Sudan with his eyesight failing, to meet his death on the battlefield.

The polite puzzlement with which reviewers had received the first version became outright hostility when they read the second. 'His chief defect is ignorance of life,' wrote J. M. Barrie in one of the kinder reviews. 'This seems a startling charge to bring against one whose so-called knowledge of life has frightened the timid. But it is true. Dick Heldar's views are Kipling's views.' Dick Heldar was little more than a two-dimensional mouthpiece and Maisie a blurred cipher. Nothing rang true. As in his own confused relationship with Flo Garrard, Ruddy had indulged himself with imagined feelings which had no basis in reality. 'We see at once that his pathos is potatoes,' was Barrie's final judgement. 'It is not legitimate.'[24]

A month after completing the revised version of *The Light That Failed* in late August 1890, Ruddy heard that Professor Alex Hill had died suddenly in India. Having digested the news and its impli-

cations he followed the example of his creation Dick Heldar and
fled. 'We regret to hear that Rudyard Kipling has broken down
from overwork,' reported the *Athenaeum* on 4 October. 'He has
been ordered to take a sea voyage and sailed on the P&O steamer
Shannon for Naples.' In *Something of Myself* Kipling offered this
explanation: 'The staleness and depression came after a bout of real
influenza, when all my Indian microbes joined hands and sang for
a month in the darkness of Villiers Street. So I took ship to Italy.'
This was nonsense, for the bout of flu had occurred months earlier, during the darkness of the preceding winter. What caused him
to take ship was the realisation that the woman whom he had so
assiduously courted as a married woman was now a widow – and
on her way home to America by way of England. For two years he
had worshipped Edmonia Hill as a soul-mate, secure in the knowledge that she was unavailable. The prospect of her reappearance in
his life as a real and available woman seems to have filled him with
panic. He needed to get away to clear his mind.

Little is known about the sea voyage other than that Ruddy visited the Sorrento villa of Lord Dufferin, now British Ambassador
in Rome. He was back in London before the end of October and
a month later met Edmonia Hill and her sister Carrie Taylor as
they passed through London on their way home to the United
States. But Ruddy's mind was now hardened and there seems to
have been no question of his returning to the romantic intimacy
which had once meant so much to him, never mind taking it a
stage further. The two sisters came and went, apparently without
reawakenings on either side. The last meeting took place at the sisters' hotel on 5 December, and Ruddy and Edmonia never again
met face to face.

It was while in this state of self-denying withdrawal from the
opposite sex and very much in the tenor of 'He travels the fastest
who travels alone' that Ruddy found a kindred male spirit in
Wolcott Balestier, an intense young American not that much older
than himself – twenty-nine years to his twenty-five – who shared
his passion for literature and who was equally determined to make

his mark. The two met in early March 1890 at a soirée at the home of the popular novelist Mrs Humphry Ward and each proceeded to dazzle the other, the one with his prodigious talent, the other with his American charm and brio. Balestier was then working in England as an agent negotiating contracts between English authors and an American publishing house notorious for its piracy of British authors' work, but he had previously spent three solid years at Lovells as a magazine editor and he knew the business inside out. He took Ruddy's side in a copyright quarrel with Harper and Sons, arranged for the authorised edition of *Life's Handicap* to be published in America, and went out of his way to provide a sympathetic ear whenever Ruddy needed to talk.

A curious letter to an unnamed recipient, accidentally filed among the papers of Kay Robinson in the Kipling Collection at the University of Sussex, was almost certainly written by Ruddy to Wolcott Balestier after their first meeting. Its dating of 9 March 1890 places it after Ruddy's encounter with Flo Garrard in the street and before he sent his terse appeal to his parents. In it Ruddy thanked his correspondent for his 'beautiful sympathy and insight' but rejected his counsel of perfection:

> Where I come from they taught me (with whips of circumstance and the thermometer at 110 in the shade) that the only human being to whom a man is responsible is himself . . . Pray for me, since I am a lonely man in my life, that I do not take the sickness which for lack of understanding I should call love. For that will leave me somebody else's servant – instead of my own. My business at present, so far as I can feel, is to get into touch with the common folk here, to find out what they desire, hope or fear and then after the proper time to speak whatever may be given to me . . . From this ideal I make no doubt I shall lamentably fail.[25]

According to their mutual friend Edmund Gosse, Balestier boasted of having made a 'personal conquest' of Kipling and of securing his agreement to collaborate with him on his next novel 'within a week' – a claim that has encouraged at least one biographer to see Balestier as a predatory homosexual and Kipling as a repressed one unwilling to face the fact.[26] This ignores the most remarked upon feature of Balestier, which was the effect he had on people. Henry James wrote of his 'extraordinary subtlety of putting himself in the place of the men – and quite as easily, when need was, of the women of letters'.[27] Arthur Waugh, who worked for him as his assistant, afterwards remembered his 'chameleon power with people'.[28] That power Balestier put to good effect in placing his friendship at Ruddy's disposal, and his reward was an intimacy at least as close as that which Ruddy had earlier enjoyed with Kay Robinson on the *CMG*, and probably a great deal closer.

So well did the two get on together that they decided to collaborate on a novel, to be set partly in the American West and partly in India. One account of the writing of *The Naulahka: A Story of East and West* has Balestier typing away while Kipling paces the room, 'each composing, suggesting, or criticising in turn, and the mind of each stimulating the other'.[29] However, Ruddy's troubles with *The Light That Failed* and his other work meant that it was not until the start of 1891 that real progress began to be made, Wolcott reporting to a friend that the book was 'as American as a roller blade and as Indian as a juggernaut'.[30]

In its original form the Naulakha was a marbled pavilion in Lahore Fort reputed to have cost nine *lakhs* of rupees to build. As misspelled in the title of the novel it was a jewelled necklace belonging to the princely state of Rhatore which the American Nicholas Tarvin sets out to steal, partly to influence a railroad boss into building a railway station for his hometown in the Midwest but also to win back his beloved, Kate Sheriff, who has turned him down and is now a medical missionary in Rhatore. Like Maisie in *The Light That Failed*, Kate is a 'new woman' who wants to go her own way. The story ends happily, with Nicholas winning Kate back – but only after she recognises that she is not ready to work with the Indian women whose lot she wants to better. Published in April 1892, *The Naulahka* was more credible than *The Light That Failed*, but still a disappointment to readers whose appetites had been whetted by *Life's Handicap*. As before, Tarvin and his beloved had failed to come alive on the page. Brilliant at portraying life's rougher characters in his short stories, Ruddy appeared incapable of working on a larger canvas. Something in his nature or his upbringing – and it is tempting to blame the withdrawal of love and the absence of loving adult role-models in his Southsea years – had left him emotionally stunted, unable to deal with the full range of human feelings. He understood the pleasures of the flesh as found in the arms of Appledore fish girls, Lahore courtesans, Putney tarts and Simla matrons, but shrank from real human intimacy, preferring as his womanly ideal the Maiden, virginal and compliant: Flo Garrard as she ought to be and not as she was. Unable to reconcile the one with the other, Ruddy exalted in his fiction what he was unable to find in his life.

From 1890 onwards Wolcott Balestier was visited in London by members of his family, including his two younger sisters, Carrie and Josephine, both of whom came and went over the months, taking it in turns to act as his housekeeper. Josephine was the prettier of the two, Caroline the clever one, stern-faced and strong-minded. Ruddy met them frequently and was made welcome in their family circle. He flirted with both sisters in a light-hearted way without, it seems, showing a preference for one over the other. But Carrie was the most literary-minded of the two and the most determined, as enthusiastic a literary groupie as Alice Macdonald had been a Pre-Raphaelite groupie a generation earlier. She was, in Henry James's words, 'a little person of extraordinary capacity . . . remarkable in her force, acuteness, capacity, and courage – and in the intense – almost manly nature of her emotion'.[31] She took great pleasure in meeting her brother's famous friends, and as the collaboration on *The Naulahka* progressed she began to make herself useful to both its authors as a collator, encouraging Ruddy to join 'the typewriter fold' and helping him keep his papers in order. At twenty-seven she was two years Ruddy's senior, not a great age difference but enough for him to see her as an older woman of the sort he could trust and relate to. 'He is so refreshingly unEnglish,' wrote Carrie to Josephine in January 1891. 'And for some unknown reason I have never had any shyness with him and I can be myself when he is about which is a great relief.'[32] Although marriage can hardly have been in either party's mind at that time, it is noteworthy that when Alice Kipling first set eyes on Carrie Balestier that summer she exclaimed, 'That woman is going to marry our Ruddy.'

For reasons unexplained that may have had to do with Lockwood's two royal commissions, Alice and Lockwood Kipling were now renting a small flat in Brighton, where Ruddy joined them from time to time, eager for 'ten hours of hot sunshine'[33] – and thinking seriously of returning to India. According to Trix, it was at Brighton as Ruddy sat at their table working on a new poem that he asked rhetorically what it was he was trying to say and was told by his mother, 'And what should they know of England who only England know?' The line provided the cornerstone for 'The English Flag', which calls on the 'street-bred people' of England to remember that their great empire had been won at a price. The four winds of the cardinal points bear witness to the expansion of British hegemony overseas, each calling in turn for the English people to 'Go forth' and do their bit. 'Me men call the Home-Wind for I bring the English home,' declares the East Wind:

> The reeling junks behind me and the racing seas before,
>   I raped your richest roadstead – I plundered Singapore!
> I set my hand on the Hoogli; as a hooded snake she rose,
>   And I flung your stoutest steamers to roost with the startled
>   crows.
>
> But never the lotos closes, never the wild-fowl wake,
>   But a soul goes out on the East Wind that died for
>   England's sake –

Man or woman or suckling, mother or bride or maid –
  Because of the bones of the English the English flag is
    stayed.

It was the first time since 'Ave Imperatrix' that Kipling had written a poem that was unashamedly imperialist. The poem's sentiments accorded perfectly with W. E. Henley's nationalist views and he ran 'The English Flag' in what was now the *National Observer*, soon afterwards making it the opening poem in a popular anthology entitled *Lyra Heroica*. By this means 'The English Flag' became rooted in the minds of two generations of Victorian and Edwardian schoolchildren. So seductively lyrical is its form that it is easy to overlook the fact that it is essentially a hymn to conquest.

In June 1891 Ruddy joined the Balestier family at a holiday cottage they had taken on the Isle of Wight, where his contact with Wolcott's two sisters grew more intimate by the day. A month earlier Edmund Gosse, a staunch ally of both Balestier and Kipling, had publicly called on Ruddy to renew himself by returning to his travels. 'Go east, Mr Kipling,' he wrote in a critical article in the *Century Magazine*. 'Go back to the Far East . . . Come back in ten years' time with another precious and admirable budget of loot.' Ruddy was now fast approaching a point of no return in his relationship with the elder of the two Balestier sisters and he resolved the issue by opting to take Gosse's advice. 'My need was to get clean away and re-sort myself,' was how he explained himself in his autobiography. He evidently hoped that Wolcott Balestier would come with him: the first draft of 'The Long Trail', written at this time, shows that the appeal contained in the poem to 'pull out on the trail again' was initially directed not to a 'dear lass', as subsequently published, but to a 'dear lad'. 'Your English summer's done,' reads part of the first verse:

Ha' done with the Tents of Shem, dear lad,
  We've seen the season through,

> And it's time to turn on the old trail, our own trail, the out
>   trail,
>   Pull out, pull out, on the Long Trail – the trail that is always
>   new!

In the event Ruddy travelled alone, setting sail in mid-August 1891 on board the steamship *Moor*, bound for the 'clean sunshine' of the Cape, the first leg of a world voyage that would take him by way of New Zealand into the South Pacific.

It was a journey made without purpose – other than a vague hope to meet up with Robert Louis Stevenson on Samoa – and without companions – other than a sexual fling with a woman passenger on the leg to Australia. After two weeks in New Zealand, Ruddy had had enough and turned about. In mid-December he disembarked at Colombo, crossed to the Indian mainland, and after four days and nights in trains was back in Lahore, 'the only real home I had yet known', where not only his parents but also his old school chum Lionel 'Stalky' Dunsterville and his beloved bearer Kadir Baksh, 'pearl among khitmatgars', were on hand to greet his return.

Ruddy was back among his own people in the land where he was most himself. The community that only two years earlier had looked down upon him as a young pup now fêted him as a celebrity, and his own paper carried a report on his return. He revisited his old haunts in and around the city – 'there, arrogant and unashamed was Lalun's naughty little house' – and was easily prevailed upon to write an account of his return to Lahore for the *CMG*. He was less happy to learn that George Chesney, on behalf of the *Pioneer*'s management in Allahabad, had sold the rights on all his writings in the *Pioneer* and the *Week's News* to his old friend Émile Moreau for £1500. Although George Allen intervened from his retirement in England to make a gift to his former protégé of the copyright to all the short stories and poetry which had appeared in the pages of the *Pioneer*, the *Civil and Military Gazette* and the *Week's News* (an act of generosity that Allen's heirs did not appreciate), the matter continued to rankle. A peacemaking suggestion from Chesney that Ruddy might like to stay on in India to write some more 'Letters of Marque' for the *Pi* was rejected out of hand.

Whatever Ruddy's further plans may have been, they were disrupted by the arrival of a telegram at Bikaner House on Christmas Eve. According to Edmund Gosse, it came from Carrie Balestier and was short and to the point: 'WOLCOTT DEAD STOP COME BACK TO ME STOP.'

The news that his dearest friend had died of typhoid while on a business trip to Dresden left Ruddy grief-stricken. His Indian years should have hardened him to sudden death, but he had never been able to come to terms with it. Shocked and unnerved, he immediately booked a passage on the first available homeward-bound ship out of Bombay. He left his bewildered parents on Christmas Day and two days later boarded a Lloyd Triestino steamer bound for Europe. It seems entirely fitting that the only person to witness his final departure from the land of his birth was the Goan ayah – 'so old but so unaltered' – who had nursed him as a boy, and who bade him farewell 'with blessings and tears'.[34]

12

'Try as he will'

WEDDINGS AND FUNERALS, VERMONT
AND SUSSEX, 1892–9

Try as he will, no man breaks wholly loose
From his first love, no matter who she be.
Oh, was there ever sailor free to choose
That didn't settle somewhere near the sea?

Rudyard Kipling, 'The Virginity', *The Years Between*, 1914

The day after Ruddy arrived in London he took out a special marriage licence and a week later, on 18 January 1892, in a subdued ceremony witnessed by few friends and fewer relatives, he and Carrie Balestier were married at All Souls Church, Langham Place. According to Edmund Gosse, it was as if Ruddy had been 'hurried into matrimony, like a rabbit into its hole . . . At 2.8 the cortège entered the church and at 2.20 left it . . . Both bridegroom and bride are possessed by a very devil of secrecy and mystery.'[1] Henry James, who gave the bride away, was equally mystified. Writing to his brother William, he commended Carrie as 'a hard devoted little person whom I don't in the least understand his marrying. It is a union of which I don't forecast the future though I gave her away at the altar in a dreary little wedding with an attendance simply of four men – her mother and sister prostrate with influenza.'[2]

After a week's honeymoon as guests of Brown's Hotel the

newly-weds sailed off to America, although not before Ruddy had tacked two new poems to the beginning and end of his *Barrack-Room Ballads*: at the front an embarrassing encomium to the memory of Wolcott Balestier – 'E'en as he trod that day to God so walked he from his birth, / In simpleness and gentleness and honour and clean mirth' – and as an *envoi* a revised version of 'The Long Trail' complete with sex change, in which he set out his hopes of sharing the future with Carrie:

> The Lord knows what we may find, dear lass,
>   And the Deuce knows what we may do –
> But we're back once more on the old trail, our own trail, the
>   out trail,
>   We're down, hull down on the Long Trail –
> The trail that is always new.

By the time these verses were published in March 1892 the Kiplings were well into the first leg of their honeymoon tour, which took them across America and Canada and then to Japan, where a bank crash and the loss of all Ruddy's savings forced them to turn about. In June *The Naulahka* was published, and in August the couple settled in Balestier country at Brattleboro, in the hills of Vermont. For a year they rented a cottage from Carrie's surviving brother, Beatty, while they set about building a house for themselves – an austere, ark-like structure which Ruddy named Naulakha. 'I love this People,' Ruddy had written after his first tour through the United States, and, although the lawlessness and disorder of American society troubled him, he believed these negative qualities to be more than offset by the rugged individualism of the American common man – in particular, those who embodied the American pioneer spirit: frontiersmen, hunters and farmers, whom he labelled 'captains courageous'. These 'unhandy men' were 'set, silent, indirect in speech, and as impenetrable as that other eastern farmer who is the bedrock of another land', by which he meant India and the Indian *ryot*. Indeed, in its tensions and contradictions the United States reminded him of British India, and he convinced himself that he could be as much at home here as he had become in the Punjab. Bliss Cottage was little more than a rustic log cabin, and here he and Carrie lived as pioneers, installing a stove and piling up spruce boughs, so that 'When winter shut down and sleigh-bells rang all over the white world that tucked us in, we counted ourselves secure.'[3]

This was a time of uncomplicated joy for both Ruddy and Carrie, made all the sweeter by the birth of a daughter, Josephine, at the end of the year. 'You can guess how happy we are,' he wrote to W. E. Henley in London five days later. 'All things are going so excellently. Her chin is mine and the rest is dough but there's no doubt about the chin. Nor unluckily about the temper which is anything but civilised.' He also explained why he had sent his old patron no new work for publication recently: 'I've been neglecting prose for verse and besides I've struck a vein of animal yarns that is leading me further afield than I thought.'[4]

During the summer Ruddy had been too busy travelling to write much fiction, but by the autumn Carrie's developing pregnancy had set him thinking about children and childhood, reawakening his own inner child, long dormant. In answer to a request for children's stories from Mary Mapes Dodge, editor of the *St Nicholas Magazine*, he sent her 'The Potted Princess',[5] based on his and Trix's Bombay childhood and their Goan ayah's talent for soothing her charges through story-telling. In the accompanying letter he asked Mrs Dodge if she was interested in some more children's tales he was working on. The first of these, subsequently published in the *St Nicholas Magazine* as 'Collar-Wallah and the Poison Stick',[6] drew on his observation of a troop of langurs in Simla, strengthened by further insights into monkey behaviour contained in his father's *Beast and Man in India: a Popular Sketch of Indian Animals in their Relations with the People* – a delightful bestiary, lavishly illustrated with Lockwood Kipling's own sketches, which Ruddy had encouraged Macmillan to publish some months earlier. A second story he proposed to Mrs Dodge would be about 'a small boy who got a blessing and a ghost-dagger from a Thibetan lama who came down from Thibet in search of a miraculous river that washed away all sin (the river that gushed out when the Bodhisat's arrow struck in the ground) and how these two went hunting for it together – the old priest with his priestly tam o'shanter hat and the young English child.'[7] Within a week the small boy who was to accompany the lama on his search had acquired a name: 'If the children think fit we'll try another [story] – the tale of the Thibetan lama and Kim o' the Rishti[,] for I would sooner make a fair book of stories for children than a new religion or a completely revised framework of our social and political life.'[8]

These are the earliest known references to *Kim*. However, from two further surviving letters written over the succeeding weeks it is clear that Ruddy then put Kim and his Tibetan lama to one side – because his mind was now entirely focused on something altogether more atavistic: the Indian jungle and its denizens, human and wild. Every European child raised in India with an ayah heard stories drawn, directly or indirectly, from the much-loved *Jatakas*, tales of birds and beasts and men, and their interactions, based on ancient Buddhist moral tales. In Lahore Ruddy would have been hard put to avoid recent translations of these tales from the original Pali into English: Rhys Davids's *Buddhist Birth Stories or Jataka Tales* had been published in 1880 and Victor Fussboll's more comprehensive *Folktales of India: the Pali Jataka* in 1884.

However, the most direct means of their transmission to both Lockwood and Rudyard Kipling was the formidable educationist and women's emancipator Mrs Flora Annie Steel. Ruddy had first come to know Mrs Steel in Lahore when she was in her mid-thirties, the wife of a Punjab Civilian but better known throughout Upper India as an amateur actress, the 'Infant Phenomenon'. In February 1884 she had come to Lahore to act in a performance of *Winning a Husband*, which Ruddy reviewed for the *CMG*. In that same year Mrs Steel published *Wide-awake Stories for Children*, based on Punjabi folk tales which were themselves largely derived from the *Jatakas*. Her work as inspector of schools for the Punjab Government brought her into contact with the Kiplings, and it is impossible to believe that her forthright views on the status of Indian women and on corruption in high places did not impress themselves on the younger Kipling. Mrs Steel then made the mistake of taking on the Government of the Punjab, claiming that official posts were being bought and sold, and she was punished by having her husband posted to the other end of the Punjab. She herself refused to budge from Lahore and eventually a High Court judge had to be brought in to resolve the dispute, which he did, but at the cost of her husband's career. So in 1888 the Steels retired to England, where Mrs Steel began to write more seriously, first *The Complete Indian Housekeeper and Cook*, dedicated to 'The English Girls to whom fate may assign the task of being House-Mothers in Our Eastern Empire', and then a series of novels set in the Punjab: *From the Five Rivers*, *Miss Stuart's Legacy* and *The Potter's Thumb*, all published in 1893–4.

Flora Annie Steel's work was accomplished enough for Ruddy to declare her to be 'a beautiful writer and she <u>knows</u>',[9] and she was close enough to his father to ask him to collaborate with her on a reissue of her *Wide-awake Stories* under the new title of *Tales of the Punjab*. Lavishly illustrated by Lockwood Kipling throughout with delightful engravings and pen-and-ink sketches of birds, beasts and enchanted humans, the book was published by Macmillan in 1894. However, long before *Tales of the Punjab* appeared in print both text and drawings had exercised a profound influence on Ruddy's writing.

A further inspiration at this same time came from Rider Haggard's *Nada the Lily*, published in serialised form in the summer of 1892, which drew on a Zulu story of a wild boy who ran with a pack of wild dogs. It led directly to Ruddy's writing 'In the Rukh', which he described as 'a tale about Indian Forestry work which included a boy who had been brought up by wolves'. The *rukh* is the Indian forest interior, where Gisborne of the Woods and Forests and his chief, Muller, encounter a mysterious jungle-dweller 'naked except for the loin-cloth, but crowned with a wreath of the tasselled blossoms of the white convolvulus creeper . . . his brown skin glistening in the sunlight'. He gives his name as 'Mowgli', describes himself as without parents, home or caste, and proceeds to demonstrate to the two Europeans his complete mastery over the jungle. Then it emerges that Mowgli has been suckled by a she-wolf and raised as a wolf cub, and still lives among a pack of wolves that are 'my playmates and my brothers, children of the mother that gave me suck . . . Children of the father that lay between me and the cold at the mouth of the cave when I was a little naked child.'[10]

This first rather clumsy-footed foray into the Indian jungle opened up all sorts of possibilities. By Thanksgiving 1892 Ruddy was writing enthusiastically to Mrs Dodge to tell her that an elephant tale was complete, a tiger story was in the process of being written and a wolf tale would follow on. The first was 'Toomai of the Elephants',[11] the second 'Tiger-Tiger'[12] – 'a tale of the man eater who was ignominiously squelched in his lair by the charge of the village buffaloes under the command of the little boy herd' – and the third was to be a companion-piece to the tale about the jungle-dweller Mowgli already told in 'In the Rukh' and would be entitled 'Mowgli's Brothers': '<u>He</u> was a wolf boy (we have them in India) but being caught early was civilised. His brothers the wolves followed his career respectfully and afar . . . from village to village till at last Mowgli's too faithful retainers became a nuisance and . . . the upshot was that he went out into the moonlight and explained things to these four grey wolves of Oude and they saw the justice of his demands and left him in peace.'[13]

Fortunately for children's literature, Ruddy's initial outlines for 'Tiger-Tiger' and 'Mowgli's Brothers' were abandoned as he delved deeper into the matter of Mowgli's imagined beginnings. Ruddy had always delighted in the company of small children but the birth of his 'first beloved' Josephine had lifted him to a condition of happiness such as he had never experienced, and in this state of euphoria he was able to loosen the restraints of adulthood and slip back into the shape-shifting innocence of his childhood days, imagining himself into an Eden-like nursery populated by fearsome beasts into which a naked, helpless man-child is abandoned. And what greatly facilitated this return to childlike ways was the arrival in Brattleboro in June 1893 of Lockwood Kipling, bringing with him what must have been a very large portmanteau stuffed with his Indian drawings and a small library of Indian books that included Flora Annie Steel's *Wide-awake Stories*.

Thanks to the efforts of friends in high places such as Walter Lawrence, now Private Secretary to Lord Dufferin's successor, Lord Lansdowne, Lockwood Kipling had been permitted to retire early on a full pension in recognition of his public services. For reasons that can only be guessed at but which may have had their roots in a mother's extended sulk over a son's unsuitable match, Lockwood came on to America alone, leaving Alice in England to look for an affordable retirement home – eventually secured as a modest 'snail-shell of a house' in Tisbury, near the Wiltshire cathedral city of Salisbury. There is a hint in Edith Plowden's unfinished MS 'Fond Memory' that Alice Kipling's mercurial nature did not serve her well in India once the Dufferins' golden age had ended and her children had gone – and that she never recovered her sparkle. The shadows of depression were closing in on her, just as they were on her daughter Trix.

In Brattleboro father and son worked together in the closest harmony. Indian service tended to harden the views of most *koi hais* but Lockwood Kipling seems to have been an exception, in that he retired with his even temper further mellowed. Almost eighteen years of close proximity with men like the master craftsman Bhai Ram Singh, who accompanied him to England on his royal contracts, had taught Lockwood to look more kindly on India's pre-Islamic Buddhist and Hindu cultures. His later Indian drawings are suffused with humanity and 'a wisdom beyond earthly wisdom' born of 'experience and adversity'. Something of this greater

THE PRAYER

OF FAITH

SHALL SAVE

THE SICK

Hindu couple with sick child, J. L. Kipling (National Trust)

understanding seems to have been imparted to his son as the two sat smoking their pipes and plotting out fresh stories together, initially in Ruddy's new house Naulakha and then, a year later, in Tisbury.

The frontispiece to Flora Annie Steel's *Tales of the Punjab* is a full-page pen-and-ink drawing by Lockwood Kipling showing a little Indian boy in turban and loincloth playing a flute. He squats under a tree filled with birds and monkeys, surrounded on every side by 'the beasts of the forest, and the birds of the air, and the fishes of the pond' drawn by his music. In the story it illustrates,

'Little Anklebone', the little boy is a shepherd eaten by wolves and reduced to an ankle bone, but Lockwood has chosen to illustrate him whole. Here is the archetype of both Mowgli the man-cub and Kim, 'little friend of all the world'.

Father and son are known to have mulled over *Kim* together in Vermont, but he failed to grow and so was put to one side in favour of Mowgli, the infant who is found by Father Wolf and saved from the jaws of the ravening tiger Shere Khan, most feared of all jungle creatures.[14] Suckled by Mother Wolf, accepted as a brother by her own cubs, Mowgli is brought before the Wolf Pack, led by Akela the great grey Lone Wolf, where Bagheera the Black Panther and Baloo, 'the sleepy brown bear who teaches the wolf cubs the Law of the Jungle', speak up for him. Despite being an alien presence in the jungle, Mowgli is permitted to enter the Wolf Pack. Akela foresees a 'time of need' when the man-cub may be of help, so she orders Baloo and Bagheera to take Mowgli away and train him in the Laws of the Jungle. So begins 'Mowgli's Brothers', finished in December 1893, which became the first of the three Mowgli tales in *The Jungle Book*, afterwards followed by another five collected in *The Second Jungle Book*.

According to Carrie's diary, Ruddy now confided to her that he had experienced the 'return of a feeling of great strength, such as he had when he first came to London'. Kipling himself put it rather differently when he came to look back on this most fruitful period. Again his Daemon took charge, in the form of a Zen-like directness that allowed him to set his innermost thoughts on to the page without intervention from his outer consciousness: 'The pen took charge, and I watched it begin to write stories about Mowgli and animals, which later grew into the *Jungle Books*. Once launched there seemed no particular reason to stop, but I had learned to distinguish between the peremptory motions of my Daemon, and the "carry-over" or induced electricity, which comes of what you might call mere "frictional" writing. Two tales, I remember, I threw away.'[15] It was that Daemon, surely, that guided Ruddy's pen when he wrote in 'The King's Ankus' of the growing Mowgli wrestling with Kaa, the big Rock Python, before they took their evening swim:

> Sometimes Mowgli would stand lapped almost to his throat in Kaa's shifting coils, striving to get one arm free and catch him by the throat. Then Kaa would give way limply, and Mowgli, with both quick-moving feet, would try to cramp the purchase of that huge tail as it flung backward feeling for a rock or stump.

They would rock to and fro, head to head, each waiting for his chance, till the beautiful statue-like group melted into a whirl of black-and-yellow coils and struggling legs and arms, to rise up again and again . . . 'Good hunting!' Kaa grunted at last; and Mowgli, as usual, was shot away half a dozen yards, grasping and laughing. He rose with his fingers full of grass, and followed Kaa to the wise snake's pet bathing place – a deep, pitchy-black pool surrounded with rocks, and made interesting by sunken tree stumps. The boy slipped in, Jungle-fashion, and dived across; rose, too, without a sound, and turned on his back, his arms behind his head, watching the moon rise above the rocks, and breaking up her reflection in the water with his toes. Kaa's diamond-shaped head cut the pool like a razor, and came to rest on Mowgli's shoulder. They lay still, soaking luxuriously in the cool water.

As we read them today the Mowgli stories in the two *Jungle Books* are interspersed with other tales, of which two are worthy but unconvincing stories set in the Canadian Arctic Circle and another five are set in India. Of the latter, four are *pukka* animal tales, including two masterpieces of storytelling: the grim fight to the death waged in a bungalow compound between cobras and mongoose in 'Rikki-Tikki-Tavi', and the even grimmer 'Undertakers', in which three scavengers – an adjutant crane, jackal and crocodile – reflect on the follies of men as they guard a river-crossing on the Ganges. They look back nostalgically to the summer of 'thirty seasons ago' when all the river predators feasted on the bodies of the English dead as they floated downriver, and lament the fact that an iron railway bridge under construction will deprive them of food in the future. The dating of the Mutiny year of 1857 to thirty years earlier shows that the first draft of this story was written not in Vermont but in Allahabad in 1887.

Equally out of place in this collection is 'The Miracle of Purun Bhagat', which tells of a Bombay University-educated Brahmin, Purun Dass, who rises through the ranks to become prime minister of an Indian state and to be fêted by London society as a Westernised, progressive Indian – only to turn his back on the world to become a wandering *sanyassi* or Hindu holy man. He settles into a Himalayan mountain shrine and communes with the birds and beasts in the manner of St Francis. The benign Kipling who wrote this is very far removed from the hardliner who had railed so loudly against Hindu philosophy and Hindu intellectuals in his Allahabad days. It could be that fatherhood had mellowed him, or that his father's influence had taught him tolerance. But there is a sting at the end of the tale, for one night Purun Bhagat is roused by a langur and realises that a landslide is about to crash down upon the sleeping village below. Seizing a firebrand he scrambles down the hillside to rouse the villagers and save their lives. Kipling seems to be saying that the Hindu creed of passivity and acceptance of fate, worthy as it is, is not enough; that in a crisis it is the Western notion of action and intervention that saves the day.

Arresting as they are, 'Rikki-Tikki-Tavi', 'The Undertakers', 'The Miracle of Purun Bhagat' and the other non-Mowgli tales are trespassers in the *Jungle Books*. By being interleaved between the Mowgli stories they cloak Kipling's achievement, which is that the eight Mowgli tales and associated verses together form a cohesive eight-chapter novel with its own unifying philosophy. The Free People in Mowgli's jungle are not the *Bandar-Log*, the anarchic 'monkey-people' who think of themselves as free but who squabble and fight among themselves, but those creatures who voluntarily submit themselves to the discipline of the Law of the Jungle. Without that Law, as followed by the members of the Wolf Pack, and as taught to Mowgli by Baloo and Bagheera, there can be no order. It requires little stretching of the imagination to read into this a metaphor for British rule in India, with the British as the members of the Wolf Pack and the Indians in the role of the *Bandar-Log*. This philosophy seems to have had its roots in Ruddy's mixed feelings about both American society and British India, and his belief that what kept these fractured societies from falling apart was the rule of law firmly applied, as exemplified by the British in India and as summarised – perhaps rather *too* summarily – in his poem 'The Law of the Jungle', which makes its point in the opening quatrain:

> Now this is the Law of the Jungle – as old and as true as the
> sky;
> And the Wolf that shall keep it may prosper, but the Wolf
> that shall break it may die.
> As the creeper that girdles the tree-trunk the Law runneth
> forward and back –
> For the strength of the Pack is the Wolf, and the strength of
> the Wolf is the Pack.

The Law of the Jungle demands absolute loyalty to the Pack and to its leader, and while parts of it, in Kipling's telling, are specifically vulpine, its conclusion was intended to have universal application:

> Now these are the Laws of the Jungle, and many and mighty
> are they;
> But the head and the hoof of the Law and the haunch and
> the hump is – Obey!

The paradox, which Rudyard Kipling never fully addresses or resolves, is that while he recognised the necessity of the Law and made much of it, he himself wanted no part of it, but demanded for himself the licence to stand outside the Law, even to mock it and challenge it.

A further product of this happy period in Lockwood Kipling's company was 'The Bridge-Builders',[16] a deeper exploration of the tensions between Western rationalism and Eastern mysticism touched on in 'The Miracle of Purun Bhagat'. Back in 1887 Ruddy had reported for the *CMG* on the completion of a new bridge over the Ganges at Benares, the ceremonial opening of which by Lord Dufferin had had to be postponed due to a severe flood. This provided the basis for another of the unfinished tales Ruddy took with him when he finally left Allahabad in 1889, to be brought out three years later and given depths which the younger Ruddy could never have conceived. 'The Bridge-Builders' tells the story of Findlayson of the Public Works Department, who with the assistance of his Native gangmaster Peroo has been constructing the 'great Kashi Bridge over the Ganges', soon to be declared open by the Viceroy. Findlayson is a practical man, his beliefs rooted in modern science. His bridge is 'raw and ugly as original sin, but pukka – permanent', like British India itself, and he is immensely proud of his achievement: 'He looked back on the humming village of five thousand work-men; upstream and down, along the vista of spurs and sand; across the river to the far piers, lessening in the haze; overhead to the guard-towers – and only he knew how strong those were – and with a sigh of contentment saw that his work was good.' By con-trast, Peroo the Hindu knows the power of Mother Ganga at flood time and fears that the building of the bridge has angered the god-dess.

The floodwaters duly rise: 'The river lifted herself bodily, as a snake when she drinks in midsummer, plucking and fingering along the revetments, and banking up behind the piers till even Findlayson began to recalculate the strength of his work.' When the moment of crisis arrives Peroo offers Findlayson some pellets of opium, which he swallows unthinkingly. Under its influence he acts without thought to his safety and he and Peroo are washed downriver and on to a sandbank. They shelter beside an aban-doned Hindu shrine, where they are joined by a number of wild animals, each an avatar of a Hindu god, who dispute among them-selves over the effect the bridge will have on them and whether it should be allowed to stand. When woken from his stupor by the chill of dawn, Findlayson claims to have suffered a fever: 'It seemed that the island was full of beasts and men talking, but I do not remember.' Peroo, however, remembers everything and is able to conclude, 'Now I am wise.' They are rescued and find the bridge intact, but it is Peroo who gains from the experience and Findlayson who is humbled, even if his engineering has triumphed over the river.

'The Bridge-Builders' can be read as a struggle between the natural and supernatural, of East confronting West, and of new India challenging the old – but also as a fusion of opposites, a merging of the real and the fabulous. It can equally be interpreted as an endorsement for the power of drugs to lift the mind on to a higher plane of consciousness. A psychiatrist might also make something of the fact that two of Rudyard Kipling's most powerful Indian stories ('The Bridge-Builders' and 'In Flood-Time') involve death-dealing and life-altering river floods, and three ('The Bridge-Builders', 'The Undertakers' and 'The Strange Ride of Morrowbie Jukes') involve netherworlds set on shifting sands or sandbanks where the Law does not apply.

At Naulakha father and son worked side by side, the one writing his tales, the other drawing sketches to decorate and illustrate them. Together with Carrie and baby Josephine they might almost have been a new Family Square. In September Lockwood returned to England and the atmosphere changed, in large part because Carrie's determination to run things her way had put a strain on the Kiplings' relations with the other members of the Balestier family and their neighbours. Three bitter months marooned in deep snow was as much as Ruddy and Carrie could endure, and in January 1894 they fled to the warmth of Bermuda – where, characteristically, Ruddy buttonholed in the street a sergeant from the Royal Berkshire Regiment and secured an invitation to tea in his married quarters. Fourteen years earlier the sergeant had been present at the Maiwand disaster in the Second Afghan War and had seen his colonel and the other wing of his regiment overwhelmed while he and the rest retreated in panic back to Kandahar. Rudy coaxed the story out of him and turned it into cruel, honest poetry in 'That Day':

I 'eard the knives be'ind me, but I dursn't face my man,
  Nor I don't know where I went to, 'cause I didn't 'alt to
    see,
Till I 'eard a beggar squealin' out for quarter as 'e ran,
  An' I thought I knew the voice an' – it was me![17]

A trip to England in the summer to show off his sixteen-month-old daughter to his mother reinforced Ruddy's conviction that literary London held no more charms for him. He visited old friends and old haunts, but felt alienated and unable to connect. He attended a formal banquet honouring the newly ennobled Lord Roberts, lately retired from India, and was astonished by the reception given to the pair of them. His tribute to 'Bobs' Roberts – 'There's a little red-faced man, / Which is Bobs, / Rides the tallest 'orse 'e can – / Our Bobs' – had recently appeared in the newspapers to universal praise, and when these two little men entered the banqueting hall side by side they were given a standing ovation directed as much towards the younger man as the grizzled old warrior. No less unsettling was a return to Westward Ho!, where Ruddy represented USC's old boys at a ceremony marking the retirement of his beloved guru Cormell Price and was observed 'silently looking into the past'.[18]

For most of their time in England Ruddy and Carrie lived in a rented house near his parents at Tisbury, allowing Ruddy to commune daily with his father for almost three months before they returned to Vermont in August. 'Heaven was kind to me in England,' he wrote to an American correspondent, 'where I was safely delivered of several poems, four new jungle tales and a piece of broad farce.'[19] The last *Jungle Book* story was completed back in Vermont, with Ruddy finally writing to Mary Mapes Dodge on 18 June 1895 that he had 'this week finished the last of the New Jungle books with the words "and this is the last of the Mowgli tales because there are no more to be told." Now we must try new things.'[20]

Among the new things tried were two Indian tales conceived as further tributes to the empire-building work of Anglo-Indians of the same mould as Findlayson the engineer hero of 'The Bridge-Builders', all three being subsequently collected and published in 1898 in the aptly named *The Day's Work*. The more readable of the two is 'The Tomb of His Ancestors', which begins with a private joke that the Kiplings' friends would have enjoyed: 'Some people will tell you that if there were but a loaf of bread in all India it would be divided equally between the Plowdens, the Trevors, the Beadons, and the Rivett-Carnacs. That is only one way of saying that certain families serve India generation after generation as dolphins follow in line across the open seas.' The Chinns are one such family, the brighter ones going into the ICS and the duller ones joining the Police or the Forest Service. John Chinn the Younger follows family tradition and finds himself administering the Satpura hills of Central India, inhabited by tribal Bhils, where his father and grandfather served before him. The Bhils are up in arms against the Government's vaccination programme – until John Chinn goes out into the jungle to take on the vengeful spirit of his ancestor 'Jan Chinn' in the form of a giant man-eating tiger, which he shoots and kills.

Far more ambitious is 'William the Conqueror', in which the 'William' of the title is not a man but the mannish sister of a Punjab official for whom she keeps house. After four hard years in India in which she has survived cholera and typhoid, William wears her hair 'cropped and curling over her head', walks in 'long, easy strides', prefers a 'dingy old riding-habit' to dresses, will 'never set foot on the ground if a horse were within hail', likes to sit on chairs with 'one foot tucked under her . . . rolling cigarettes for her brother', loves to talk shop, speaks fluent Urdu and Punjabi, and looks at men 'squarely and deliberately between the eyes – yea, after they had proposed to her and been rejected'.

The story is divided between Lahore and a district in southern India where a state of famine has been declared which promises to be as bad as the mismanaged 'Big Famine' of Lord Lytton's time. William's brother and her brother's friend Scott of the Punjab

Irrigation Department are sent south to help out. William goes with them and soon finds herself as involved in famine relief work as her menfolk, to the extent of taking on some of Scott's work when he goes down with fever. They all work manfully through the Hot Weather until the Rains break, by which time Scott and William are in love. As they return to the Punjab the latter knows she has found her destiny: 'Here was the land she knew and loved, and before her lay the good life she understood, among folk of her own caste and mind.'

During the writing of 'William the Conqueror' Carrie noted in her diary that Ruddy had 'got the hang of quite a new sort of woman' who was 'turning out stunningly'.[21] William is indeed a far more rounded and believable heroine than those Ruddy had tried and failed to portray in *The Light That Failed* and *The Brushwood Boy* but she is not, as several Kipling biographers have suggested, an idealised version of Edmonia Hill. Far from it. To put it plainly, William is no more than a man in a skirt.

A dry spell followed. Efforts to get *Kim* going again were started and abandoned. Their second child, Elsie, looking 'ridiculously like her mother', was born in February 1896, by which time Carrie's relations with her prickly brother Beatty were approaching breaking point, while Ruddy for his part was becoming increasing vexed by what he saw as the US Government's growing belligerence towards his own country, to say nothing of the behaviour of American reporters, who regarded him as public property. Ruddy found refuge in his friendship with their family doctor, James Conland, who as a young man had served on the cod-fishing fleets of the Grand Banks off Newfoundland. This led to the two of them exploring the doctor's old haunts in Boston and Gloucester, and to the writing of Ruddy's third novel, *Captains Courageous: a Story of the Grand Banks*, first published in instalments in *McClure's Magazine* over the winter of 1896–7. Its author confided to a friend that it was 'plain narrative done from the inside and . . . a corker', adding that 'I always told you I could write a tale.'[22] The critics' judgement was that it was rich in local detail but lacked conviction, particularly in its characterisation of the main protagonist: the unlikeable rich man's son Harvey Cheyne, who is rescued from drowning by cod fishermen and over the course of eight chapters at sea in their company becomes a better man for it.

In early May 1896 angry words were exchanged between Ruddy and his brother-in-law in a country lane, resulting in Beatty being brought to court and a great deal of hostile reporting in the press. 'Rud a total wreck,' Carrie noted in her diary a week later. 'Sleeps all the time. Dull, listless, and weary. These are dark days for us.'[23] Within weeks they had decided to quit Vermont for England. On their last day at Naulakha friends came to say goodbye and found Carrie in tears and Ruddy 'frozen in misery'. The latter was quoted as saying, 'There are only two places where I want to live – Bombay and Brattleboro. And I can't live in either.'[24]

On 1 September the family boarded a steamship bound for Southampton and from there moved into Rock House, a large country mansion set high on the cliffs at Maidencombe in south Devon, with spectacular views across Torbay to Portland Bill sixty miles away. A return to the county he had known in the happier years of his boyhood led Ruddy to invoke those years afresh in his imagination. In mid-December he wrote to 'Uncle Crom' Price about the doings of the Old USCs he had met or heard of, adding that he was 'deep in a school tale, in which Dunsty [Dunsterville], Beresford, Crofts and all the rest of them come in. There's a lovely scene of you in your study . . . I've never worked the mine of material I accumulated at Westward Ho! But come down and you shall hear it read.'[25] This was 'Slaves of the Lamp', the first of the *Stalky & Co.* stories, published in *Cosmopolitan* in April 1897. It does not seem to have crossed his mind that in writing about his fellow pupils and their masters in barely disguised form he was trespassing on their privacy.

Despite the pleasure Ruddy found in writing his *Stalky* tales, and however much he professed to feel at home, neither he nor Carrie was at ease in Rock House. Within weeks of occupying it they found themselves in the grip of what Kipling afterwards described as a 'brooding Spirit of deep, deep Despondency within the open, lit rooms . . . a growing depression which enveloped us both in a gathering blackness of mind and sorrow of the heart, that each put down to the new, soft climate and, without telling the other, fought against for long weeks'.[26] When at last in February 1897 Ruddy discovered that Carrie hated the house as much as he, they chose to forfeit six months' rent for a happier home. Something of the darkness of that time may have been preserved in the eleven stark lines written in April 1897 at the behest of Ruddy's cousin Phil Burne-Jones, who had followed in his father's footsteps as an artist after failing to complete his degree at Oxford. When they first met as adults in 1889 after his return to London Ruddy had thought Phil a bit of a 'phool', but eight years later he found him more likeable and agreed to help further his career by providing a text to the centrepiece of an exhibition at the New Gallery in London. The painting showed a man sprawled unconscious on a couch with a beautiful, sharp-toothed woman in a white shroud lowering over him – with just a hint of a leer on her lips. The only explanation offered was the caption, *The Vampire*, and Ruddy's text, which ran in full:

> A fool there was and he made his prayer
>   (Even as you and I!)
> To a rag and a bone and a hank of hair
>   (We called her the woman who did not care)
> But the fool he called her his lady fair –
>   (Even as you and I!)
>
> Oh, the years we waste and the tears we waste
>   And the work of our head and hand
> Belong to the woman who did not know
>   (And now we know that she never could know)
> And did not understand!

The sub-text, of which Ruddy must surely have been aware, was that the painting was of the actress Mrs Patrick Campbell, who had rejected Phil's advances. Phil must have hoped that his famous cousin's name would help to sell the picture, but it was the eleven stark lines, published in the *Daily Mail* two weeks before the painting was even exhibited, that received all the attention, helping to advertise the fact that the author of 'Danny Deever', 'Arithmetic on the Frontier' and other chill reminders of human frailty was back in England.

The big event in 1897 was the celebration of Queen Victoria's Diamond Jubilee. It was also the year in which Rudyard Kipling became the first poet to command a mass audience. In early April, with Carrie and the family settled into a hotel in Kensington, he was elected to the Athenaeum under the club's rule for the admittance of eminent persons without balloting, and on the day of his election he dined with Lord Milner, Cecil Rhodes, Sir Sidney Colvin, Sir Walter Besant and Moberly Bell, editor of *The Times*. Over the course of the previous year Bell had published in his paper a number of poems of what Ruddy had taken to calling 'a national character', afterwards collected in *The Seven Seas*. Offered gratis, these public verses elevated Kipling to the status of a national weathervane, a poet who spoke *for* as much as *to* the British people on national and international issues, even when his views were in conflict with those of the government of the day. Inevitably Moberly Bell wanted something for *The Times* to mark the Jubilee, and after much grumbling Ruddy obliged. On 15 June Carrie noted in her diary that he was working on a poem called 'White Man's Burden', which he then put to one side in order to try a different approach on the theme of imperial hubris, constructed around a single phrase lodged in his head: 'Lest we forget'.

With both sets of verses still unfinished Ruddy went down to Spithead for a fortnight with the Royal Navy, gathered for the Jubilee Review as the greatest armada the world had ever seen. Thrilled though he was by this display of naval strength, he was dispirited by all the patriotic fervour whipped up by the Jubilee celebrations, and on his return to land went back to work on the second of the two poems, soon afterwards submitted to Moberly Bell with the remark that it was 'about time we sobered down'. The poem was immediately published under the title 'Recessional'. The impact of this solemn call for national humility before God was immediate and unparalleled. Ruddy's agent, A. P. Watt, wept when he first read the verses and declared his client to be 'the only rightful heir to the mantles of Shakespeare, Milton, and Tennyson'. Sir Walter Besant probably got it right when he wrote: 'You caught the exact feeling – what all people with the Puritanic touch in us wanted to have said and couldn't say. That is genius.'[27]

Much as Ruddy savoured the public acclaim, the birth in mid-August of a first male child, named John after his grandfather, meant a great deal more. He and Carrie had just taken a five-year lease on The Elms, a house overlooking the green at Rottingdean in Sussex and within a cricket ball's throw of Ned and Georgie Burne-Jones's cottage, North End House, on the other side of the green. Within this wider circle of relatives and friends visiting from London something of the contentment Ruddy had known in Vermont returned, although not enough to dispel entirely his bouts of 'darkness and gloom'. Crom Price came to stay with Ned Burne-Jones, a close friend since their grammar school days together in Birmingham, and his company gave Ruddy encouragement to further plunder and embellish his Westward Ho! days in more *Stalky* tales. But Ruddy's continuing depressions, the winter darkness and what he described in his autobiography as a growing unease about the way political events were shaping led him to take his family to winter in South Africa at the start of 1898.

A return to sunlight at the Cape brought back the delights of 'the life unaltered our childhood knew' (see Chapter 2, pp. 36–8) and with the renewal of warmth he began to write the *Just So Stories*: simple spoken tales intended to delight his own children. By the spring these had taken on a life of their own, to be tested out on his return to Sussex on other young members of the Macdonald clan, including Margaret Burne-Jones's daughter, Angela Mackail, then aged eight:

> The *Just So Stories* are a poor thing in print compared with the fun of hearing them told in Cousin Ruddy's deep unhesitating voice. There was a ritual about them, each phrase having its special intonation which had to be exactly the same as last time and without which the stories are dried husks. There was an inimitable cadence, an emphasis of certain words, an exaggeration of certain phrases, a kind of intoning here and there which made his telling unforgettable.[28]

In South Africa Ruddy had been taken up by Cecil Rhodes, and in his admiration for the man and his loathing for the Dutch Boers, representing the worst excesses of colonialism, he willingly allowed himself to be seduced by Rhodes's vision of Africa under Anglo-Saxon rule. His return to England in April coincided with America's little proxy war with Spain over Cuba, which ended with the United States becoming colonial rulers in all but title of Cuba and the Philippines. Since he viewed America as Britain's natural ally in its role as global lawgiver, Ruddy was pleased to see it sign up to membership of the imperial club. Dusting down the verses abandoned the previous summer, he reworked them into a call to the United States to join with Britain in its self-appointed task of extending the blessings of the Law to the far corners of the earth:

> Take up the White Man's burden –
>   Send forth the best ye breed –
> Go bind your sons to exile
>   To serve your captives' need;
> To wait in heavy harness
>   On fluttered folks and wild –

Your new caught sullen peoples,
Half devil and half child.[29]

Whatever their intent, the verses of 'The White Man's Burden' were among the clumsiest Kipling ever penned, their sentiments among the crudest: at best a call to the Anglo-Saxon world to do its painful duty by spreading its higher values to the rest of the world, at worst a hymn to aggressive white supremacy. Critics and biographers alike have scratched their heads over the incongruity of these lines being written seemingly in tandem with 'Recessional' in the Jubilee summer of 1897, but it is worth remembering that the final polish to 'The White Man's Burden' was only given in November 1898, at a time when Ruddy was feeling unusually low, still grieving for a close relative and reeling from a second no less devastating blow.

The first disaster was the sudden death of his Uncle Ned, who suffered a heart attack at The Grange in mid-June 1898. This was the first real loss Ruddy had suffered since the death of Wolcott Balestier seven years earlier, and he took it hard. After an all-night vigil in which the men of the family stood two-hour watches, Ned Burne-Jones's ashes were buried in the churchyard at Rottingdean in a ceremony Ruddy found harrowing, made all the worse by seeing Uncle Crom 'broken to pieces'. He and his Uncle Ned had exchanged long, heartfelt and even scabrous letters over the years, and as soon as the opportunity arose Ruddy went through his uncle's papers, removing and destroying the lot, together with as many of his letters to his Aunt Georgie as he could lay hands on. Carrie's diary shows that Ruddy subsequently found solace in returning to work on *Kim*, an early outline or draft of which he sent to his father in Tisbury for comments. In late September Alice Kipling came to stay with her sister in Rottingdean, bringing with her that same draft, together with Lockwood's notes. Very soon afterwards the second disaster hit the Kiplings: the mental break-down of their beloved 'Maiden'.

In her first novel, *The Heart of a Maid*, published under the pseudonym 'Beatrix Grange' in 1891 as No. 8 in Wheeler and Co.'s Indian Railway Library series, Trix had written of the incompatible temperaments of the book's heroine May and her husband Percy: 'He was naturally self-contained and undemonstrative. May would have liked him to be passionate. She had married him not for her own sake, but for his . . . Sometimes the very sound of her husband's slow, monotonous voice made her clasp her hands together in silent, intense irritation. Half this was purely physical, but it was none the less very real and hard to bear.' It is impossible to judge to what extent this portrayal of a doomed marriage was based on her own, but it is surely no coincidence that in her second novel, *A Pinchbeck Goddess*, published in 1897, the only character that rings true is Lilian, married to a man who shows no affection towards her and who retreats into sullen silence whenever he is challenged. 'We don't speak the same language, he and I,' Lilian tells a sympathetic friend. 'It wouldn't be fair to tell my own people, for they really love me and it would make them unhappy; besides . . . my husband's family would say it was all my own fault.' In the novel Lilian's unhappiness ends when she becomes pregnant, but for Trix there was no happy ending.

A Fleming relative afterwards came close to confirming the accuracy of Trix's picture of her marriage:

> She and Uncle Jack, though deeply attached, scarcely shared one thought or pleasure. He was Army to the toe-tips and looked on all writing or painting as rather riff-raff stuff . . . Our family looked down on the marriage as a very Bohemian alliance, an opinion they had to modify later when all her relations, Baldwins, Poynters, Burne-Jones, not to say Kipling himself achieved a good measure of fame . . . but by then the damage had been done. I think the split in her affections, real love for her husband and real yearning for her own relations and all the fun they had in the world of life and letters[,] was too much for her.[30]

Suffering from what sounds very like classic bipolar disorder, Trix was brought back to England by her husband to be looked after by her mother in Tisbury, where she then experienced a severe psychotic episode in the late autumn of 1898, alternating between 'mutism' and long bouts of 'almost constant talk . . . nearly all nonsense'. Alice Kipling seems initially to have been in denial, but in early November she was forced to admit to her son that Trix needed professional care. On 18 November 1898 – just four days before Carrie noted in her diary that a final draft of 'The White Man's Burden' had been completed to her husband's satisfaction – Ruddy wrote to his uncle Alfred Baldwin explaining that his mother was taking Trix to a Dr Colenso in London where 'she would be dosed and dieted and generally looked after' for three weeks: 'If she does not kill herself before the 22nd we shall at least have the satisfaction of knowing that she will then seriously enter upon the care of herself. I shall then take steps to introduce a specialist . . . The main point is not to flutter the mother.'[31]

Trix failed to respond to this course of treatment and had to be installed in a nursing home, where she remained for more than a year, her mother noting that 'There are times in every day when she is her own bright self and then she suddenly changes and drifts away into a world of her own – always a sad one – into which I cannot follow her.'[32] Although Trix recovered sufficiently to be able to return with Jack Fleming to India in 1902 she suffered several relapses, the most serious following the death of her parents in the winter of 1910–11, and she remained in fragile mental health thereafter for much of the rest of her life.

In the gloomy winter months following Trix's breakdown Ruddy stayed with his parents at The Gables in Tisbury to give his mother support. He also continued to work on *Kim* with his father: 'Under our united tobaccos it grew like the Djin released from the brass bottle, and the more we explored its possibilities the more opulence of detail did we discover . . . Between us, we knew every step, sight, and smell on his casual road, as well as all the persons he met.' *Kim* became a refuge, providing therapeutic release for both men, and on his return to his own family at The Elms, Rottingdean, at Christmas Ruddy continued to work on the book: 'The sou'-westers raged day and night, till the silly windows jiggled their wedges loose. But I was quite unconcerned. I had my Eastern sunlight and if I wanted more I could get it at "The Gables", Tisbury.'[33]

The writing of *Kim* continued into the New Year of 1899, at which point it was decided that rather than proceeding to South Africa as planned the family should instead go to America to see Carrie's parents. Alice Kipling's fears for their health in risking a winter crossing of the Atlantic were dismissed, and on 20 January the five Kiplings and a nanny set sail from Liverpool. A fortnight later they docked in New York with everyone in the party suffering from coughs and colds. Almost immediately the condition of little Josephine and Elsie grew worse and they were diagnosed as suffering from whooping cough. Then Ruddy developed pneumonia, which spread to both lungs. By 24 February he had fallen into a delirium. After eight days of hovering on the brink he was declared by the doctors to be out of danger – but as his condition improved, so that of Josephine deteriorated. The death on 6 March of the daughter who was 'the delight of his heart' was kept from him by Carrie and his friends for some weeks for fear of the shock killing him.

It took Ruddy the better part of four months to recover his strength and his nerve. Six months after setting out for America he and his depleted family returned to their home at Rottingdean to rebuild their lives. His parents and his Aunt Georgie helped them to readjust, with Lockwood Kipling noting to a friend that 'The house and garden are full of the lost child and poor Rud told his mother how he saw her when a door opened, when a space was vacant at table – coming out of every green dark corner of the garden – radiant – and heartbreaking.'[34]

So many letters of condolence and good wishes had been received that Ruddy and Carrie were forced to reply through the press in a general letter of thanks. But among those who wrote and who received a personal letter in return was Mrs Edmonia Hill – their first exchange of letters since the breakup in late 1890. 'Be thankful that you never had a child to lose,' Ruddy told her. 'I thought I knew something of what grief meant till that came to me. My "fame" never was of any use to me anyway, and now it seems more of an irony than ever.' He spoke of never returning to America but of the possibility of going back to India: 'There isn't much news of India in my life. Now and again I hear of an old name – but not often. It has all changed. The Curzons want me to come out and stay with them – but Viceroys are not exactly my line. This fool-sickness of mine which had the bad taste to leave me and take my little Maiden (I wish you could have seen her) makes it I believe impossible for me to stay in England through the winters: so I suppose I may as well try India as any other place.' He closed his letter with a brief postscript: 'I am afraid this is rather badly written but the fact is that I don't do much writing nowadays.'[35]

What made Ruddy's loss harder to bear was what he regarded as his betrayal by friends, among them Kay Robinson and George 'M'Turk' Beresford. Robinson had made the mistake of publicly quoting at length from Ruddy's reply, written in Lahore in April 1886 (see Chapter 8, p. 207), after Robinson had urged him to seek literary fame in England. This breach of his privacy provoked Ruddy into demanding the return of the letter, which Robinson did with good grace, promising never again to write another word of their past acquaintance and adding that 'All that I have written has been in the spirit of the warmest friendship and admiration; and I was naturally proud that, although everyone used to laugh both at Allahabad and Lahore when I said you would be quickly recognised as one of the greatest poets of recent times, my judgement has been so completely justified.'[36] Ruddy did not respond, and their friendship ended there.[37]

It was from this time, according to Kipling's niece Angela Thirkell, that the shutters came down. Writing in 1932 when her uncle was still alive, she stated that 'There has been the same charm, the same gift of fascinating speech, the same way of making everyone with whom he talks show their most interesting side, but one was only allowed to see these things from the other side of a barrier and it was sad for the child who used to be free of the inner courts of his imagination.'[38]

But the compulsion to write was still there, and in the late summer of 1899 Ruddy resumed work on the *Just So Stories*. It was a year and a half before he felt able to refer obliquely to his lost daughter, imaged as a half-glimpsed free spirit with eyes 'bright as diamonds and bluer than the sky above' roaming the Wealden downs in his poem 'Merrow Down', included among the verses in *Just So Stories*:

> For far – oh, very far behind,
>   So far she cannot call to him,
> Comes Tegumai alone to find
>   The daughter that was all to him!

Envoi: 'In the faith of little children'

KIM AND AFTER, 1899–1936

> Came the Whisper, came the Vision, came the Power with the
>   Need,
>   Till the Soul that is not man's soul was lent us to lead.
> As the deer breaks – as the steer breaks – from the herd where
>   they graze,
>   In the faith of little children we went on our ways.
> Then the wood failed – then the food failed – then the last
>   water dried –
>   In the faith of little children we laid down and died.
>
> Rudyard Kipling, A Song of the English, 1893

In the late summer of 1899 Ruddy wrote to his agent, A. P. Watt, asking him to return the manuscript of *Mother Maturin*, which for some years had been lodged with him for safe keeping. Taking what little could be salvaged from the 350 pages written a decade earlier and abandoning the rest, Ruddy returned to work on *Kim*, knowing now that this was his best chance of fulfilling the task he had set himself many years earlier, to write the great Indian novel. With characteristic candour Alice Kipling had once remarked to her son that 'You know you couldn't make a plot to save your soul', but Ruddy had now stopped worrying about the novel's structure, having decided that *Kim* should unfold in the same picaresque style as Cervantes' *Don Quixote*. 'Kim took care of himself,' he wrote of this final stage of the novel's development. 'The only trouble was to keep him in bounds.' By November of that year Ruddy was able to read an early draft of *Kim* to his Aunt Georgie over at North End House.

The Boer War now intervened. On 12 October 1899 the British Government declared war on Kruger and his Boers in the Transvaal, and Ruddy at once felt impelled to do his bit by rallying the British public behind the troops. 'Rud is absorbed with excitement and anxiety over the troops in Africa,' Carrie noted in her diary. His response appeared in the *Daily Mail* on 31 October in the form of 'The Absent-Minded Beggar', his barrack-room-style ballad about 'a gentleman in khaki ordered south'. At Ruddy's request it carried no copyright and within days was being sung in music halls and drawing rooms to a tune 'guaranteed to pull teeth out of barrel-organs' composed by Sir Arthur Sullivan. But by mid-December British garrisons at Mafeking, Kimberley and Ladysmith were under siege as British forces suffered a series of reverses in open battle. In January Lord Roberts was called in to take over as Commander-in-Chief, and with his arrival the Indian Army gained a greater say in the running of the campaign.[1]

As he wintered in Cape Town with his family Ruddy became increasingly caught up in the war, and his determination to be physically involved was finally realised when he and a group of like-minded gentlemen-journalists contrived to set up a local propaganda newspaper in Bloemfontein. There were those, including his Aunt Georgie and his cousin by marriage Jack Mackail, who were dead set against the war and saw Kipling's part in it as imperial propagandising at its worst. But for Ruddy it was a case of good colonialism versus bad, and as the Boers were first starved into defeat and then appeased by the Liberal Government elected to power in 1906 his public poetry grew ever more strident and insufferable, to the point where it became, in Henry James's damning phrase, all 'steam and patriotism'.[2] But on the human level the South African War gave Ruddy the opportunity to assuage his grief through practical effort. At long last he was afforded the opportunity to play the role of special correspondent in a theatre of war, to be the man of action his physical short-comings had always prevented him from becoming. The war allowed him to stand shoulder to shoulder as a comrade among the military men he most admired, and when he discovered that these same men saw him as their champion, his exhilaration was hard to contain. 'Never again will there be such a paper,' he wrote of his few weeks on the *Friend of the Free State*. 'Never again such a staff. Such larks.'[3]

The Boer War helped restore Ruddy in body and mind. He returned to England in April re-energised, and at once sat down in his study at The Elms in Rottingdean to complete the writing of *Kim*, which he did over the course of the next twelve to fourteen weeks. Entries in Carrie's diary record that it was finished by 7 August, after which negotiations began immediately for the novel's publication, initially in serial form chapter by chapter in *McClure's Magazine* in America, beginning in December 1900, and in Britain in *Cassell's Magazine* from January 1901, with the book publication to follow in the autumn.

What is so bizarre about this final stretch is that Kipling came straight from the front line of a war, his mind filled with images of soldiering, and immediately flung himself into the completion of a novel about a boy's search for identity. Part of the explanation may lie in the two verses which Kipling wrote on completing the final proof corrections to the text – verses which he then used to head one of the chapters of *Kim* when published in book form:

> Something I owe to the soil that grew –
>   More to the life that fed –
> But most to Allah Who gave me two
>   Separate sides to my head.

> I would go without shirts or shoes,
>   Friends, tobacco or bread
> Sooner than for an instant lose
>   Either side of my head.[4]

A lot has been said about these verses and the way in which they sum up, in Christopher Hitchens's apt phrase, 'a man of permanent contradictions'.[5] Those contradictions are at their most glaring in *Kim*, but it is also in *Kim* that they are successfully resolved. Like his creator, the boy Kimball O'Hara has two separate sides to his head. His being is divided between Britain (bearing in mind that Ireland was at this time part of Great Britain) and India. His father's papers sewn into the leather amulet case hanging round his neck prove Kim's Britishness, but in almost every other respect he belongs to India, being 'burned black as any native' and speaking the vernacular 'by preference' and his mother-tongue only in 'clipped uncertain sing-song'. Even though he may be joking when he asks the Afghan horse-trader Mahbub Ali if he, Kim, is a Hindu, Kim's question is part of his search for identity. He does not know what he is, and the need to know becomes increasingly important to him. But as the tale and his quest unfold it becomes apparent that the two aspects of Kim are opposed and seemingly irreconcilable, as are the ruler and the ruled, the brown and the white, the rational and the intuitive. It seems that Kim can be one or the other but not both.

However, Kim goes on to demonstrate his capacity for survival through his extraordinary ability to slip effortlessly from one guise into another – a gift which Mahbub Ali and his employers in the Government of India's intelligence services recognise and use to their advantage. Then Kim is claimed as one of *their* kind by two clergymen, a Methodist and a Catholic, and even though he finds them bigoted and ignorant of Indian ways he feels the pull of his race and submits to being schooled as a sahib – until the call of the Indian side of his head becomes irresistible, at which point he resumes his role as the *chela* or disciple of his Buddhist Lama from Tibet. As Kim journeys across northern India on foot, by train and by bullock cart, he continues to ask himself, 'What is Kim?' and he remains a 'mixture o' things', first one thing and then the other – until the final crisis comes. He survives to become – what?

Biographers and literary critics tend to shy away from the ending of *Kim*, but most take the line that it has quite deliberately been left open and ambiguous: Kim will most probably become a sahib, or he just might choose to stay with the Lama as his disciple. The question of Kim's identity remains unresolved.

But the fact is that *Kim* sprang from the pen of the champion of Britain's imperial quest, hot from the South African war and deeply frustrated by what he saw as his Government's failure to defend its hard-won Empire by refusing to equip its armies properly, denying support to its empire-builders and giving succour to its enemies by failing to suppress armed rebellion. Ruddy returned home to Rottingdean determined to put out the message that Britain's imperial mission was under threat – and nowhere more so than in India, cornerstone of the empire. Like every Anglo-Indian of that era he had been infected by the paranoia of the advance of the Russian bear and the belief that India's North-West Frontier was its Achilles heel: the gateway through which the Cossack hordes would pour down upon the Indian plains. That paranoia reached fever pitch in the 1890s, thanks to the celebrated encounter between Captain Francis Younghusband and Colonel Grombtcheski high on the Taghdumbash Pamir in the summer of 1889 and the warnings of experts like General Sir Henry Brackenbury, Director of Military Intelligence, who made public his fears that 'in consequence of the want of a defined policy for meeting further Russian aggression . . . we shall find Russian troops occupying the passes of the Hindu Kush'.[6]

The continuing presence of his parents in the Punjab had helped to sustain Ruddy's interest in events on the North-West Frontier. Beginning in Chitral in 1895 there had been a series of tribal uprisings along the frontier each more serious than the last, culminating in 1897–8 in a general frontier uprising throughout Malakand and Tirah, where it took a combined British and Indian Army force of 40,000 fighting men more than six months to subdue a dozen of the strongest Pathan tribes. The fear of another frontier uprising to follow, supported by Russia, was very real, and Ruddy had already given voice to it in October 1898 in his poem 'The Truce of the Bear', in which he stressed the need for constant vigilance:

Over and over the story, ending as he began –

   There is no truce with Adam-zad, the Bear that looks like a
   Man![7]

All these fears Ruddy reflected in *Kim* by making the defence
of British India its central political theme, romanticised into the
'Great Game'– the hidden struggle between the Great Powers
across central Asia with India as the prize, fought out by 'players'
from both sides: spies seeking to extend Russia's control by sub-
version, and counter-spies working to frustrate their aims. In *Kim*
he envisaged an elite force of secret agents dedicated to defending
British India from its external enemies and its traitors within, 'players of the Game' drawn from every race and religion: Mahbub Ali
the Afghan horse-trader; Hurree Chunder Mookerji the Bengali
Babu; the lean Maratha identified only as E.23; the Simla curio
dealer and 'healer of sick pearls' known as Lurgan-Sahib who is
patently not a pukka sahib; and their controller, the shadowy
Colonel Creighton. All have entered at risk to their lives into 'the
Great Game that never ceases day and night, throughout India',
knowing that 'the Game is greater than the players of the Game'.
The orphan boy Kim is duly recruited into their ranks and with
his help India's enemies in the shape of two bogus explorers, one
Russian and one French, are prevented from fomenting a conspiracy among the frontier tribes.

This is what the imperial, conservative, reasoning side of
Kipling's head envisaged when he sketched out his ideal *Kim*: a
colourful, picaresque *Boy's Own* adventure in which the boy
Kimball O'Hara, for all his Indianness, learns what it is to be a
sahib and understands that his future is to serve both the Indian
people and British India as long as the Great Game continues to
be played.

That may well have been Ruddy's intention, but in the writing
a combination of circumstances caused the practical, sensible side
of Kipling to gave way to the other side of his head: the intuitive,
dark, elemental side which harked to his Daemon and within

which his child nature resided, his real self undimmed, the good Kipling. The change had begun with Ruddy's rediscovery of his child self with the birth of his first-born, followed by his seeking refuge in that same childhood after her death six years later. But scarcely less significant was the return of the father Ruddy had lost at the age of six, in the role of guru.

The only letter from son to father known to have survived the bonfires was written in 1888 when Ruddy learned that he would not be returning to the family home in Lahore. Written in blank verse, it purports to be from 'Halim the Potter to Yusuf His Father and Master Craftsman in the walled city of Lahore', and is a tribute to the father he acknowledges as his mentor and guide, expressed in potter's terms:

> Thy hint, thy council and thy touch . . .
>> My workmanship thou saidst – and I believed.
> It was so small a touch, so slight a word.
>> I threw the wet clay – marred it. Now I see!

> The hand went and the clay thereafter fell
>> Uncouthly. These two months have shown the truth.

More than a decade later the Pater returned to stand at his son's shoulder, again offering hint, council and touch, and placing at his son's disposal his encyclopaedic knowledge of India. Lockwood Kipling was on hand at almost every stage in the writing of *Kim*. Even as the final proofs were being checked he was there, modelling terracotta plaques in low bas-relief of the ten most important characters in the story, to be inserted as sepia plates in the first editions of *Kim*. 'He would take no sort of credit,' wrote his son of his contribution. 'There was a good deal of beauty in it [*Kim*], and not a little wisdom; the best in both sorts being owed to my Father.' In *Something of Myself* Kipling implies that Lockwood was at his side when painful cuts had to be made, including 'a half-chapter of the Lama sitting down in the blue-green shadows at the foot of a glacier, telling Kim stories out of the *Jatakas*, which was truly beautiful but, as my old Classics master would have said, "otiose", and it was removed almost with tears'.[8] The removal of this scene at a very late stage shows how the role of the Lama had grown in the writing – and all the signs are that this was Lockwood Kipling's doing; that the Lama and his Buddhist philosophy were the greatest of the many gifts which Lockwood brought back from India for his son.

Lockwood makes his presence felt in *Kim* from the start – as the white-bearded, pipe-puffing curator of the building in Lahore known locally as the *Ajaib Gher* or Wonder House. He is on hand to welcome the Tibetan Lama to his museum and to guide him through the Buddhist exhibits, revealing a detailed knowledge of Buddhist history and iconography that amazes the Lama. Under his curatorship the Punjab Museum had grown into one of the world's most important repositories of early Buddhist art from the Gandhara civilisation, largely thanks to archaeologists like Lockwood's colleague Aurel Stein. In 1898 in the wake of the Malakand Campaign Stein had excavated Buddhist monastic sites in the hitherto forbidden tribal areas of Swat, and in January of that same year the uncovering of inscribed Buddha relics in a stupa close to India's border with Nepal had completed a cycle of remarkable discoveries in that region which had begun with the finding of the Buddha's long-lost birthplace at Lumbini – an event of huge significance to Buddhists since it was one of the four great pilgrimage sites associated with the life of the Buddha. It had not gone unnoticed by Lockwood Kipling that a few miles west of Lumbini had also been discovered the ruins of Kapilavastu, the city where the Buddha had been raised as Prince Siddhartha, and from which he had fired the arrow which gave rise to the Spring of the Arrow – which now became the ultimate goal of the Lama's quest in *Kim*.

It was Lockwood Kipling, too, who had kept up with the latest developments in Tibetan Buddhist studies, which owed a great deal to the work of two enthusiasts: Dr Austine Waddell of the

Indian Medical Service and a Bengali boarding-school headmaster, Sarat Chandra Das. In Darjeeling both men had studied under Tibetan religious teachers as well as learning from an earlier generation of explorer-spies known as the 'Pundits', hill-men recruited and trained by the Survey of India at its headquarters in Dehra Dun, a place well known to the Kiplings since it was where Jack Fleming had his base.[9] Although never secret agents in the modern sense, the Pundits had mapped Tibet and central Asia at risk of their lives, and included among their number was Sarat Chandra Das – who provided the model for Babu Hurree Chunder, the 'oily, effusive and nervous' secret agent who proceeds to turn the Kipling stereotype of the effete, subversive babu on its head by revealing himself as a man of courage and action.

Dr Waddell's *The Buddhism of Tibet or Lamaism* was published in 1897 and Sarat Chandra Das's account of his illicit travels in Tibet in 1899. Both works came as a shock to those who knew Buddhism through the writings of Rhys Davids, Monier Williams and the Theosophists, in that they portrayed Tibetan Buddhism as a perversion of Buddhism and Tibetan lamas as anything but masters of higher consciousness. These conflicting perceptions explain the only false note in *Kim* – when the gentle Lama declares to the museum's curator that he has come to India from his Tibetan lamasery alone because 'it was in my mind that the Old Law was not well followed; being overlaid, as thou knowest, with devildom, charms and idolatry'. Lockwood Kipling was steeped in the early Buddhism portrayed in the Gandharan sculptures and basalt reliefs which he had cared for in his museum, and it was this purer philosophy, drawing on the verses of Arnold's *Light of Asia* and Max Müller's translation of the *Dhammapada*[10] scriptures, which he passed on to his son in Tisbury and Rottingdean.

In the early chapters of *Kim* the boy's surrogate parent is Mahbub Ali, the manliest of father-figures, who provides him with hot meals and money. Devout Muslim Sufi though he is, Mahbub Ali refuses to give alms to 'cursed unbelievers' and he has none of the instinctive tolerance of Kim, who alone among the children playing on the great gun Zam-zammah shows charity towards the strange Tibetan Lama and so seals his own fate. As 'Little Friend of All the World' Kim is strictly neutral and takes no more interest in the Lama's religion than in the 'few score' other religions he has encountered, but like the Elephant's Child in the *Just So Stories* he has ''satiable curtiosity' which leads him to follow the Lama: 'The lama was his trove, and he purported to take possession.' The feminine unassertiveness of the Lama is unlike anything he has experienced but he accepts the role of the Lama's *chela* or disciple with equanimity, using it as his cover while continuing to work closely with Mahbub Ali. Despite his Afghan background the horse-trader is portrayed as a devoted loyalist of the British Raj, as are Lurgan Sahib and Babu Hurree Chunder. In *Kim* these three major players of the Game fill the same roles as Baloo, Baghera and Kaa in the *Jungle Books* as they teach Kim the Law.

But as the novel unfolds and Kim journeys deeper into the Indian interior, we find him rejecting the Law, or at least that version of the Law taught at St Xavier's boarding school and practised by his fellow players of the Game. The masculine element, so dominant in the first half, now begins to give way to the feminine, exemplified by the increasing importance Kipling accords to two maternal figures: the wealthy widow known as the *Sahiba* who mothers Kim through a fever, and the hill-woman known as the Woman of Shamlegh. The significance of these two characters is almost always downplayed by the mostly male critics and commentators who have passed literary judgement on *Kim*: the Woman of Shamlegh turns out to be the same woman so cruelly let down by her white lover in 'Lispeth', written fourteen years earlier. The younger Ruddy had predicted for her a miserable fate as a 'bleared, wrinkled creature, exactly like a wisp of charred rag', but the older and wiser man has transformed her into a proud and commanding matriarch with two husbands in tow. It is no accident that at the point in the book where Kim and his Lama leave the plains Kipling opens the chapter with an unacknowledged Hindu saying: 'Who goes to the Hills goes to his mother.' Kim is entering feminine territory and from now on these two quintessentially Indian ayah or surrogate mother-figures dominate the story, supported by the gentle Lama and the effeminate plump Babu. And it is no accident that from this point onwards British India and the British, represented throughout by male authority figures, pale into the background, never to reappear. When finally Babu Hurree Chunder comes to sit at the feet of the Lama, he reveals his Westernisation to be no more than skin-deep:

> He himself had been taught by the Sahibs, who do not consider expense, in the lordly halls of Calcutta; but, as he was ever first to acknowledge, there lay a wisdom behind earthly wisdom – the high and lonely lore of meditation. Kim looked on with envy. The Hurree Babu of his knowledge – oily, effusive, and nervous – was gone. . . There remained – polished, polite, attentive – a sober, learned son of experience and adversity, gathering wisdom from the lama's lips.

Kim himself has no time for higher thoughts until, with his duty to Creighton-Sahib and the Great Game done, he and the Lama begin the final stage of their journey, which is to allow the Lama to find the object of his spiritual pilgrimage: 'The River of the Arrow'. Kim now realises that he has deceived the Lama by pretending to be what he was not. Overcome by 'strain, fatigue, and the weight beyond his years', he breaks down in a fever. He is taken in a litter to the Sahiba's house, where she first gives him an opiate that makes him sleep for thirty-six hours and then nurses him back to health. But when Kim struggles to get back into the world again he experiences what can only be described as his moment of enlightenment:

> He looked upon the trees and the broad fields, with the thatched huts hidden among crops – looked with strange eyes unable to take up the size and proportion and use of things – stared for quite half an hour. All that while he felt, though he

could not put it into words, that his soul was out of gear with his surroundings – a cog-wheel unconnected with any machinery . . . The breezes fanned over him, the parrots shrieked at him, the noises of the populated house behind – squabbles, orders, and reproofs – hit on dead ears.

'I am Kim. I am Kim. And what is Kim?' His soul repeated it again and again.

He did not want to cry – had never felt less like crying in his life – but of a sudden easy, stupid tears trickled down his nose, and with an almost audible click he felt the wheels of his being lock up anew on the world without. Things that rode meaningless on the eyeball an instant before slid into proper proportion . . . They were all real and true – solidly planted upon the feet – perfectly comprehensible – clay of his clay, neither more nor less. He shook himself like a dog with a flea in his ear, and rambled out of the gate. Said the Sahiba: 'Let him go. I have done my share. Mother Earth must do the rest.'

Kim lies down under a banyan tree, where he feels the 'good, clean dust' between his toes and pats it between his hands – 'the hopeful dust that holds the seeds of all life'. Then he sleeps: 'And Mother Earth was as faithful as the Sahiba . . . His head lay powerless upon her breast, and his opened hands surrendered to her strength. The many-rooted tree above him, and even the dead man-handled wood beside, knew what he sought, as he himself did not know.'

Now Mahbub Ali reappears to reclaim the boy for the Great Game, and as Kim sleeps he and the Lama dispute over who shall have him. 'It is his right to be cleansed from sin – with me,' argues the Lama, and he suggests that Mahbub Ali might like to join them. Amused by the Tibetan's insolence Mahbub Ali backs off. The Lama then wakes Kim and tells him that his search for the River of the Arrow is over. On account of the merit acquired in his search, the river has come to him. Finally, in what is the novel's penultimate paragraph, the Lama tells Kim that, like a true Bodhisattva who having broken free of the wheel of existence nevertheless returns to help others achieve enlightenment, he has come back for him: 'Son of my Soul, I have wrenched my Soul back from the Threshold of Freedom to free thee from sin – as I am free, and sinless! Just is the Wheel! Certain is our deliverance! Come!' The novel closes with the Lama smiling, 'as a man may who has won salvation for himself and his beloved'.

There is no ambiguity here. What few commentators and critics have been unable to accept is that the novel ends not with Kim torn between duty and faith, British India and Indian India, West and East, action and contemplation, but with Kim a committed disciple of a Tibetan Buddhist Lama. He has found himself and he has made his choice. The struggle between the two sides of Kim's head ends with a clear victory for the better side. A book that began as a political allegory about the defence of British India and, by implication, of Western values, has become the vehicle for a very different Law, that of the Buddhist *Dharma*.

What most commentators do agree on is that as a novel *Kim* finds a perfect balance between seemingly irreconcilable opposites, that its protagonists are as fully realised as its portrayals of urban Lahore and of rural India up and down the Grand Trunk Road, and that the India brought to life is suffused with warmth, the work of a man who loved India deeply. The novelist Kingsley Amis described *Kim* as 'one of the greatest novels in the language', the critic Angus Wilson as 'the culmination and essence of all the transcendence that Kipling gained from his Indian experience'. The no less distinguished Bengali man of letters Nirad Chaudhuri thought *Kim* 'great by any standards that ever obtained in any age of English literature', going on to speak of 'Kipling's vision of a much bigger India, a vision whose profundity we Indians would be hard put to it to match even in an Indian language, not to speak of English. He had arrived at a true and moving sense of that India which is almost timeless, and had come to love it.' Even Edward Said, the scourge of Orientalists and Orientalism, went so far as to declare *Kim* to be of 'great aesthetic merit', albeit a 'masterwork of imperialism'.[11]

In December 1900 the first chapter of *Kim* was published in *McClure's Magazine* in America, and on the thirtieth of that month Rudyard Kipling celebrated his thirty-fifth birthday. Half his life was over. He had always appeared older than his age but he now looked and acted like a man in his late forties, his eyes sunk and overhung by bushy eyebrows, his mouth lost behind a walrus moustache, to all intents a dry old stick, animated only when he could forget himself among children or in the company of people he felt he could trust. When *Kim* first appeared in book form in October 1901 it produced an enthusiastic response from Kipling's former admirer Henry James, who rejoiced at his return to his art and urged him to abandon his political verses, 'by which I mean chuck public affairs, which are an ignoble scene, and stick to your canvas and your paintbox. There are as good colours in the tubes as ever were laid on, and <u>there</u> is the truth. The rest is humbug. Ask the Lama.'[12]

But Kipling chose not to ask the Lama. *Kim* was the last real victory of the intuitive, Indian side of his head. It was also Kipling's farewell to India, to his childhood, perhaps even to his Daemon – although he himself believed that it returned to him once more when he wrote *Puck of Pook's Hill* for his two surviving children at their new home, Bateman's, in East Sussex, in 1904. India had been the paradise garden of his childhood, his land of lost delight. He had returned at sixteen but with his Bombay childhood locked and hidden away, finding his parents' India to be a land of darkness filled with night terrors and lurking death. But by degrees he had rediscovered the art of moving between worlds as he had as a child – and in doing so had learned to love India again, despite himself; discovered also the delights of risk-taking and shock-making and how to exploit his fears by turning them to his advantage. He learned also to listen to both sides of his head, one of which told him that all was chaos without the Law while the other said let go and let your instincts be your guide, drawing strength from both sides.

Leaving India behind, he remained bound to India, so that the best of what he imagined and wrote had its roots in the dark side of his head and what he had seen and heard in India. And the further he moved away from India in time as well as space, the stronger became that side of the head that was least Indian and most law-abiding and British. The balance was lost – only to be recovered when his love for his first-born and his grief at her loss took him back to 'the life unaltered our childhood knew'. With his father's guidance he learned to 'undo what the North has done' and so let back in all 'the sights and the sounds and smells / That ran with our youth in the eye of the Sun' – the flotsam and jetsam of twelve years of Indian living – just long enough to create and write the celebration of childhood that is *The Jungle Book* and the celebration of India that is *Kim*.

Rudyard Kipling lived on to celebrate his seventieth birthday quietly with Carrie at Bateman's. He died on 18 January 1936, the forty-fourth anniversary of their marriage. After *Kim* he had continued to write poetry, fiction, and what he termed 'verses of a national character'. Of the poetry, 'If – ', 'The Glory of the Garden', 'The Smugglers', 'The Way Through the Woods', 'My Son Jack', and perhaps half a dozen more poems continue to be loved and valued. Of the fiction, if we exclude his writing for children there are plenty of well-crafted stories but very little that really holds the imagination except in fits and starts, and absolutely nothing of worth linked to India. With *Kim* he had said it all.

Notes

Book titles are given in shortened form, the full version being found in the Bibliography. The Kipling family are designated by their initials: RK: Rudyard Kipling; JLK: John Lockwood Kipling; AK: Alice Kipling; ATF: Alice 'Trix' Fleming.

A number of Rudyard Kipling's collected works have been similarly abbreviated: *SM*: *Something of Myself*; *DD*: *Departmental Ditties*; *PTH*: *Plain Tales from the Hills*; *BRB*: *Barrack-Room Ballads*.

Of other main works or archives frequently cited: *CMG*: *Civil and Military Gazette*; *KJ*: *Kipling Journal*; Pinney, *Letters*, Vol. I/Vol. II/Vol. IV: Thomas Pinney, *The Letters of Rudyard Kipling*, Vols. I, II and IV; Rutherford, *Early Verse*: Andrew Rutherford, *Early Verse of Rudyard Kipling*; Carrington, *RK*: Charles Carrington, *Rudyard Kipling*; Lycett, *RK*: Andrew Lycett, *Rudyard Kipling*; Birkenhead, *RK*: Lord Birkenhead, *Rudyard Kipling*; APAC, BL: Asia, Pacific and Africa Collection at the British Library; Sussex: University of Sussex Library Special Collections.

Preface: Blowing the Family Trumpet
1 RK to Mrs Edmonia Hill, Lahore 14 May 1888, from a copy, RK Papers, Sussex, collected in Pinney, *Letters*, Vol. I.

Introduction: 'Seek not to question'
1 W. J. Clarke ('G. F. Monkshead'), *Rudyard Kipling*.
2 K. M. Wilson, 'The Manuscript of "The English Flag"', *KJ*, March 1986.
3 Angela Thirkell, *Three Houses*.
4 Kipling's act of kindness failed to prevent this same deranged individual from taking a half-hearted pot-shot at him as he emerged from the Athenaeum some years later.
5 ATF, Edinburgh 14 May 1939, to her cousin Florence Macdonald, quoted in Lorna Lee, *Trix*.
6 RK to Lionel Dunsterville, Bateman's 20 November 1927, KP, Sussex, collected in Pinney, *Letters*, Vol. IV, quoted in Lycett, *RK*.

7 Mrs Elsie Bambridge in a memoir written for Charles Carrington, published as the 'Epilogue' in Carrington, *RK*.

8 ATF, June 1940, to her niece Mrs Elsie Bambridge, quoted in Lorna Lee, *Trix*.

1 : 'Mother of cities': Bombay and a Beginning, 1865–7

1 Among them Watson's cast-iron frame 'birdcage', imported from England to become Bombay's first modern hotel. In 1896 it screened the Lumière Brothers' cinematograph, laying the foundation stone of Bollywood and the world's largest film industry.

2 ATF, 'My Brother, Rudyard Kipling', *KJ*, December 1947.

3 Edith Macdonald, *Annals*.

4 Frederick M. Macdonald, *As a Tale that is Told*.

5 Kay Robinson, 'Rudyard Kipling in India', *Pearson's Magazine*, June 1896.

6 Sir John Maynard, 'Now Let Us Praise Famous Men', *KJ*, September 1961.

7 Frederick M. Macdonald, op. cit.

8 Sir Walter Lawrence, *The India We Served*.

9 Kay Robinson, 'Kipling in India', *McClure's Magazine*, July 1896.

10 Trix's view of this can be found on p. 44.

11 Frederick M. Macdonald, op. cit.

12 Ibid.

13 Edward Burne-Jones to Cormell Price, Tate Gallery Archive, quoted in Judith Flanders, *A Circle of Sisters*.

14 Georgiana Burne-Jones, *Memorials of Edward Burne-Jones*, Vol. I.

15 Edith Plowden, 'Fond Memory, 1875–1910', unpublished MS, Baldwin Papers, Sussex.

16 Edith Plowden, 'Rudyard Kipling's Parents in India', *KJ*, July 1938.

17 John Craig, 'John Lockwood Kipling: the formative years', *KJ*, December 1974 and March 1975; also Bryan Diamond, 'John Lockwood Kipling and the Victoria and Albert Museum', *KJ*, December 2003.

18 Govt. of Maharashtra State Archives, Bombay Education Department, Vol. 2 1865 Comp. No. 49.

19 Sir John Kaye, *A History of the Great Revolt*.

20 H. G. Keene, 'Anglo-Indians', *Sketches in Indian Ink*.

21 Sir Bartle Frere, 1868, quoted in *Ladies in the Sun*, ed. J. K. Stanford.

22 From a letter written by Charlotte Roberts, wife of an ICS officer, in September 1862, quoted in Zoe Yalland, *Boxwallahs*.

23 *Gazetteer of Bombay City and Island*, Vol. I, 1909.

24 Minute of the EICo Court of Directors, 1755.

25 *Pioneer*, 18 July 1870.

26 From which the rough cotton overalls worn by British jack tars took their name.

27 J. M. Maclean, *Maclean's Guide to Bombay*.

28 Dr Hewlett's 1864 Census Report, 1872.

29 J. M. Maclean, op. cit.

30 *Pioneer*, 8 March 1865.

31 *Pioneer*, 8 February 1865.

32 J. H. Rivett-Carnac, *Many Memories*.

33 Quoted without source by Mildred Archer, 'Lockwood Kipling and Indian Decorative Arts', *Apollo*, April 1986.

34 Capt. W. E. Gladstone Solomon, 'Lockwood Kipling and the Bombay School of Art', *KJ*, October 1927.

35 Letter from G. Terry to the Director of Public Instruction, 19 May 1875. Public Works Dept., Bombay No. 111 of 1875.

36 See her letter to Mrs Rivett-Carnac of 28 August 1870 in which she blames the fever suffered by her husband and son as 'due to the swamp in which we live', JLK Papers, Sussex.

37 *Pioneer Mail*, 20 June 1870.

38 Quoted without source by Arthur R. Ankers, *The Pater*.

39 JLK to Edith Macdonald, 12 December 1866, JLK Papers, Sussex.

40 RK, 'To the City of Bombay', *The Song of the Cities*, 1894.

41 Capt. W. E. Gladstone Solomon at a meeting of the Kipling Society, reported in *KJ*, March 1933.

42 Edith Plowden, 'Fond Memory, 1875–1910', unpublished MS, Baldwin Papers, Sussex.

43 RK, 'The Son of His Father', *Land and Sea Tales for Scouts and Guides*, 1923.

44 Lyall Papers, APOC, BL, MSS. Eur. F132, quoted in E. M. Collingwood, *Imperial Bodies*.

45 Edith Macdonald, 'Some Memories of my Cousin', *KJ*, July 1938.

46 JLK to Edith Macdonald, 12 December 1866, JLK Papers, Sussex.

47 ATF, 'My Brother Rudyard Kipling', *KJ*, December 1947.

48 Charles Eliot Norton, in a biographical note to a 1900 edition of *PTH*. This American scholar was a friend of Alice and Lockwood Kipling.

2: 'Youth in the eye of the sun': Bombay and Expulsion from Eden, 1867–71

1 RK, *SM*.

2 ATF, 'Through Judy's Eyes', unpublished MS, ATF Papers, Sussex.

3 RK, 'Song of the wise children', 1899.

4 J. R. B. Jeejeebhoy, in a letter to the *Times of India*, 21 January 1936.

5 Capt. W. E. Gladstone Solomon, 'Lockwood Kipling and the Bombay School of Art', *KJ*, October 1927.

6 JLK to Edith Macdonald, 12 December 1866, JLK Papers, Sussex.

7 Sharada Dwivedi and Rahul Mehrotra, *Bombay: the City Within*. See also the same authors' *Fort Walks*.

8 Capt. W. E. Gladstone Solomon, op. cit.

9 The details are given in Ankers, *The Pater*, giving JLK Papers, Sussex, as its source. The letter referred to has a page missing, apparently mislaid or stolen since consulted by Ankers.

10 J. H. Rivett-Carnac, *Many Memories of Life in India*.

11 RK, *SM*.

12 The story is best told in Judith Flanders, *A Circle of Sisters*.

13 Edith Plowden, 'Fond Memory, 1875–1910', unpublished MS, Baldwin Papers, Sussex.

14 Hannah Macdonald, Diaries, Baldwin Papers, Sussex, quoted in Pinney, 'Rudyard Kipling's First English Residence', *KJ*, December 1985.

15 Louisa Baldwin to Agnes Poynter, 9 November 1868, Baldwin Papers, quoted in Pinney, 'Rudyard Kipling's First English Residence', *KJ*, December 1985.

16 Frederick M. Macdonald, *As a Tale that is Told*.

17 Edith Macdonald, 'Some Memories of my Cousin', in *KJ*, July 1938.

18 ATF, 'My Brother Rudyard Kipling', *KJ*, December 1947.

19 ATF, in a letter, *KJ*, October 1945.

20 According to a Bombay informant, this ayah was named Mary and was from Mangalore on the Malabar coast south of Bombay. She subsequently served as ayah to other European families, as did her daughter after her.

21 RK, *SM*.

22 RK, ibid.

23 RK, 'Tods' Amendment', *PTH*, 1888.

24 ATF, 'Through Judy's Eyes', unpublished MS, ATF Papers, Sussex.

25 ATF, 'My Brother Rudyard Kipling', *KJ*, December 1947.

26 ATF, 'Through Judy's Eyes', unpublished MS, ATF Papers, Sussex.

27 RK, 'His Majesty the King', *Wee Willie Winkie*, 1890.

28 AF to Stanley Baldwin, 27 March 1945, Baldwin Papers, Sussex, quoted by Lycett, *RK*.

29 'That boy again', *Pioneer*, 5 December 1885.

30 JLK, *Pioneer*, 9 May 1870.

31 Edith Plowden, 'Fond Memory, 1875–1910', unpublished MS, Baldwin Papers, Sussex.

32 Col. A. R. D. Mackenzie, *Mutiny Memoirs*.

33 *Pioneer*, 30 January 1865.

34 Sir Alfred Lyall, 'The Anglo-Indian Novelist', first published in the *Edinburgh Review*, October 1899, afterwards reprinted in his *Studies in Literature and History*, 1915.

35 *Pioneer*, 28 February 1882 and 26 October 1882. Meadows Taylor was the author of *Confessions of A Thug*; *Tara: A Mahratta Tale*; *Ralph Darnell*; and

The Fatal Amulet. G. H. Keene had published *Under the Rose: Poems Written Chiefly in India*; *The Death of Akbar and Other Poems*; *Peepul Leaves: Poems Written in India*; and *Poems Original and Translated*. General Sir George T. Chesney had written *A True Reformer*; *The Dilemma: A Tale of the Mutiny*; *Indian Polity*; and *The Private Secretary*. The High Court judge Sir Henry S. Cunningham was best known for his *Chronicles of Dustypore: A Tale of Modern Anglo-Indian Society*. The administrator, statistician and historian Sir William Hunter wrote extensively on a wide range of subjects.

36 RK, 'My First Book', reprinted in *KJ*, March 1960.
37 His friend and patron Harry Rivett-Carnac asserts in his autobiography that George Allen asked him to find a Bombay correspondent 'in my Bombay days', which suggests a much earlier date than 1870. However, the phrase could still be applied to Rivett-Carnac's time as Commissioner of Cotton and Commerce in Allahabad, since his duties frequently took him down-country to Bombay.
38 JLK, *Pioneer*, 30 May 1870.
39 JLK, *Pioneer*, 30 June 1873.
40 JLK, *Pioneer*, 10 May 1870.
41 RK, in his polemical (and much disliked) poem 'The Islanders', 1902.
42 JLK, *Pioneer*, 17 February 1876. The last sentence Rudyard recycled a decade later in declaring that 'Providence created the maharajas to offer mankind a spectacle'.
43 JLK, *Beast and Man in India*.
44 JLK, *Pioneer*, 8 August 1870.
45 JLK, *Beast and Man in India*.
46 Lord Reay to Lord Dufferin, 7 September 1884, Dufferin Papers MSS. Eur. F130/42e, APAC, BL.
47 Sir W. W. Hunter, *England's Work in India*.
48 JLK, *Pioneer*, 1 August 1870.
49 AK to Mrs Rivett-Carnac, Nassik 28 August 1870, JLK Papers, Sussex.
50 Quoted in Charles Eliot Norton's Foreword to the US edition of *PTH*, 1890.
51 Florence Macdonald, 'Some Memories of My Cousin', *KJ*, July 1938.
52 J. H. Rivett-Carnac, *Many Memories*.
53 G. Terry, letters to Director of Public Instruction, PWD No. 146 of 1874, dated 2 September 1874, and PWD No. 111 of 1875, dated 19 May 1875. Although dating from a period after Rudyard had been removed from Bombay, the letters illustrate the unhealthy conditions in which the Kiplings were living in 1871.

3: 'A double death': Southsea and Lahore, 1871–7

1 Hannah Macdonald, Diaries, Baldwin Papers, Sussex, quoted in Pinney, 'Rudyard Kipling's First English Residence', in *KJ*, December 1985.

2 Edith Plowden, 'Fond Memory 1875–1910', unpublished MS, Baldwin Papers, Sussex.

3 The letter was in relation to an exhibition of Indian sculpture at the South Kensington Museum and is referred to in A. W. Baldwin, *The Macdonald Sisters*, 1960.

4 ATF, letter to Stanley Baldwin, 27 March 1945, Baldwin Papers, Sussex, quoted in Lycett, *RK*.

5 ATF, 'My Brother Rudyard Kipling', recorded at the BBC on 17 April 1947, subsequently published in *KJ*, December 1947.

6 Ibid.

7 For example, Judith Flanders in her otherwise faultless *A Circle of Sisters*, 2001.

8 ATF, 'My Brother Rudyard Kipling', recorded at the BBC on 17 April 1947, subsequently published in *KJ*, December 1947.

9 Ibid.

10 Sir Gilbert Murray, *Unfinished Autobiography*.

11 ATF, 'My Brother Rudyard Kipling', recorded at the BBC on 17 April 1947, subsequently published in *KJ*, December 1947.

12 Mrs Hannah Macdonald, Diaries, Sussex, quoted in Lycett, *RK*.

13 ATF in a letter to Lord Birkenhead, Birkenhead, *RK*.

14 ATF, in a discussion at a Kipling Society meeting, in *KJ*, June 1937.

15 Miss Florence Macdonald, 'Some Memories of My Cousin', in *KJ*, July 1938.

16 ATF in a letter to Lord Birkenhead, Birkenhead, *RK*.

17 Mrs Georgie Burne-Jones to Mrs Caroline Kipling, 21 May 1907, RK Papers, Sussex.

18 Stanley Baldwin; quoted by his son A. W. Baldwin, *The Macdonald Sisters*.

19 William Yeldham, writing as 'Aliph Cheem', from 'Twaddle', *Lays of Ind*.

20 George Aberigh-Mackay, 'The Grass-Widow in Nephelogoccygia', *Twenty-One Days in India*.

21 RK, *SM*.

22 The Marchioness of Dufferin and Ava, *Our Viceregal Life in India*.

23 Extracts from *Lahore as it was and is* are given in H. R. Goulding, *Old Lahore: Reminiscences of a Resident*, 1924, based on articles for the *CMG*. See also F. A. Underwood, 'Lahore as it Was', *KJ*, December 1970.

24 Edith Plowden, 'Fond Memory 1875–1910', unpublished MS, Baldwin Papers, Sussex.

25 RK, *SM*.

26 Edith Plowden, 'Fond Memory 1875–1910', unpublished MS, Baldwin Papers, Sussex.

27 Ibid.

28 JLK, *Pioneer*, 1 November 1875.

29 ATF to Mrs Caroline Kipling, 29 November 1936, JLK Papers, Sussex, quoted in Judith Flanders, *A Circle of Sisters*.

30 Edith Plowden, 'Fond Memory 1875 –1910', unpublished MS, Baldwin Papers, Sussex.

31 Lord Derby, in Andrew Roberts, *Salisbury*.

32 Lord Salisbury, in Andrew Roberts, *Salisbury*.

33 Ibid.

34 JLK to Edith Plowden, Simla, undated, JLK Papers, Sussex.

35 Edith Plowden, 'Fond Memory 1875–1910', unpublished MS, Baldwin Papers, Sussex.

36 Ibid.

37 Ibid.

4: 'One school of many': United Services College, Westward Ho!, and Bikaner House, Lahore, 1877–82

1 Edith Plowden, 'Fond Memory 1875–1910', unpublished MS, Baldwin Papers, Sussex.

2 ATF, 'My Brother Rudyard Kipling', recorded at the BBC on 17 April 1947, subsequently published in *KJ*, December 1947.

3 RK, *SM*.

4 C. G. Beresford, 'Kipling – Some Early Influences', by 'McTurk', in *KJ*, April 1928.

5 RK, 'An English School', first published in *The Youth's Companion*, October 1893, afterwards in *Land and Sea Tales for Scouts and Guides*, 1923.

6 Lorraine Price, 'Uncle Crom: Kipling's friendship with Crom Price', *KJ*, March 1994.

7 L. C. Dunsterville, 'Stalky's School-Days', *KJ*, September 1932.

8 AK to Cormell Price, January 1878, quoted by Lycett. See also *KJ*, March 1865, and Baldwin Papers, Sussex.

9 G. C. Beresford, 'The Veritable Kipling', *KJ*, April 1930.

10 RK, 'The Last Term', *Stalky & Co.*, 1899.

11 C. G. Beresford, *School-Days with Kipling*.

12 Oscar Wilde in his review of *PTH*, in *The Nineteenth Century Magazine*, September 1891.

13 G. C. Beresford, *School-Days with Kipling*.

14 Maj. Gen. L. C. Dunsterville, 'Stalky's School-Days', in *KJ*, September 1932.

15 RK, *SM*, 1936.

16 G. C. Beresford, *School-Days with Kipling*.

17 Undated letter quoted in Arthur Baldwin, *The Macdonald Sisters*.

18 ATF, Notes, Kipling Papers, Sussex.

19 Edith Plowden, 'Fond Memory 1875–1910', unpublished MS, Baldwin Papers, Sussex. According to Miss Plowden, 'Rudyard finished the poem in 1880 at my request when we were together at Warwick Gardens'.

20 RK, 'Overheard', *Schoolboy Lyrics*, 1881.

21 RK, 'The Dusky Crew', *Schoolboy Lyrics*, 1881.

22 Mrs Edmonia Hill, note accompanying RK's letters, RK Papers, Sussex.

23 When RK presented a copy of his *Echoes* to the masters' common room at USC in 1885 he inscribed the following verses in the fly leaf:
   Placetne, Domini? – in far Lahore
   I await your verdict, 'mid the palms and roses
   Much as I did in those judgements writ of yore
   Upon my 'proses'.

24 RK to Mrs John Tavernor Perry, USC 9 March 1882, Library of Congress, collected in Pinney, *Letters*, Vol I.

25 C. G. Beresford, *School-Days with Kipling*.

26 G. C. Beresford, 'Schoolboy Lyrics and Juvenilia', in *KJ*, October 1928.

27 This famous observation was contained in a letter written at what is today Keats Grove, Hampstead, on 21 December 1817. The key passage runs: 'At once it struck me what quality went to form a Man of Achievement, especially in Literature, and which Shakespeare possessed so enormously – I mean Negative Capability, that is, when a man is capable of being in uncertainties, mysteries, doubts, without any irritable reaching after fact and reason.'

28 RK to W. C. Crofts, Lahore 18–27 February 1886, Dalhousie University, collected in Pinney, *Letters*, Vol. I.

29 Most notably Birkenhead, *RK*, and, more stridently, Martin Seymour-Smith, *Rudyard Kipling*, 1989.

30 RK, 'Ballad of the King's Daughter', probably written in 1882, set down in *Sundry Phansies*, MSS in the New York Public Library, collected in Rutherford, *Early Verse*. Oscar Wilde's 'Ode to the King's Daughter' had appeared a year earlier.

31 RK, 'Parting', set down in *Sundry Phansies*, MSS in the New York Public Library, collected in Rutherford, *Early Verse*.

32 RK, 'The Story of Paul Vaugel', *Sundry Phansies*, MSS in the New York Public Library, collected in Rutherford, *Early Verse*.

33 AK to Edith Plowden, Lahore, wrongly dated 18 November 1880 but written over a period of days in November 1879, JLK Papers, Sussex.

34 ATF, to Col. C. H. Milburn, *KJ*, December 1942.

35 T. H. Thornton and J. L. Kipling, *Lahore: A Historical and Descriptive Note*.

36 AK to Edith Plowden with a postscript by JLK, Lahore 18–24 November 1879, JLK Papers, Sussex.

37 JLK to Edith Macdonald, Violet Hill, Simla, autumn 1881, JLK Papers, Sussex.

38 ATF, 'My Brother Rudyard Kipling', recorded at the BBC on 17 April 1947, subsequently published in *KJ*, December 1947.

39 RK, 'An English School', *St Nicholas Magazine* in October 1893, collected in *Land and Sea Tales for Scouts and Guides*, 1923.

40 Carrington, *RK*.

41 AK to Edith Plowden, Lahore 18 December 1881, JLK Papers, Sussex.

42 AK to Edith Plowden, Lahore 13 March 1881, JLK Papers, Sussex.

43 AK to Edith Plowden, Lahore 28 April 1881, JLK Papers, Sussex.

44 Sir Cooper Lethbridge, in *Journal of the East India Association*, Vol. V, 1914.

45 JLK to Edith Plowden, Lahore 30 June 1882, JLK Papers, Sussex.

46 The playwright Sir Terence Rattigan claimed that it was his grandfather, Sir William Rattigan, who originally hired RK, but the Allen family has a better authenticated claim. In support of family tradition, the telegram was confirmed by Mrs Edmonia Hill, 'The Young Kipling: Personal Recollections', *Atlantic Monthly*, CLVII, 1936, and by William M. Carpenter, '"Kipling about" in London for a Week: by a Hustling American', in *KJ*, October 1928.

47 C. G. Beresford, *School-Days with Kipling*.

48 Ibid.

49 RK, 'On the Strength of a Likeness', *CMG*, 10 January 1887, collected in *PTH*, 1888.

50 RK, transcribed into Notebook 1, RK Papers, Sussex, collected in Rutherford, *Early Verse*.

51 C. G. Beresford, *School-Days with Kipling*.

5: 'As a prince entering his kingdom': Lahore and Simla, 1882–3

1 RK, 'Letters of Marque', 1888.

2 RK, *SM*.

3 A hybrid word originating in Bombay and derived from the Hindustani word for a squash-rackets court, *gend-khana* or ball-house.

4 RK, *SM*.

5 Ibid.

6 AK to Edith Plowden, Lahore 24 February 1883, JLK Papers, Sussex.

7 ATF, 'My Brother Rudyard Kipling', *KJ*, April 1948.

8 ATF to Col C. H. Milburn, 'The Homes of Rudyard Kipling', *KJ*, December 1942.

9 RK, 'A Morning Ride', Notebook 1, RK Papers, Sussex, collected in Rutherford, *Early Verse*. According to a note by RK in his Notebook 1,

it was 'Published in the *Englishman* with one howling misprint'. It has still to be located, and may predate 'A New Departure', *CMG*, 29 March 1883.

10 RK, *SM*.

11 RK to Cormell Price, Lahore 30 December 1882, Library of Congress, collected in Pinney, *Letters* Vol. I.

12 Kay Robinson, 'Rudyard Kipling in India', *Pearson's Magazine*, June 1896.

13 JLK to Edith Plowden, Lahore, undated 1883, JLK Papers, Sussex.

14 RK, *SM*, 1936, but see also his less gracious tribute in 'My First Book', reprinted in *KJ*, March 1960.

15 Kay Robinson, 'Rudyard Kipling in India', *Pearson's Magazine*, June 1896.

16 RK to Rev. George Willes, Lahore 17 November 1882, Dalhousie University, collected in Pinney, *Letters*, Vol. I.

17 RK to Crom Price, Lahore 30 December 1882, Library of Congress, collected in Pinney, *Letters*, Vol. I.

18 RK to Edith Macdonald, Lahore 14–17 August 1883, Library of Congress, collected in Pinney, *Letters*, Vol. I.

19 JLK to Edith Plowden, Lahore, undated but early 1883, JLK Papers, Sussex.

20 JLK to Edith Plowden, Lahore, undated but early 1883, JLK Papers, Sussex.

21 JLK to Edith Plowden Lahore, 1 May 1882, JLK Papers, Sussex.

22 The Bengal Civilian Thomas Bignold spoke for many when he published an anonymous poem praising his forebears for their 'taming' of India and criticising Ripon and Ilbert for their shortsightedness. Only when Indians were Anglicised and Christianised should they be given judicial and political responsibility:

When truth and learning flourish
  Loved for themselves alone;
When, last and best, this darkened land
  Our holy faith shall own:
Then may we share the fortress
  We have held six hundred years;
For India will be Britain,
  And her sons a Briton's peers.

'Our Peers', afterwards published posthumously in *Leviora: being the Rhymes of a Successful Competitor*, 1888.

23 Something of his early life is told in Charles Allen, *Soldier Sahibs*.

24 RK, 'A New Departure', in *CMG*, 29 March 1883, signed 'The Other Player'. Collected in Scrapbook 1, RK Papers, Sussex, and in Rutherford, *Early Verse*.

25 RK to Cormell Price, Lahore 1 June 1883, Library of Congress, collected in Pinney, *Letters*, Vol. I, 1990.

26 The final compromise solution allowed European defendants to have the right to claim trial by a jury made up of at least half European members. The bill came into force on 25 January 1884.

27 RK, 'Lord Ripon's Reverie', *CMG*, 15 September 1884.

28 RK to Edith Macdonald, Lahore 12–13 June 1883, Library of Congress, collected in Pinney, *Letters*, Vol. I.

29 Edward J. Buck, *Simla Past and Present*.

30 A German term misappropriated by the British in India to describe a wife living apart from her husband.

31 RK, 'Garm – a Hostage', first published in *Actions and Reactions*, 1909.

32 RK to Edith Macdonald, Lahore August 1883, Library of Congress, collected in Pinney, *Letters*, Vol. I.

33 Charles T. French, *Journal of a Tour of Upper Hindustan*.

34 Lady Balfour (ed.), *Personal and Literary Letters of Robert, First Earl of Lytton*, quoted in Pamela Kanwar, *Imperial Simla*.

35 RK, *Kim*, 1900.

36 Benmore was subsequently sold to the Government of the Punjab and in 1888 became the Civil Secretariat.

37 RK, *DD*.

38 RK, 'Out of Society', *Pioneer*, 4 July 1885.

39 RK, 'Possibilities', *Pioneer*, 19 July 1885.

40 RK, *SM*.

41 Sir Walter Lawrence, *The India we Served*.

42 Captain H. Hayes, *Among Men and Horses*.

43 Edward J. Buck, *Simla Past and Present*.

44 RK, *SM*.

45 George Allen had himself initially been seduced by Madame Blavatsky's extraordinarily powerful persona, afterwards appearing in Sir Edward Buck's account as 'Mr. A.' This humiliation may help to explain his intense dislike for Allan Octavian Hume. The full story is set down in Buck, *Simla Past and Present*.

46 Allan Octavian Hume to Lord Ripon, January 1883, Ripon Papers, Add, MSS 43616, APAC, BL, quoted in Martin Briton, *New India 1885: British Official Policy and the Emergence of the Indian National Congress*, 1969.

47 Edward J. Buck, *Simla Past and Present*.

48 RK, 'Miss Youghal's Syce', in *CMG*, 25 April 1887, collected in *PTH*, 1888.

49 Jacob apparently showed Sir Edward Buck papers which convinced him that he had acted 'as a secret agent in Government in certain circles'. Buck presumably told as much to RK. Buck, *Simla Past and Present*.

50 RK to Edith Macdonald, Lahore, 14–17 August 1883, Library of Congress, collected in Pinney, *Letters*, Vol. I.

51 RK to Mrs James Walker, 'In Memoriam July–August 1883', August–September 1883, Morgan Library, collected in Pinney, *Letters*, Vol. I.

6: 'The seething city': Lahore and the Family Square, 1883-4

1 RK to Edith Macdonald, in a verse letter entitled 'At the End of a Year', December 1883, Library of Congress, collected in Pinney, *Letters*, Vol. I.

2 RK to Edith Macdonald, Lahore 14–17 August 1883, Library of Congress, collected in Pinney, *Letters*, Vol. I.

3 RK to Cormell Price, Lahore 29 August 1883, Library of Congress, collected in Pinney, *Letters*, Vol. I.

4 RK to W. C. Crofts, Lahore 14 November 1883, RK Papers, Sussex, Library of Congress, collected in Pinney, *Letters*, Vol. I.

5 RK, 'The Dassera Festival', in *CMG*, 2 October 1883, collected in Scrapbook 1, RK Papers, Sussex.

6 'A Hustling American', '"Kipling About" in London for a Week', in *KJ*, October 1928.

7 RK, *SM*.

8 ATF, 'My Brother Rudyard Kipling', BBC 17 April 1943, subsequently published in *KJ*, December 1947.

9 ATF in a letter to the editor, *KJ*, October 1942.

10 ATF, 'My Brother Rudyard Kipling', BBC 17 April 1943, subsequently published in *KJ*, December 1947.

11 RK to Edith Macdonald, Lahore 16–28 January 1884, Library of Congress, collected in Pinney, *Letters*, Vol. I.

12 RK's political polemic 'A New Departure' was first published in the *Englishman* before being reprinted in the *CMG*, 29 March 1883.

13 Col. H. R. Goulding, *Old Lahore*.

14 RK, 'The Story of Tommy', in *CMG*, 29 September 1884, signed 'E. M.', Scrapbook 1, RK Papers, Sussex, collected in Rutherford, *Early Verse*.

15 Gen. Sir Thomas Edward Gordon gives an account of the killing at Ranikhet in *A Varied Life*.

16 From a MS in Royal Leicester Regiment Museum, reprinted in *The Green Tiger*, August 1952, and afterwards in 'Concerning "Danny Deever" and a murder at Ranikhet, India, in 1886', *KJ*, July 1954.

17 RK, 'Danny Deever', first published in Britain in the *Scots Observer* (afterwards the *National Observer*), 22 February 1890, and in India in the *Week's News*, 23 March 1890.

18 The link with the folk ballad was identified by Lord Baldwin in *The Macdonald Sisters*.

19 T. S. Eliot, *A Choice of Kipling's Verse*.

20 RK, 'Anglo-Indian Society', *CMG*, 29 January 1887, collected in Pinney, *Kipling's India*.

21 RK, *SM*.

22 RK, 'On Fort Duty', February 1884, Notebook 1, RK Papers, Sussex, collected in Rutherford, *Early Verse*.

23 RK to Edith Macdonald, Lahore 4 February 1884, Library of Congress, collected in Pinney, *Letters*, Vol. I.

24 RK to Edith Macdonald, Lahore 4 April 1884, Library of Congress, collected in Pinney, *Letters*, Vol. I. A rather different version of this episode is given in *SM*, where the bribe is remembered as 'a five hundred rupee note and a Cashmere shawl' and is returned 'at the hands of the camp-sweeper'. This has the ring of authenticity, for the young Kipling enjoyed taking and giving offence.

25 RK to Edith Macdonald, Lahore 4 April 1884, Library of Congress, collected in Pinney, *Letters*, Vol. I.

26 Rudyard Kipling and Wolcott Balestier, *The Naulahka*, 1892.

27 Kay Robinson, 'Rudyard Kipling in India', in *Pearson's Magazine*, June 1896. The poem in question, 'Ichabod', was published in the *CMG* on 9 November 1887 under the signature of 'Kingcraft' and achieved considerable notoriety. Collected in Rutherford, *Early Verse*.

28 RK, 'Mister Anthony Dawking', one of eight contributions signed 'The Traveller' published in the *CMG* in 1888 but not collected by RK in his scrapbooks. Reproduced in Charles Allen, *Kipling's Kingdom*.

29 RK to Edith Macdonald, Lahore 28 April 1884, Library of Congress, collected in Pinney, *Letters*, Vol. I.

30 E. Kay Robinson, 'Rudyard Kipling in India', *Pearson's Magazine*, June 1896.

31 Noel F. Cooke, 'The "Pioneer" of Kipling's Day', *KJ*, March 1964.

32 *CMG*, 20 March 1886.

33 RK to Edith Macdonald, Lahore 4 June 1884, Library of Congress, collected in Pinney, *Letters*, Vol. I.

34 One of the guests at Ruddy's picnic in the Shalimar Gardens may have been eighteen-year-old Adela Cory, one of three daughters of Col. Thomas Cory, the *CMG*'s one-time editor and part-proprietor. Adela was in Lahore in 1884 and, given her father's links with the newspaper and the fact that he and Alice Kipling acted together in at least one amateur production, we can take it that the Cory girls rubbed shoulders with the Kiplings. Even if the high-caste Miss Adela Cory was off-limits to Ruddy, their mutual love of poetry ought to have drawn them together. Unfortunately, there is not a jot of evidence to show that either party sought or received the attentions of the other. Adela moved with her father to Sind in 1886 and there met and married Col. Malcolm Nicholson. A decade later the Nicholsons retired to England, where Adela published *The Garden of Karma* under the pen-name of 'Laurence Hope'.

It included 'Four Indian Love Lyrics', considered at the time to be wildly sensual, including the well-known verses which begin 'Pale hands I loved beside the Shalimar, / Where are you now? Who lies beneath your spell?' See also Jennifer M. T. Carter, 'A Tale of Two Poets', *KJ*, June 2000.

35 RK, 'False Dawn', *PTH*, January 1888.

36 RK to Edith Macdonald, Lahore 11–14 June 1884, Library of Congress, collected in Pinney, *Letters*, Vol. I.

37 RK, *SM*

38 RK to Edith Macdonald, Dalhousie 14 August 1884, Library of Congress, collected in Pinney, *Letters*, Vol. I.

39 Just to confuse the issue this copy begins with the inscription 'The Mater / From Ruddy. / August 22nd 1884'. Rudyard Kipling Collection, George Arents Research Library, Syracuse University, collected in Rutherford, *Early Verse*.

40 RK, 'The Tragedy of Crusoe, C. S.', *CMG*, 13 September 1884, collected in Pinney, *Kipling's India*.

41 RK, *SM*.

42 RK to Edith Macdonald, Lahore 4 June 1884, Library of Congress, collected in Pinney, *Letters*, Vol. I.

43 Sir William Moore, *A Manual of Family Medicine*.

44 RK, 'The Moon of Other Days', *Pioneer*, 25 December 1884.

45 RK, 'The City of the Heart', *Echoes*, 1884.

46 RK to Edith Macdonald, Lahore 17 September 1884, Library of Congress, collected in Pinney, *Letters*, Vol. I.

47 A close parallel can be found in Coleridge's drug-taking and writing. On a manuscript copy of his poem 'Kubla Khan' Coleridge wrote that it was conceived 'in a sort of Reverie brought on by two grains of Opium, taken to check a dysentery'.

48 As, for example, RK to Edith Macdonald, 4–5 December 1886: 'I broke down with <u>insomnia</u> again and after a merry course of leeches and morphia injections went to Simla', Library of Congress, collected in Pinney, *Letters*, Vol. I.

49 RK to Margaret Burne-Jones, Lahore late November and early December 1885, RK Papers, Sussex, collected in Pinney, *Letters*, Vol. I.

50 Andrew Lang, *Essays in Little*.

51 RK to Edith Macdonald, Lahore 17 September 1884, Library of Congress, collected in Pinney, *Letters*, Vol. I.

7: 'The Oldest Land': The Punjab and Simla, 1885

1 Sir Mortimer Durand, head of the Foreign and Political Department under Lord Dufferin, quoted in P. Sykes, *Sir Mortimer Durand*.

2 Lord Dufferin to Sir James Stephen, Simla 28 July 1885, Stephen Papers, Cambridge University Library.

3 JLK to Edith Plowden, Lahore 16 March 1885, JLK Papers, Sussex.

4 RK to Edith Macdonald, Simla 30 July 1885, Library of Congress, collected in Pinney, *Letters*, Vol. I. The invitation was probably contained in the note from George Allen mentioned in the 5 February entry of RK's 1884–5 Diary.

5 RK, 'In the Spring Time', *Pioneer*, 20 March 1885, under the byline 'R.' The *siris* or Indian acacia flowers in early spring to produce scented white flowers; the *köil* is a bird of the cuckoo family whose distinctive two-note mating call 'ko-el', repeated several times over with increasing volume and higher pitch, is first heard in March; the *sat-bhai* or 'seven brothers' are jungle babblers which move about in small, chattering flocks, found throughout the plains.

6 RK, Diary 1884–5, Houghton Library, University of Harvard, reproduced in Pinney, '*Something of Myself*'.

7 RK, Diary 1884–5, Thursday 1 October 1885, Houghton Library, University of Harvard, reproduced in Pinney, '*Something of Myself*'. Suddhu made his first public appearance in the short story 'Section 420, I. P. C.', *CMG* 30 April 1886, republished as 'The House of Suddhoo' in *PTH*.

8 'The Vision of Hamid Ali' was published in the *Calcutta Review* in October 1885 but RK refers to its acceptance in a letter to Edith Macdonald dated 30 July 1885.

9 RK to Edith Macdonald, Simla 30 July 1885, Library of Congress, collected in Pinney, *Letters*, Vol. I.

10 RK, 'The City of Two Creeds', *CMG*, 1 October 1887, collected in Pinney, *Kipling's India*.

11 RK, 'The City of Evil Countenances,' *CMG*, 1 April 1895, collected in Pinney, *Kipling's India*.

12 RK to Mrs Isabella Burton, 7 November 1887, private collection, quoted in Lycett, *RK*.

13 RK to Lionel Dunsterville, Lahore 30 January 1886, RK Papers, Sussex, collected in Pinney, *Letters*, Vol. I.

14 RK, 'To Meet the Amir', tenth article in the series, *CMG*, 6 April 1885, collected in Pinney, *Kipling's India*.

15 RK, 'Boots', *The Five Nations*, 1903.

16 Hariot, Marchioness of Dufferin and Ava, *Our Viceregal Life in India*.

17 Ibid.

18 Sir Walter Lawrence, *The India We Served*.

19 JLK to Edith Plowden, Lahore 16 March 1885, JLK Papers, Sussex.

20 RK, 'Lispeth', *CMG* 29 November 1886, collected in *PTH*.

21 Lieut.-Gen. Sir G. F. MacMunn tells the full story in 'Kipling's India as I saw it in '33', in *KJ*, December 1933.

22 RK, 'Simla Notes', *CMG* 16 June, collected in Scrapbook 1, RK Papers, Sussex.

23 RK, 'Collar-Wallah and the Poison Stick', *St Nicholas Magazine*, February 1893.

24 JLK to Edith Plowden, Lahore 16 March 1885, JLK Papers, Sussex.

25 ATF to Stanley Baldwin, Edinburgh 27 March 1945, RK Papers, Sussex.

26 This and the earlier remark about 'heart-burning' were recollected by Sir George Birdwood of the Indian Medical Service, a great promoter of the arts in Bombay, quoted in a note in *KJ*, Dec 1941.

27 Maj.-Gen. J. C. Rimington, 'Westward Ho! Reminiscences', in *KJ*, October 1941.

28 JLK to Edith Plowden, Lahore 16 March 1885, JLK Papers, Sussex.

29 JLK to Margaret Burne-Jones; this section of his letter was dated Simla 10 October 1885 but not completed and posted until 31 January 1886, JLK Papers, Sussex.

30 RK to Edith Macdonald, Simla 30 July 1885, Library of Congress, collected in Pinney, *Letters*, Vol. I.

31 RK, 'Simla Notes', *CMG*, 29 July 1885.

32 RK, Diary 1884–5, 2 August 1885, Houghton Library, University of Harvard, reproduced in Pinney, '*Something of Myself*'.

33 RK to Edith Macdonald, Simla 1 August 1885, Library of Congress, collected in Pinney, *Letters*, Vol. I.

34 RK, Diary 1884–5, August 1885, Houghton Library, University of Harvard, reproduced in Pinney, '*Something of Myself*'.

35 RK, Diary 1884–5, August 1885, Houghton Library, University of Harvard, reproduced in Pinney, '*Something of Myself*'.

36 In these speculations I have followed the detective work of Pinney, '*Something of Myself*'.

37 From Lord Birkenhead's notes, first noted by and quoted in Lycett, *RK*.

38 RK to Kay Robinson, Lahore 30 April 1886, RK Papers, Sussex, collected in Pinney, *Letters*, Vol. I.

39 RK to W. C. Crofts, Lahore 18-27 February 1886, Dalhousie University, collected in Pinney, *Letters*, Vol. I.

40 RK to Margaret Burne-Jones, Lahore 26 September 1885, RK Papers, Sussex, collected in Pinney, *Letters*, Vol. I.

41 JLK to Margaret Burne-Jones, begun Simla 10 October 1885 but not completed and posted until 31 January 1886, JLK Papers, Sussex.

42 RK to Margaret Burne-Jones, Lahore, begun 28 November 1885, the last-quoted completed 18 December 1885, RK Papers, Sussex, collected in Pinney, *Letters*, Vol. I.

8: *'In vigil or toil or ease': The Plains and the Hills,* 1886

1 RK to Lionel Dunsterville, in a letter now lost but quoted in Carrington, *RK*.

2 RK, 'The Rupaiyat of Omar Kal'vin', *CMG*, 30 January 1886.

3 JLK to Margaret Burne-Jones, begun Simla 10 October 1885 and completed Lahore 31 January 1886, JLK Papers, Sussex, collected in Pinney, *Letters*, Vol. I.

4 RK to W. C. Crofts, Lahore 18–27 February 1886, Dalhousie University, collected in Pinney, *Letters*, Vol. I.

5 JLK to Margaret Burne-Jones, Lahore 31 January, 1886, JLK Papers, Sussex, collected in Pinney, *Letters*, Vol. I.

6 RK to Kay Robinson, Lahore 30 April 1886, RK Papers, Sussex, collected in Pinney, *Letters*, Vol. I.

7 RK to Kay Robinson, Lahore 30 April 1886, RK Papers, Sussex, collected in Pinney, *Letters*, Vol. I.

8 RK to Andrew Macdonald, Lahore, undated but February 1886, Ray Collection, Morgan Library, collected in Pinney, *Letters*, Vol. I.

9 Kay Robinson, 'Rudyard Kipling in India', *Pearson's Magazine*, June 1896.

10 Kay Robinson, 'Kipling in India', *McClure's Magazine*, July 1896.

11 RK to Kay Robinson, Lahore 30 April 1886, RK Papers, Sussex, collected in Pinney, *Letters*, Vol. I.

12 RK, 'East and West', *CMG*, 14 November 1885.

13 RK, 'The Ballad of East and West', *Macmillan's Magazine*, November 1889.

14 'Sabretache', *Tatler*, 21 February 1954, referred to in *KJ*, July 1954.

15 RK, 'A Week in Lahore', *CMG*, 19 January 1886, collected in Pinney, *Letters*, Vol. I.

16 Kay Robinson, 'Rudyard Kipling in India', in *Pearson's Magazine*, June 1896.

17 RK, 'A Popular Picnic', *CMG*, 30 March 1886, collected in Pinney, *Letters*, Vol. I.

18 RK, 'From the Masjid-Al-Aqsa of Sayyid Ahmed (Wahabi)', introductory verses to 'The Captive', *Limits and Discoveries*, 1904. The verses have no relation to the story and must have been written many years earlier. Sayyid Ahmed was the charismatic leader who introduced Arabic Wahhabism to India in 1826 and then set out to make jihad against the Sikhs and the British. In Kipling's time in India Wahhabis were involved in the Black Mountains uprising of June 1888, leading to a military campaign in the autumn. Lockwood Kipling made drawings of some Black Mountain Sayyids, most likely prisoners in Lahore Jail.

19 RK, 'A Week in Lahore', *CMG*, 11 January 1886. The possible link with 'The Story of Muhammad Din' is speculated upon in Pinney, *Kipling's India*.

20 RK, 'The Story of Muhammad Din', *CMG*, 8 September 1886, collected in *PTH*, 1888.

21 His letter is quoted in Emanul Karim, 'Rudyard Kipling and Lodge Hope and Perseverance', *KJ*, March 1974.

22 The statement is made in Laski, *From Palm to Pine*, but no source is cited.

23 RK, 'The Mother Lodge', *BRB*, 1895.

24 Col. H. R. Goulding, *Old Lahore: Reminiscences of a Resident*, 1924.

25 RK to Margaret Burne-Jones, Lahore 24 June 1886, RK Papers, Sussex, collected in Pinney, *Letters*, Vol. I.

26 ATF, 'My Brother Rudyard Kipling', BBC Radio, 19 August 1947, subsequently published in *KJ*, April 1948.

27 RK declares in one letter (27 February) that he and Robinson had 'a lively four days together', in another (24 June) that her unnamed suitor had written to him 'some weeks ago', and had 'only seen Trix for four days'. Both RK and Trix gave the suitor's age as twenty-eight, when Robinson was thirty-one, but would RK have called him 'a nice youth and a merry' if he had known he was that old?

28 'The Grave of the Hundred Dead' was evidently revised and published in the *Week's News* on 7 January 1888.

29 RK, 'Arithmetic on the Frontier', *DD*, 1886.

30 RK to W. C. Crofts, Lahore 14 September 1886, Cornell University, collected in Pinney, *Letters*, Vol. I.

31 Given in George MacMunn, 'The Original Gunga Deen', *KJ*, July 1943.

32 RK, 'Only a Subaltern', *Week's News*, 25 August 1888, collected in *Under the Deodars*, subsequently in *Wee Willie Winkie and Other Stories*, 1890.

33 RK, 'It's Oh to meet an Army man', 'De Partibus', *CMG*, 27 December 1889, collected in *Abaft the Funnel*, 1906.

34 RK, *SM*.

35 G. C. Beresford, *School-Days with Kipling*.

36 John Fraser in an interview, Birkenhead, *Rudyard Kipling*, 1978.

37 RK, 'Snarleyow', *National Observer*, 29 November 1890, afterwards collected in *BRB*, 1892.

38 RK, 'A Levéety in the Plains', *CMG*, 26 May 1886.

39 RK, Preface to *PTH*, 1888.

40 RK, 'Love-o'-Women', collected in *Many Inventions*, 1893.

41 JLK to Margaret Burne-Jones, Simla 27 July 1886, JLK Papers, Sussex, collected in Pinney, *Letters*, Vol. I.

42 Rudyard Kipling, 'My First Book', reprinted in *KJ*, March 1960.

43 George Younghusband, *Forty Years a Soldier*.

44 Sir Ian Hamilton, *Listening for the Drums*.

45 RK, 'The Mark of the Beast', *Pioneer*, 12 and 14 July 1890, and *New York Journal* in that same month, collected in *Life's Handicap*, 1891.

46 Quoted by C. E. Buckland, *Dictionary of Indian Biography*.

47 RK, 'Our Gentleman Riders', *CMG*, 20 August 1888.

48 RK, 'An Old Song', *CMG*, 15 August 1887.

49 George Younghusband, *Forty Years a Soldier*.

50 RK, 'Three and – an Extra', *CMG*, 17 November 1886, collected in *PTH*, 1888.

51 Mrs Hauksbee makes her first appearance in 'Three and – an Extra' and her last in 'Mrs Hauksbee Sits It Out', *Illustrated London News*, Christmas 1890, collected in John Whitehead, *Mrs Hauksbee & Co.*

52 John Whitehead, 'Mrs Hauksbee Rides Again', *KJ*, September 1998 and December 1998.

53 RK, 'The Education of Otis Yeare', *Week's News*, 10 March 1888, collected in *Under the Deodars*, 1889.

54 RK, 'Anglo-Indian Society', *CMG*, 29 January 1887, collected in Pinney, *Letters*, Vol. I.

55 RK to Edith Macdonald, Lahore 4–5 December 1886, Library of Congress, collected in Pinney, *Letters*, Vol. I.

56 RK, 'Christmas in India', *Pioneer*, 24 December 1886.

57 RK to Edith Macdonald, Lahore 4–5 December 1886, Library of Congress, collected in Pinney, *Letters*, Vol. I.

9: 'Forty foolish yarns': From Lahore to Allahabad, 1887–8

1 RK to Thacker, Spink and Co., Lahore 3 February 1887, Yale University Library, uncollected, referred to in Lycett, *RK*, 1999.

2 RK to Mrs Maunsell, Lahore 10 June 1887, Library of Congress, collected in Pinney, *Letters*, Vol. I.

3 RK to Mrs Isabella Burton, Lahore 26 October 1887, private collection, composite published in Pinney, *Letters*, Vol. I. Further details of this and succeeding letters to Mrs Burton are found in Lycett, *RK*.

4 Sir Ian Hamilton, *Listening for the Drums*.

5 RK to Margaret Burne-Jones, Lahore 27 September 1885, RK Papers, Sussex, collected in Pinney, *Letters*, Vol. I.

6 RK, 'For the Women', *CMG*, 18 February 1887, collected in Rutherford, *Early Verse*.

7 RK, 'What the People Said', *CMG*, 4 May 1887, reprinted in the third edition of *Departmental Ditties*, 1889.

8 Lorna Lee, *Trix*.

9 RK to Margaret Burne-Jones, Jamalpur 25 January 1888, RK Papers, Sussex, collected in Pinney, *Letters*, Vol. I.

10 Sir John Kaye, *History of the Sepoy War*, Vol. II.

11 G. H. Keene, *Handbook for Visitors*.

12 Home Secretary's Confidential Despatches, Indian Records, 1878 (APAC, BL).

13 Quoted in Lycett, *RK*.

14 RK to Margaret Burne-Jones, Jamalpur 25 January 1888, RK Papers, Sussex, collected in Pinney, *Letters*, Vol. I.

15 Ibid.

16 AK's comments were quoted by RK in a letter to Mrs Edmonia Hill, Allahabad 30 April 1888, from a copy in RK Papers, Sussex, collected in Pinney, *Letters*, Vol. I.

17 RK to Mrs Isabella Burton, Allahabad 20 January 1988, from a private collection, quoted in Lycett, *RK*.

18 Mrs Edmonia Hill to Caroline Taylor, date unknown, quoted in Lycett, *RK*.

19 RK, *SM*.

20 Ibid.

21 'Hustling American', ' "Kipling About" in London for a Week', *KJ*, October 1928.

22 W. J. Makin, *T.P.'s Weekly*, 17 August 1929.

23 T. Goodenough, *Leeds Mercury*, 30 December 1926.

24 W. J. Makin, *T.P.'s Weekly*, 17 August 1929.

25 RK, *SM*.

26 RK, 'The Epics of India', *CMG*, 24 August 1886, collected in Pinney, *Letters*, Vol. I.

27 RK, 'A Real Live City', *Pioneer*, 2 March 1888, collected in *From Sea to Sea*, 1890.

28 RK, 'The Song of the Women', *Pioneer*, 17 April 1888.

29 RK to Mrs Edmonia Hill, April 1888, from a copy in RK Papers, Sussex, collected in Pinney, *Letters*, Vol. I.

30 RK to Mrs Edmonia Hill, 8 May 1888, from a copy in RK Papers, Sussex, collected in Pinney, *Letters*, Vol. I.

31 RK, 'Dray Wara Yow Dee', *CMG*, 28 April 1888, collected in *In Black and White*, 1889.

32 RK to Mrs Edmonia Hill, 11 May 1888, from a copy in RK Papers, Sussex, collected in Pinney, *Letters*, Vol. I.

33 Sir William Hunter to RK, July 1888, quoted in F. H. Skrine, *The Life of Sir William Wilson Hunter*.

34 Sir William Hunter, *The Academy*, 1888.

35 RK to Mrs Edmonia Hill, 15 May 1888, from a copy in RK Papers, Sussex, collected in Pinney, *Letters*, Vol. I.

36 RK to Mrs Edmonia Hill, 1 June 1888, from a copy in RK Papers, Sussex, collected in Pinney, *Letters*, Vol. I.

37 *Auteur du Mariage* (1883) and *Auteur du Divorce* (1886) by 'Gyp', the pseudonym of Madame de Mirabeau, Comtesse de Martel de Janville (1849–1932), who wrote more than 120 novelettes.

38 RK, *SM*.

39 Andrew Wilson, *Abode of Snow*.

40 I am indebted to D. C. Kala for much of this information, contained in his recently published book *Frederick Wilson*.

10: *'Who travels the fastest': Simla, Allahabad and an ending*, 1888–9

1 RK to Mrs Edmonia Hill, 9–10 July 1888, from a copy in RK Papers, Sussex, collected in Pinney, *Letters*, Vol. I.

2 RK to Mrs Edmonia Hill, 27 June 1888, from a copy in RK Papers, Sussex, collected in Pinney, *Letters*, Vol. I.

3 RK to Mrs Edmonia Hill, 28 June–1 July 1888, from a copy in RK Papers, Sussex, collected in Pinney, *Letters*, Vol. I.

4 RK to Mrs Edmonia Hill, 15 July 1888, incomplete letter, from a copy in RK Papers, Sussex, collected in Pinney, *Letters*, Vol. I.

5 JLK to Edith Plowden, Effingham 28 August 1888, JLK Papers, Sussex.

6 RK to Mrs Edmonia Hill, 13 July 1888, incomplete letter, from a copy in RK Papers, Sussex, collected in Pinney, *Letters*, Vol. I.

7 RK to Mrs Edmonia Hill, undated incomplete letter, probably late July 1888, from a copy in RK Papers, Sussex, collected in Pinney, *Letters*, Vol. I.

8 RK, *SM*.

9 RK, 'One Viceroy Resigns', *Pioneer*, 7 December 1888, collected in later editions of *DD*.

10 AK to Lord Dufferin, 17 December 1888, Dufferin Papers, PRO Northern Ireland, quoted in Lycett, *RK*.

11 RK, *SM*.

12 Mrs Edmonia Hill, Hill Papers, Cornell University, quoted in Lycett, *RK*.

13 RK to Mrs Edmonia Hill, 6 October 1888, from a copy in RK Papers, Sussex, collected in Pinney, *Letters*, Vol. I.

14 RK, 'A Celebrity at Home: Mrs S. A. Hill at Belvidere House, Allahabad', unpublished MS, Baldwin Papers, Sussex.

15 Mrs Edmonia Hill, 'The Young Kipling', *Atlantic Monthly*, April 1936.

16 Birkenhead, *RK*.

17 Sir Charles Ross Alston, related in K. Jamilludin, *The Tropic Sun*.

18 W. J. Makin, *T.P.'s Weekly*, 17 August 1929.

19 RK, 'The Drums of the Fore and Aft', *Wee Willie Winkie*, December 1888.

20 RK, 'The Masque of Plenty', *Pioneer*, 26 October 1888, collected in *RK's Verse*.

21 RK, 'The Enlightenment of Pagett, MP', *Contemporary Review*, June 1890.

22 RK, 'The Head of the District', *Macmillan's Magazine*, January 1890, collected in *Life's Handicap*, 1891.

23 RK to Mrs Edmonia Hill, probably 6 February 1889, from a copy in RK Papers, Sussex, collected in Pinney, *Letters*, Vol. I.

24 RK to Mrs Margaret Mackail, NWP Club, Allahabad 11–14 February 1889, RK Papers, Sussex, collected in Pinney, *Letters*, Vol. I.

25 RK, *SM*.

26 RK to Mrs Edmonia Hill, probably 26 February 1889, from a copy in RK Papers, Sussex, collected in Pinney, *Letters*, Vol. I.

27 RK to Mrs Edmonia Hill, 26 February 1889, from a copy in RK Papers, Sussex, collected in Pinney, *Letters*, Vol. I.

28 RK to Kay Robinson, Lahore 13 April 1886, RK Papers, Sussex, collected in Pinney, *Letters*, Vol. I.

29 This was one burnt bridge too many, and as soon as he had the funds he bought the copyright back for the then considerable sum of £1200.

11 : *'Life and Death . . . and Love and Fate':*
London and fame, 1889–91

1 RK, undated articles printed in the *Pioneer*, Scrapbook 1, RK Papers, Sussex, quoted in Carrington, *RK*.

2 RK to Mrs Edmonia Hill, Wellesley 13 September 1889, from a copy in RK Papers, Sussex, collected in Pinney, *Letters*, Vol. I.

3 Quoted in Carrington, *RK*, the source being a letter from Lockwood de Forest, an American collector of Indian art whom Lockwood Kipling had met in Lahore.

4 RK to Mrs Edmonia Hill, The Grange 25 October 1889, from a copy in RK Papers, Sussex, collected in Pinney, *Letters*, Vol. I.

5 RK to Miss Caroline Taylor, Embankment Chambers 9 December 1889, from a copy in RK Papers, Sussex, collected in Pinney, *Letters*, Vol. I.

6 RK, *SM*.

7 RK, 'A Legend of Great Honour', *CMG*, 11 and 13 January 1890, subsequently published in England as 'My Great and Only'.

8 Desmond Chapman-Huston, *The Lost Historian*.

9 RK, *SM*.

10 RK to Mrs Edmonia Hill, Embankment Chambers 3–25 December 1889, from a copy in RK Papers, Sussex, collected in Pinney, *Letters*, Vol. I.

11 JLK to Edith Plowden, 29 Wynnstay Gardens, Kensington, undated but autumn 1890, JLK Papers, Sussex.

12 RK to Mrs Edmonia Hill, Embankment Chambers early November 1889, from a copy in RK Papers, Sussex, collected in Pinney, *Letters*, Vol. I.

13 RK, *SM*.

14 Ibid.

15 RK to Mrs Edmonia Hill, Embankment Chambers 3–25 December 1889, from a copy in RK Papers, Sussex, collected in Pinney, *Letters*, Vol. I.

16 Ibid.

17 RK to Mrs Edmonia Hill, Embankment Chambers 2 January 1890, from a copy in RK Papers, Sussex, collected in Pinney, *Letters*, Vol. I.

18 RK, 'In Partibus', *CMG*, 23 December and *Pioneer*, 25 December 1889, collected in *Abaft the Funnel*, 1909.

19 RK to Mrs Edmonia Hill, Embankment Chambers February 1890, from a copy in RK Papers, Sussex, collected in Pinney, *Letters*, Vol. I.

20 RK's next (surviving) letter was sent on 30 July 1899 in reply to Edmonia Hill's letter of condolence.

21 Quoted without source in Birkenhead, *RK*.

22 Ibid.

23 JLK to Edith Plowden, 29 Wynnstay Gardens, Kensington, undated but late summer 1890, JLK Papers, Sussex.

24 J. M. Barrie in *Contemporary Review*, quoted in Carrington, *RK*.

25 RK to an unidentified recipient, Embankment Chambers 9 March 1890, in RK Papers, Sussex, collected in Pinney, *Letters*, Vol. II.

26 Martin Seymour-Smith, *Rudyard Kipling*.

27 Henry James, 'Wolcott Balestier: a Portrait', *Cosmopolitan*, May 1892.

28 Arthur Waugh, *One Man's Road*, quoted in Wilson, *The Strange Ride of Rudyard Kipling*.

29 Will Cabot in *Vermont Phoenix*, 13 November 1891, quoted in Carrington, *RK*.

30 Wolcott Balestier to W. D. Howells, 18 February 1891, Harvard, quoted in Lycett, *RK*.

31 Henry James in two letters, to Mrs Sands and Edmund Gosse, quoted without source in Carrington, *RK*.

32 Carrie Balestier to Josephine Balestier, January 1891, Dunham, quoted in Lycett, *RK*.

33 RK to George Allen, January 1891, Dalhousie University, collected in Pinney, *Letters*, Vol. II.

34 RK, *SM*.

12: 'Try as he will': Weddings and funerals, Vermont and Sussex, 1892–9

1 Edmund Gosse to R. W. Gilder, 18 January 1892, quoted in Lycett, *RK*.

2 Henry James to William James, 6 February 1892, Houghton Collection, Houghton Library, Harvard, quoted in Carrington, *RK*.

3 RK, *SM*.

4 RK to W. E. Henley, Brattleboro 3 January 1893, Berg Collection, New York Public Library, collected in Pinney, *Letters*, Vol. II.

5 RK, 'The Potted Princess', *St Nicholas Magazine*, January 1893.

6 RK, 'Collar-Wallah and the Poison Stick', *St Nicholas Magazine*, February 1893.

7 RK to Mary Mapes Dodge, Brattleboro 15 October 1892, Princeton University, collected in Pinney, *Letters*, Vol. II.

8 RK to Mary Mapes Dodge, Brattleboro 24 November 1892, Princeton University, collected in Pinney, *Letters*, Vol. II.

9 RK to R. U. Johnson, Naulakha 20 December 1895, Dalhousie University, collected in Pinney, *Letters*, Vol. II.

10 RK, 'In the Rukh', *Many Inventions*, June 1893.

11 RK, 'Toomai of the Elephants', *St Nicholas Magazine*, December 1893, collected in *The Jungle Book*, 1894.

12 RK, 'Tiger-Tiger', *St Nicholas Magazine*, February 1894, collected in *The Jungle Book*, 1894.

13 RK to Mary Mapes Dodge, Brattleboro 21 October 1892, Princeton University, collected in Pinney, *Letters*, Vol. II.

14 It is odd that the Bengal tiger, alone among the *Jungle Book*'s larger beasts, should have been saddled with so many negative qualities. Kipling seems to have taken his cue from R. A. Sterndale, Bengal Civilian and renowned *shikari*, who in his *Denizens of the Jungle*, 1880, wrote about a tiger he named 'Shere Ali', both cowardly and cruel in his killing.

15 RK, *SM*.

16 RK, 'The Bridge-Builders', *Illustrated London News* Christmas number 1893, collected in *The Day's Work*, 1898.

17 RK, 'That Day', first published in 1896 edition of *BRB*.

18 Gen. A. S. Little in a letter to Lord Birkenhead, quoted in Birkenhead, *RK*.

19 RK to E. L. White, Naulakha 17 August 1894, Ray Collection, Morgan Library, collected in Pinney, *Letters*, Vol. II.

20 RK to Mary Mapes Dodge, Naulakha 18 June 1895, Princeton University, collected in Pinney, *Letters*, Vol. II.

21 Mrs Carrie Kipling, Diary 21 March 1895, RK Papers, Sussex.

22 RK to Robert Barr, 11 March 1896, quoted without source in Lycett, *RK*.

23 Mrs Carrie Kipling, Diary, 13 May 1896, RK Papers, Sussex.

24 Carrington and Lycett give different accounts of the encounter, both taken from the same source. Lycett cites Molly Cabot, 'The Vermont Period: Rudyard Kipling in Vermont', *English Literature in Transition*, 29/2, 1986.

25 RK to Cormell Price, Rock House 18 December 1896, Library of Congress, collected in Pinney, *Letters*, Vol. II.

26 RK, *SM*.

27 Both letters are quoted in Carrington, *RK*.

28 Angela Thirkell, *Three Houses*.

29 The final draft was noted as finished by Carrie Kipling on 22 November 1898. Copies were then sent to Theodore Roosevelt and *McClure's*

Magazine. It appeared in *The Times* on 4 February and in the New York *Sun* and *Tribune* on 5 February 1899.

30 Mrs Katherine Crossley, 'Impressions of Trix', in '"Aunt Trix": Mrs Alice Macdonald Fleming, Some Recollections by Gwladys Cox', Lorna Lee, *Trix: Kipling's Forgotten Sister*.

31 RK to Alfred Baldwin, The Elms 18 November 1898, Dalhousie University, collected in Pinney, *Letters*, Vol. II.

32 AK to Mrs Georgina Burne-Jones, 6 March 1899, JLK Papers, Sussex, footnote in Pinney, *Letters*, Vol. II.

33 RK, *SM*.

34 JLK to Sally Norton, 22 July 1899, JLK Papers, Sussex, quoted in Lycett, *RK*, 1999.

35 RK to Mrs Edmonia Hill, The Elms 30 July 1899, Library of Congress, collected in Pinney, *Letters*, Vol. II.

36 Kay Robinson to RK, 19 December 1899, RK Papers, Sussex.

37 Kay Robinson was now building a new career for himself as a writer on nature. He became a devoted pantheist and 1903 founded the *Countryside* magazine which he edited for many years before his death in 1928.

38 Angela Thirkell, *Three Houses*.

Envoi: 'In the faith of little children': Kim and after, 1899–1936

1 Another beneficiary was George Allen's North-West Tannery in Cawnpore, which made the boots for the Indian Army, although Sir George himself had now retired to a country estate in Sussex with the knighthood he had so long craved. He died in 1900.

2 Henry James to Grace Norton, 15 December 1897, Harvard, quoted in Lycett, *RK*.

3 Quoted without source in Carrington, *RK*.

4 RK, 'The Two-Sided Man'. The two verses are as printed at the head of Chapter 7 in *Kim*. The poem was subsequently revised and enlarged before collection in *Songs from Books*, 1913.

5 Christopher Hitchens, *Love, Poverty and War*.

6 Charles Allen, *God's Terrorists*.

7 RK, 'The Truce of the Bear', *Literature*, October 1898, collected in *The Five Nations*, 1903.

8 RK, *SM*.

9 For the full story of the Pundits, see Charles Allen, *A Mountain in Tibet*, John Keay, *Where Men and Mountains Meet*, and Patrick Hopkirk, *Trespassers on the Roof of the World*.

10 Max Müller, *Sacred Books of the East*, Vol. XI, 1881.

11 Angus Wilson, *The Strange Ride of Rudyard Kipling*; Nirad Chaudhuri, 'The Finest Story about India – in English', *Rudyard Kipling: the Man,*

his Work and his World, ed. John Gross, 1972 ; Edward Said, 'Kim: the Pleasures of Imperialism', *Raritan*, 1987.

12 Henry James to RK, 30 October 1901, Harvard, quoted in Lycett, *RK*, 1999.

A Glossary of Indian and Anglo-Indian Words

Definitions given in *italics* are taken from the glossary found in the 1897 edition of *Departmental Ditties*, the work of J. Lockwood Kipling.

Act – To deputise, thus 'to do an act'.

ADC – Aide-de-Camp.

Adjutant-crane – Largest stork in N. India, known for its upright stance and measured gait.

Afghan business – Second Afghan War of 1878–80.

Afridi – tribesman from one of the largest of the Pathan tribes.

Ajaib-ghur, Ajaib-ghar – 'House of wonders', name given to the Lahore Museum.

Allah ho Akbar – 'God is Great', opening phrase of the Muslim call to prayer.

Anglo-Indian – Originally used to describe Britons living in India, after 1900 used to designate a person of mixed Indo-British ancestry, *see* Eurasian.

Anna – One-sixteenth of a rupee, thus 'eight annas to a rupee' to describe a Eurasian.

Annandale – *A valley near Simla – the Simla Racecourse, Cricket, and Recreation Grounds*.

Ayah – Child's nurse, lady's maid, der. Portuguese.

Baba – Baby, orig. English, thus 'baba-*logue*'– 'baby people', 'missy baba' – 'little miss'.

Baboo, babu – *A title such as 'Mr', used frequently to signify a Bengali clerk*; originally a term of respect but increasingly used as a pejorative term by Anglo-Indians to describe semi-Anglicised Indians, particularly Bengalis.

Babul – Thorny mimosa with yellow flowers.

Bagh – Enclosed formal garden; but also tiger, *see* also *shere*.

Bagheera – Panther.

Bahadur – Champion, brave.

Baloo – Brown bear.

Bandar, bundur – monkey.

Bandobast, bandobust, bundobast, bundobust – Tie up loose ends, arrangement, thus 'let's make a bundo'.

Bania, bunnia, bunya – *A corn and seed merchant or dealer*; also money-lender, thus '*banyakiraj*' – 'rule of the money-lender', term used to describe the British Raj.

Baradari – Muslim monument with twelve entrances.

Bazaar, bazar – Native market.

BB&CI – Bombay, Baroda and Central India railway.

Bearer – Personal servant or valet, originally torch or palanquin bearer.

Benmore – *The old Simla Assembly Rooms.*

Bhang – Indian hemp or cannabis in processed form.

Bhai – Brother, thus *bhai-bhand* – brotherhood, *see* also Boy.

Bheesti, Bheesty, Bhistee – water-carrier, also employed to sprinkle water from goatskin *mussack* over dusty ground.

Bibi – Lady, often used to describe kept mistress, thus *bibi khana* – lady's house, kept woman's quarters.

Bobs – General Sir Frederick Roberts, later Lord Roberts, known as 'Bobs Bahadur' – 'Robert the Champion'.

Box-wallah – Door-to-door pedlar, thus derog. term for British business-men in India.

Boy – Call for servant, der. *bhai* – 'younger brother'.

Brandypawni – Brandy and soda-water, favourite tipple in Clubs.

Brahmin – *A member of the priestly caste* of Hindus, thus ICS, *see* also Heaven-Born.

Budlee, budli – Substitute or acting servant, often used jokingly to describe an 'acting' appointment.

Bund – Raised embankment, thus Apollo Bunder in Bombay.

Bungalow – Country house, der. *bangla* – 'country', properly, simple single-storey building with verandah.

Burka, boorka – Outdoor garment worn by Muslim women to cover them-selves.

Burra – Big or senior, thus *burra sahib* – senior man; *burra*-mem – wife of senior man; *burra khana* – Big dinner party, *burra deen* – big day, thus Christmas Day, *burra* bungalow – senior officer's house, *burra* peg – double tot of whisky or brandy.

Bursat – *The rains, which set in about the middle of June – the first of them is known as the 'chota bursat', or small rains – after which there is generally a break before the regular monsoon sets in.*

Butcha, batcha – Baby, thus *tum soor ka butcha* – 'you son of a pig', phrase much favoured by Tommies.

Byle – *A bullock.*

Calcutta–Simla – Axis of the Government of India until 1912, with Calcutta the seat of government during the Cold Weather and Simla in the Hot Weather.

Cantonment – Military quarter of the Station, usually found some distance outside the Native town and separated from it by a Maidan or exercise ground, pron. 'cantoonment'.

Chaprassi, chuprassi – Office peon, so called because of the brass *chapras* or buckle worn.

Chela – Young disciple, der. 'house slave'.

Cheroot – Short Indian cigar.

Chick – Split bamboo screen.

Chief – Boss.

Chirag – Simple lamp.

Chit – Note or certificate, der. *chitti*, thus 'chit up' – 'approach someone in authority' (poss. der. of 'chat up').

Chokra – Boy, often applied to inexperienced junior sahib – *see* Chukkeroo.

Chowk – Wide central street, der. *chauk*, equivalent to the English mall.

Chota – Small or junior, thus *chota* sahib – junior sahib or sahib's son, *chota hazri* – little breakfast or morning tea, *chotee bolee* – small talk or children's talk, *chota bungalow* – assistant's house, *chota* peg – single tot of whisky or brandy.

Chuckeroo – Youngster, der. *chokra*.

Chummery – Shared household, usually of bachelors, der. chum.

Civil and Military – the two ruling castes of British India, officers of the Government of India's civil, political, police and other services and of the British Army and Indian Army.

Civilian – Government of India administrative officer, *see* ICS, Heaven-Born.

Civil List – Warrant or Order of Precedence, otherwise known (confusingly) as the Green, Red or Blue Book.

CMG – The *Civil and Military Gazette*, printed in Lahore.

Civil Lines – The official quarter of a Station, built outside the Native town, comprising government offices and the residences of senior government officials.

Club – Private sports club owned by its members and thus exclusive, usually taken to mean the Station club exclusive to the Civil and Military.

Cold Weather – The winter months from October to mid-March.

Collector – Chief administrator of a District, one of whose duties was the collection of revenue, formerly a *Tahsildar*, also known in some regions as Deputy Commissioner, *see* District.

Commissioner – Senior administrator presiding over a Division comprising several Districts.

Competition-Wallah – Indian Civil Servant after entry by competition was introduced in 1856.

Compound – Enclosed ground or garden surrounding a residence, der. Portuguese.

Congress – The Indian National Congress formed in 1873, afterwards becoming a political party.

Coolie, Cooly – *Hired labourer or burden carrier*, der. *Koli* caste in Western India.

Country – Term used to describe people and objects of Indian origin, often with pejorative overtones, thus 'country-born' – European born in India, 'country-bred'– European educated in India, 'country-made' – 'goods made in India', by definition inferior.

Covenanted servant – Civil officer entered into a formal contract with the Secretary of State for India, specifically the ICS.

CP – Central Provinces

Curry and Rice – Popular book of this title published in 1858, thus 'curry and rice days' of mid-nineteenth-century India.

Dak, dawk – *'Post', i.e., properly, transport by relays of men and horses; and thence the mail or letter post, as well as arrangement for travelling or for transmitting articles by such relays.*

Dak-bungalow – A rest house for the accommodation of travellers.

Deodar – *The 'Cedrus deodarus' of the Himalayas*; lit. 'tree of God'.

Dhaee, dhai – Wet nurse.

Dhal, dhall – Lentils.

Dhangi – Small rowing boat, thus dinghy.

Dhobi, dhoby – Washing, thus *dhoby*-wallah – washerman, *dhobi* itch – skin irritation, supposedly derived from excessive use of starch.

Dhoolie, doolie – Covered litter suspended from a pole.

Dibs – *A slang term for money* – *rupees*.

Din, deen – Faith (Muslim), thus religion.

District – Main administrative unit in British India, 250 in number, administered by a District Magistrate.

Duftar, dufter – Book, journal, record – sometimes used instead of *duftar khana* for 'the office', see also *Cutcherry*.

Durbar – Court or levee held by ruler.

Durzee, darzi – Tailor, thus '*durzee*-bird'.

Eid – Muslim festival marking the end of Ramadan.

Ekka – Unsprung cart pulled by one pony, der. *ek* – one.

Englishman – Calcutta newspaper, rival to the *Pioneer*.

Eurasian – Person of mixed British and Indian ancestry, replaced in 1900 by 'Anglo-Indian'.

Fakir – Ascetic or holy man.

Ferash – *A species of date tree, der. faras*

Frontier – The Frontier was always India's North-West Frontier, also known as NWF.

Furlough – Leave of absence, usually taken as Home leave.

Gallibat – Small sailing boat, thus jolly-boat.

Ganja – Indian hemp or cannabis.

Gareeb parwa – 'Protector of the poor', phrase much used by beggars and supplicants.

Gentleman-ranker – Gentleman enlisted in the British Army as a private soldier.

Ghat – *A mountain pass, a landing place or a ferry*; thus 'burning-ghat', where the Hindu dead are cremated.

Ghari, gharry – Carriage, thus *ghora ghari* – horse-drawn sprung hackney carriage.

Ghora – Horse.

GIP – Grand Indian Peninsula railway.

Gora logh – White men.

Grass widow – Wife temporarily separated from her husband, usually in the Hills.

Griff, griffin – Newcomer to India, orig. obscure.

Great Game – Anglo-Russian rivalry and espionage played out on and beyond India's northern frontiers.

Gup – Gossip.

Gymkhana – Sports meeting or sports club, der. *gend-khana* – ball-house or squash racket court.

Hafiz – *A guardian, governor, preserver.*

Hakim – Muslim doctor.

Half-caste – Person of mixed Indo-European origins.

Hathi – Elephant.

Hazur, hazoor – Presence, term of respect.

Hawa-khana – 'To eat the air', to take an evening stroll.

Heaven-born – Term used to describe *Brahmins*, thus ICS.

Hills – Mountains of India, thus Hill-station – British settlement and sanatorium established mainly in the Himalayan foothills.

Hindustan, Hindoostan – Land of the Hindus, but originally northern and central India east of the Indus.

Hindustani – 'More properly Urdu . . . the language of the educated people of all Central and Northern India . . . lingua franca left by all the conquering Moslem invaders from Central Asia . . . the one language in which the mercenary conquerors of many languages could communicate . . . It grew up on the basic language of Aryan India with a vocabulary that is largely Persian and Arabic, but with a grammar that is Hindi . . . normally written in the Devanagri character which reads from left to right.' Sir George MacMunn, from 'Kipling's Hindustani', *Kipling Journal*, April 1941.

Home – Anglo-Indian term for Britain.

Hooka, hookah – Pipe by which tobacco smoke is drawn through a coolant of rose water, also known as 'hubble-bubble'.

Hot Weather – The summer months from mid-March to the end of September.

Hubshi – Ethiopian, derog. term for black man.

IA – Indian Army.

ICS – Indian Civil Service, *see* Heaven-Born, *Brahmins*.

IFS – Indian Forestry Service.

IMS – Indian Medical Service.

IP – Indian Police.

IPS – Indian Political Service.

Izzut, Izzat – honour, reputation.

Jadhoo, jadhu – Magic, thus *Jadhoo-ghar* – magic house, name allegedly given by Indians to Masonic Lodges.

Jakko – A mountain peak in the Punjab – one of the highest of the Himalaya on which Simla is situated.

Jat – Cultivator people of Punjab.

Jemadar – The second native officer in a company of Sepoys.

Jezail – A heavy Afghan rifle, fired with a forked rest.

Jampan, jhampan – Open litter on wheels, thus *jhampani* – litter or rickshaw puller.

Jinriksha – *see* rickshaw.

John Company – Nickname of Honourable East India Company, der. *jehan kampani* – 'honoured company'.

Jungi Lat Sahib – Lord of the Army, Commander-in-Chief.

Jungle – *Forest, or other wild growth*; thus, *jungli* – wild; also, *jungli-wallah* – forest officer, *jungle-morgi* – Jungle fowl, *see* also *Rukh*.

K – Knighthood, ideally a KCB rather than a KCSI (Knight Companion of the Order of the Star of India) or a KCIE (Knight Companion of the Order of the Indian Empire), infinitely preferable to a CIE (Commander of the Indian Empire) or CSI (Companion of the Order of the Star of India).

Kafila – Camel caravan.

Kafir, kaffir – An unbeliever in the Moslem faith, hence Kafiristan in north-eastern Afghanistan.

Kala jugga – 'Dark place', secluded corner of dance hall.

Kalka – A village in the Punjab, at the foot of the Himalays, on the road from Umballa to Simla.

Kerani – Old-fashioned term for clerk used in Punjab, *see Babu.*

Khana – House or room, thus *khansamah* – chief servant at table, house steward, usually a Muslim, but in Bengal a cook.

Khan – Muslim tribal chief or headman, honorific title.

Kharif – Harvest after the summer monsoon.

Khitmatgar – *Table servant* – *a Mahommedan who will also perform the duties of a valet;* senior servant, butler, often referred to as 'khit'.

Khud – *A precipitous hill side, a deep valley.*

Khyberee – *An Afghan tribe inhabiting the Khaibar pass, in Afghanistan.*

Koel, Köil – *The Indian nightingale;* more properly Indian cuckoo, *Eudynamys orientalis.*

Koi hai – 'Who's there?', thus term used for an old India hand.

Kutcha – Raw, unripe, thus unfinished, substandard.

Lakh – One hundred thousand, usually of rupees, *see Naulakha.*

Lal gora – 'Red white [face]', Indian term for British ordinary soldier.

Lama – Religious superior in Tibetan Buddhism, usually taken to mean any Tibetan monk.

Langur – *The great white-bearded ape, much patronised by Hindus, and identified with the monkey-god Hanuman.* More correctly, a species of long-tailed monkey larger than the more common *Rhesus macaque.* According to Sterndale's *Natural History of Mammalia of India,* 1884, 'an animal of very developed social instincts'.

Lat Sahib – Lord Sahib, usually the Governor-General and Viceroy.

Log, loghe – Species, people, thus *sahib-logue* – sahibs, *bandar-log* – monkey people.

Loot – Plunder, der. *lut.*

Lunkah – Prized cheroot from South India.

Ma-Bap – 'Mother-father,' thus '*ap mai ma-bap hai*' – 'you are my mother and father', honorific form of address used by supplicants.

Maharaja – Hindu ruler of an Indian state entitled to a gun salute.

Mahratta – *The name of a famous Hindu race,* now spelled Maratha, hill people of the Deccan and Western Ghats, today Maharashtra.

Mahout – Elephant driver.

Maidan – Green, area of open land usually sited between Native city and Station.

Mali, Malli – Gardener.

Masher – Man who forces himself on women.

Masjid – Mosque.

Memsahib – 'Madam sahib', commonly used for European lady.

Minar – Tower of mosque, used for call to prayer.

Moorgi khana – 'Hen house', ladies' area of Club.

Mela – Fair, festival.

Mehta, mehtar – Prince, term used ironically to address sweeper of low or untouchable caste.

Mlech, mleccha – *One without caste.* Name given to Huns and other foreign invaders by early Indian chroniclers.

Mofussil – Rural interior of India, thus 'mofussilite' – inhabitant of *mofussil*, also name of the *Mofussilite* newspaper, founded in Agra in 1845, succeeded in 1865 by the *Pioneer.*

Mohurram – Shia Muslim month of fasting to commemorate martyrdom of Hussain, grandson of Prophet Mohammed.

Mohur – Mughal gold coin.

Moulvie – Muslim cleric more learned than a *Mullah.*

Muezzin – Muslim caller to prayer.

Mulki Lat Sahib – 'Lord of the Land', the Viceroy of India.

Mullah – Muslim cleric.

Munshi – Language teacher, writer of letters.

Mussulman – 'One who submits', thus Muslim.

Nag, naag – Snake, spec. cobra, snake-god.

Naik – Indian Army equivalent of corporal.

Native – Native Indian, but excluding Europeans born in India, thus Native quarter or Native city.

Nauker-log – House servants.

Naulakha – Nine lakhs, name given to marbled pavilion in Lahore Fort; *The Naulahka*, written jointly by Rudyard Kipling and Wolcott Balestier, misspells the word.

Nullah – Ditch, ravine.

Nungapunga – Naked, from *nunga* – unclothed.

NWF – North-West Frontier.

NWP – North-Western Province, with Agra as its capital, which in 1858 became the North-Western Provinces and Oude, later shortened to United Provinces, with Allahabad as its capital.

Om mane padme/i hum – Tibetan Buddhist mantra usually translated as 'Hail, jewel in the lotus'.

Oont – Camel.

Padre – Name given to all Christian ministers in India, regardless of sect.

Pagal – Mad, thus *pagal-khana* – picnic, *pagal-nautch* – fancy-dress party.

Pahari – Hillman.

Pariah – Outcaste, thus pi-dog.

Pathans – Muslim tribes of Afghan origin inhabiting North-West Frontier.

Peg – *A term used for a brandy (or other spirit) and soda.*

Pendal, Pandal – Shed.

Peliti – *A well-known confectioner*, with branches in Calcutta and Simla.

Pi – The *Pioneer*, founded 1865, leading newspaper of North India.

Poodle-faker – Womaniser, esp. in the Hills; thus 'poodle-faking'.

Pop – Popular social event held in Simla on Mondays with tea and musical turns.

Postheen, poshteen – Afghani wool-lined coat with a tendency to smell in hot weather.

Pugri, pagaree – Turban.

Punjab – 'Land between five rivers', thus the land between the five rivers that fed the Indus, a Sikh kingdom incorporated into British India as a Province; thus 'Punjabi', native of Punjab.

Pukka – Ripe, complete, finished, first-class.

Punkah – *A large swinging fan suspended from the ceiling and pulled by a cooly* or *punkah-wallah*.

Purdah – Curtain, thus the screening of women from public view in Indian households, thus *purdahnashin* – to take the veil.

Rabi – Crops sown after the spring rains.

Raj – Rule, sovereign government, thus British crown rule in India from 1857 to 1947.

Raja, Rajah – *A native chief*; more accurately, a Hindu ruler, demoted by the British to the status of princes or chiefs.

Rains – Summer monsoon, breaking in eastern India in about late May or early June.

Ranken – *Ranken & Co., a well-known firm of tailors*, with a branch in Simla.

Ressaldar, rissaldar – native cavalry officer.

Rest house – *see* 'dak bungalow'.

Rickshaw – *A contraction of 'Jinny rickshaw', a two-wheeled conveyance drawn by a cooly* – *imported from Shanghai*; more accurately, introduced from Japan as the 'jin-rick-sha' in about 1880.

Roti – Bread.

Rukh – Forest, as opposed to jungle.

Rupee – Silver coin, Indian equivalent of shilling.

Ryot – *A tenant of the soil; an individual occupying land as a farmer or cultivator – a native agriculturist.*

Sahib, saheb – Lord, master, companion, gentleman, commonly used to denote a European.

Salaam alaikum – 'Peace be unto you', standard Islamic greeting.

Salwar-kameez – Blouse and baggy trousers worn in Punjab by (mostly) Muslim women.

Samadh – Hindu/Sikh cenotaph.

Sangar, sungar – Stone breastwork.

Sanyassi – Hindu ascetic.

Sat-bhai – *(lit. The seven brothers), a species of thrush, so called from the birds being gregarious, and usually seven of them are found together.*

Sarai, serai – *A place for the accommodation of travellers, a khan, a caravansary.*

Satrap – Governor, orig. of a Persian province.

Screw – Pay.

Season – British India enjoyed the Cold Weather Season in winter and the Simla Season in summer.

Sepoy, sipahi – Indian infantry soldier.

Shah – Ruler.

Shaitan – Satan, devil.

Shamiana – Decorated awnings or screens.

Shauk, shoke – Hobby or pursuit.

Shere – Tiger, but *see* also *Bagh*.

Shikar – Sport, hunting, chase, prey, game; thus *Shikari* – hunter.

Sikh – *A 'disciple', the distinctive name of the disciples of Nānak Shāh, who in the sixteenth century established that sect, which eventually rose to warlike prominence in the Punjab, and from which sprung Ranjāt Singh, the founder of the brief kingdom of Lahore.*

Simkin – *A Hindustani corruption of the word 'champagne'.*

Sircar, Sirkar – The Government of India.

Sirdar – Commander, honorific title partic. among Sikhs.

Siris – *The tree Acacia, a timber of moderate size, best known in the Upper Provinces.*

Snider – rifle.

Sowar – Indian cavalry trooper.

Spoon – To make love in a sentimental manner, also used as a noun.

Station – A district or divisional headquarters, also wherever British officials gathered and worked, usually sited outside Native town or city; *see* Hill-station.

Stunt – Indian pronunciation of Assistant.

Subadar – *The chief native officer of a company of Sepoys.*

Sub chiz, sub cheez – Everything.

Sudder – Chief court.

Syce, sais – Groom.

Suttee, sati – *The rite of widow-burning; i.e., the burning of the living widow along with the corpse of her husband, as formerly practised by people of certain castes among the Hindus, and eminently by the Rājputs.*

Swadeshi – Home-spun cotton goods.

A Glossary of Indian and Anglo-Indian Words

Talukdar – Landed gentleman.

Tamarisk – *A graceful, feather-like shrub; is covered with numberless spikes of small pink flowers when in blossom.*

Tamasha – Spectacle, fuss.

Tat, tatoo – Indian pony, der. *tattu* – pack pony.

Tazea, taziya – Symbolic tombs of martyrs carried by Shia faithful in *Moharram* processions.

Tiffin – Light luncheon.

Tikka-gharri – Box-like hired carriage.

Tonga – *A two-wheeled car drawn by two ponies curricle fashion, and used for travelling in the hills.*

Topee, topi – Hat, thus *sola topee* – sun helmet made from pith of *sola* plant, *topi-wallah*s – the British in India.

Tour – To travel through one's area of responsibility, usually the District, traditionally undertaken in the Cold Weather.

Tulwar, talwar – *A sabre, used by the Sikhs*; also by Pathans

Tum-tum – Dog-cart, der. obscure.

Upper Provinces/Upper India – in Kipling's day a hangover term from the time when northern India was known to the British as the Upper Provinces of Bengal or Upper Hindustan.

Urdu – Turkish word for 'horde', thus language of the camp, lingua franca of Northern India; see *Hindustani*.

Vazier, wazier – Chief minister in Muslim state.

Vedas – Ancient holy texts of Brahminism.

Verandah – Covered deck or platform surrounding bungalow; der. Portuguese.

Wah! – Exclamation of satisfaction or pleasure.

Wahabee, Wahhabi – derog. term for the followers of an extreme Muslim sect.

Waler – *Horses imported from New South Wales are called Walers* – usually horses suitable for light cavalry.

Wallah – Man.

Zam-zammah – The 'Hummer', the name given to Lahore's giant cannon, of uncertain meaning der. orig. from Arabic.

Zenana, zanana – *The apartments of a house in which the women of the family are secluded.*

Select bibliography

Rudyard Kipling: early collected work to 1901
and later works referred to

United Services College Chronicle, 1881–3.

Schoolboy Lyrics, Lahore, 1881.

Civil and Military Gazette, Lahore, 1882–94.

Echoes, 'by Two Writers' (RK and Alice 'Trix' Kipling), Lahore, 1884.

The Pioneer, Allahabad, 1883–94.

Quartette: The Christmas Annual of the Civil and Military Gazette, 'by Four Anglo-Indians' (RK with Alice, Lockwood and 'Trix' Kipling), Lahore, 1885.

Departmental Ditties and Other Verses, Lahore, 1886.

The Week's News, Allahabad, 1888–91.

Plain Tales from the Hills, Allahabad, 1888.

Soldiers Three: Stories of Barrack-Room Life, Indian Railway Series, No. 1, Allahabad, 1888.

The Story of the Gadsbys: A Tale Without A Plot, No. 2, 1889.

In Black and White: Stories of Native Life, No. 3, 1889.

Under the Deodars: In Social Bye-Ways, No. 4, 1889.

The Phantom 'Rickshaw and Other Stories, No. 5, 1889.

Wee Willie Winkie and Other Child Stories, No. 6, 1889.

Letters of Marque, Allahabad, 1889.

Mine Own People, 1890 (suppressed).

The City of Dreadful Night and Other Places, 1891 (suppressed).

'Turnovers' from the 'Civil and Military Gazette' January–December 1888, 1891 (suppressed).

The Light That Failed, 1891.

Life's Handicap; Being Stories of Mine Own People, 1891.

City of Dreadful Night, 1892 (suppressed).

The Smith Administration, 1892 (suppressed).

Barrack-Room Ballads and Other Verses, 1892.

The Naulahka: A Novel of West and East (RK and Wolcott Balestier), 1892.

From Tideway to Tideway, 1892–5.

Many Inventions, 1893.

The Jungle Book, 1894.

My First Book, ed. Jerome K. Jerome, 1894.

The Second Jungle Book, 1895.
Captains Courageous: A Story of the Grand Banks, 1897.
The Day's Work, 1898.
A Fleet in Being, 1898.
From Sea to Sea: Letters of Travel 1887–89, 1899.
Stalky & Co., 1899.
Kim, 1901.
Just So Stories, 1902.
The Five Nations, 1903.
Traffics and Discoveries, 1904.
Puck of Pook's Hill, 1906.
Collected Verse, 1907.
Actions and Reactions, 1909.
Abaft the Funnel, 1909.
Songs from Books, 1913.
The Years Between, 1914.
Land and Sea Tales for Scouts and Guides, 1923.
The Brushwood Boy, 1926.
Something of Myself, 1936.
Andrew Rutherford, ed., *Early Verse by Rudyard Kipling 1879–89: Unpublished, Uncollected, and Rarely Collected Poems*, 1986.
Thomas Pinney, ed., *Kipling's India: Uncollected Sketches 1884–88*, 1986.
Thomas Pinney, ed., *The Letters of Rudyard Kipling, Vol. I: 1872–89*, 1990; *Vol. 2: 1890–99*, 1990.
Thomas Pinney, ed. *Rudyard Kipling: 'Something of Myself' and other Autobiographical Writings*, 1991.

Kipling Collection Papers consulted at the University of Sussex Library Special Collections

RK, notebook 1881–2, containing 52 poems in his own hand, RK Papers 24/1.
RK, notebook 1882–4, containing 58 poems in his own hand, RK Papers 24/3.
RK, volume of articles, stories and verses pub. in *CMG* 1884–6, RK Papers 28/1.
RK, volume of articles, stories and verses pub. in *Pioneer* 1885, RK Papers 28/2.
RK, volume of articles, stories and verses pub. in *CMG* 1886–7, RK Papers 28/3.
RK, volume of articles, stories and verses pub. in *Civil and Military Gazette*, *Pioneer*, *Week's News* and other journals 1887–91, RK Papers 28/4.
RK, Bound volume of articles, stories and verses pub. in English and US newspapers and periodicals, 1892–1910, RK Papers 28/5.

JLK and AK, letters to RK 1890, JLK Papers 1/7.
JLK and AK, letters to Edith Plowden 1880–1900, JLK Papers 1/10–11
AK, letters to Margaret Burne-Jones 1885–6, JLK Papers 1/1.
AK, letter to Edith Macdonald, 1866, JLK Papers 1/8.
AK, letter to Mrs Rivett-Carnac, 1870, JLK Papers 1/13.
JLK, letters to Duke of Connaught, JLK Papers 1/14
JLK, cuttings from *Pioneer* 1870–97, JLK Papers 28/19-21.
ATF, Notes on Flo Garrard and *Schoolboy Lyrics*, RK Papers 32/32
ATF, 'Through Judy's Eyes', Typescript MS, ATF Papers 1/8.
Mrs 'Carrie' Kipling, extracts from diaries 1892–1908 by Charles Carrington, Carrington Papers 1/8-9.
Edith Plowden, 'Fond Memory 1875–1910', MSS, Baldwin Papers 1/11-20.

Contemporary Sources

Anon., *Sleepy Sketches: or, How We Live, and How We Do Not Live, from Bombay*, 1887.
Sir Edwin Arnold, *The Light of Asia*, 1879; *On the Indian Hills*, 1881; *Pearls of Faith*, 1883; *Lotus and Jewel*, 1887.
N. W. Bancroft, *From Recruit to Staff Sergeant*, 1885.
James Barrie, 'Mr Kipling's Stories', *Contemporary Review*, Vol. LIX, March 1891.
Theodor Beck, *Essays on Indian Topics*, Pioneer Press, 1888.
George C. Beresford, 'Kipling at United Services College, Westward Ho!', *Cambridge Magazine*, April 1899; *School-Days with Kipling*, 1936.
Wilfred Scawen Blunt, *My Diaries: being a Personal Narrative of Events, 1888–1914*, 1921.
Bombay Asiatic Journal, 1838.
Edward J. Buck, *Simla Past and Present*, Second Edition, 1924.
C. E. Buckland, *Dictionary of Indian Biography*, 1906.
Georgiana Burne-Jones, *Memorials of Ed Burne-Jones*, Vol. I, 1904.
Calcutta Review, 'General Literature', Vol. 78, No. 156, 1884; 'General Literature', Vol. 91, No. 181, 1890.
'Casual', *That Reminds Me*, CMG Press, 1922.
John Cave-Brown, *Incidents in Indian Life*, 1886.
Phil Robinson, ed., *The Chameleon: An Anglo-Indian Periodical of Light Literature*, 1871–3
W. J. Clarke, *Rudyard Kipling: An Attempt at Appreciation*, 1899.
W. E. Coleman, 'Critical Historical Review of the Theosophical Society: an Exposé of Madame Blavatsky', *The Religio-Philosophical Journal*, 1893.
J. P. Collins, 'Rudyard Kipling at Lahore', *Nineteenth Century and After*, Vol. CXXI, Jan. 1937.
Col. Arthur Cory, *Shadows of Coming Events: or The Eastern Menace*, 1876; reprinted as *The Eastern Menace*, 1881.

R. N. Cust, *Pictures of Indian Life Sketched with the Pen from 1852 to 1881*, 1881; *Sorrows of Anglo-Indian Life, by a Sufferer*, 1889.

Sarat Chandra Das, *Religion and History of Tibet*, 1881; *Indian Pandits in the Land of Snow*, 1893.

T. W. Rhys Davids, *Buddhism*, 1886; *Buddhist Birth Stories or Jataka Tales*, 1880.

Col. Newnham Davies, *Jadoo*, 1898.

Hariot, Marchioness of Dufferin and Ava, *Our Viceregal Life in India: Selections from my Journal 1884–88*, 1889.

Lord Dufferin, Dufferin Papers, Clandeboye and Belfast.

Gen. Lionel C. Dunsterville, *Stalky's Reminiscences*, 1928.

G. R. Elsmie, *Thirty-Five Years in the Punjab, 1858–1893*, 1907.

'An Ex-Civilian', *Life in the Mofussil*, 1889.

Alice 'Trix' Fleming (née Kipling), (as 'Beatrice Grange'), *The Heart of a Maid*, 1891; *A Pinchbeck Goddess*, 1897; 'Some Childhood Memories of Rudyard Kipling', *Chambers's Journal*, March 1939.

William H. C. Folsom, *Fifty Years in the North-West*, Pioneer, 1888.

Charles Forjett, *Our Real Danger in India*, 1877.

Charles T. French, *Journal of a Tour of Upper Hindustan*, 1853.

Victor Fussboll, *Folktales of India: the Pali Jataka*, 1884.

T. Goodenough, 'Rudyard Kipling in Allahabad', *Leeds Mercury*, 30 December 1926.

Gen. Sir T. E. Gordon, *A Varied Life: a Record of Military and Civil Service, of Sport and Travel in India, Central Asia and Persia, 1849–1902*, 1906.

Henry R. Goulding, *Old Lahore: Reminiscences of a Resident, with which is reproduced a Historical and Descriptive Account by the late Mr T. H. Thornton*, CMG Press, 1924.

Govt. of the Bombay Presidency, *Gazetteer of Bombay City and Island*, Vol. I, 1909.

Govt. of the Punjab, *Gazetteer of the Simla District*, 1888–89; Punjab District Gazetteers.

Hilda Gregg, 'The Indian Mutiny in Fiction', *Blackwood's Edinburgh Magazine*, Vol. 161, No. 400, February 1897.

Rider Haggard, *Nada the Lily*, 1892.

Gen. Sir Ian Hamilton, *Listening for the Drums*, 1944.

Capt. Horace Hayes, *Among Men and Horses*, 1894.

Edmonia Hill, 'The Young Kipling', *Atlantic Monthly*, Vol. 157, April 1936.

Sir William W. Hunter, *The Imperial Gazetteer of India*, 1881; *England's Work in India*, 1881; *India of the Queen*, 1887.

Indian Charivari, Calcutta, dates unknown.

Sir John Kaye, *History of the Sepoy War*, 1859; *History of the Great Revolt*, 1880.

George Henry Keene, *A Servant of John Company*, 1897; *A Handbook for Visitors to Lucknow with Preliminary Notes on Allahabad and Cawnpore*, 1875.

John Lockwood Kipling, *Beast and Man in India: A Popular Sketch of Indian Animals in their Relations with the People*, 1891.

John Lang, *Wanderings in India and Other Sketches*, 1859; *Essays in Little*, 1891.

Cuthbert Larking, *Bandobast and Khabar*, 1888.

Col. W. F. B. Laurie, *Sketches of Some Distinguished Anglo-Indians: with An Account of Anglo-Indian Periodical Literature*, 1875.

Sir Walter Roper Lawrence, *The India We Served*, 1928.

Sir Alfred Comyn Lyall, *The Life of the Marquis of Dufferin and Ava*, 1905.

Edith Macdonald, *Annals of the Macdonald Family*, 1923.

Frederick Macdonald, *As a Tale that is Told*, 1919.

A. R. D. Mackenzie, *Mutiny Memoirs, Being Personal Reminiscences of the Great Sepoy Revolt of 1857*, Pioneer Press, 1892.

James Mackenzie Maclean, *Maclean's Guide to Bombay*, 1875.

W. J. Makin, 'In the Club at Allahabad', *T.P.'s Weekly*, August 17 1929.

'G. F. Monkshead' – see W. J. Clarke.

Gen. Sir William Moore, *A Manual of Family Medicine and Hygiene for India*, 1893.

Max Müller, *Sacred Books of the East*, Vol. XI, 1881.

Sir Gilbert Murray, *Unfinished Autobiography*,

Charles Eliot Norton, 'The Poetry of Rudyard Kipling', *Atlantic*, Vol. LXXIX, Jan 1897.

Edward F. Oaten, *A Sketch of Anglo-Indian Literature*, 1908.

'Observer', *An Anglo-Indian Microcosm: A Sketch of Anglo-Indian Society*, Pioneer Press, 1886.

Edward E. Oliver, *Across the Border or Pathan and Biloch*, illus. by J. Lockwood Kipling, 1890.

'Pericles', *Three Chapters on the Future of India*, Pioneer Press, 1875.

The Pioneer newspaper, Pioneer Press, 1865–95; *Punjab Notes and Queries*, Pioneer Press, 1883–6; *The Seditious Character of the Indian National Congress*, Pioneer Press, 1888.

'Pukhtana', *Our Political, 1849 and 1879: Two Sketches Founded on Fact*, CMG Press, 1880.

J. P. Rawlins, *Under the Indian Sun*, CMG Press, 1897.

Lord Ripon, Ripon Papers, Cambridge University Library.

J. H. Rivett-Carnac, *Many Memories of Life in India*, 1910.

Field-Marshal Lord Roberts, *Forty-One Years in India*, 1905.

E. Kay Robinson, 'Rudyard Kipling in India', *Pearson's Magazine*, June 1896; 'Kipling in India: Reminiscences by the Editor of the Newspaper on Which Kipling Served at Lahore', *McClure's Magazine*, July 1896; 'Rudyard Kipling as Journalist', *Literature*, March 1899.

David Ross, *The Land of the Five Rivers and Sindh*, 1883.

Alfred Percy Sinnett, Editor *Pioneer* 1872–81, *The Occult World*, 1881; *Esoteric Buddhism*, 1883.

Select bibliography

Flora Annie Steel, *Garden of Fidelity: An Autobiography*, 1929.

Sir James Stephen, Stephen Papers, Cambridge University Library.

R. A. Sterndale, *The Afghan Knife*, 1879; *Denizens of the Jungle*, 1880; *Seonee*, 1887.

W. O. Swanston ('A Volunteer'), *My Journal: or, What I Did and Saw between the 9th June and 25th November 1857, with an Account of General Havelock's March from Allahabad to Lucknow*, 1858.

Angela Thirkell, *Three Houses*, 1931.

Thomas Henry Thornton and J. Lockwood Kipling, *Lahore: A Historical and Descriptive Note*, 1876.

Martin Towelle, *Towelle's Hand Book and Guide to Simla*, 1877.

United Indian Patriotic Association, *Showing the Seditious Character of the Indian National Congress and the Opinions Held by Eminent Natives of India*, Pioneer Press, 1888.

L. A. Waddell, *The Buddhism of Tibet or Lamaism*, 1897.

Sir William Wedderburn, *Allan Octavian Hume: Father of the Indian National Congress 1829–1912*, 1913.

Week's News, Pioneer Press, 1888–9.

H. G. Wells, *The New Machiavelli*, 1911.

Oscar Wilde, review, *Nineteenth Century Magazine*, September 1891.

Andrew Wilson, *Abode of Snow*, 1890.

Sir George Younghusband, *The Story of the Guides*, 1908; *Forty Years a Soldier*, 1923.

Col. Henry Yule and A. C. Burnell, *Hobson-Jobson: A Glossary of Colloquial Ango-Indian Words and Phrases*, 1884.

Secondary sources

(articles in the *Kipling Journal* are too numerous to be listed)

F. S. Aijazuddin, *Lahore: Illustrated Views of the Nineteenth Century*, 2004.

Charles Allen, *Kipling's Kingdom: His Best Indian Stories*, 1987; *A Mountain in Tibet*, 1978; *God's Terrorists: the Wahhabi Cult and the Hidden Roots of Modern Jihad*, 2006.

Arthur R. Ankers, *The Pater*, 1988.

Earl (Arthur) Baldwin, *The Macdonald Sisters*, 1960.

Muhammad Baqir, *Lahore Past and Present*, 1952.

Vaughan Bateson, *Something More of Kipling*, 1938.

C. A. Bayley, *The Local Roots of Indian Politics: Allahabad 1880–1920*, 1975.

Lord Birkenhead, *Rudyard Kipling*, 1975.

Martin Briton, *New India 1885: British Official Policy and the Emergence of the Indian National Congress*, 1969.

Mary Burnett, *The Ilberts in India 1882–86*, 2000.

Margarita Burns, *The Indian Press: a History of the Growth of Public Opinion in India*, 1940.

Charles Carrington, *Rudyard Kipling: His Life and Work*, 1955.

Desmond Chapman-Huston, *The Lost Historian: Sydney Low*, 1936.

Cora L. Diaz De Chumaceiro, 'On Rudyard Kipling's Loss of Ayah', *Psyart: an online journal of the psychological study of the arts*, February 2003.

John Coates, *The Day's Work: Kipling and the Idea of Sacrifice*, 1997.

Bernard Cohen, 'Representing Authority in Victorian India', in E. Hobsbawm and T. Ranger, eds., *The Invention of Tradition*, 1983.

E. M. Collingwood, *Imperial Bodies: the Physical Experiences of the Raj 1800–1947*, 2001.

Louis Cornell, *Kipling in India*, 1966.

Mike Davis, *Late Victorian Holocausts: El Niño Famines and the Making of the Third World*, 2001.

Sir Henry Mortimer Durand, *A Life of Sir Alfred Comyn Lyall*, 1913.

Sharada Dwivedi and Rahul Mehrotra, *Fort Walks: Around Bombay's Fort Area*, 1999; *Bombay: the Cities Within*, 2001.

T. S. Eliot, *A Choice of Kipling's Verse*, 1941.

Judith Flanders, *A Circle of Sisters: Alice Macdonald, Georgiana Burne-Jones, Agnes Poynter and Louisa Baldwin*, 2001.

David Gilmour, *The Long Recessional: the Imperial Life of Rudyard Kipling*, 2002.

Allen J. Greenberger, *The British Image of India: a Study in the Literature of Imperialism*, 1969.

John Gross, ed., *Rudyard Kipling: the Man, his Work and his World*, 1972.

Reginald Harbord, *The Readers' Guide to Rudyard Kipling's Work* Vols. I-VIII, now in the process of being updated as the *New Readers' Guide* by the Kipling Society under the editorship of John Radcliffe and George Webb, published in instalments on the Society's web-site at www.kipling.org.uk ('Readers' Guide').

Christopher Hitchens, *Love, Poverty and War*, 2005.

Peter Hopkirk, *Quest for Kim: In Search of Kipling's Great Game*, 1996; *Trespassers on the Roof of the World*, 1977.

Robert Hyam, *Empire and Sexuality*, 1990.

Shamsul Islam, *Kipling's Law: A Study of his Philosophy of Life*, 1975.

K. Jamilludin, *The Tropic Sun: Rudyard Kipling and the Raj*, 1974.

Tim Jeal, *Baden-Powell*, 1989.

D. C. Kala, *Frederick Wilson: 'Hulson Sahib' of Garhwal 1816–83*, 2006.

Pamela Kanwar, *Imperial Simla: the Political Culture of the Raj*, 1990.

Peter Keating, *Kipling the Poet*, 1994.

John Keay, *The Gilgit Game*, 1979; *Where Men and Mountains Meet*, 1982.

Sandra Kemp, *Kipling's Hidden Narratives*, 1988.

Omar Khan, *From Kashmir to Kabul: the Photographs of William Baker and John Burke 1861–1900*, 2002.

Kipling Society, *The Kipling Journal*, 1927–2007.

Select bibliography

Sean Lang, 'Saving India Through Its Women', *History Today*, September 2005.

Marghanita Laski, *From Palm to Pine: Rudyard Kipling Abroad and at Home*, 1987.

Lorna Lee, *Trix: Kipling's Forgotten Sister*, 2004

Sir Roper Lethbridge, 'The Press in India', *Journal of the East India Association*, New Series, Vol. V, 1914.

Sir Alfred Comyn Lyall, *The Life of the Marquis of Dufferin and Ava*, 1905; *Studies in Literature and History*, 1915.

Andrew Lycett, *Rudyard Kipling*, 1999.

Philip Mason, *Kipling: the Glass, the Shadow and the Fire*, 1975.

Partha Mitter, *Much Maligned Monsters*, 1992.

B. J. Moore-Gilbert, *Kipling and 'Orientalism'*, 1986.

Peter Mudford, *Birds of a Different Plumage: a Study of British-Indian Relations*, 1974.

Adam Nicholson, *The Hated Wife: Carrie Kipling 1862–1939*, 2001.

Harold Orel, *A Kipling Chronology*, 1990.

Mark Pafford, *Kipling's Indian Fiction*, 1989.

Norman Page, *A Kipling Companion*, 1984; *From Bombay to Southsea: the Two Childhoods of Rudyard Kipling*, 2002.

Bishambhar Nath Pande, *Allahabad Retrospect and Prospect*, 1955.

Neil Philip, ed., *The Illustrated Kipling*, 1988.

W. F. C. C. Plowden, *Records of the Chichele Plowdens*, 1914.

Violet Powell, *Flora Annie Steel: Novelist of India*, 1981.

M. Naeem Qureshi, 'A Museum for British Lahore', *History Today*, September 1997.

K. Bhaskara Rao, *Rudyard Kipling's India*, 1967.

F. Reid and D. Washbrook, 'Kipling's Kim and Imperialism', *History Today*, Vol. 32,1982.

Andrew Roberts, *Salisbury: Victorian Titan*, 1999.

Andrew Rutherford, ed., *Kipling's Mind and Art*, 1964.

Edward Said, *Introduction* and *Notes* to *Kim*, 1987.

Martin Seymour-Smith, *Rudyard Kipling*, 1989.

Edward Shanks, *Rudyard Kipling: A Study in Literature and Political Ideas*, 1940.

F. H. Skrine, *The Life of Sir William Wilson Hunter*, 1901.

J. K. Stanford, *Ladies in the Sun*, 1962.

John Whitehead, ed., *Mrs Hauksbee and Co: Tales of Simla Life by Rudyard Kipling*, 1998.

Angus Wilson, *The Strange Ride of Rudyard Kipling: His Life and Works*, 1977.

Lewis D. Wurgaft, *The Imperial Imagination: Magic and Myth in Kipling's India*, 1983.

Zoe Yalland, *Boxwallahs: The British in Cawnpore 1857–1901*, 1994.

Kenneth Young, ed., *The Diaries of Sir Robert Bruce Lockhart*, 1973.

Select bibliography of Anglo-Indian Verse and Fiction c. 1857–90

'A. B. C. S.', *Current Repentance*, Calcutta 1885.

George Aberigh-Mackay ('Ali Baba'), sketches for *Vanity Fair* 1878–9 pub. as *Twenty-One Days in India, being the Tour of Sir Ali Baba*, 1879; sketches for *Bombay Gazette* pub. as *The Teapot Series: Serious Reflections by a Political Orphan*, 1880.

Edward Aitken, ('E. H. A.'), sketches for *Times of India* pub. as *Tribes on my Frontier*, 1883: *Behind the Bungalow*, 1889: *Naturalist on the Prowl*, 1896.

'Ali Baba' – see George Aberigh-Mackay.

'Aliph Cheem' – see Walter Yeldham.

Alexander Allardyce, *The City of Sunshine*, 1877.

'Alpha', *Some Railway Servants and Other Sketches*, CMG Press, 1890.

Anon., *Gowry: An Indian Village Girl*, 1876.

Anon., *The Indian Heroine*, 1877.

Anon., *How Will It End?*, 1887.

Anon., *Lotus: A Psychological Romance*, 1888.

Anon., *The Lover's Stratagem*, 1889.

Anon., *The Morlands: A Tale of Anglo-Indian Life*, 1888.

Anon., *New Tale of a Grandfather: or, How Herat Was Lost and Won*, 1885.

Anon., *The Rajah's Heir*, 1890.

Anon., *Told On the Verandah: Passages in the Life of Colonel Bowlong, Set Down By His Adjutant, c.* 1890.

Captain George Atkinson, *Curry and Rice on 40 Plates, or the Ingredients of Social Life at Our Station in India*, 1859; *Indian Spices for English Tables; ie Rare Relish of fun from the far east, being the adventures of 'our special correspondent in India'*, 1860.

D. Aubrey, *Letters from Bombay*, 1884.

A. J. Bamford, *Turbans and Tails, or Sketches in the Unromantic East*, 1888.

J. Barras, *Rama: A Sensational Story of Indian Village Life*, 1886.

'Paul Benison'– see John Walter Sherer.

Thomas Frank Bignold, *Leviora: Being the Rhymes of a Successful Competitor*, 1888.

Frederick Boyle, *Legends of the Bungalow*, 1882.

Lady Annie Brassie, *Sunshine and Storm in the East*, 1880.

'H. Broughton' – see George Trevelyan.

Geraldine Butt, *Verses*, CMG Press, 1884.

Henry James Byron, *Aladdin,* CMG Press, 1882.

Mrs H. M. Cadell (Jessie Ellen Nash), *Ida Craven*, 1873.

Robert C. Caldwell, *The Chutney Lyrics: A Collection of Comic Pieces in Verse on Indian Subjects*, 1871.

'C. A. L.' – see Sir Alfred Comyn Lyall.

Gen. Sir George Chesney, *A True Reformer*, 1873; *The Dilemma: A Tale of the Mutiny;* 1880; *Indian Polity*, 1882 ; *The Private Secretary*, 1884.

'Owen Christian' – see Henry Curwen.

'C. L. T.' – see Lionel James.

'C. M. a Bombay Walla' – see C. J. MacDowall

'M. J. Colquhoun' (Mrs Charles Scott), *Under Orders*, 1882; *Primus in India*, 1885; *Every Inch a Soldier*, 1888.

F. M. Crawfurd, *Mr Isaacs: A Tale of Modern India*, 1882.

'Tom Cringle' – see William Walker.

Mrs B. M. Croker, *Proper Pride*, 1882; *Pretty Miss Neville*, 1883; *Someone Else*, 1885; *Diana Barrington*, 1888: *A Romance of Central India*, 1888; *Two Masters*, 1890; *A Third Person*, 1893, etc.

Sir Henry S. Cunningham, *Wheat and Tares: A Tale*, 1862; *Chronicles of Dustypore: A Tale of Modern Anglo-Indian Society*, 1877; *The Heriots, The Coeruleans: A Vacation Idyll*, 1887; *Sybilia*, 1889, etc.

Henry Curwen (ed. *Times of India*), (as 'Owen Christian'), *Poems*, 1885; *Zit and Xoe*, 1886; *Lady Bluebeard*, 1888; *Dr Hermione*, 1890.

Edith Cuthell ('An Indian Exile'), *In Tent and Bungalow*, 1890; *Indian Idylls*, 1892, etc.

William Dalton, *The White Elephant*, 1860; *Phankor the Adventurer*, 1862.

Tim Daly (poss. pseud.) ('F. E. W.'), *Sketches of Native Life*, 1869; *Mess Stories*, 1872.

George Dick, *Fitch and His Fortunes: An Anglo-Indian Novel*, 1877.

Sir Henry Durand ('John Roy'), *Helen Trevelyan: or, The Ruling Race*, 1892.

'E. H. A.' – see Edward Aitken.

Robert H. Elliott, *Written on Their Foreheads*, 1879.

'F. E. W.' – see Tim Daly.

J. F. Fanthorne ('J. F. F.'), *Mariam*, 1886.

G. M. Fenn, *Begumbagh: A Tale of the Indian Mutiny*, 1890.

Arthur Brownlow Fforde, *The Trotter: A Poona Mystery*, 1890; *The Subaltern, the Policeman and the Little Girl: An Anglo-Indian Sketch*, 1890; *The Maid and the Idol*, 1891; *The Little Owl*, 1893, etc.

Mrs E. M. Field, *Here's Rue for You*, 1883; *Bryda: A Story of the Indian Mutiny*, 1888.

Mrs H. A. Fletcher, *Poppied Sleep*, 1887.

'Forrest, R. E.' – see Maj.-Gen. D. H. Thomas.

'Gillean' – see J. N. H. Maclean.

Geraldine Glasgow, *Black and White*, 1889.

'Maxwell Gray'– see Mary Tuttiett.

James Grant, *First Love and Last Love: A Tale of the Indian Mutiny*, 1868; *Only An Ensign: A Tale of the Retreat from Kabul*, 1871.

J. Percy Groves, *The Duke's Own*, 1887.

Ian Hamilton, *The Ballad of Hadji*, 1888.

Beaumont Harrington, *Ashes for Bread*, 1884.

'H. G. K.' – see Henry George Keene.

W. A. Hunter, *The Trial of Muluk Chand: A Romance of Criminal Administration in Bengal*, 1888.

J. R. Hutchinson, *More Than He Bargained For: An Anglo-Indian Tale of Passion*, 1887.

'An Indian Detective', *A Romance of Indian Crime*, 1885.

'An Indian Exile' – see Edith E. Cuthell.

William W. Ireland, *Randolph Methyl: A Story of Anglo-Indian Life*, 1863.

Henry C. Irwin, *Rhymes and Renderings*, 1885.

P. W. Jacob, *Hindoo Tales*, 1873.

'J. A. N.' – see John R. Denning.

'J. F. F.'– see J. F. Fanthorne.

Henry George Keene ('H. G. K.'), contrib. to *Pioneer* and *Chameleon*; *Under the Rose: Poems Written Chiefly in India*, 1868; *The Death of Akbar and Other Poems*, 1875; *Peepul Leaves: Poems Written in India*, 1879; *Poems Original and Translated*, 1882; as 'J. Smith, Junior', *Sketches in Indian Ink*, 1891.

Charles Arthur Kelly, *Delhi and other Poems*, 1872.

'Kentish Rag' – see Bernard R. Ward.

W. H. G. Kingston, *The Young Rajah: A Story of Young Life and Adventures*, 1876.

Maj. Charles Kirby, *The Adventures of An Arcot Rupee*, 1867.

'A Lady', *The Brahmin's Prophecy*, 1875.

John Lang, ('Mofussilite'), ed. The *Mofussilite* from 1845, novels serialised in the *Mofussilite*: *Too Clever By Half: or, The Harroways*, 1852; *The Wetherbys, Father and Son: or Sundry Chapters of Indian Experience*, 1853; *Will He Marry Her?* 1859; *Who Was the Child?*, 1859; *My Friend's Wife: or, York, You're Wanted*, 1859.

L. K. Laurie ('Pekin') (contrib. to *Pioneer*); *Sketches in the C. P.: or, Sketches in Prose and Verse*, 1881.

Mary E. Leslie, *India and Other Poems*, 1856; *Sorrows, Aspirations and Legends of India*, 1859, *Sacred Lyrics and Sonnets: Heart Echoes from the East*, 1861.

S. K. Levett-Yeats, *The Heart of Denise*, 1889; *The Romance of Guard Mulligan*, 1893; *The Widow Lamport*, 1894.

'Lunka', *Whiffs: Anglo-Indian and Indian*, 1891.

Sir Alfred Comyn Lyall (contrib. to *Calcutta Review, Englishman* etc.), *Verses Written in India*, 1889.

C. J. MacDowall ('C. M. a Bombay Walla'), *The Chutney Papers: Society, Shikar and Sport in India*, 1884.

J. N. H. Maclean ('Gillean'), *The Ranee: A Legend of the Indian Mutiny*, 1887.

H. F. Manisty, *Horama: A Poem in Indian Exile*, 1890.

Florence Marryat (afterwards Mrs Ross-Church), *Love's Conflict*, 1865; *For Ever and Ever*, 1866; *Gup: Sketches of Anglo-Indian Life and Character*, 1868; *Nelly Brooke*, 1869; *Veronique*, 1869, etc.

Philip Meadows Taylor, *Confessions of A Thug*, 1839; *Tippoo Sultan*, 1840; *Tara: A Mahratta Tale*, 1863; *Ralph Darnell*, 1865; *The Fatal Amulet*, 1872; *Seeta*, 1872; *The Story of my Life*, 1877; *A Noble Omen*, 1878.

'Mirza Moorad Alee Beg "Gaekwaree"', *Lalun the Beragun, or The Battle of Panipat: A Legend of Hindoostan*, 1884.

'A Moffusilite' (but not John Lang), *The Confessions of Meajahn, Darogah of Police*, 1869.

'Moffusilite' – see John Lang.

Lady Sydney Morgan (Sydney Owenson), *Luxima, The Prophetess: A Tale of India*, 1859.

'M. W.', *How Will It End? The One in Madness, Both in Misery: A Story of Anglo-Indian Life*, 1887.

'N. J. A.' – see J. R. Denning.

William N. Norris, *No New Thing*, 1883.

John B. Norton, verses inc. *Nemesis: a Poem in Four Cantos*, 1861.

Ivan O'Bierne, *Jim's Wife*, 1889; *The Colonel's Crime*, c. 1890; *Doctor Victor*, 1891, etc.

E. O'Donovan, *Merv: A Story of Adventure and Captivity*, 1883.

Diana Oldenbuck, *A Legend of Spur and Spear*, 1889.

C. P. A. Oman, *Eastwards: or, Realities of Indian Life*, 1864.

'Our Domestic Novelist', *The Perilous Adventures of the Knight Sir Tommy*, 1871.

'Owen Christian' – see Henry Curwen.

James Payne, *A Confidential Agent*, 1881.

'Pekin' – see L. K. Laurie.

H. A. B. Pittard, *Poems*, 1884.

R. Planche, *The Discreet Princess*, 1873.

'A Planter's Mate', *A New Clearing: A Medley of Prose and Verse*, 1884.

J. Pomeroy, *Home from India*, 1869.

Iltudus Prichard, *The Chronicles of Budgepore: or, Sketches of Life in Upper India*, 1871.

Capt. Mayne Reid, *The Cliff Climbers: or, Lost in the Himalayas*, 1864; *The Lost Mountain: A Tale of Sonora*, 1883; *The Star of the Empire*, 1886.

Capt. R. Reid, *Revelations of an Indian Detective*, 1885.

Phil Robinson (ed. *Pioneer*), (as 'Ronin'), *Nugae Indicae: On Leave in my Compound*, 1871; as 'Chameleon' ed., *The Chameleon, An Anglo-Indian Periodical of Light Literature*, 1871–4; *In My Indian Garden*, 1878; *Under the Punkah*, 1881; *Chasing a Fortune: Tales and Sketches*, 1884; *Tigers at Large*, 1885.

Horatio B. Rowney, *The Young Zemindar*, 1883.

'John Roy'– see Sir Henry Durand.

John Walter Sherer ('Paul Benison'), *The Conjurer's Daughter*, 1880; *At Home in India*, 1882; *Images of Indian Days*, 1885; *Worldly Tales*, 1886.

Maud Sheridan, *Elaine's Story: A Tale of the Afghan Frontier*, 1879; *Lady Hastings: An Indian Story*, 1880.

Herbert Sherring, *Light and Shade: Tales and Verse*, 1884.

Alfred Percy Sinnett (ed. *Pioneer*), *Karma: A Novel*, 1886.

C. H. Sisson, *Once in a Way: A Jubbalpore Miscellany*, 1866.

'John Smith' – see H. G. Keene.

'Son Gruel', *What We Met in the Mufussil*, 1887.

Flora Annie Steel, *Wide-awake Stories for Children*, 1884; *Tales of the Punjab*, illus. by J. Lockwood Kipling, 1894; *From the Five Rivers*, 1893; *Miss Stuart's Legacy*, 1893, *The Potter's Thumb*, 1894, etc.

Charles Swynnerton, *The Adventures of Rajah Rasalu*, 1884.

C. H. Tawney, *The Kathakosha or Treasury of Stories*, illus. by J. Lockwood Kipling, 1895.

Maj.-Gen. D. H. Thomas ('Forrest, R. E.'), *The Touchstone of Peril*, c.1889; *Eight Days: A Tale of the Indian Mutiny*, 1891, etc.

D. H. Thomas, *The Touchstone of Peril*, 1886.

Septimus S. Thorburn, *David Leslie: A Story of the Afghan Frontier*, 1879.

Sir George Trevelyan, (as 'H. Broughton'), *The Dawk Bungalow: or, Is His Appointment Pucka?*, 1863; *The Competition Wallah*, 1864.

William Walker, *Tom Cringle's Letters on Practical Subjects Suggested by Experiences in Bombay*, 1863; *Jottings of an Invalid*, 1865.

Elliot Walters, *Gutter and Mansion: or, Shadows of Anglo-Indian Life, A Tale*, 1890.

William Waterfield, *Indian Ballads and Other Poems*, 1865.

H. B. M. Watson, *Marahuna: A Romance*, 1888.

William Trego Webb, ('William Trego'), *Indian Lyrics*, 1882.

'Jane Williams', *Lilian: A Racy Indian Novel*, 1888.

Bernard Wycliffe, *The Musulman's Lament Over the Body of Tipoo Sultan*, 1864.

Major Walter Yeldham ('Aliph Cheem'), *Lays of Ind*, 1871; *Lays of Ind*, new ed., 1873; *Lays of the Sea-Side*, 1887.

Yoke-Wright, *A Double Wedding*, 1885.

Charlotte M. Yonge, *The Young Step-Mother, c.* 1860; *The Clever Woman of the Family, c.* 1865.

Index